SAMUEL BUTLER

SAMUEL BUTLER

A Biography

Peter Raby

University of Iowa Press
Iowa City

To my family

CONTENTS

CONTENTS

Acknowledgements

I here record my thanks to the many people who helped me while I was researching and writing this book: with information, references and suggestions, with encouragement, and with hospitality. I owe a special debt of gratitude to the .following: Professor Hans-Pieter Breuer, who has been exceptionally generous with his knowledge of Butler, Thomas Cocke, Don Cupitt, Brian Lake, Richard Luckett, Andrew Motion, Murray Pollinger, Arthur Sale, Dr Elinor Shaffer, and Stephen Tompkins. I thank Mr and Mrs Groome, of the Old Rectory, Langar, the Headmaster of Shrewsbury School, and Librarian, Mr James Lawson. I also thank everyone who assisted me in New Zealand, especially the following: Dr P.B. Maling, Mr and Mrs Graham Peacock and Mr Leonard Tripp at Orari Gorge, Mr and Mrs John Acland at Mount Peel, Mr and Mrs Mark Acland at Mount Somers, Mr and Mrs Urquhart at Erewhon, and Mr and Mrs Prouting at Mesopotamia (Mr Prouting flew me in his helicopter to the site of Butler's hut in Forest Creek – an unforgettable experience).

I am grateful to the Trustees of the Smuts Foundation, and to Homerton College, Cambridge, for assistance towards a study trip to New Zealand.

The librarians, curators and staff of the following were unfailingly helpful: The British Library; The University Library, Cambridge; King's College, Cambridge; The Chapin Library, Williams College, Williamstown, Massachusetts; The Canterbury Museum, Christchurch; The Canterbury Public Library, Christchurch; The Alexander Turnbull Library, Wellington; and especially St John's College, Cambridge, where Mr Malcolm Pratt gave me the benefit of his extensive knowledge of Butler and the Butler Collection.

For permission to quote from copyright material I am grateful to the following: Major Richard Butler; The Master and Fellows of St

John's College, Cambridge; The Provost and Scholars of King's College, Cambridge; The Chapin Library, Williams College, Williamstown, Massachusetts; The British Library; Shrewsbury School; The Canterbury Museum, Christchurch; The Alexander Turnbull Library, Wellington. I should like to thank the following for permission to reproduce illustrative material: Major Richard Butler (1, in text p. 14); The Canterbury Museum, Christchurch, New Zealand (2, in text p. 85); The Master and Fellows of St John's College, Cambridge (3, 4, 7, 9, 10, 11, 14, 15, 16, 17, 18, 21, 22, 23, 24, 25, 26 and in text pp. 198, 199, 201, 202); Shrewsbury School (in text p. 40); The Tate Gallery, London (12); The Alexander Turnbull Library, Wellington, New Zealand (4, 8, in text p. 80); The Chapin Library, Williams College, Williamstown, Massachusetts (11); Alice Worsley (13) and Elizabeth Raby (20).

At The Hogarth Press, I would like to mention Marian Covington, and a special thanks to my editor, Jenny Uglow. Finally, all my family, above all my wife Liz.

Gintrac, Lot – Swaffham Bulbeck, Cambridge

Abbreviations

For ease of reference the following editions are cited within the text:

AO *The Authoress of the Odyssey* (London, 1922)

AS *Alps and Sanctuaries of Piedmont and the Canton Ticino* (London, 1913)

E *Erewhon* (Harmondsworth, 1970)

ER *Erewhon Revisited* (London, 1908)

EV *Ex Voto* (London, 1928)

FH *The Fair Haven* (London, 1913)

FL *The Family Letters of Samuel Butler 1841–1886* (London, 1962)

FY *A First Year in Canterbury Settlement* (London, 1863)

LH *Life and Habit* (London, 1910)

M *Samuel Butler: A Memoir* by Henry Festing Jones, 2 vols (London, 1919)

N *The Note-Books of Samuel Butler, Volume I (1874–1883)*, edited by Hans-Peter Breuer (London, 1984)

S *Letters between Samuel Butler and Miss E.M.A. Savage 1871–1885* (London, 1935)

SS *Shakespeare's Sonnets Reconsidered* (London, 1927)

WF *The Way of All Flesh* (London, 1966)

CHAPTER 1

Origins

'The Three Most Important Things a man has are briefly, his private parts, his money, and his religious opinions.'[1] The statement, with the sting in its tail, comes from an outwardly conventional Victorian, bowler-hatted and black-suited. Was it conceived during Family Prayers, and recorded, like so many of Samuel Butler's notes and aphorisms, in the Reading Room of the British Museum?

Butler remains one of the great unclassifiable minds of the nineteenth century, with a reputation that rises and falls but obstinately resists definition. His versatility and curiosity led him into many areas of life and thought: religion, science, literature, art. He was artist and photographer, as well as novelist, critic, and philosopher, sheep farmer, company director and property developer. But his claim on our interest has additional support in the modern writers who were influenced by and interested in him: Shaw, first and foremost; H.G. Wells, Lytton Strachey, the Woolfs, E.M. Forster, Ivy Compton-Burnett, Robert Graves, James Joyce.

Combative, lucid, honest, with a mischievous sense of humour which surfaced at most inappropriate moments, Butler developed his intellectual muscle by questioning received ideas and attitudes. Betrayed as a child, he resolved never to be 'humbugged' again, while perplexingly playing the role of the archetypal English gentleman: public school and Cambridge; chambers in Clifford's Inn; British Museum, Royal Academy, correspondence columns of the *Athenaeum*. But a formative summer as an unpaid curate in the slums of London, long months on an emigrant ship and four years as a sheep farmer in New Zealand provided a second, less conventional education. He felt uneasy in the drawing-rooms of well-connected 'nice' people, preferring the atmosphere of public houses and music halls.

In his irreverent autobiographical novel, *The Way of All Flesh*, published after his death, in 1903, Butler created a new kind of being fit for the modern world, Ernest Pontifex (Ernest Priest). Writing about Ernest's education, which was parallel to his own, he exclaims: 'What a lie, what a sickly debilitating debauch did not Ernest's school and university career now seem to him, in comparison with his life in prison and as a tailor in Blackfriars.' (WF368) For all the bachelor, middle-class security of his London chambers and his comfortable routine, Butler lived in close awareness of the less affluent and more bohemian. For his pleasures, he would make his weekly visit to Madame Dumas in Islington, or take the steamer for a day trip to Margate or Clacton, or accompany his servant Alfred to the pantomime.

One can mock, as Malcolm Muggeridge did in his caustic study of Butler, *The Earnest Atheist*, Butler's reliance on his cheque book and his meticulous book-keeping by double entry; but he was living in a tightly knit, urban society that put a monetary value on everyone and everything, in spite of denials to the contrary. Money was luck, and freedom. Butler's nostalgia for the pastoral simplicity of the eighteenth century, partly expressed in the utopia of his novel *Erewhon*, or in his affection for the healthy, good-looking peasants of the Italian Alps, was fed by his intimate contact with the realities of London; and every day, like a good Victorian but in his own highly sceptical way, he thought about the impact of religion and the nature of God.

When Butler escaped from England and landed in New Zealand as a young immigrant of twenty-four, he climbed the volcanic hills that surround Port Lyttelton harbour to have a sight of his new country. The Canterbury Plains, lovely in colouring, stretched away into the distance, where his eye was met by the extensive blue line of the Southern Alps. As soon as he saw the mountains, he longed to cross them.

Within a few weeks, he had fulfilled his wish, and returned. It was a pattern he would repeat on several occasions during his years in South Island, most memorably in his courageous explorations of the headwaters of the Rangitata river which formed the foundation of the fictional journey over the range and on into 'Erewhon'. The impulse to explore and discover, preferably in isolation, characterised his restless cast of mind. If some grand obstacle loomed on the horizon, mysterious and forbidding – the Anglican God, the Victorian family, Darwin, Homer – he set out to investigate for himself; and he would come back from these mental expeditions, having mapped out the territory to his own satisfaction, to announce to an uninterested world that the mystery had been solved. In his final years, Butler became acutely conscious of the symmetry of his literary career; it began in 1872 with *Erewhon* and ended in 1901 with *Erewhon Revisited*, the emotional climax of which is set on the very summit of a mountain range, in the shadow of giant statues guarding the pass into the magical country beyond.

The rhythm of Butler's life, in an age when travel was suddenly available and cheap, was punctuated by journeys. The railway and the steamship made the whole world more accessible to mid-nineteenth-century England, and when Butler was planning to emigrate, fleeing the twin spectres of his father and ordination, he considered, in rapid succession, the merits of Liberia, the Cape and British Columbia. In the end New Zealand offered the advantage of being as far away from England in space and time as was practical, and proved to be his most significant journey. But every setting out was matched by a return. England, and the English society, which so confounded and oppressed him, kept calling to him; and however hard he strained at the ties that held him, he would be drawn, quietly but inexorably, back to his base at Clifford's Inn, to the circle of his close friends, even, in spite of his loud protests to the contrary, to his family. In London he would work at his books, his painting or his music until his eyes failed and his brain reeled. Then he would pack his bags again and go, in summer to the Alps, at Easter or Whitsun to Boulogne, or on Thursdays and Sundays to Gad's Hill or the Downs.

He enjoyed travelling light. The British Museum was his library. He could find a piano anywhere, and in any event carried most of Handel in his head. Yet his rooms at Clifford's Inn were stuffed with objects, the walls crowded with photographs, sketches and paintings. He kept piles of his own unsold books, stacks of manuscripts, letters, notebooks, boxes of glass negatives. He lived among the residue of his own life, a lumber-room existence from which little was discarded because everything had meaning. His memory was equally retentive. He recalled images, incidents, casual encounters and conversations, and recorded them in his notebooks and correspondence, and he kept pressed copies of most of his letters. Even when travelling, he laid down a trail of forwarding addresses, *postes restantes* and trusted hoteliers to ensure that he maintained contact with his friends and with his family.

It is in his relations with his family that Butler's paradoxical nature is most evident. His father was his intimate enemy. He felt rejected by his mother. He claimed to dislike his sisters. He hated his brother. He left England in pique and hurt to escape from the stifling incomprehension of his parents and what he believed they stood for; yet he wrote to them at great length from New Zealand, and when they proudly edited his letters and published them, he turned on them after correcting the proofs and rejected the book, *A First Year in Canterbury Settlement*, as being infected with the taint of the family home, Langar. But he could not let them go. On occasions, he was barred from the house; on others, he threatened to leave, never to meet again. He always returned, and was present at the deathbeds of his mother and his father. The combat was resolvable in one sense only by death, and, in another, by fiction.

The Way of All Flesh is the story of Butler's elemental conflict with his family. V.S. Pritchett described it as one of the time-bombs of literature, 'lying in Butler's desk at Clifford's Inn for thirty years, waiting to blow up the Victorian family and with it the whole great pillared and balustraded edifice of the Victorian novel'.[2] The book follows the path of much of Butler's own early development closely, and is undeniably, if selectively, autobiographical. He purged himself during the long process of its creation. He wrote it partly out of resentment and remembered hate; but he turns the irony as savagely on himself as on his parents and sisters, and on the whole ethos of Victorian values which he abominated and yet knew himself to be inescapably a part of.

The novel is an exercise in demythologising the family, both as an institution and in personal terms. It is the detailed, intimate record of Butler's memories, nightmares and dreams, an extended gloss on the naive painting, 'Family Prayers', which he painted in 1864 and which was his first attempt to open up the dark, locked room of his childhood. Like Ingmar Bergman, who also survived an upbringing in which sin and punishment prevailed over grace and forgiveness, Samuel Butler transformed his painful experience of childhood into art. Bergman, discussing the great film makers, commented: 'When film is not a document, it is dream.'[3] Butler's novel is dream disguised as document.

4

However much Butler strove to recreate himself, he was hyper-conscious of being the product of his parents, grandparents and ancestors; and he spent much of his life investigating his origins. The key figure in the family was Samuel's grandfather and namesake, Headmaster of Shrewsbury public school and Bishop of Lichfield, who died when he was four. It was Samuel's birthday, and a village woman who did sewing at Langar Rectory brought him a little pot of honey. 'My father came in, told us grandpapa was dead, and took away the honey saying it would not be good for us.'

Samuel had only one direct memory of his grandfather, less ominous: 'I had a vision of myself before a nursery fire with Dr Butler walking up and down the room watching my sister Harrie and myself.' (M1.19) The 'portrait' of Dr Butler in *The Way of All Flesh*, translated into George Pontifex, a successful publisher of religious works, is ambivalent. His fictional epitaph (WF110):

HE NOW LIES AWAITING A JOYFUL RESURRECTION
AT THE LAST DAY
WHAT MANNER OF MAN HE WAS
THAT DAY WILL DISCOVER

hints at Butler's uncertainty about his own judgment of him. When he eventually inherited a dinner service of silver plate, presented to Dr Butler when he became Bishop of Lichfield, he decided to sell it.

I took it to a silversmith's in the Strand, or rather got them to send some one to see it; he said it was very good, but of a period (1836) now out of fashion.

'There is one especial test of respectability in plate,' he remarked; 'we seldom find it but, when we do, we consider it the most correct thing and the best guarantee of solid prosperity that anything in plate can give. When there is a silver venison dish we know that the plate comes from an owner of the very highest respectability.'

My grandfather had a silver venison dish.

To this note Butler added a P.S., after he had written the monumental *The Life and Letters of Dr Samuel Butler*:

When I wrote the above, I knew nothing about my grandfather except that he had been a great schoolmaster – and I did not like schoolmasters; and then a bishop – and I did not like bishops; and that he was supposed to be like my father. [He does not need to add, 'and I did not like my father'.] Of course when I got hold of his papers, I saw what he was and fell head over ears in love with him. Had I known then what I know now, I do not think I could have sold the plate; but it was much better that I should, and I have raised a far better monument to his memory than ever the plate was. (M2.50–1)

Butler fell in love more easily with the dead than with the living.

Dr Samuel Butler was born in 1774. His father, William, was a linen-draper in Kenilworth, Warwickshire; his mother, Lucy, was the youngest daughter of Nathaniel Broxsell, a builder from Shepton Mallet in Somerset. The first three chapters of *The Way of All Flesh* draw on this background of solid, provincial trade and idealise it in a semi-pastoral picture of eighteenth-century stability. In reality, the Butler family had once had rather more elevated connections. But William Butler, the eldest of five sons, must have crossed his father in some way, so he never inherited the family house and property. Dr Butler, in notes on his own life, records that he was originally intended for trade. According to a family tradition, a retired army captain, Captain Don, who lodged with the Butlers, urged them to send him away to school; and in 1783, when he was just nine, he began his formal education at Rugby.

Dr Butler's education, first at Rugby and then at St John's College, Cambridge, was the formative element in the career not only of himself but of his son Thomas and grandson Samuel. His social background set him apart from most of the other boys. A contemporary – Apperley, who later wrote as 'Nimrod' in the *Sporting Magazine* – recalled that 'Butler was most unpopular in the school. In fact, partly because he was the son of a small shopkeeper . . . and at Rugby as a foundation boy, and partly on account of his churlish temper, we in the same boarding house voted him nothing better than a snob, and the meanness of his personal appearance gave a colour to our proceedings.' The possible cause of this unpopularity is then revealed: 'Never would he offer to do us a verse or two, or construe us over; but he would sit with his elbow on his knee, and his face resting on one hand and a book in the other, and never open his mouth.'[4] He may have been precociously fluent in Greek and Latin, but his main interests were reading novels and plays, and fishing (he nearly lost the end of his nose in a hunt for a pike). Butler warmed to his grandfather's lack of ease with his fellow schoolboys, and his instinctive dislike of formal study.

Dr Butler's promise as a classicist was evident. He was also a young man who attracted the confidence of his elders. Dr James, the headmaster of Rugby, took a close, almost fatherly, interest in his career; and it was through an accidental introduction to Dr Parr, the foremost scholar of the day, that in 1791 he entered St John's College, Cambridge, as a sizar, rather than Christ Church, Oxford. It was a change that he regretted at the time, but one which brought him substantial professional advantages in the future. His academic record was distinguished: Browne Medallist, Latin Ode 1792–93, Greek Ode 1794; Craven Scholar, 1793 (ahead of Coleridge and the future headmaster of Eton, Keate); fourth senior optime, and first Chancellor's medal, 1796; elected Platt Fellow of St John's, 1797. The glittering prizes that fell to Dr Butler must have seemed horribly daunting to the next two generations of Butlers who followed him to St John's.

Almost equal to his academic achievement was Dr Butler's ability to manage money. His branch of the family had fallen on relatively hard times. However, a legacy came his way from an uncle on his mother's side while he was still at school, in the form of a reversionary interest in some property at Shepton Mallet. At twenty-one, he considered selling his interest to buy an annuity for his parents. They dissuaded him, and the reversion remained in his control. Property tended to stick to his fingers: Samuel, whose life at times seemed dominated by pound notes, or the lack of them, commented a little wistfully on George Pontifex's 'pecuniary characteristics': 'It may be said that he acquired these by sitting still and letting money run, as it were, right up against him, but against how many does not money run who do not take it when it does, or who, even if they hold it for a little while, cannot so incorporate it with themselves that it shall descend through them to their offspring?' (WF114) Butler's fantasy of being born from an egg wrapped round with ten or twenty thousand pounds in Bank of England notes represented an entirely serious aspiration. One of the more remarkable aspects of Dr Butler's career, passed exclusively as an academic, schoolmaster and clergyman, was his steady acquisition of property and wealth.

Dr Butler's engagement to Harriet Apthorp, the fifth daughter of a clergyman, brought a letter full of dire financial warnings from Dr James, horrified at his protégé's intention to marry solely on the expectations of income derived from taking private pupils. The catalogue of potential hazards that he unfolded included the price of pork, highway rates, the cost of bed furniture, and the uncontrollable appetites of boys and servants. Instead, he recommended a mastership at an endowed school. Dr Butler had already considered the possibility of Shrewsbury school; at Rugby, he could only hope to become an assistant master. Shrewsbury had fallen on hard times, and there had been a move on the part of local people to promote an Act of Parliament in order to establish a new governing body. When the Act was passed in 1798 and St John's College, Cambridge, was entrusted with the appointment of the Master, Dr Butler was elected. He immediately married, and took up his duties on 1 October 1798. He was twenty-four.

He remained at Shrewsbury for thirty-eight years. When he took office, there were, by different accounts, some three or four boys, or only a single scholar. To his successor, he passed on a roll of one hundred and sixty boarders, together with eighty or so dayboys. He succeeded in restoring Shrewsbury to the status of one of the nationally recognised public schools, alongside Eton, Harrow, Winchester, Westminster, Rugby and Charterhouse. Most notably, he instituted a remarkable tradition of scholarship, so that a growing stream of his Salopian pupils won first-class honours and prizes particularly at Cambridge. So advanced were some of his best scholars that Kennedy, his successor at Shrewsbury, won the Cambridge Porson prize while still in the school's sixth form. From Oxford came accusations, hotly denied, of cramming; while from Cambridge Dr Wordsworth, Master of Trinity, commented that Dr Butler came to Cambridge 'year after year, just as a first-rate London milliner makes a yearly visit to Paris to get the fashions'.[5]

The regular success of Dr Butler's pupils in examinations may have evoked jealousy and criticism, but it also invited emulation. The headmaster of Harrow and one of his assistant masters visited Shrewsbury to observe Dr Butler teach, and to find the answers to a string of questions about 'curriculum and method': 'If there be a

8

royal road to learning you have certainly found it, and your long, merited, and universal success makes us very anxious to follow you there.'[6] The road may not have been unduly narrow, at least in intention. In Dr Butler's own words, 'If a classical school were a place where nothing else has to be done for eight or nine long years than to hammer the words of a language (and that a dead one) into a boy's brains, I should say it was indeed a singular contrivance for misspending the time.'[7] A former pupil, the Rev. R.W. Evans, in proposing a toast to 'the memory of Dr Butler' some years after his death, recalled 'his plain and sincere teaching', 'his paternal kindness', 'the interesting form in which he clothed his instruction and allured us on', and 'the exquisite taste with which he directed our attention to the beauties of the authors which we were reading, and which he impressed into our minds'.[8] Charles Darwin had rather different memories, claiming that he learnt absolutely nothing except by amusing himself by reading and experimenting in chemistry. Nicknamed Gas, he was once publicly rebuked by his headmaster 'for thus wasting my time over such useless subjects; and he called me very unjustly a "poco curante," and as I did not understand what he meant it seemed to me a fearful reproach'.[9] The system that Dr Butler installed was predominantly the curriculum and routine that his grandson Samuel was later to experience.

If the final outcome and balance of Dr Butler's headmastership was highly creditable, there were less satisfactory aspects. He was known as a stern disciplinarian, too fond at first of thrashing his boys, and he endured several turbulent periods. He also had a difficult, even bizarre relationship with his Second Master, Jeudwine. An early disagreement arose, swelled and refused to heal; and for thirty-seven years Headmaster and Second Master communicated only by letter, usually in the third person. Samuel Butler's propensity for nursing a grievance had a clear precedent. A pro-Jeudwine faction existed in Shrewsbury, and Dr Butler's reflections on the main events of his life included this note of painful experience: 'Bitter ill-treatment at Shrewsbury – a hard pill to digest, but truly a wholesome one, which brought me acquainted with mankind, and turned my thoughts from overweening vanity.'[10]

Dr Butler took responsibility for all the classical teaching in the upper school (that is, for the greater part of the curriculum), a task he approached with almost missionary zeal. Blomfield, the Bishop of

Chester, was shocked on a visit to Shrewsbury to observe the head-master cutting his pen before the end of the morning service, so as to be ready to correct the boys' exercises. In addition, together with his wife, he supervised a boarding house, which earned him a good income even if it involved him in correspondence with parents like Dr Darwin about the number of blankets on each boy's bed. He still found time for academic study, and for writing two frequently reprinted school books, *Modern and Ancient Geography* and *An Atlas of Ancient Geography*. Like his grandson, when he discovered a need or omission, he set to work and filled it himself.

While he was headmaster he also accumulated an impressive array of ecclesiastical offices and, more crucially for his family, property. Once he had established Shrewsbury school on a more even financial basis, he began to invest his surplus income in land. 'In spite of heavy demands I have had upon me,' he informed the Master of St John's, 'to the extent of £14,000 and upwards (of which a very considerable sum must be sacrificed), and notwithstanding the settle-ment of my three children in marriage and other heavy drawbacks made to secure a large landed property to my eldest grandson, in which I have been obliged to make great investments at a very low rate of interest, and have consequently much reduced my income, on the average of the last ten years I have been enabled, though keeping a carriage and living in good style, to put by full £4000 a year.'[11]

Among his purchases was a farm at Harnage, near Shrewsbury, where he raised the meat and vegetables for his three boarding houses; the Whitehall, the 'large landed property' referred to above, an estate in the Abbey Foregate on the east of the Severn with a substantial seventeenth-century house; land to the north of the town at Coton Hill; and several plots in Shrewsbury itself. Considering that he started out with a salary of £120 a year and a handful of boys, this represented a considerable entrepreneurial achievement. The three children whose marriage settlements made such heavy demands were two daughters, Mary and Harriet, and a son, Thomas. The daughters, appropriately enough, married Shropshire arch-deacons. Mary became the second wife of Edward Bather, vicar of Meole Brace on the outskirts of Shrewsbury. Harriet married John Lloyd, and had three children: the eldest's involvement in the White-hall property would lead to prolonged family tension.

Thomas, Dr Butler's son, was born on November 28th, 1806. The pattern of his career was wholly predictable. His godfather was Dr Parr, who had been responsible for diverting Dr Butler from Christ Church to St John's. His education was at Shrewsbury. The inevitable progression of St John's College, Cambridge, ordination, schoolmastering and a vicarage began to unroll.

Life for the Headmaster's son at Shrewsbury cannot have been easy. One of Thomas's grandchildren described him as having been 'greatly in subjection to his father', 'always under his eye and his control'; later, he expressed a wish to go into the Navy, but was 'compelled by his father to take orders'.[12] Many of the pressures that Samuel later so vehemently resented and resisted were suffered, and apparently accepted, by his father.

At school Thomas was a contemporary of Erasmus and Charles Darwin, whose father was a Shrewsbury doctor. Writing to Charles from Cambridge, Erasmus commented on the Shrewsbury school examinations in February, 1825: 'The examination turned out as I expected in one respect, but how in the name of heaven T.B. came to be where he is I cant conceive.'[13] In August Thomas Butler was placed highest in the school, and went up to St John's in the autumn. The following year he was a candidate for the Bell Scholarship. He dutifully sent the papers, with his answers, to his father, whose reply contrived to blame while faintly praising.

Your verses are fair – not surpassingly good – not bad; the fourth stanza is the worst.

Your Latin prose is but moderate; it is too verbose, and the right phrase is often missed, though sometimes caught.

Your Xenophon in the last sentence is very wrong.

But then you must recollect that others were liable to make faults as well as you. I hear that you have done yourself credit, and from what I see I am convinced of it.

A postscript from Tom's sister hints at the authoritarian stance which dominated family relationships: 'Papa seems quite satisfied with you, and therefore you may be easy on that score.'[14] The rest of her letter reveals an apparently happy domestic scene: anecdotes about one of the matrons, an evening party with some of the boys, commissions for Tom to fulfil in the Cambridge shops – four pounds of mangel-wurzel seed, and two new Cambridge calendars from Deighton's. Her next letter, written in the knowledge that Tom had come second to another Salopian (Shrewsbury old boy), anticipates his return as conquering hero: 'You should have heard the huzzas of the boys, and have seen the capers and frolics and delight of us all . . . And now we can talk of nothing but the delight of seeing you, which will be worth all the rest . . . Mamma says every minute she wants to see you. If she eats an egg, it is "in honour of Tom". If she takes wine, it is to drink your health, and almost whenever she opens her mouth it is to talk of you. Mrs Bromfield too is crazy to see you; so is papa, and so are John and Harriet.'[15] Tom was welcomed back to the family, but his father remained more inclined to be appeased by merit than moved by affection.

One glimpse of Thomas Butler as an undergraduate is of interest both for its own sake, and in the light of Samuel's later dealings with Darwin. The Darwins and Butlers maintained courteous, if slightly formal, relations. Tom was an undergraduate at St John's when Charles Darwin was at Christ's; inevitably, with so many Salopians at Cambridge, they had friends in common. In July and August 1828 Tom joined Darwin on a reading party in Wales together with two other St John's men, an undergraduate, John Herbert, and a Fellow, George Butterton, who was to tutor Darwin in mathematics. Butterton, another Shrewsbury star, proved 'a very dull man', according to Darwin: 'I got on very slowly.'[16] In insectology, however, the tour was much more successful. Fired by his cousin William Fox, Darwin was beginning to collect insects; and after he had left the party he wrote to Herbert with a detailed shopping list of beetles: 'These 2 last insects are *excessively rare*: & you really will *extremely* oblige me by taking all this trouble pretty soon: Remember me most kindly to Butler, tell him of my success, & I daresay both of you will easily recognize these insects: I hope his caterpillars go on well. . . . Fox remarked what deuced goodnatured fellows your friends at Barmouth must be; & if I did not know that you & Butler were so I would not think of giving you so much trouble.'[17] The holiday remained a landmark. In 1834 Herbert wrote to Darwin, by then on the *Beagle*, to describe a holiday in Dolgellau and recalled 'the limping way in which I walked down the hill some 5 yrs before with you & Butler . . .'[18] The friendships, and with them the stimulus of original, lively minds, faded; the principal residue was the taste for botany with which Darwin had inoculated Butler and which remained with him all his life.

An aura of unfulfilled promise hovers around Thomas Butler. He was placed seventh in the First Class of the Classical Tripos in 1829, and ordained deacon that same year. He then returned to Shrewsbury, and served as an assistant master to his father, and curate to his brother-in-law, Archdeacon Bather, at Meole Brace. Two years later he married Fanny Worsley. His meeting with her arose, unsurprisingly, from the Shrewsbury connection. Fanny's family came from Bristol, where her father was in business as a sugar refiner, and she came to Shrewsbury to visit her aunt and uncle Hutchings, who had moved there to enable their sons to attend the school as dayboys; the Hutchings were neighbours to Tom's other sister, Harriet. Marriage on an assistant schoolmaster's salary was an unattractive prospect, but in 1834 Thomas was presented to the living of Langar-with-Bramston by the Lord Chancellor, Lord Brougham, a piece of patronage engineered by his father. Langar is a small village some ten miles east of Nottingham, in the diocese of Lincoln. He was to live there for the next forty-two years.

CHAPTER 2

Langar

When you visit Langar today, it is hard to imagine that life there was ever, at least for the clergyman's family, other than comfortable and contented. The village curves up a small rise, and the rectory commands the crest with views over the surrounding Vale of Belvoir, in the heart of the Midlands. The house is spacious, early Georgian, built of warm red brick, with extensive walled gardens between it and the church. The church itself, the 'cathedral of the Vale of Belvoir', is of honey-coloured stone; but, as the note in Pevsner warns, 'unfortunately so vigorously restored in the 1860s by the Rev. Thomas Butler that little of the original surface remains'.[1] The landscape is pleasantly unspectacular: slight undulations, narrow streams, rich pastures, well-treed even now. There Thomas and Fanny Butler brought up four of their children: Harriet (Harrie), Samuel, born on December 4th, 1835, Thomas, and Mary (May); while in the churchyard is the grave of William, who followed Thomas and died when still a baby.

'H. & S. Butler in their wheelbarrows.' Sketch by Anna Worsley

The family was neither isolated nor friendless: Butler, in *The Way of All Flesh*, gives the impression that their acquaintance was almost exclusively with other clergy families, but that does not seem borne out by other references and correspondence. There were constant comings and goings, especially with the Worsley relations, and neighbouring families, like the Halls of Whatton, remained lifelong friends. Certainly, there was no poverty. Yet both Samuel and his younger brother Thomas were in different ways profoundly unhappy, and each rebelled violently against their parents, and principally against their father, who to others seemed a benign and respected man.

The first important event in Samuel's life was his baptism, a sacrament whose effectiveness he would later analyse in detail. He was fond of commenting that the ten months' gap between birth and baptism 'was a very risky business, because during all those months the devil had the run of him'.

Dr Butler was the cause of the delay. He was in the process of resigning the headmastership of Shrewsbury, and organising the appointment of his former pupil, Kennedy, as his successor. For some time he had been nursing hopes of a bishopric, like a cleric in a Trollope novel, relying on the influence of Brougham, the Lord Chancellor. One vacancy passed him by, and then came a double blow: Lord Melbourne's government was dismissed, and when he returned to power in March, 1835, he formed an administration without Dr Butler's patron. However, the Prime Minister had indeed been impressed by Butler's claims and abilities, and quickly nominated him to a bishopric, though the actual see was not decided upon immediately. The pause enabled Butler to complete the school year at Shrewsbury, before his consecration on July 3rd, 1836, as Bishop of Lichfield, the diocese in which he had worked as Archdeacon. He eventually found time to visit Langar in September in order to baptise Samuel in person, and to stand as godfather to him.

Apart from his name and presence, Dr Butler made two other contributions: a phial of Jordan water, and a turbot sent down from Grove's of Bond Street for the christening dinner. When the cover was removed from the dish, the Bishop noticed with horror that the turbot had been mishandled in the kitchen, and turning to his daughter-in-law exclaimed: 'Good God, Fanny, it's skinned!' (N235) In these slightly inauspicious circumstances, Samuel's christening was celebrated.

Samuel Butler recorded his childhood in *The Way of All Flesh*. Although it is not of course true in every particular, it is, both on his own and others' account, an extremely faithful record of actual events, incorporating with scrupulous care letters, inscriptions, topography, incidents. It is a prototype of English autobiographical novels; it was not to see the light till after he and most now living were dead, he confided to his friend Charles Gogin, 'so that I am telling the truth the whole truth and nothing but the truth. . . .'[2] It is also highly selective, and the portraits should be regarded as 'drawn from' their originals, commentaries on an individual's perception rather than attempts at objective portrayals. If Thomas and Fanny Butler are on trial as Theobald and Christina Pontifex, as it often seems they are, then we hear very little in their defence. But the imaginative and emotional force of this part of the novel makes it disturbingly convincing. Cowed and subjugated as a child, Samuel sustained an intense hurt, which he locked away until he was able to express some part of it in a manuscript that he once regarded as his *magnum opus*.

There are two passages especially in which Samuel attempts to express his early feelings towards his parents. The first is a generalised description of how Theobald and Christina fulfilled their duty in rooting out all signs of self-will in their children:

Before Ernest could well crawl he was taught to kneel; before he could well speak he was taught to lisp the Lord's prayer, and the general confession. How was it possible that these things could be taught too early? If his attention flagged or his memory failed him, here was an ill weed which would grow apace, unless it were plucked out immediately, and the only way to pluck it out was to whip him, or shut him up in a cupboard, or dock him of some of the small pleasures of childhood. Before he was three years old he could read and, after a fashion, write. Before he was four he was learning Latin, and could do rule of three sums.

As for the child himself, he was naturally of an even temper, he doted upon his nurse, on kittens and puppies, and on all things that would do him the kindness of allowing him to be fond of them. He was fond of his mother, too, but as regards his father, he has told me in later life he could remember no feeling but fear and shrinking. Christina did not remonstrate with Theobald concerning the severity of the tasks imposed upon their boy, nor yet as to the continual whippings that were found necessary at lesson times. Indeed, when during any absence of Theobald's the lessons were entrusted to her, she found to her sorrow that it was the only thing to do, and she did it no less effectually than Theobald himself; nevertheless she was fond of her boy, which Theobald never was, and it was long before she could destroy all affection for herself in the mind of her first-born. But she persevered. (WF117–18)

Christina's unkindness is excused because it follows the path laid down by Theobald; and because it can be explained as springing from the highest intentions, however misguided: 'For Ernest, a very great future – she was certain of it – was in store. This made severity all the more necessary, so that from the first he might have been kept pure from every taint of evil.' (WF118) Theobald is allowed no such latitude. He 'had never liked children'. Ernest is given no room for pause: 'When Ernest was in his second year, Theobald, as I have already said, began to teach him to read. He began to whip him two days after he had begun to teach him.' (WF120) The general approach is then exemplified in a savagely ironic scene observed by the narrator Overton, Butler himself in the guise of a family friend. The setting is a Sunday evening, when the children, as an especial treat, are to be allowed to choose and sing their hymns. Ernest's choice of 'Come, come, come; come to the sunset tree' proves fatal, for he is unable to pronounce 'come' to his father's satisfaction.

'Now, Ernest, you are not taking pains: you are not trying as you ought to do. It is high time you learned to say "come," why, Joey can say "come," can't you, Joey?'

'Yeth, I can,' replied Joey, and he said something which was not far off 'come.'

'There, Ernest, do you hear that? There's no difficulty about it, nor shadow of difficulty. Now, take your own time, think about it, and say "come" after me.'

The boy remained silent for a few seconds and then said 'tum' again.

I laughed, but Theobald turned to me impatiently and said,

'Please do not laugh, Overton; it will make the boy think it does not matter, and it matters a great deal'; then turning to Ernest he said, 'Now Ernest, I will give you one more chance, and if you don't say "come," I shall know that you are self-willed and naughty.'

He looked very angry, and a shade came over Ernest's face, like that which comes upon the face of a puppy when it is being scolded without understanding why. The child saw well what was coming now, was frightened, and, of course, said 'tum' once more.

'Very well, Ernest,' said his father, catching him angrily by the shoulder, 'I have done my best to save you, but if you will have it so, you will,' and he lugged the little wretch, crying by anticipation, out of the room. A few minutes more and we could hear screams coming from the dining-room, across the hall which separated the drawing-room from the dining-room, and knew that poor Ernest was being beaten.

'I have sent him up to bed,' said Theobald, as he returned to the drawing-room, 'and now, Christina, I think we will have the servants in to prayers,' and he rang the bell for them, red-handed as he was. (WF124–5)

At family prayers, Theobald reads from the Book of Numbers, about the man who was found gathering sticks on the Sabbath, and was stoned to death as the Lord commanded Moses. The awful lore of the Old Testament ran in Langar Rectory, just as it had done in Shrewsbury. Thomas Butler, with the triple authority of father, clergyman and schoolmaster, merely applied the principles he had seen practised, and had no doubt personally experienced. Dr Butler may have softened a little towards the end of his Shrewsbury régime; but even so his correspondence is sprinkled with apologia: 'Your son had been flogged twice, and twice only, when you saw him, and each time with neither more nor less than the usual degree of punishment, which consists of six cuts with a few twigs of loose birch held in the hand ... With regard to allowance being made for your son's backwardness, I have only to state that ample allowance has always been made for the backwardness of him and of every backward boy; but to great backwardness he joins great idleness, and it is necessary for any master who means to do his duty faithfully to a boy or his

parents, to correct this when he sees fit . . .'³ Thomas Butler in his
turn did his duty, and with such immoderation and insensitivity that
Samuel associated learning with punishment, while all his feelings
towards his father were overlaid by fear and resentment. Some commentators have tried to excuse the treatment Samuel experienced as
no more than common Victorian practice, adding disingenuously that
Samuel was a delicate child physically, as well as highly sensitive.
Long before Samuel was in a position to compare his upbringing
and education with that of others, or to begin to make sense of and
so control his reaction to it, he had suffered an acute emotional
deprivation which he struggled to come to terms with all his life:

> He never liked me, nor I him; from my earliest recollections I
> can call to mind no time when I did not fear him and dislike
> him; over and over again I have relented towards him, and said
> to myself that he was a good fellow after all; but I had hardly
> done so when he would go for me in some way or other which
> soured me again. (N231)

The father taught him language, and the son's sad profit was to know
how to curse him.

Towards his mother, Samuel's feelings were more ambiguous. In a
later chapter of *The Way of All Flesh* there is an analysis of Christina's
domestic confidence trick with Ernest. 'Whenever his mother wanted
what she called a confidential talk with him she always selected the
sofa as the most suitable ground on which to open her campaign.
All mothers do this; the sofa is to them what the dining-room is to
fathers. In the present case the sofa was particularly well adapted for
a strategic purpose, being an old-fashioned one with a high back,
mattress, bolsters and cushions. Once safely penned into one of its
deep corners, it was like a dentist's chair, not too easy to get out of
again.' Having wheedled from Ernest all she wanted to know, she
'afterwards got him into the most horrible scrape by telling the whole
to Theobald'. (WF197–9) The sensuous, feminine associations of
the sofa – his mother's hand on his, her repeated kisses, the stroking
of hair – lured him like a siren's voice; but again and again he would
find himself instead in the harsh masculinity of the hated dining-
room, heavy with memories of Latin and Greek lessons and redolent
of a particular kind of varnish.

Butler's sense of betrayal by his mother colours his handling of Christina: betrayal of the son to the father, but also betrayal of the son in the name of a false view of religion, and so a betrayal to spiritual death. The idea of death is never far away in Butler's descriptions of his perpetual combat with his parents. In the sofa episode, he wrote of 'the mangled bones of too many murdered confessions' which were 'lying whitening round the skirts of his mother's dress'. (WF200)

Another major sequence is the long quotation of a letter that Fanny Butler actually wrote at Langar to her two sons when she was pregnant with her younger daughter, May. This letter was preserved and given to Samuel on his mother's eventual death in 1873. In the event of her death in childbirth, it was intended to be opened when Samuel reached the age of sixteen, when it would have served as a spiritual breastplate to arm him against the temptations of the world. The preamble is sufficiently ironic: 'When this is put into your hands will you try to bring to mind the mother whom you lost in your childhood and whom, I fear, you will almost have forgotten? You, Ernest, will remember her best, for you are past five years old, and the many, many times that she has taught you your prayers and hymns and sums and told you stories, and our happy Sunday evenings will not quite have passed from your mind . . .' As she warms to her theme, the twin motifs of obedience to the earthly father and of self-denial to the heavenly, and the implied connection between the two, become clearer and sharper, like commandments written on stone:

> You know (for I am certain that it will have been so) how he has devoted his life to you and taught you and laboured to lead you to all that is right and good. Oh, then, be sure that you *are* his comforts. Let him find you obedient, affectionate and attentive to his wishes, upright, self-denying and diligent; let him never blush for or grieve over the sins and follies of those who owe him such a debt of gratitude, and whose first duty it is to study his happiness. You have both of you a name which must not be disgraced, a father and a grandfather of whom to show yourselves worthy; your respectability and well-doing in life rest mainly with yourselves, but far, far beyond earthly respectability and well-doing, and compared with which they are as nothing, your eternal happiness rests with yourselves. You *know* your

duty, but snares and temptations from without beset you, and
the nearer you approach to manhood the more strongly will you
feel this. With God's help, with God's word, and with humble
hearts you will stand in spite of everything, but should you leave
off seeking in earnest for the first, and applying to the second,
should you learn to trust in yourselves, or to the advice and
example of too many around you, you will, you must fall . . .
(FL40–2,WF133–4)

Fanny Butler came from a Unitarian background, joining the
Church of England only before her marriage. Her letter combines
the narrower doctrines of each tradition, stressing the difficulty of
achieving eternal happiness and the insidious ease of failure. The
potential timing of the letter's reception, and the implications of
certain phrases – 'but snares and temptations from without beset
you, and the nearer you approach to manhood the more strongly will
you feel this' – suggest an association of Mammon with sexual
licence: an anxiety amply justified in the case of Tom, and, more
circumspectly, by Samuel. Its chief thrust, however, is the rigidity
and narrowness of the kind of religion preached from Langar pulpit
and reinforced in dining-room and drawing-room, and the qualities
which characterise it: humility, obligation, debt, duty, self-denial.
'How,' asks Butler through the persona of Overton, 'was it possible
that a child only a little past five years old, trained in such an
atmosphere of prayers and hymns and sums and happy Sunday
evenings – to say nothing of daily repeated beatings over the said
prayers and hymns, etc., about which our authoress is silent – how
was it possible that a lad so trained should grow up in any healthy
or vigorous development, even though in her own way his mother
was undoubtedly very fond of him, and sometimes told him stories?'
(WF136) Fanny Butler's religious views, and her respectful devotion
towards her husband, were the two most damning indictments
Samuel could bring against her.
   She was seen in a very different light by the rest of the family.
Her granddaughter recalled her as 'a dear motherly woman sitting
knitting' by the drawing-room fire, giving each child a sweet from a
bottle of 'goodies' at bedtime.[4] Her letters reveal an affectionate,
humorous woman, secure in her well-ordered world of family and
parish life. In contrast to her brother's dark memories, May wrote a

poem when she eventually left Langar listing the flowers and trees and ivied steps, and picturing the children bringing buds of woodbine to their mother's lap.[5] Into this alternative view fits the story of Crib, the little black family dog, who trotted into church to fetch the cook because the kettle was boiling. For Samuel, at least in retrospect, the family relationships were stiff and restrictive. In later life he found himself more at ease among the unsophisticated and uneducated, among country people and foreigners. He would go walking in the villages around London, calling at inns and farms, in search of some lost innocent world, and often in search of eggs. In *The Way of All Flesh* he contrasts the lore of Langar Rectory with that of the cottage. Overton goes to buy eggs in the village, and a cottager's wife begins to wrap them up:

> This operation was carried on upon the ground in front of the cottage door, and while we were in the midst of it the cottager's little boy, a lad much about Ernest's age, trod upon one of the eggs that was wrapped up in paper and broke it.
>
> 'There now, Jack,' said his mother, 'see what you've done, you've broken a nice egg and cost me a penny – here, Emma,' she added, calling her daughter, 'take the child away, there's a dear.'
>
> Emma came at once, and walked off with the youngster, taking him out of harm's way.
>
> 'Papa,' said Ernest, after we had left the house, 'why didn't Mrs Heaton whip Jack when he trod on the egg?'
>
> I was spiteful enough to give Theobald a grim smile which said as plainly as words could have done that I thought Ernest had hit him rather hard.
>
> Theobald coloured and looked angry. 'I dare say,' he said quickly, 'that his mother will whip him now that we are gone.' (WF128–9)

The incident may be fictional; the yearning for kindness and affection was real. Samuel found this where he could: as a child among the servants, like the family nurse, Anne Wade, or with pet kittens, and even aunts, and in adult life through a series of emotionally charged friendships. He learned not to expect anything of the kind from his immediate family. The precept in the book of guidance for parents reportedly used by Thomas and Fanny, 'Break your child's will early, or he will break yours later on', destroyed his capacity to love. Years of conflict and reflection brought about a strictly limited measure of understanding, which surfaces in some of Samuel's later notes. For example, 'MY MOST IMPLACABLE ENEMY from childhood onward has certainly been my father. I doubt not whether I could not make a friend of my brother more easily than I could turn my father into a cordial genial well-wisher; and yet I do not for a moment doubt the goodness of his intentions from first to last.' (N222) In fact, the apparent generosity of the concluding concession is momentary, lasting only until one recalls the traditional association of 'good intentions'. Equally appalling is the enmity between brother and brother, so casually disclosed. The full force of the struggle is expressed in a note, 'Family, Fables of the Erinyes', which constructs a general principle from the Langar experience:

The Ancients attached such special horror to the murder of near relations because the temptation was felt on all hands to be so great that nothing short of this could stop people from laying violent hands upon them. The fable of the Erinyes was probably invented by fathers and mothers and uncles and aunts. (N221)

In the middle-class clerical Langar of Samuel's memory only negative things seemed to happen, or were recalled. No evocation of the beautiful Langar garden occurs in *The Way of All Flesh*, either as refuge or as alternative world. Innocence scarcely breathed before experience intervened. It seems characteristic that one of Samuel's most vivid recollections, 'Bees at Langar Drawing-room Paper', has an 'indoors' setting, and records frustration and deception:

The paper at Langar was at one time of a pattern full of roses, red and white, or camellias, I forget which. I have seen the bees come in on a summer's afternoon and try flower after flower of them, going from sofa to ceiling and then down the next row. They find it impossible in the presence of so many of the associated ideas to believe in the absence of the one they set most store by – honey. (N164)

He makes little reference to the surrounding countryside, or to visitors and holidays. Samuel Butler was less fortunate than his contemporary, William Hale White, 'Mark Rutherford'. White, whose Calvinistic Sunday was a 'season of unmixed gloom', nevertheless experienced those 'perfect poetic pleasures which the boy enjoys whose childhood is spent in the country, and whose home is there', fishing and bathing in the Ouse in summer, skating and playing football in the winter.[6] Samuel's early childhood was recollected as essentially isolated, friendless and confined.

One memorable exception to the pattern of domestic confinement was the expedition the whole family made to Italy in 1843. After Dr Butler's death in 1839, his son was at last comfortably off. In later life Dr Butler had made several journeys through Europe to Italy, so establishing a family tradition, and the Langar party's first excursion was a leisurely affair, partly by train, partly in their own carriage. They went as far as Liège by rail, then by road to Cologne, by rail again to Basel, and on through Switzerland to Parma, Modena, Bologna and Florence to Rome. There they passed half the winter. 'It was my father's birthday and we were all in Rome for the winter of 1843. To celebrate the day (November 28th) we children were taken to the top of St Peter's. I was then just a week under 8 years of age and have a vivid recollection of the event.' Significantly, it was his father's birthday, not his own, whose celebration Samuel remembered. The Butlers moved south to Naples, and in both cities Samuel had lessons in Italian, one part of his education of which he did approve. 'Signora Capocci (I think her name was), who used to teach us Italian at Naples, told us of a poor dear young friend of hers who had had a great misfortune. Her words impressed me:

' "Povero disgraziato!" she exclaimed. "Ha ammazzato il suo zio e la sua zia" (Poor unfortunate fellow! he has murdered his uncle and his aunt).'[7]

Sympathy for a man who had murdered his relations appealed to Samuel and stayed in his mind with other images: a monk rolling down a staircase like a sack of potatoes, bundled into the Corso in broad daylight by a man and his wife; Cardinals kissing Pope Gregory XV's toe in the Sistine chapel; and the beggars who ran after the carriage all day long, crying 'Eretici!' when they were given nothing. His affection for Italy was instinctive: he 'liked to remember that at the age of eight he had fallen in love with Italy at first sight, and that he remained faithful to her for the rest of his life.' (M1.27)

Other legacies from Dr Butler filtered through to Samuel's consciousness. 'As a boy I used sometimes to taste claret at my father's dinner-table when there was a party or guests in the house. I got the taste well into my head. I never tasted claret again for years but, when I did, I found it quite different: much more like weak port wine. I could not make it out and supposed my memory was at fault. But a few years ago I was dining with my old college friend Jason Smith . . . and after dinner there was some wine which I at once recognised as the claret of my infancy. There was no mistake about it. I asked Jason what the wine was. He said it was Château Lafitte and very fine. I have no doubt my father when I was a boy was finishing up my grandfather's cellar.' (M1.29)

But the Bishop's death did not liberate his son. Thomas Butler busied himself conscientiously with his parish duties; he revised his father's school books, the *Geography* and the *Atlas*; he worked on the collection of dried plants, which he would eventually present to the Shrewsbury museum in 65 volumes; and he proceeded with the serious business of his children's education. The children, and particularly Samuel, did not thrive: they were 'white and puny; they were suffering from *home-sickness*'. (WF138) To polish Samuel in preparation for Shrewsbury, he was sent in 1846, when he was ten, to a private school near Coventry. He made little reference to his time there, apart from the boredom of churchgoing. 'When I was at school at Allesley the boy who knelt opposite me at morning prayers, with his face not more than a yard away from mine, used to blow pretty little bubbles with his saliva which he would send sailing off the tip of his tongue like miniature soap bubbles; they very soon broke, but they had a career of a foot or two. I never saw anyone else able to get saliva bubbles right away from him; and though I have endeavoured for some five and fifty years to acquire the art, I never yet could start the bubble off my tongue without its bursting. Now things like this really do relieve the tedium of church . . .' (M1.31–2) At Allesley he went on with the Eton Grammars, the books that his father had thrashed into him, so that when he moved on to Shrewsbury he knew both Latin and Greek grammars perfectly – only to find in his new school that he had to learn Kennedy's

Grammar instead. This he never mastered, a misfortune which he later claimed to be grateful for.

There is a wry irony in the image of Samuel slaving away at the wrong grammar; but most of his memories were painful: the dead body of his baby brother William – 'The only one of my relations with whom I never quarrelled' (M2.414) – lying naked on a bed; the birthday present of birds' eggs and honey removed from him on the news of his grandfather's death; the daily treadmill of learning lessons or Catechism by rote. As he commented, 'the general impression which the Catechism leaves upon the mind of the young is that their wickedness at birth was but very imperfectly wiped out at baptism, while the mere fact of being young savoured more or less distinctly of sin.' Butler associated these personal miseries with the role his father played in the public life of the church: the rectory, rather than the church itself, was the source of mischief. The description of the service in chapter 14 of *The Way of All Flesh* has the detailed sharpness of significant memory:

Even now I can see the men in blue smock frocks reaching to their heels, and more than one old woman in a scarlet cloak; the row of stolid, dull, vacant plough-boys, ungainly in build, uncomely in face, lifeless, apathetic . . .

They shamble in one after another, with steaming breath, for it is winter, and loud clattering of hobnailed boots; they beat the snow from off them as they enter, and through the opened door I catch a momentary glimpse of a dreary leaden sky and snow-clad tombstones . . .

They bob to Theobald as they pass the reading desk ('The people hereabouts are truly respectful,' whispered Christina to me, 'they know their betters.') and take their seats in a long row against the wall. The choir clamber up into the gallery with their instruments – a violoncello, a clarinet, and a trombone. I see them and soon I hear them, for there is a hymn before the service, a wild strain, a remnant, if I mistake not, of some pre-Reformation litany.

The memory turns into a lament for some lost and indefinable expression of religious experience:

Gone now are the clarinet, the violoncello and the trombone, wild minstrelsy as of the doleful creatures in Ezekiel, discordant, but infinitely pathetic. Gone is that scarebabe stentor, that bellowing bull of Bashan, the village blacksmith, gone is the melodious carpenter, gone the brawny shepherd with the red hair, who roared more lustily than all, until they came to the words, 'Shepherds with your flocks abiding,' when modesty covered him with confusion, and compelled him to be silent, as though his own health were being drunk. They were doomed and had a presentiment of evil, even when first I saw them, but they had still a little lease of choir life remaining, and they roared out:

but no description can give a proper idea of the effect. (WF92–4)

The narrator, Overton, records a later visit to the church, where there was now a 'harmonium played by a sweet-looking girl with a choir of school children around her', chanting the canticles to the most correct of chants and singing Hymns Ancient and Modern; later in the evening he sees 'three very old men come chuckling out of a dissenting chapel, and surely enough they were my old friends the blacksmith, the carpenter and the shepherd', with a look of content that convinces him they have been singing songs of Sion. Butler would not have wished to substitute Dissent for the Established Church; but the contrast emphasises the divisions and tensions that permeated the rural parishes of the mid-nineteenth century: social, intellectual and spiritual divisions, which the Church of England through its representative the Rector scarcely touched. The banishment of the 'wild minstrelsy' is symbolic of the Church's failure to reach the people, rather as Hardy noted in *Under the Greenwood Tree*: 'People don't care much about us now! I've been thinking we must be almost the last left in the county of the old string players? Barrel-organs, and the things next door to 'em that you blow wi' your foot, have come in terribly of late years.'[8] George Eliot also recorded the controversy about church music when she described the Rev. Amos Barton climbing into the pulpit to silence the choir's wedding psalm by announcing a hymn 'to some meeting house tune'.[9] Butler, whose emotions were always called into play in the presence of music, sensed instinctively his father's arid life. Whereas Amos Barton walked, with the sleet driving in his face, along roads black with coal dust to the workhouse, Butler imagined his father 'trudging through muddy lanes and over long sweeps of plover-haunted pastures to visit a dying cottager's wife' with meat and wine and spiritual consolation; and then, like Amos Barton, he returned to the safety of his rectory and the welcome of his admiring wife, conscious that he had done his duty, but with a deep sense of dissatisfaction. (WF95) The stiff and joyless atmosphere that Butler experienced is conveyed by his own painting, 'Family Prayers'. Each member of the group, family or servant, seems to be lost, not in wonder or praise, but in vacancy and isolation.

CHAPTER 3

Shrewsbury

In the autumn of 1848, Samuel Butler began his public school education at Shrewsbury. Since there was as yet no railway line from Shrewsbury to the Midlands, the cross-country journey was usually made by coach, a tedious and uncomfortable trip. If the account in *The Way of All Flesh* is accepted, Samuel travelled on this first occasion with his parents in the family carriage. At the other end the terrifying prospect of Dr Kennedy awaited him.

For some temperaments, the family associations might have been encouraging. This was the school that Butler's grandfather had built up into the most academically prestigious of the day; it was the school where his own father had finally headed the examination list, and where he had lived and taught in his turn. The Headmaster, Dr Benjamin Hall Kennedy, was his grandfather's star pupil and chosen successor, and had preceded Thomas Butler by only three years at St John's. Samuel was surrounded by Butler property and relations; across the English Bridge to the east lay the great Tudor house of the Whitehall, where one paternal aunt, Mrs Lloyd, lived with her children; a mile and a half to the south was the village of Meole Brace, the home of his favourite Aunt Bather. If Samuel, like young Ernest Pontifex, had heard 'awful accounts of Dr Skinner's temper, and of the bullying which the younger boys . . . had to put up with at the hands of the bigger ones' (WF143), at least he would be safe from the attentions of his father.

Samuel, however, identified books with unhappiness, and Kennedy with his father. Kennedy becomes, in the novel, the ominously named Skinner, and his library a place of terror: 'the room where new boys were examined and old ones had up for rebuke or chastisement. If the walls of that room could speak, what an account of blundering and capricious cruelty would they not bear witness to!' (WF144) The room was 'as depressing from its slatternliness as from its atmosphere of erudition'. Dust rose from the Turkey carpet when Ernest and his father ominously stumbled over a hole:

> The walls were covered with book shelves from floor to ceiling, and on every shelf the books stood in double rows. It was horrible. Prominent among the most prominent upon the most prominent shelf were a series of splendidly bound volumes entitled *Skinner's Works*.
>
> Boys are sadly apt to rush to conclusions, and Ernest believed that Dr Skinner knew all the books in this terrible library, and that he, if he were to be any good, should have to learn them too. His heart fainted within him. (WF146)

Kennedy, besides representing authority, was volatile, tempestuous, idiosyncratic, energetic, enthusiastic. He never succeeded in winning Butler's trust, nor in instilling confidence into him. Writing years later to W.E. Heitland, Butler confessed: 'I was physically puny and timid, and Kennedy's March temperament was so distressing to me that I was virtually on strike during the whole time I was under him, but your description of him is perfectly just, and I am sure nothing set him so much against me as the conviction that nothing would induce me to come out of my shell in his presence – this piqued him – but if ever in an impulsive moment I did come out, he always touched my horns.'[1] This was Butler at his more objective, or perhaps merely more tactful. In fiction he treated him more severely, describing him as 'a passionate half-turkey-cock, half-gander of a man whose sallow, bilious face and hobble-gobble voice could scare the timid, but who would take to his heels readily enough if he were met firmly . . .' (WF143) How could such a man understand that he was making his money by corrupting youth?

Shrewsbury school, the scene of this campaign of corruption, was then situated next to the castle, on high ground, at the narrow neck of land where the Severn bends like a horse-shoe around the town of Shrewsbury. The main building, now the Public Library, dates from 1630, with the older Riggs Hall behind it. Philip Vandyck Browne's drawing of 1833, which shows the main school and the Headmaster's house to its left, gives the impression of cloistered calm, with the groups of small boys in caps, the praepostors (the prefects) in hats, and the mortar-boarded, gowned masters. The picture might have been designed to illustrate the prospectus:

> The spirit and intent of this discipline is, to prepare boys gradually for the right use and true enjoyment of liberty, by making its enlargement dependent on conduct and exertion: – to give the fullest encouragement to goodness and industry: the utmost discouragement to their opposites: – to make good example influential: – to detect, repress, and, when needful, to remove, evil example: – to bring boys into frequent communion with the Masters: to aim at forming, not only good scholars, but also right-principled and useful men.[2]

What the drawing does not reveal is that on one side the life of the town washed right up against the school: 'The Bounds of the School are strictly limited, on the town side, but extend a mile and a half into the country. . . . None but a praepostor is allowed to go into the town without permission, except during the hour from 1 to 2 o'clock, when a boy in the Lower Sixth or Upper Fifth may go, on business, to a certain limit.' Shrewsbury was a thriving market town which expanded with the arrival of the railway in 1848, and offered any number of temptations. As Kennedy reminded parents, 'the efficacy of this, or any other, discipline may be impaired in various ways, but especially by a large amount of pocket-money being supplied to boys without reference to their merit. Pocket-money thus indiscriminately bestowed, encourages idleness; and to this source are distinctly traced the worst evils which public schools have to encounter.'[3] The Shrewsbury tactic was to limit pocket-money, allowing it to be supplemented by 'merit money', on a scale which related to a boy's Form, and varied by the quality of his work and behaviour. Most pocket-money was spent on food. The worst evils that Ernest Pontifex was forced to admit to, when his father conducted his infamous inquisition into the morals of each boy in the school, were smoking, drinking beer at the 'Swan and Bottle', and swearing and obscene language. Butler's comment on Ernest, that he 'was generally more inclinable to moderate vice than to immoderate virtue' (WF156), is likely to be accurate about himself. He never had enough money to indulge himself too freely. After learning that he was made 'pitiably sick by an amount of beer which would have produced no

31

effect upon a stronger boy' (WF159), he dropped the habit, as there was little fun in it. He therefore never drank much alcohol, but he certainly acquired his lifelong taste for tobacco while at school.

No letters survive from Butler's first year, though the novel contains one from his alter ego, Ernest. Significantly, the major topic is the Latin translation test: 'Dr Skinner made me do about the horse free and exulting roaming in the wide fields in Latin verse, but as I had done it with Papa I knew how to do it, and it was nearly all right, and he put me in the fourth form under Mr Templer, and I have to begin a new Latin grammar not like the old, but much harder. I know you wish me to work, and I will try very hard.' (WF154)

Butler's academic confidence was crushed by the change in grammars. In other areas of school life, he did not fare much better. He was reserved by temperament, his physique was small, and he had been given few opportunities for learning how to make friends easily. At thirteen Ernest 'was a mere bag of bones, with upper arms about as thick as the wrists of other boys of his age; his little chest was pigeon-breasted; he appeared to have no strength or stamina whatever'. (WF156) He found himself painfully knocked about at football, and was useless at cricket. Games at Shrewsbury were voluntary, so he mostly kept out of them. There was one sport, though, which he enjoyed, and that was the institution of the 'hounds', a form of cross-country drag hunt organised by the boys, and barely tolerated by Kennedy because most of the traditional 'meets' took the boys well out of the school bounds. Butler's light build was well suited to running and walking. His stamina, and the pleasure he took in physical exercise of this kind, stayed with him all his life.

The diaries of John Coker Egerton, who left Shrewsbury in 1848 just as Butler arrived, give a vivid account of school life, but from a very different perspective.[4] Egerton had a strong affection for the place, for the masters and for his contemporaries. His diaries do not, of course, invalidate Butler's account; in fact, they make Butler's inability to feel at ease even more poignant, for the entries build up a convincing picture of a stimulating existence. Interspersed with the details of cricket matches, swimming, rowing, football, meetings of the 'hounds', are accounts of concerts in the town (including a visit by Guilia Grisi); of hearing Charles Kemble reading *Hamlet*; of visits to the Assizes, and the Races; of meetings of the Debating Society and Fancy Dress Balls; of taking supper or wine or coffee with one of the masters. The diaries also record less-authorised visits to shops and public houses: 'I was "encouraged" at Mother Wade's'; 'Went to see a badger baited at a rat-catcher's in the town'; 'After afternoon church I walked to the Fox my first time'. It was a robust, demanding kind of life. The praepostors and senior boys organised the games and societies, negotiated with the Doctor about the hounds or the Fancy Dress Ball, maintained the school traditions: 'In the evening the ceremony of roasting which is inflicted on all the new members of Head Room took place. Memo: nothing terrible.' The margin between success and confidence, and failure and fear, in such a society is narrow. Butler, physically slight, immature, shy, and without a ready supply of pocket-money to buy breakfasts or suppers at Mother Wade's, at first did little more than survive.

Even so, he exaggerated his own academic shortcomings and timidity in his portrait of Ernest, which reflects, as he admitted, what he felt to be the case rather than the facts. In the Midsummer examinations for Form IV in 1849, he was placed fourth in classics, sixth in mathematics, and fourth in French, and duly moved up into the Fifth Form the following year. The school curriculum was organised around a detailed system of half-yearly examinations, each with an accompanying printed syllabus, marks, and merit marks, which had been originally instituted by Dr Butler. This system regulated progress and promotions for the ensuing half-year. Merit marks ('Good Classical Work for a fortnight, gains 1 Merit Mark, Good French Work for two months, 1 Merit Mark') contributed to extra half-holidays, or even up to five days' extra holiday (especially welcome when each term lasted nineteen weeks). There was also the incentive of merit money, controlled by the weekly classics and mathematics marks, and further modified by merit and penal marks. The maximum for a boy in the Lower Fifth was 4s 6d: 'several boys got four shillings and few less than sixpence, but Ernest never got more than half-a-crown and seldom more than eighteen pence; his average would, I should think, be about one and nine pence, which was just too much for him to rank among the downright bad boys, but too little to put him among the good ones.' (WF160)

Butler's surviving school letters, all to his mother, are less pessimistic, though they do convey a sense of strained dutifulness:

I thought of you many times yesterday and hope that you are not more tired than may be reasonably be expected . . . Here is the geography and history paper that Papa may see the sort of things that are asked I hope the map may give me some advantages as I'm certain no one else did one. I got up most of the things the night before but forgot that cape Athos was Monte Santo and that Sinus Pelasgiacus was gulf of Volo. My fountain Pirene was wrong. I placed Acheron too in Boeotia. But else I was correct. NB the scribbling was not done at school. I think I have done a good examination and shall know on Saturday . . . I shall be a monitor this half year; that is shall have in turn to call over in our hall (about every three weeks) and on the strength of that have a Exercise excused; and to be allowed to go home a day earlier and sit up till 10 o'clock and have a room with fire and gas of an evening to sit in. Which is not bad but the reverse. With love to yourself and every one about the place.

The letter ends, as do all these early letters, 'I remain Your affectionate Son S. Butler'; as though conscious of the impersonality, he adds a P.S.: 'About the place means Tom Harry May Miss Logie Papa and in fact all within 10 miles round.' (FL42–3) Another letter from the spring of 1851 sounds much more buoyant: Tom, at home because of measles – 'What a very lucky dog that Tom is I should like the measles to come to Shrewsbury' – is given detailed advice as to what parts of Latin and Greek grammar to learn. Then the letter expands:

We are to have a fancy ball; I am not coming out à la Mr Tupman as a brigand with green velvet breeches well spangled though certainly not possessing either of the disadvantages which the aforesaid gentleman possessed namely being neither too old nor too fat. There is to be an oratorio got up with all the Manchester choir etc. (the first information is *true* the 2nd I hold to be slightly apocryphal but still there is a semblance of truth about it.) (FL43–4)

This seems more like the Shrewsbury that Egerton records; and it is necessary to reconcile the interior, psychological sense of inferiority and oppression explored in *The Way of All Flesh* with the sardonic sophistication of the fifteen year old Samuel Butler, who played his role more convincingly than perhaps he realised. Years later, the ambivalence surfaced in his regular attendance at old boys' dinners, equally regularly regretted; while in his notes he thought it worth recording that the different sized bog-holes in the school latrines were known as 'The Doctor', 'Mrs Kennedy', and 'Lottie' (their eldest daughter).

In the autumn of 1851 Tom joined him at Shrewsbury. Samuel's letter of September 25th to his mother, who was away from home at Portsmouth, is an interesting mixture: partly dutiful, partly practical (checking up on the hamper arrangements), but it also reveals a growing capacity for self-analysis: cool, ironic, and conscious of his audience.

> I am glad you like your quarters: but can fancy how acceptable a letter must be. In the first place Tom and I think that a hamper at the end of November just before coming home is rather a paradox and therefore if it could be managed to be sent whilst Aunt Bather is at home she would see about it and it could come about a week after long holiday which begins Tuesday it would be very pleasant provided it was convenient; the inside would be left to Aunt Bather provided only that among other things it contains a *veal pie.*

He then adds a message to his father (ferns and plants formed a kind of neutral territory throughout Butler's life in his relations with him):

> Please tell Papa when next you see or write that I found the 'Adiantum nigrum' (by the way you can't translate Adiantum therefore don't lie awake to think about it) growing on Haughmond hill and as it is almost exclusively a seaside fern it is rather a curious thing to find here . . .

The news of his academic progress is more positive, though his anecdote about Kennedy shows how incompatible they were:

> I do flatter myself that I am improving slowly in my exercises; in my theme the other day I talked of babies finding a great

35

difficulty in walking the Dr. turned it to me and observed, 'any Baby could find it easy to make such Latin as this; why you cant saaoar' (spreading his arms as if he was going to fly) 'You hop from twig to twig and seem afraid to venture two steps beyond the nest' this refers to my sentences being too short but still he gave me a better opinion of it and did not punish me (there being no absolute errors of commission). My verses too (tho' they had a false quantity) he said were rather more in 'the spirit of the thing,' so I begin to have a better hope. I get on very smoothly with Mr Brown I really think him a very clever little man in other respects besides drawing his conversation is always very sensible. (FL44-5)

Philip Vandyck Browne was the drawing master. He had been at Shrewsbury since Dr Butler's time, and told Samuel that he had driven round the archdeaconry of Derby with him during two successive summers, and 'sketched every church at his desire'. Drawing was an option, taken during 'open time'. Butler's love of art, and the instinct that later crystallised into his ambition to become an artist, were nourished by Browne. The more immediate outcome of his influence is a series of watercolours, mostly dated 1854, of Shrewsbury and Langar.

Butler's other great delight, a second oasis in the dry academic routine, was music, and in this he was encouraged by his favourite Aunt Bather. 'My great delight was to get her to play the overtures to Rodelinda and Atalanta, which were her stock pieces.' (M1.35-6) Handel offered the advantages of being accessible, orthodox, and almost sacred. Aunt Bather owned four volumes of Clarke's *Beauties of Handel*, and left them to Samuel. Novello had begun to publish cheap editions, and Samuel would sell a schoolbook to a second-hand dealer and buy a number of the *Creation* or *Elijah*.

His love of Handel was given stimulus from another, and more unexpected, quarter. Carrie Bridges, whose brother George would eventually marry Harriet Butler, was staying at Langar when Sam and Tom came home from Shrewsbury for a half-term weekend. Mrs Butler described the scene in a letter to the absent May: Sam and Tom 'look famously well. Sam has grown half an inch and Tom a quarter. They were both confirmed a few days before they left. We are a most happy family party . . . The boys and Carrie have made excellent friends already. They were a little shy of each other at first, but music is a glorious bond of union; and Carrie plays Handel to Sam half the day.' Sam, continuing the letter, wrote more matter-of-factly: 'The rain has just begun and therefore a walk which Miss Bridges and I were to have taken is prematurely ended. Neither she nor I am very sorry, I guess, for we shall stop in and strum at the piano.'[5] The 'happy family party' may have been wishful thinking on the part of the mother; but Carrie Bridges's playing of 'The King shall rejoice' was wonderfully refreshing: the other news in the letter concerned the growth of the ferns in the drawing-room, the health of the parish invalids, and the progress of the new vestry. The music of Handel became one of the major influences and loves of Samuel's life: ' . . . of all dead men Handel has had the largest place in my thoughts. In fact, I should say he and his music have been the central fact in my life ever since I was old enough to know of the existence of either music or life . . . I believe I am not exaggerating when I say that I have never been a day since I was 13, without having had Handel in my mind many times over.' (N243) Butler took every opportunity to play music, either on St Mary's church organ, or surreptitiously on the piano in the Shrewsbury music-seller's shop.

Aunt Bather meant far more to Butler than a means to music, though the association with Handel intensified the bond. In *The Way of All Flesh*, Miss Alethea Pontifex is partly modelled upon the personality of Butler's later friend, Miss Savage; yet the role she plays in the novel in easing the pressures of Roughborough and discreetly encouraging Ernest was undertaken for Samuel by his aunt: 'A better, kinder soul never breathed; however much she preached she was always kind to me . . .' He records one of her gentle reproofs:

One day she saw me eating bread and butter and honey. Brought up as she was during the early days of Dr Butler's married life, while he was still poor, no doubt she had been allowed bread and honey or bread and butter, but not bread and butter and honey. Such extravagance alarmed her; and she said that it was not heard of in her youth, neither among the young people whom she knew, nor yet, as far as she could gather, in any class of society.

'Why, my dear,' she said, 'don't you remember, "The queen

37

was in the parlour eating bread and honey"; she was not eating bread and butter and honey.'

To which I, being I suppose then about 14 or 15, replied that the Bible expressly enjoined us to eat butter with our honey.

'Butter and honey,' it said, '*shalt* thou eat.'

Whereon she dropped the subject. (M1.35–6)

Butler learned to construct an alternative life for himself. He went through the motions of academic training without ever becoming absorbed by it, rose slowly to the rank of praepostor, and played his role in institutions like the hounds, and the 'Royal Salopian Steeplechases', distance and hurdle races in which each runner was given the name of a horse and owner. He was Senior Whip to the hounds in 1852, and Huntsman for the 1853 season, though he was 'incapacitated by illness, and Mr Wickham reigned in his stead'.[6] He wrote to tell his sister Harriet about the May races: 'I am a steward but shall not run; not that I [am] not well enough or otherwise incapacitated but the stewards are not expected to run as they have the pacing of the ground and the height of the hurdles.' (FL47) In his last year, Butler was not only a steward but also took part. There is a note in a scrapbook of the Rev. Alfred Paget, a much-liked mathematics master, that in the Derby Stakes, 'Three times round and the distance', Mr Clarke's 'bk h Vesuvius – S. Butler –' came fifth. The horses' names were chosen with care. On another occasion, Butler was 'Backbiter': his quick temper and cutting tongue were already in evidence.

Butler had no mask to conceal his unhappiness. Like Ernest, he even gave credit to his turkey cock headmaster for noticing something was wrong. ' "Pontifex," said Dr Skinner, who had fallen upon him in hall one day like a moral landslip, before he had time to escape, "do you never laugh? Do you always look so preternaturally grave?" The doctor had not meant to be unkind, but the boy turned crimson, and escaped.' (WF186) Butler made his various escapes: into music and painting and into the same kind of dreams that he satirised in his mother in his portrait of Christina. Some of this dreaming took the form of worshipping images, unattainable idols, a practice that he continued and suffered from all his life. The friends he made at school were not the ones he wanted: Ernest 'did not much care about the boys who liked him, and idolised some who kept him as far as possible at a distance'. (WF187)

Similarly, the first girl who attracts Ernest's attention in *The Way of All Flesh* is beyond his reach. His awareness of her is given a musical context, an echo of Carrie Bridges: Ernest goes down to the drawing-room to play the piano before breakfast so as not to disturb his papa and mama, and finds Ellen 'sweeping the drawing-room floor and dusting while he was playing'. Ellen has a clear, but high complexion, grey, beautifully shaped eyes, lips full and restful, figure perfect but 'erring if at all on the side of robustness'. She is an idealised reflection of those girls of natural, simple beauty who attracted Butler's admiration at intervals, but Ellen, having fallen and become pregnant, is sternly banished from Battersby vicarage, away from Ernest's adolescent yearning. (WF188–92)

By 1853, Butler's priority was his preparation for St John's: 'I got 3s 6d merit money the other day; the Dr. says I improve; and I'm sure that I do . . . I am working among other mathematics some equation papers of St John's college: very hard: called the 7 devils: they are 7 in number and extremely difficult; they quite stump me.' (FL46–7) But his father's plans for another family expedition to Italy, this time without Samuel, prompted reconsideration. His letters show how much he minded being left behind. 'I answer you soon,' he wrote to his sister Harriet, 'for fear that you and mama should think that I am weeping because I am not to go; I agree with Papa that time now *cannot* be spared, and I assure you I am making the most of it and working very hard; don't think that I shouldn't like to go; but the fact is I *can't* and theres an end of it; don't think this is sham resignation for it is not; the thing I regret most is the lengthy separation from you all . . .' He moves on to more neutral schoolboy items: he has been lying vegetating in the sun on the ball court hill – but 'only once a week and that Sunday'; one of the praepostors has shot a lot of rooks and made them into a pie; the rats are squeaking under the wainscot. (FL47–8)

He also mentioned he had been to tea with Aunt Bather, who appears to have intervened tactfully on his behalf, judging from his next letter home:

I know that both of you would take me if you could, and did not resolve against it without mature consideration; that is the

yᵉ way in which Mr Paget doth attempt to cram yᵉ boys

Drawing by Samuel Butler, 1852, from the scrapbook of the Reverend
A.J. Paget

reason that I did not once ask you to take me: Auntie asked me to write down my views of the case on a piece of paper 'pro's' on one side 'con's' on the other; I did not ask her to send them to you and I do not know whether she did; only do not think, if she has, that I have been grumbling behind your backs for I have certainly not; as, indeed, I think she would tell you.

Samuel was being groomed for classical honours, and the ultimate prize of a fellowship. The choice lay between missing the trip, and staying on for a further year at Shrewsbury. Samuel, meeting Kennedy, managed to ask him if he had had a letter from his father; but he just replied, 'Yes I have – and written to him.' 'I asked no more: literally not daring so to do; pray let me hear the result *post haste*. I almost hope to have a line tomorrow so as to be either killed or cured at once.' Kennedy, and Canon Butler, relented. Samuel missed the autumn half-year, travelling through Switzerland with the rest of his family to Rome and Naples, and taking up his study of Italian.[7] He returned to Shrewsbury in the new year of 1854 to continue his preparation. In the school class list for Midsummer, he was placed seventh in the Upper Sixth and won no prizes. However, after his admission to St John's for the Michaelmas term, he was able to write to his father that he had been awarded a scholarship. The Shrewsbury classical machine had done its job.

Butler's obstinacy about the European trip, contact with the art and language of Italy, and even the series of watercolours, point to a growing consciousness of independent powers. As Ernest leaves Roughborough for the last time by train, Butler describes him as looking right into the middle of the sun, veiled by grey mist, 'as into the face of one whom he knew and was fond of'.

At first his face was grave, but kindly, as of a tired man who feels that a long task is over; but in a few seconds the more humorous side of his misfortunes presented itself to him, and he smiled half reproachfully, half merrily, as thinking how little all that had happened to him really mattered, and how small were his hardships as compared with those of most people. Still looking into the eye of the sun and smiling dreamily, he thought how he had helped to burn his father in effigy, and his look grew merrier, till at last he broke out into a laugh. Exactly at this moment the light veil of cloud parted from the sun, and he was brought to *terra firma* by the breaking forth of the sunshine. (WF220–1)

Samuel Butler's own life was about to begin.

CHAPTER 4

St John's

For Butler, Cambridge was 'the first place where he had ever been consciously and continuously happy'. After the cramped companionship of Shrewsbury, and the suffocating domestic life at Langar, St John's offered a framework of independence and freedom within which he could expand. At last he found some protection against the intrusions of external authority: 'How can any boy fail to feel an ecstasy of pleasure on first finding himself in rooms which he knows for the next few years are to be his castle?' Assured of his right to the most comfortable chair, without having to cede it to mamma or papa or sister, free to smoke at will, free above all to be alone when he wished, he rejoiced in the new world that his years on the classical and mathematical treadmill had earned: 'Why, if such a room looked out both back and front on to a blank dead wall it would still be a paradise, how much more then when the view is of some quiet grassy court or cloister or garden...' (WF221–2) His rooms were on D staircase, in New Court. In an essay published towards the end of his time at Cambridge, Butler described his homecoming to 'dear old St John's' after a European walking tour:

From my window in the cool of the summer twilight I look on the umbrageous chestnuts that droop into the river; Trinity library rears its stately proportions on the left; opposite is the bridge; over that, on the right, the thick dark foliage is blackening almost into sombreness as the night draws on. Immediately beneath are the arched cloisters resounding with the solitary footfall of meditative students, and suggesting grateful retirement. I say to myself then, as I sit in my open window, that for a continuance I would rather have this than any scene I have visited during the whole of our most enjoyed tour, and fetch down a Thucydides, for I must go to Shilleto at nine o'clock tomorrow.[1]

The bachelor model of paradise was firmly imprinted.

Fired by his surroundings, Butler took up his studies with renewed enthusiasm. He was admitted to St John's as a pensioner, the largest category of undergraduate, on May 2nd. In November he was able to begin a letter to his father with casual understatement: 'The scholarships came out this morning and I have got one; only 5 freshmen have; how much mine is worth I do not know; but shall some day I suppose.' (FL49) Canon Butler retained a portion of his son's awards, which included a Shrewsbury Exhibition. 'I am exceedingly pleased with the unexpected addition to my income by your giving me half the £35,' Butler wrote with veiled irony. 'I have always contrived to make my present carry me thro' and I cannot say that I have had anything to complain of on the score of money at my university career so far. But another £4 per term will be very acceptable and I am not likely either to spend £6 extra on the strength of it or let the £4 remain idle in my pocket. I am very much obliged to you for it.' (FL53) The meticulous accountancy and defensive self-justification will become familiar. Butler was always quick to respond to his father's challenges, seeming to gain strength each time he was crossed.

But, for a while, such tensions were relatively minor. Butler enjoyed sharing his mildly sardonic view of college life with his father: he allowed himself only the occasional barb, such as the reference to lack of cash, or 'tin':

I have to swear thro' thick and thin tomorrow at 9 but as I believe that you are only required to swear that you'll be a good boy and not beat the master and senior fellows (which were I to attempt I dont think I should succeed in doing) and that you have not got any tin, another fact which my conscience will permit me to assent I shall not make any bones about the oaths.

I go to Parkenson in Euclid on Tuesday Thursday and Saturday mornings from 8 to 9. To Headlam on Mondays Wednesdays and Fridays at the same hour; To Mayor's *voluntary* composition lectures three times a week for two hours at a time; and to Reyner arithmetic twice a week: Parkenson and Headlam and France are awfully jolly dons far the nicest in the college: Reyner and Mayor are brutes. Bateson stopped me in the courts a day or two ago and let me dandle his two fat fingers and was very kind. I go to Aunt Susan's quite once a week and she has told me never to go on Saturdays. (FL49–50)

At that period, an undergraduate's studies were almost entirely based within his college. St John's, with 292 undergraduates in 1858, was the second largest college (Trinity had 473; no other college more than 100) and organised the mathematical teaching into two rival 'sides', with a separate scheme of lectures, each preparing candidates for the Mathematical Tripos. Mathematics was still the dominant study. Before entering for the Classical Tripos, Butler, like every other candidate for honours, had to achieve a certain standard in mathematics, hence the emphasis on Euclid and arithmetic. Because there was no entrance examination, and because the curriculum at public or grammar school varied so widely, much of the college teaching was elementary and repetitive; so any 'reading man' who aimed at achieving a reasonably high place in a Tripos 'coached', seeking out private individual tuition which was a considerable additional expense.

Even in the wider world of Cambridge, Butler found himself surrounded by school and family connections. Francis France, Tutor and President, had been head boy at Shrewsbury, and had been taught by Butler's grandfather; William Bateson, the Senior Bursar, elected Master in 1857, was a Salopian; Richard Shilleto, who coached Butler at a later stage of his Cambridge education and who was denied a fellowship because of his early marriage, was yet another product of Dr Butler's classical training; while J.E.B. Mayor came from the Kennedy era at Shrewsbury.

News, visits, hampers, parcels of wine, passed between Langar and Cambridge. Aunt Susan was Samuel's Great-aunt Susannah Apthorp, his grandmother's unmarried sister. He preferred her to another family connection, the widow of a Nottinghamshire clergyman: 'I hate Mrs Parry and she bothers me to walk which I sometimes but rarely do.' (FL50) Carrie Bridges came to Cambridge, and Butler was able to find a chaperone so that he could show her his rooms, which were full of plants from Langar, including a flourishing woodsia. There were other social obligations, stoically endured. When

Butler was joined at St John's by his brother Tom in 1856, they were 'let in for a tea-party' at Shilleto's: 'this bitterly cold thaw is not certainly tempting weather to stir out in, much less at night and on such an errand, but nevertheless it must be done. Tom has never been there before and I don't fancy he'll want to go again. The Harvey Goodwin's asked me to an evening party on Wednesday. I went as I could not help myself: it too was exquisitely dull.' (FL57) Tom, usually referred to in terms of mild disparagement, did not interfere much in his brother's life; he left Cambridge without taking his degree. These well-intentioned offers of hospitality and friendship, however unappreciated at the time – and Butler never overcame his unease at formal social gatherings – established some basis for future relationships. By the time Butler came to write his grandfather's life, Shilleto had been transformed into 'my kind and illustrious old friend'.

The undergraduates' day began at seven, with morning chapel. College lectures were usually over by twelve, and about half-past one, according to Butler's contemporary T.G. Bonney,[2] reading men shut up their books, took a very light lunch (often only bread and butter) and went out for some exercise. At St John's, rowing flourished; and many undergraduates followed Charles Simeon's advice to check every day that the third milestone from Cambridge was in place. In the summer, Byron's Pool made a pleasant bathing place, or the hardier, including Butler, would run down to Sheep's Green and swim before chapel. 'We have had a great deal of wet lately,' he told May, 'but yesterday a complete change seems to have set in, and the heat was tremendous. I am very glad of it, for our early bathing had dwindled to a very few (I have been a most unflinching adherent) owing to the daily encreasing chilliness of the water: and as I consider it a grand institution I don't like seeing it decay.'[3] In winter he enjoyed skating, or expeditions to the riverside hamlet of Upware, five miles from anywhere, where he was a member of the 'Republic Society'.

It was, naturally enough, in the company of his contemporaries that Butler began to relax and to develop his personality and his distinctive frame of mind. There were plenty of Salopians to form a large network of acquaintances, and their names occur in Butler's letters home, usually in connection with their chances for various scholarships and prizes. His closer friends, though, were drawn from a variety of backgrounds: prospective lawyers and bankers as well as scholars and clergymen, with rowing as one of their common interests. He soon became a 'not unpopular member of the best set of his year'. (WF223).

A letter to his mother helps to define both the 'best set' and the kind of men Butler found uncongenial. Mrs Butler's enquiries about friends were, in Samuel's opinion, seldom disinterested; she was casting in a naive attempt to entice prospective husbands in the direction of Harriet or May. One contemporary she asked about, Lys, had cut him dead as mutton, notwithstanding his endeavours: 'whatever company I was in I always spoke to him when we met, tho' he might be with the most atrocious cads. Lys is good enough himself, he is only gawky and uncouth, but he is never a man that I could ever become in any way intimate with, and so I suppose considering me a "bloated aristocrat", in company with all the rest of the Lady Margaret boat club, he has determined to have none of us . . .' (FL60–1) Butler, too slight of build to be a successful oar, enjoyed coxing, and in time coaching, the college boats. In 1857, a mistake on the third night nearly lost the college the Headship.[4] The float on the starting line got wrapped round the rudder strings, checking the boat till the rings gave way. The boat was by then lying straight across the river, but the number 7 backed water, and Lady Margaret sprinted away with Second Trinity almost overlapping. If they had been bumped, Butler would have been held responsible. As things turned out, he commented, 'I get praise for coolness and good steering as much and more than blame for my accident and the crew are so delighted at having rowed a race such as never was seen before that they are satisfied completely . . . another inch and I should have never held my head again.' (FL58–9) In May he was again coxing the first boat, and his description reflects the confidence he felt at being part of a successful crew:

With good luck we shall remain easily head of the river, to the great chagrin of the First Trinity boat club . . . Just when matters were looking rather lugubrious for us, some beautiful freshmen got ripe under my assiduous coaching, and we now do the course in less time than any other boat.

As we go over the course every day, there are plenty of gigs and traps running by our sides, and men, too, timing us and noticing every stroke; one feels very big and responsible with the knowledge that if you steer a foot too wide round a corner or don't keep the boat's head *quite* straight, but budge a *little little* bit to the one hand or the other, your misdeed is looked upon with untellable satisfaction or the contrary by heaps of foes or friends of the boat. (FL61)

This strain of hearty, uncomplicated, collegiate athleticism reveals an unexpected aspect of Butler. Certainly, he seems to have relished being supposed a 'bloated aristocrat' in the company of men like Joseph McCormick, later rector of St James's, Piccadilly, who won a rowing blue, and William Marriott, afterwards a barrister, M.P. and Privy Councillor, with whom he planned a walking trip to visit the churches of Normandy. Other friends included Henry Hoare, George Paley, Jason Smith and another future barrister, Joseph Green, who accompanied him on a walking tour through the Dauphiné to Switzerland and Italy in June, 1857.

Butler published an account of this tour in the St John's magazine, *The Eagle*. There had been no undergraduate journal before *The Eagle* was founded in 1858. Butler was one of the original editors, and contributed an essay 'On English Composition, and Other Matters' to the first number, his earliest published work.[5] He argued that the style of English authors in the seventeenth century was 'more terse and masculine than that of those of the present day, possessing both more of the graphic element, and more vigour, straightforwardness, and conciseness'. Butler lays down a number of rules for writing: 'forgetfulness of self, and carefulness of the matter in hand'; a preference for plain narration; the principle of taking care of the matter, and letting the words take care of themselves; not talking about what you do not understand. These are rules that he would not find much reason to alter in years to come. His second contribution, 'Our Tour', sets out to show how far you could travel through Europe on £25. It begins as a highly practical commentary on railways and hotels – Butler would have been an excellent journalist – interspersed with the unusual incidents and observations of the bizarre that delighted him. But when the travellers leave Grenoble and head up the Romanche valley into the mountains, Butler begins to lose himself and take the reader with him:

Leaving our trap at Briançon and making a hasty breakfast at the Hotel de la Paix, we walked up a very lonely valley towards Cervières. I dare not say how many hours we wended our way up the brawling torrent without meeting a soul or seeing a human habitation; it was fearfully hot too, and we longed for *vin ordinaire*; Cervières seemed as though it never would come – still the same rugged precipices, snow-clad heights, brawling torrent, and stony road, butterflies beautiful and innumerable, flowers to match, sky cloudless. At last we are there; through the town, or rather village, the river rushes furiously, the dismantled houses and gaping walls affording palpable traces of the fearful inundations of the previous year, not a house near the river was sound, many quite uninhabitable, and more such as I am sure few of us would like to inhabit. However, it is Cervières such as it is, and we hope for our *vin ordinaire*; but, alas! – not a human being, man, woman or child, is to be seen, the houses are all closed, the noonday quiet holds the hill with a vengeance, unbroken, save by the ceaseless roar of the river.[6]

Butler became more expansive on holiday, released from the strain of keeping up a role, and this trip offered most of the ingredients which made him feel happy: a congenial companion, simple food and wine, mountains and mountain flora, foreigners (ideally, Italians), unusual architecture and customs. He liked the idea of being the first, or one of the first. Cheap rail travel was making Europe wonderfully accessible to the middle-class English tourist; but the kind of long-distance walking that Butler and Green undertook that summer, over unfrequented passes with scarce and rough accommodation, was more adventurous than most. On this occasion he returned contentedly enough to the little paradise of his Cambridge room, and took down his Thucydides.

Butler was now working hard and systematically with a First in mind. His mentor, Richard Shilleto, the distinguished Greek scholar, was one of the most sought-after coaches in Cambridge. An early marriage ruled out the Trinity fellowship he seemed destined for; heavy drinking is reported to have blocked his nomination as Regius Professor of Greek. At one stage he was teaching twelve students every day, six days a week. His method was narrow, rigid, and highly successful; and even to secure Shilleto's services was a mark of distinction. 'Shilleto said he should not take me this term,' Butler wrote to his father on October 23rd, 1857, 'as he has made it an invariable rule never to take men in their last term unless they were going to be *very* high, such men as Snow &c. So I told him that he would please to break that regulation on the spot, to which he succumbed without a moment's hesitation. The very next time I went to him however, being in a communicative mood he said he hoped I should get a first but it all depended on my exertions during the next 3 months and that very likely I shouldn't. No one of you wants a first class half so much as I do: so you need not fear my becoming inflated by any hopes held out but rather rejoice that I am being encouraged which I think a great invigorator when sparingly applied.' (FL62) Butler was working so hard that his eyes had become inflamed and he was forced to give up reading by candle light:

> Daylight reading does not in the least affect them so I have been out of bed by a quarter past 5 every morning lately and into bed by 10 at night, get a cup of tea by 6 in the morning and read till nine, breakfast and amusement till 10, read from 10 to one, go to Shilleto ½ past 6 to ½ past 7 (I don't care about that at all.)
>
> Well then there is music from 1 to 2 and exercise from 2 to 4 and music from 4 to 5 and dinner at 5; so when I come back from Shilleto I am pretty glad to have done the day's work. Of course drawing goes to the dogs. I am exceedingly well in every respect but my eyes, and they are mending. (FL62–3)

Butler kept on with his music, though he did not give as much time to it as he would have liked: 'I shall have no visible result to show on the pianoforte and have scarcely played a dozen hours the whole term, Sunday included.' (FL57) But in his last year, the prompting of his friends led to more regular practice under a music master, who said he lacked execution and told him not to play any more Bach for the present: 'The music master is a very nice fellow and very strict and has got a nasty way of caricaturing your style of playing (in what I think a most unfair manner tho' I submit with all the meekness of a lamb without a word of argument).' (FL62)

So preparation for the Classical Tripos continued, with the long hours of study relieved by music and the Lady Margaret boat club, by visits to Stittle's Nursery Gardens for strawberries and skating expeditions on the Cam. Until the results were known, the precise shape of the future could conveniently be ignored: whatever it might be, however, it was assumed that ordination would follow. The family tradition supported it; it was the inevitable accompaniment of college fellowship or school headmastership; a third of Cambridge under-graduates came from clergy families. Butler seems to have experi-enced little in the way of religious doubt as an undergraduate. Never-theless, his almost pathological dislike of and contempt for the Evangelicals may have concealed misgivings that he found it difficult to articulate. Although Charles Simeon had died in 1836, his influ-ence in the university was still strong, one particularly active colony being among the sizars of St John's, which he described in *The Way of All Flesh*:

> Behind the then chapel of this last-named college there was a 'labyrinth' (this was the name it bore) of dingy, tumbledown rooms, tenanted exclusively by the poorest undergraduates, who were dependent upon sizarships and scholarships for the means of taking their degrees . . .
>
> In the labyrinth there dwelt men of all ages, from mere lads to grey-haired old men who had entered late in life. They were rarely seen except in hall or chapel or at lecture, where their manners of feeding, praying and studying, were considered alike objectionable; no one knew whence they came, whither they went, nor what they did, for they never showed at cricket or the boats; they were a gloomy, seedy-looking *confrérie*, who had as little to glory in in clothes and manners as in the flesh itself.
>
> Unprepossessing then, in feature, gait and manners, unkempt and ill-dressed beyond what can be easily described, these poor fellows formed a class apart, whose thoughts and ways were not as the thoughts and ways of Ernest and his friends, and it was among them that Simeonism chiefly flourished. (WF232–3)

The sneering, snobbish tone of these paragraphs betrays the 'repel-lent attraction' that the Sims had for Butler; he nowhere alluded to the fact that his own grandfather entered St John's as a sizar. The gawky and uncouth Francis Lys, who eventually went out to Madras as a missionary, sounds like a Sim, in contrast to the bloated aristocracy of the Lady Margaret boat club, though in an earlier generation many rowing men were Sims – the Magdalene 1st boat was known as The Tea Kettle, because of a preference for tea over ale, and the 2nd Trinity boat as the Hallelujahs. The St John's Sims went about at night dropping tracts into the letter boxes of men they thought ripe for conversion, and Butler circulated a parody:

> Beware! Beware! Beware! The enemy sowed tracts in the night, and the righteous men tremble.
>
> 2. There are only 10 good men in John's; I am one; reader, calculate your chance of salvation.
>
> 3. The genuine recipe for the leaven of the Pharisees is still extant, and runs as follows: – Self-deceit ⅓ + want of charity ½ + outward show ⅓, humbug ∞, insert Sim or not as required. Reader, let each one who would seem to be righteous take unto himself this leaven.[7]

Butler, who saw things in black or white and was either vehemently for or against an attitude, was well-cast in the role of Saul as persecutor or possible convert. The description of the Simeonite gathering in *The Way of All Flesh*, where the handsome, courteous Evangelical preacher from London, the Rev. Gideon Hawke, preaches on the text 'Saul, Saul, why persecutest thou me?', suggests a basis of experience: 'The virtue lay in the man more than in what he said; as for the last few mysterious words about his having heard a voice by night, their effect was magical; there was not one who did not look down to the ground, nor who in his heart did not half believe that he was the chosen vessel on whose especial behalf God had sent Mr Hawke to Cambridge.' (WF243–8)

The personal implications for Butler, and what he really believed in, were coming closer and closer to the surface. His golden time at Cambridge was drawing to an end. He sat for the Classical Tripos in 1858, and achieved his First Class, being placed 12th equal, good enough for an academic career should he wish one. For the last time he coxed the 1st boat in the Mays. He then moved down to London, and spent six months as an unpaid assistant to the Rev. Philip Perring, a former pupil of Dr Butler at Shrewsbury, and a curate at St James's, Piccadilly. Butler took lodgings in Heddon Street, off

Regent Street, and found himself in a new and quite unexpected
world.

CHAPTER 5

London: the Prodigal Son

The six months or so that Butler spent in London, between the autumn of 1858 and the spring of 1859, were crucial to his development. He went there to gain some experience of parish work before returning to Cambridge to read for the Voluntary Theological Examination. 'I lived among the poor and worked among them,' he commented later, 'but soon discovering that I could not take the teaching of the Church as seriously as I thought a clergyman ought to take it . . .'[1] By the time he left, he knew that he did not want to be ordained. He also knew that he did not believe the religion in which he had been brought up. He spent most of the rest of his life working out what he did believe in.

The radical change is simpler to describe than to explain. There are no surviving letters from the period, and relatively few direct allusions in his later notes and writing. His fictional treatment suggests that he found the experience traumatic: his lodgings in Heddon Street are transformed into 'Ashpit Place', and his antihero Ernest re-enacts the fall: brought to the edge of ruin by the charms of Miss Snow, the Drury Lane 'actress', he assaults her respectable neighbour Miss Maitland during a pastoral visit and is sentenced to six months' imprisonment with hard labour in Coldbath Fields. Butler's later close friend and biographer, Henry Festing Jones, claimed that there was nothing in Butler's life to correspond to the Miss Maitland incident (M1.60–1), by which he meant that Butler was already sufficiently sexually and socially experienced to know the difference between a 'respectable' girl and one of a different sort.[2] Jones shared Butler's mistress for some years, and shared Butler's intimate confidences: Butler was not reticent in private about sex. The clumsy, unsuccessful pass is symbolic: the earnest young man has simply got everything wrong.

Butler discovered that his education and upbringing, privileged, sheltered and narrow, gave him no qualifications whatsoever for the job he had undertaken. He found the mass of people supremely indifferent to religion, at least to the religion represented by the Church of England. The believers he met tended to be Nonconformists, whose arguments were much more convincing than his own. When one of the young men in his evening class asked him why a good and all-powerful God should have permitted the existence of evil, he is reported to have replied: 'My good man, don't you see? If Adam had not eaten the apple you would now be in the Garden of Eden; whereas, things being as they are, you have a chance of Heaven, which is a much better place.' (M1.60) He then found out that most of the boys in his class had never been baptised; far more shocking, baptism apparently had no measurable effect on their character or behaviour: those who had been baptised seemed no better – nor worse – than those who had not. Butler was, if not innocent, then extraordinarily naive, as he freely admitted. He had accepted unquestioningly a whole bundle of dogmas, stock answers and prejudices: he confessed later to his aunt, Mrs Worsley, that he turned down an invitation to their house that winter because he was afraid it was a sin to eat with Unitarians on Christmas Day. (FL104) As the months passed, he realised that he must jettison everything that he had been told, and work things out for himself. He began by making a detailed scrutiny of the Greek New Testament, analysing the inconsistencies and variations in the Gospel narratives.

Other experiences of the world influenced his image of himself. Soon after he had taken his degree, he travelled north to examine at a school in Bolton. Learning that he was intending to claim only his second-class rail fare, the Headmaster reprimanded him: 'Young man, there are two classes of people in this world: there are those who prey, and there are those who are preyed upon; never you belong to this latter.' (N182) So he charged first-class fare, and travelled second, and the bonds of Langar loosened slightly.

Butler now faced the dilemma of telling his parents, no simple task especially for someone so unsure of his own ground. He emphasised his misgivings about ordination: there was no way he could unburden himself of his more personal doubts. What his father gave he took, he explained to his mother in his role of prodigal son: 'for that capital so laid out I can show good interest – especially during the six months I was in Heddon Street; true I fear the interest is not such as *you* like, but it is such as I feel all precious to me though I see that this storm has been brought about by no other means. But for this I should have been quietly ordained and none of this sad business would ever have come about.' (FL77–8) In the spring of 1859 he went down to Torquay, in Devon, where his family was staying on a protracted visit during his sister Harriet's engagement to George Bridges. There it was agreed (at least in Butler's view) that he should return to St John's, see if he could attract some coaching, and, if no opening appeared at his own college, try for a fellowship elsewhere in Cambridge. As he noted in 1901, 'If I had remained at St. John's I should probably have got a fellowship. Stanwell of my year, also a Johnian, got one; he was only 20th in the first class whereas I was bracketed 12th. I cannot doubt that the fellowship he got would have been given to me. *I am very glad it never was*, for like enough I should have stuck on in Cambridge till now!' (FL65)

Butler's plan was designed to buy time. A fellowship would never have suited him, as it would have entailed studying and lecturing in the classics, which held little interest for him. His father, on further reflection, saw the scheme as full of danger; an opportunity to linger in Cambridge, surrounded by unreliable and subversive companions, on the security of an allowance he had rashly offered. He had no inkling of the spiritual and intellectual turmoil in which his son found himself, and simply pressed for a firm and practical way of earning a living: Samuel was, after all, twenty-three. His letter of March 9th set the tone for a correspondence in which both men consistently achieved the least helpful interpretation of the other's position:

Today your letter has come. It does not strike me as satisfactory. I don't want you to be a schoolmaster any more than I want you to be ordained. But I mean you to do something for your living for your own sake. And if you can show me anything else that you like better, the sooner it is done the better I shall be pleased.

If you say 'I'm very well content as I am and would rather live on my allowance and improve my mind', I shall not sanction your throwing away your best years, so I shall cut your allowance down.

I don't want to force upon you any life that is objectionable

56

to you but I do want to drive you to halt no longer between two opinions and to choose some course. The college life you are now leading seems the worst sort for opening your mind. (FL64)

Butler was extremely hurt by this letter, as he confessed to his mother, especially by the implication that he was sponging off his father. His reply put forward a provocative alternative: 'What say you to my going to Liberia for instance and seeing what kind of a place it is, and whether or no cotton growing there is likely to pay . . .' (FL65) In one respect, the wild Liberian notion worked, for his father was at least prompted into a grudging remark: 'I don't want to drive you into a line of life you dislike. Neither will I object to your staying up till October.' (FL67) But the sudden introduction of emigration certainly made him question his son's judgment. He refused to allow Samuel any more time; he wanted a clear path, a stated objective; he wanted him to read for a specific purpose and with some direction, namely the Voluntary Theological Examination and the Carus Prize for Greek. Butler certainly wished to read, but for his own darker and inexpressible purposes. Also, having 'read so much at subjects which I never cared a straw about I am naturally anxious to make use of opportunities you gave me to apply what little I may have learnt to practical use in subjects wherein I take a lively interest . . .' (FL69) He wanted, in fact, to go on with his music, and particularly to take drawing lessons at the Cambridge school of art. With some understandable reluctance, he gradually revealed that art was the profession he really wished to explore and felt he had some talent for, rather than any of the astonishing menu of alternatives canvassed: schoolmastering, bookselling, the army, the law, farming, diplomacy, even homoeopathic medicine.

The correspondence, speeding between Cambridge, Torquay and Langar, is still painful to read, for it reveals an anguish in Butler's mind that he was unable to articulate, let alone communicate; he clearly longed for an understanding and affectionate relationship, while every exchange emphasised the impossibility of achieving it. Some of his letters and interpretations would have tried the patience of most fathers. Canon Butler, irritable by temperament, made gestures in the direction of tolerance, but between him and his son was an unbridgeable divide. Butler could not define in terms that his father would accept what his instincts urged him towards: art, music,

writing, philosophy. Any hint in the direction of creativity or originality was curtly dismissed: 'I have no objection to your taking up
drawing as an amusement – I said that long ago. But as to the wild
scheme of making it a profession with no knowledge whatever how
far it may answer, and to the neglect and ruin of every other prospect,
to this I will give no countenance at all – not for my sake but for
yours.' (FL81) The 'artist scheme' was, in Canon Butler's eyes, the
worst of all possible choices, undoubtedly because of the moral
danger in which he assumed his son would be placed. The leap from
holy orders to artist's studio would throw him into very dangerous
society. He might learn to draw well enough to be encouraged to go
on, but that was not the same as becoming a painter. Excellence
alone would give 'station and respectability' to his career: 'Meanwhile
your society is cast in with a set of men who as a class do not bear
the highest character for morality, are thrown into the midst of the
most serious temptations and if it is possible that you may stand, it
is also possible that you may fall. I can't consent to it.' (FL88–9)

If Canon Butler failed to appreciate his son's latent creativity, he
could not begin to understand the nature of his theological questioning. Urged to clarify his objections, Butler did his best, though
reluctantly, because he knew how much it would grieve his parents.
He cited Article XV as the passage he specially objected to:

'But all we the rest, though baptised and born again in Christ,
yet offend in many things' (James iii.2); 'and if we say that we
have no sin we deceive ourselves and the truth is not in us' (I
John i.8). Believing for my own part that a man can, by making
use of the ordinary means of grace, attain a condition in which
he can say, 'I do not offend *knowingly* in any one thing either
habitually or otherwise and believe that whereas once on a time
I was full of sin I have now been cleansed from all sin and am
Holy even as Christ was holy upon earth.'
   . . . I know not how to put my thoughts in less strong language
and yet express them fairly and fully: I grant that to beings of
finite intelligence like ourselves there will be, it may be, certain
sins of ignorance which we could not be fairly chargeable for
having committed, having many been educated to such and
such a belief and never had the means of discovering the

falsehood thereof – but that no sin that is known to be sin will appear in him that is incorporate with Christ.

Two notes, the first by his father, signal the importance of this letter of May 9th, 1859. 'This I believe just the doctrine held by Pelagius but the Article seems to me not only supported by the quotation but wisely framed in almost the words of the quotations for John and James. Thomas Butler.' To which Butler, at the close of his life, replied: 'I do not know which is the more comic in its own melancholy way – my letter or my father's note.' (FL73–4)

Butler concentrated on the area that had so perplexed him in London at his evening class: the relationship between baptism and grace. Broadly, he could not accept a religion that based itself upon the fundamental wickedness of humanity, whose practice was centred on the injunction, 'Thou shalt not', and whose doctrine pointed to the eternal divide of heaven and hell. Although the way he defined his objection may be comical, the shock to his consciousness, to his self-image and to his image of the world was violent. His experience, however tenuous, of the intense faith preached by the Sims only made him more vulnerable. Just when he was open to the powerful attractions of personal commitment, he found the foundations, not the building, to be flawed.

The issues that Butler successively grappled with – the status of the Bible, the nature of life after death, the Virgin Birth, the Resurrection – were already controversial, and remain so today. His education had insulated him from current theological and philosophical debate. He appeared ignorant that Coleridge, for instance, reflecting the seminal biblical criticism of Germany, had already confronted these problems; or that F.D. Maurice's more recent essay on 'Eternal Life and Eternal Death', which had led to his dismissal from King's College, London, in 1853, affirmed the very position he was struggling to express to his father. Butler seldom found comfort or confirmation in the ideas of his near-contemporaries. He preferred to wrestle on his own. The pursuit of ultimate truths, however, was postponed because of the urgent need to settle his immediate future. Canon Butler's next broadside raised the emotional temperature still higher: 'If you choose to act in utter contradiction of our judgment and wishes and that before having acquired the slightest knowledge of your powers which I see you overrate in other points, you can of course act as you like. But I think it right to tell you that not one sixpence will you receive from me after your Michaelmas payment till you come to your senses.'

After agreeing that the army was an unsuitable career – the risk of Samuel 'getting into difficulties' with his superior officers was too great, though the 'necessity for obeying' was tempting, even when balanced by the expense of buying a commission – he laid down his terms crisply:

It is best to be clear and distinct. I will not contribute to your going abroad. I will continue your allowance as far as £100 a year in law. I should have heavy fees and expenses to pay which will not allow me to do more. Neither am I disposed to sacrifice the other children to you. If you will not take that profession and can get a tutorship, good. If you can get a mastership in a school, good but not so good. If you can devise another plan of your own I'll hear it but under no fetter to accede. You take no notice of my last letter which yet required an answer.

God give you a seeing eye one day.

Still your affectionate Father. (FL74–5)

Money, never far from centre stage in the Butler family dramas, assumed a dominant role. In a long letter to his mother, still in Torquay (written on the assumption that it would be immediately forwarded to Langar), Butler began to assert his autonomy. He claimed that he had 'duties to myself to perform even more binding on me than those to my parents', and announced histrionically that he would reject the pounds, shillings and pence and go in search of bread his own way.

No man has any right to undertake any profession, for which he does not honestly believe himself well qualified, to please any other person. I should be preferring the hollow peace that would be patched up by my submission (for you could never forget that this submission had been obtained by money pressure), and the enjoyment of more money, to undergoing the great risk and trial which I see before me. I am old enough by this time to know my own mind, and deliberately accede to my father's proposal that I should receive no more from him if I refuse to do what he wishes; it is fair play – I don't question his right to do what he likes with his own. I question his wisdom greatly, but neither his motives nor his determination to stick to them. (FL75–8)

Butler's options were diminishing: he would be granted an allowance to pursue either the law or schoolmastering, both anathema to him; his own choices lay between emigration or art. He claimed he had £270; he would make it last three years, and then borrow from friends until he could make a living; or he would borrow against his eventual interest in the Whitehall property at Shrewsbury.

Butler was especially bitter about the Whitehall property. By his grandfather's will, the whole estate had been left to Samuel, after life interests to his Aunt Lloyd and to his father. However, at their instigation, he had been persuaded to agree to sell the house itself and some land to his cousin, Thomas Lloyd, in 1857: as he noted in 1901, 're the sale of the Whitehall Shrewsbury to my cousin. How they bamboozled me!' (FL62) The entail had accordingly been lifted, the sale concluded, the proceeds reinvested, and the entail replaced. In the event, the town of Shrewsbury expanded with the prosperity brought in part by the railway, land values rose sharply, and Butler would have been substantially better off had the estate remained intact. He remained convinced that he should never have been faced with the invidious choice of agreeing to the sale or causing offence within the family.

All through the summer the dispute smouldered, springing up from time to time in a blaze of rhetoric and abuse: 'tyrant', 'martyr', 'disinherit', 'gross impropriety'. Various alternative occupations were investigated, including an editorial position on a newspaper, which prompted a letter heavy with paternal disparagement:

I have no objection in the world to your accepting the kind and liberal offer of Mr Midglay if only you feel and are competent. But I have it your church principles will stand in your way (of course Mr M. should know what they are), and I fear what you call speaking out may ruin the paper. Neither do I know at all how conversant you are with political knowledge. Altogether I fancy more judgment and maturity are wanted than you possess, and if the paper comes to grief its upholders must change their editor or give it up at once.

With this borne in mind I have no obstacle to put in your way – and will aid your little plan, but rapid and sound judgment is wanted in it. (FL84–5)

Finally, farming emerged as a kind of compromise, allied to emigration. The combination met with a more reasoned, even favourable, response: 'I will therefore so far consent to emigration that I will continue your allowance while you are away for 12 months and then advance capital needful.' New Zealand was proposed. 'You mention New Zealand to which I shall make no objection,' replied his father, proceeding at once to spell out its disadvantages: 'It is however I believe about 5 months passage and takes near 12 months therefore to get an answer to a letter. This is a serious drawback in any case but especially where there is uncertainty and indefinite money matters to be arranged. Would the Cape suit you? It's only 6 weeks I believe, and communication any time much easier. Even Columbia is nearer than New Zealand and has I believe a good prospect, but you are less fitted for it, for it is a newer country.'

In the same letter, Canon Butler produced one last and surprising rabbit, astonishing in view of his earlier strictures: diplomacy. 'I would use every effort and Wm. Lloyd has kindly promised the same to get an appointment as attaché to some Embassy. Of course in the first instance in a subordinate post. You are quick at languages and know something of Italian and French. It must however be a *sine qua non* that if you take this line (and I'm not sure that it can be got for you) you should make it your profession and not a mere vehicle for seeing art and practising it as your object.' (FL88–9) Butler ignored this bizarre suggestion, and obediently, but now scarcely bothering to suppress his irony, replied by return of post: 'I gratefully and gladly accept your kind consent to my emigrating. I hope by the exercise of prudence and industry to make a sufficient sum of money to enable me to return home at the end of some ten or dozen years.' Already he was planning to cross Canada and be over the Rocky Mountains before the end of October, and suggested setting off on 15 August, in ten days' time: it would be his constant endeavour to make his parents feel that in consenting to his departure for a considerable time, they would have gained a son rather than lost one.

Once the decision was agreed, they all cooled down. More advice and discussion led to the choice of New Zealand, where the Canterbury Association, with the Archbishop as president, had been set up to develop a settlement on Church of England principles. The Butler and Worsley connections were put to work, and letters of introduction and recommendation began to arrive. Towards the end of September Butler said his goodbyes at Langar, and moved to London to stay with his Uncle and Aunt Worsley in Taviton Street, in Bloomsbury. He left his prayer book behind at home, but May found it and forwarded it to him. He thanked her, and added: 'I trust you will not think *too* much of me, but am sure that I shall think *very* much indeed of all at Langar, and often I am sure we shall be thinking of one another at the same time and in the same way.'³ May learned after from Mrs Hall that Samuel said his greatest grief on going away was leaving her, which surprised, pleased and saddened her. She wished she had known it before.⁴

Butler had originally booked his passage on the *Burmah*, but reluctantly cancelled it on his cousin Richard Worsley's advice when changes were made to the passenger accommodation: a stroke of luck, or providence, since the *Burmah* was lost on the voyage. He spent a busy last week. His new ship, the *Roman Emperor*, was lying in the East India docks before leaving from Gravesend. He chose fittings for his cabin: a table and chair, a square of carpet, looking glass, lamp, washing stand and water filter. He had his photograph taken. He made crucial calls on New Zealand contacts, notably James Edward Fitzgerald, the first Superintendent of Canterbury Province, who was the official agent and emigration commissioner in London: Fitzgerald promised to deliver letters of introduction in person at Gravesend. He did the rounds of his friends, including Philip Perring. He even learned that a neighbour of a Cambridge friend had taken the next cabin to his – a farmer's daughter 'of pleasant exterior' called Buss – 'what a name!' He trusted she was engaged and going out to be married.⁵

On Friday, September 30th, on a cold, windy, rainy day, he was rowed out from the pier at Gravesend to his ship. None of his family came to see him off. Having clambered over the ship's side, Butler was taken aback by the apparently inextricable confusion:

. . . the slush upon the decks, the crying, the kissing, the mustering of the passengers, the stowing away of baggage still left upon the decks, the rain and the gloomy sky created a kind of half amusing, half distressing bewilderment, which I could plainly see to be participated in by most of the other landsmen on board – honest country agriculturists and their wives looking as though they wondered what it would end in – some sitting on their boxes and making a show of reading tracts which were being presented to them by a methodistical looking gentleman in a white tie . . .

And so the afternoon wore on, wet, cold, and comfortless – no dinner served on account of the general confusion – fortunately I was able to seize upon some biscuits. The emigration commissioner was taking a final survey of the ship and shaking hands with this, that, and the other of the passengers – fresh arrivals kept continually creating a little additional excitement – these were of saloon passengers who were alone permitted to join the ship at Gravesend. By and by a couple of policemen made their appearance and arrested one of the passengers, a London cabman, for debt. He had a large family and a subscription was soon started to pay the sum he owed. Subsequently a much larger subscription would have been made in order to have him taken away by any body or anything . . .

At last some food was served. Butler went down to his cabin and started to unpack and arrange his books. He smoked a couple of pipes and went up on to the poop. There was no sound except 'the clanging of the clocks from the various churches of Gravesend, the pattering of rain upon the decks, and the rushing sound of the river as it gurgled against the ship's side'.[6]

When he finally went to bed, for the first time in his life he did not say his prayers. The rites of passage had begun, and the ties with Langar were loosened further. 'The night before I had said my prayers,' he recorded, 'and doubted not that I was always going on to say them, as I always had done hitherto. That night, I suppose, the sense of change was so great that it shook them quietly off.' (N184)

CHAPTER 6

The New Chum

The happiness that Butler had tasted at Cambridge, which had been soured by the doubts and disagreements of the last year, slowly returned as the emigrant ship sailed south. Distance from his family, distance from the oppressive conventions of Victorian England – conventions both of social habit and of mind – released his energy.

His account of his experiences was later published in *A First Year in Canterbury Settlement*.[1] There is a vitality in his descriptions of the long voyage towards the promised land, and a renewed optimism and curiosity. His health was good, and he was spared the miseries of seasickness. In the privacy of his cabin, he settled down in the relative comfort of his folding armchair to read his books and write his journal; his chief study was Gibbon's *Decline and Fall*, volumes two and three of which he especially recommended for anyone thinking of taking holy orders. He enjoyed an evening rubber of whist, had lessons on the concertina, played shuffleboard, and even organised and conducted the small choir: 'We practise three or four times a week; we chant the Venite, Glorias, and Te Deums, and sing one hymn. I have two basses, two tenors, one alto, and lots of girls, and the singing certainly is better than you would hear in nine country places out of ten. I have been glad by this means to form the acquaintances of many of the poorer passengers.' (FY23) This item seems aimed at his readers in Langar. The Te Deums and Venites take their place among vivid descriptions of sky and sea, and the incidents and details that punctuated the routine of the voyage: the burial of a consumptive girl, the capture of a shark, the multitude of birds in the southern seas. The route took them to the south of Australia and 'Van Diemen's Land', then to Stewart's Island and north up the east coast of South Island to Port Lyttelton.

New Zealand held out to young men the promise of freedom: 'They were all so delighted with the prospect of the untrammelled life before them that they felt it necessary to make some gesture of contempt for the conventions they had left behind, so the first evening ashore they built a huge bonfire, piled on it their top hats and tail coats, and danced in a ring round the blazing fire.'[2] Everything about the new world was notable, with its strange mixture of the exotic and the familiar. 'Oh, the heat!' wrote Butler,

> the clear transparent atmosphere, and the dust! How shall I describe everything – the little townlet, for I cannot call it town, nestling beneath the bare hills that we had been looking at so longingly all the morning – the scattered wooden boxes of houses, with ragged roods of scrubby ground between them – the tussocks of brown grass – the huge wide-leafed flax, with its now seedy stem, sometimes 15 or 16 feet high, luxuriant and tropical-looking – the healthy clear-complexioned men, shaggy-bearded, rowdy-hatted, and independent, pictures of rude health and strength – the stores, supplying all hetero- geneous commodities – the mountains, rising right behind the harbour to a height of over a thousand feet – the varied outline of the harbour now smooth and sleeping . . . (FY31)

Washing his hands before dinner at the Mitre, he was disconcerted to overhear through the scrim partition a snatch of conversation:
'Have you washed yet?'
'No.'
'Don't you mean to wash this year?'
'No.'
When his neighbours turned out to be clean and respectably dressed, he realised they were sheep farmers talking shop. After dinner, so foreign and yet so English, and a second shock on finding that beer cost sixpence a glass, he and a companion set off up the steep bridle path to scale the Port Hills, which separate Lyttelton from Christchurch and the Canterbury plains.

The hills are volcanic, brown and dry; dotted with tussock, flax, and a great deal 'of a very uncomfortable prickly shrub, which they call Irishman' (FY32) which Butler did not like the look of. The hill was so steep, and the sun so hot, that Butler put his knapsack on the back of the packhorse that made a daily trip; and then, at the summit, he could pause and look at the scattered houses of

Christchurch, dotted about on the swampy ground beside the river Avon; and beyond the plains to that long, blue, lofty, even line of the mountains, 'like the Jura from Geneva or the Berwyn from Shrewsbury'. (FY33)

Butler had no very clear idea how he was to earn a living, let alone make his fortune, in New Zealand. It was pioneer country. The settlement itself was ten years old, and Christchurch had the raw potential of a frontier town. He put up at the Lyttelton Hotel in Oxford Terrace, and listened to the talk of sheep, horses, dogs, cattle, paddocks and bush. These were precisely the topics Butler wanted to hear about. With the help of his letter of introduction from Fitzgerald, he invested £55 of his modest means in a bay horse, named Doctor, a good river-horse, and very strong. Thus supplied with this absolute necessity for life in the settlement, he began to explore the country around Christchurch, which gave him an inkling of the kind of life he might soon be living:

> Next morning, I rode some miles into the country, and visited a farm. Found the inmates (two brothers) at dinner. Cold boiled mutton and bread, and cold tea without milk, poured straight from a huge kettle in which it is made every morning, seem the staple commodities. No potatoes – nothing hot. They had no servant, and no cow. The bread, which was very white, was made by the younger. They showed me, with some little pleasure, some of the improvements they were making, and told me what they meant to do; and I looked at them with great respect. These men were as good gentlemen, in the conventional sense of the word, as any with whom we associate in England – I daresay, de facto, much better than many of them. (FY37)

The notion of a gentleman creating a new life for himself by the sweat of his own brow appealed to Butler; but he was spared the test of a truly long-term commitment by the arrival, within days, of £2000 from England, the first instalment of a total of £5000 which his father offered to give him. He never managed to sound particularly grateful for this arrangement, justifying his attitude by the argument that his father was well able to afford it. Inevitably, too, the outstanding £3000 provided ground for future antagonisms and misunderstandings. But the possession of capital made all the difference to his New Zealand prospects. As he admitted later, without it he would have been confined to the same kinds of profession open to him in England. With its security, he was able to contemplate four main possibilities: to buy a quantity of sheep, place them on some squatter's run and receive a share of the wool proceeds; to buy the goodwill of an established sheep run; to buy land, lay it down with English grass, and stock it; or – the most challenging option – to ride out and discover suitable land, rent it from the Commission, and gradually develop and stock it himself. It was this last course that Butler decided to investigate.

It was a bold choice. Butler knew nothing about sheep, or any other form of farming. He could scarcely ride. His upbringing, apart from his continental walking holidays, had been unrelievedly domestic; and his undergraduate days had given him a taste for comfort, and a certain admiration for, even envy of, the elegant and the sophisticated. On the other hand, it might be argued that to anyone who had survived the physical and emotional rigours of an English public school education, most other hardships would seem relatively trivial. Butler's will was highly resilient, and he had formidable powers of endurance.

When he first climbed the Port Hills, Butler's eye had been drawn to the mountains, 'the distant Apennines, that run through the middle of the island'; and he longed to 'get on the other side of them'. He met a sheep farmer, J.C. Watts Russell, who owned a run in the back country, behind the Malvern hills; Russell agreed to take Butler with him on a short expedition into the remoter valleys, prospecting for sheep country that had not yet been taken up.

This first expedition, in March, 1860, initiated Butler into many aspects of New Zealand life. He learned to ride, and to trust his horse. For the first time he saw a sheep killed, and came to accept the fact that the same knife both killed the beast and carved the mutton for dinner. He had his first experience of life in the bush. After spending a day crossing the plains, while the mountains slowly drew nearer, they made their way up the Waikitty Valley, dined at the station owned by George Harper, and arrived at the end of the first phase of their journey by moonlight, at the Lake Coleridge station homestead:

Here we were bona fide beyond the pale of civilisation; no

boarded floors, no chairs, nor any similar luxuries; everything was of the very simplest description. Four men inhabited the hut, and their life appears a kind of mixture of that of a dog and that of an emperor, with a considerable predominance of the latter. They have no cook, and take it turn and turn to cook and wash up, two one week, and two the next. They have a good garden, and gave us a capital feed of potatoes and peas, both fried together, an excellent combination. Their culinary apparatus and plates, cups, knives and forks, are very limited in number. The men are all gentlemen and sons of gentlemen, and one of them is a Cambridge man, who took a high second-class a year or two before my time . . . He regarded me as a somewhat despicable new-comer (at least so I imagined), and when next morning I asked where I should wash, he gave rather a French shrug of the shoulders, and said, 'The lake.' I felt the rebuke to be well merited, and that with the lake in front of the house, I should have been at no loss for the means of performing my ablutions. So I retired abashed and cleansed myself therein. Under his bed I found Tennyson's *Idylls of the King*. So you will see that even in these out-of-the-world places people do care a little for something besides sheep. (FY50)

The Cambridge man was William Rolleston, a future Superintendent of the Province and Government Minister.

Leaving civilisation behind them, Butler and Russell rode across rough country and entered the Aroca branch of the Harper river, intending to follow it to its source and hoping to find a saddle that would lead them to new ground. They camped on a flat on the edge of the bush, lit a fire, tethered the horses, boiled tea, and supped.

The night was warm and quiet, the silence only interrupted by the occasional sharp cry of a wood-hen, and the rushing of the river, whilst the ruddy glow of the fire, the sombre forest, and the immediate foreground of our saddles and blankets, formed a picture to me entirely new and rather impressive. Probably after another year or two I shall regard camping out as the nuisance which it really is, instead of writing about sombre forests and so forth . . .' (FY53)

They used their saddles for pillows, strapped blankets around themselves, and settled down for the night. But Butler found the scene too novel to sleep. Just as he was drifting off he would look up and see the stars; and then he gradually discovered he had underestimated the amount of blankets he needed, and had failed to choose a spot with a hollow for his hipbone. But he concealed his discomfort from his companion, anxious to be accepted as an 'old chum' as quickly as possible. The next morning, they moved on; the mountains, glaciered and magnificent, closed in, the river dwindled, and they were in the grandest Alpine scenery. Butler thought it needed 'a chalet or two, or some sign of human handiwork in the foreground'; as it was, the scene struck him as too savage. It was a true wilderness, untouched by any sign of human occupation. Maoris had travelled through some of the Alpine passes on their way to the west coast; but there were few Maoris surviving in South Island, and none in this area. Butler and Russell were the first white men to penetrate so far into the Aroca fastnesses.

Leaving their horses, and pushing on up through a belt of black birch, full of parroquets, they emerged on to the moraine of an old glacier to be confronted by frightful precipes and glaciers. Two thousand feet above them was a saddle, but its covering of snow prevented them climbing it, as they had left their blankets and provisions behind with the horses. Moreover, the real purpose of the journey was commercial, rather than scientific. They had satisfied themselves that there was no sheep country worth renting, and that the mountains they were among were not the main back-bone range, but only offsets. Back at the camp site, Butler put into practice what he had learned of the art of sleeping rough: he slept in his clothes, and made sure he had a hollow for his hip. At dawn, he found the mountains 'pale as ghosts, and almost sickening from their death-like whiteness'. (FY57–8) They retraced their route to the Lake Coleridge station, burning the scrub on the flats behind them as they rode down. The journey had been a rigorous initiation into the wildness of the back country, taking Butler into unmapped, virgin territory. The solitude struck him repeatedly.

He had learned a great deal about safety and survival, and the incentive of finding new country drew him back to the upper valleys. Almost immediately, he made another expedition in the

same area, this time on his own, up the Waimakiriri. He under-
went a condensed course in the art of crossing rivers, threading
his way across the many channels of the braided river with the
help of a rapidly acquired appreciation of the dangers, and
complete trust in his horse, Doctor. He proved that he and
Russell had been correct in supposing that the snow-covered
saddle was not a true pass, but only led to the next river
above the Rakaia. He also sensed that another route held more
promise:

I saw one saddle low enough to be covered with bush, ending
a valley of some miles in length, through which flowed a small
stream with dense bush on either side. I firmly believe that this
saddle will lead to the West Coast; but as the valley was impass-
able for a horse, and as, being alone, I was afraid to tackle the
carrying food and blankets, and to leave Doctor, who might
very probably walk off whilst I was on the wrong side of the
Waimakiriri, I shirked the investigation. (FY62)

This saddle was later named Arthur's Pass, and became the main
route to the west coast gold fields.

In April, with another companion, Butler rode up the Rangitata
River. Some twenty miles or so above the Mount Peel station, they
turned up into the Forest Creek tributary which struck him as an
ugly, barren-looking place: a deep valley between two high ranges
which were not entirely clear of snow for more than three or four
months. Starting from the bottom of this valley on a clear frosty
morning – so frosty that the tea-leaves in their pannikins were frozen,
and their outer blankets crisped with frozen dew – they reached a
shingle bed at the top of the range after seven hours of arduous
climbing. Butler decided to climb a peak a few hundred feet higher
than where they were resting on the shingle:

I saw snowy peak after snowy peak come in view as the summit
in front of me narrowed, but no mountains were visible higher
or grander than what I had already seen. Suddenly, as my eyes
got on a level with the top, so that I could see over, I was struck
almost breathless by the wonderful mountain that burst on my
sight. The effect was startling. It rose towering in a massy

parallelogram, disclosed from top to bottom in the cloudless sky, far above all the others.

As he commented, 'If a person says he *thinks* he has seen Mount Cook, you may be quite sure that he has not seen it. The moment it comes into sight the exclamation is, "That is Mount Cook!" – not "That *must* be Mount Cook!" There is no possibility of mistake.' (FY65–6)

Butler mocks himself for admiring a mountain that is of no use for sheep, and asks pardon for this occasional outbreak of the old Adam, the scenery-loving tourist. But his energy and persistence had revealed a large tract of country on the upland slopes of the Bush Stream watershed, between the Sinclair and Two Thumb Ranges. He returned to Christchurch, and on April 16th personally registered a claim to Run 353, supported by a sketch map.[3] This, though marginal sheep country in itself, formed the nucleus around which Butler's later holdings clustered.

In May he made one further expedition, following the Hurunui to its source, but found no land worth taking up. The terrain was difficult – the pack-horse rolled over more than once – and the weather deteriorated; it was too late in the season for long excursions. He decided to build a hut on Forest Creek and live there for the winter, and so discover at first hand whether the country was suitable for sheep in the severest conditions.

The site that Butler chose for his hut is, even today, a desolate spot; a convenient place to camp, but scarcely to live. Forest Creek runs in a valley that is wide where it joins the Rangitata, but eight miles further up it is narrow and closed in by the slopes of the Ben McLeod and Sinclair mountains sweeping up on either side. On a terrace where Butler's Stream joins Forest Creek from the south, and where there is grazing for the horses, Butler began to build what was known as a 'V' hut. He had ridden in with an old Irishman and a 'cadet',[4] and as many stores and supplies as could be carried on a single pack-horse. Somehow he sent a message to his friend John Baker in Christchurch, who applied for another 5000 acres of adjacent land on his behalf. As the site of his hut was actually on the boundary of a run belonging to Tripp and Acland, his neighbours, he also applied to buy the freehold of a small block, 10 by 20 chains.

A V hut – more understandably, an inverted V – is a roof set down without any walls on the ground: Butler's was 12 foot long by 8 foot broad. On May 20th it was ready to sleep in; and the next day Butler crossed the Rangitata with his cadet, leaving the Irishman in solitary possession: the cadet was to collect fresh supplies of meat from a neighbouring station, while Butler rode to Christchurch to fetch stores and a second cadet. Returning to the Rangitata ten days later, after a two day delay on the banks of the swollen Rakaia, he discovered a party of men who had been detained there for over a week. They had a bullock and dray, in which the cadet and the meat rode, the latter distinctly the worse for wear. Divided by anxiety for the abandoned Irishman and the dangers to the cadets in the river crossing, Butler decided to make the attempt, giving strict instructions to his companions not to follow him until he had safely negotiated each branch of the river. There were several near mishaps, including one particularly unpleasant episode when his horse sank to her belly in a quicksand, and Butler had to break all the rules of river crossing and lead her to the shore. A cat, which Butler was nursing in a bag on the pommel of his saddle, came in for a sousing; but as soon as he remounted she could be heard purring reassuringly through the bag.

Eventually, the group negotiated the Rangitata and made their way up Forest Creek through the night and the heavy rain, to find the hut a revolting mess. The thatch had been either insufficient or wrongly laid, and the ground was soaked and soppy with mud. They had tea, fried some of the disagreeably high beef, and wrapped themselves in blankets to sleep in spite of the rain dripping through the roof and the raw, cold atmosphere.

Conditions soon improved. 'Oh! what fires we made – how soon the snow grass dried! – how soon the floor, though even now damp, ceased to be slushy! – then we humped in three stones for seats – on one of which I am sitting writing while the others are at work upon the house . . .' A new tin kettle was a great acquisition, very 'beneficial', according to the Irishman; and in the evening the cat, who had done her work by ridding the place of rats, slipped in under the thatched door to lick Butler's face and purr. But as winter progressed, it became clear that the original country could not on its own make a satisfactory sheep run; it needed to be worked in conjunction with country that was clear of snow throughout the year.[5]

It is difficult to establish how long Butler actually remained at

Forest Creek. The Irishman, a great character, was anything but a handyman, and Butler was obliged, half regretfully, to send him away; while both cadets left quite quickly. He is unlikely to have stayed on his own for longer than was necessary to observe the weather conditions. There is a Tripp family tradition that Butler was employed for some time as a cadet at Mount Peel. In the words of Charles Tripp's son Bernard, 'my father was a practical man and, as you can well imagine, Butler's "theories" combined with an insatiate desire to go "exploring" did not coincide with my father's conception of station management, so, before very long, the cadetship came to an end.'[6]

His stay at the Tripps', would have been an ideal opportunity to learn something of sheep-station management before embarking on a full-scale venture. But Butler would not have been an easy candidate for a cadetship, and expressed reservations about the system; he also suggested an alternative: 'Let a man pay not only for his board and lodging, but a good premium likewise, for the insight that he obtains into up-country life, then he is at liberty to work or not as he chooses . . .' (FY70) He may have made some such arrangement with Tripp and Acland; certainly, despite his reputation for being impractical he quickly learned the principles of running a sheep station.

Butler must also have spent some time in Christchurch, at the crucial period when the Waste Lands Board were making decisions about boundaries and allotments of land. While he sat writing on his stone in the V hut, he had considered building a house, bringing up a dray and erecting a yard. However, he had seen a much better site for a permanent homestead, on a stretch of land adjacent to his own. On September 6th he applied for Run 387, made up of islands in the wide bed of the Rangitata; and on September 22nd Run 242, originally allotted to Owen and Carter and declared stocked, was transferred to Butler's name. It was to this site, in the low foothills overlooking the Rangitata between Bush Stream and Forest Creek, that he set off on Tuesday, October 2nd, 1860, with a bullock and dray loaded with all the requirements of a new station: 'Flour, tea, sugar, tools, household utensils few and rough, a plough and harrows, doors, windows, oats and potatoes for seed, and all the usual denizens of a kitchen garden . . . about a ton and a half.' (FY81) He gave the place the name that it bears today: Mesopotamia.

CHAPTER 7

Mesopotamia

Leaving Christchurch behind him, Butler meandered across the Canterbury plains on his one-hundred-and-twenty-mile journey, learning about the ways of bullocks as he went. He had armed himself with a tracing of the government map, showing the allotted boundaries, because a neighbouring runholder, Caton, had recently put up a small hut for his shepherd on the very place he had earmarked for his new home. Butler had inherited a highly developed sense of property. Setting his men to work to build a sod hut, he rode straight to Mount Potts on the other side of the Rangitata, where he knew Caton to be, and offered him financial compensation for his hut – such as it was – and sheepyard. Caton 'threatened fiercely, and would hear no reason'. (FY102) Although Butler was sure that Caton had not bought the freehold, he was equally certain that he meant to do so as soon as possible and so, determined to forestall him, he set off back to Christchurch the same afternoon, planning to travel through the night.

The Ashburton River, however, was running high, the night was dark, and even Butler was apprehensive. He camped down, waited for daylight, and set off at dawn. He had not gone far when he glanced round and saw a rider a quarter of a mile behind who turned out to be Caton. He waited for him, and the two rode side by side for some miles, neither mentioning the real reason for their journeys. It was early on Wednesday morning: the Board was due to meet the next day, and would deal with business in the order of the applications entered in the book at the Land Office, which closed at four and opened at ten. Knowing Caton could not possibly arrive in Christchurch before four, Butler decided he would not hurry, and allowed Caton to ride ahead. Then his horse went lame. He borrowed another, and finally reached town by seven in the morning. At twenty to ten he made his way to the Land Office, expecting to find Caton waiting, and anticipating a row.

To his surprise, the office doors were open. Butler looked in the book – and there was Caton's name, entered unfairly ahead of time. To Butler's even greater surprise he found his own name below Caton's, entered the previous day, he learned later, by his own solicitor, Henry Wynn Williams. Caton's deceit was self-evident. Wynn Williams added some notes to Butler's version of the affair in *A First Year in Canterbury Settlement*: 'I remember this well. It was quite a matter of chance. I knew he was prospecting for country and thought it as well to put his name down.' Caton, he added, 'a great scoundrel', 'ought to have been prosecuted, but his solicitor was Crown prosecutor!'[1] The Commissioners needed little persuasion. Butler made his case, secured the freehold, and went off to relieve the tension by playing Bach fugues on Wynn Williams's piano. With the principle of the freehold established, Caton came to terms about the hut and yard, and over the succeeding months made agreements to transfer three runs bordering the Rangitata to Butler. By the end of March, 1861, his holdings amounted to over 40,000 acres.

He was heavily occupied over the next two months supervising the building of his sod hut, negotiating for land, stocking his runs, and bringing up supplies. He engaged a shepherd called Cook, and left much of the day to day work to him. By the end of the year, he was preparing another expedition, partly, no doubt, with a view to discovering more sheep country, but also drawn by the sight of the upper reaches of the Rangitata, backed by high mountains and fed by glaciers, 'distinctly visible to the naked eye, but through the telescope resolvable into tumbled masses of blue ice . . .' (FY76)

His companion was his friend the surveyor John Holland Baker, who arrived at Mesopotamia for Christmas: 'three of us sat down to Christmas dinner and our names were Butler, Baker, and Cook . . .'[2] In January they began to explore the upper branches of the Rangitata, the Havelock, Clyde and Lawrence Rivers. They followed the Lawrence to its source and then climbed up to a saddle at its head, 'coming out on top of the range right opposite what was later known as the Whitcombe Pass'.[3] From there, they looked down on to the Rakaia headwaters below, and, deciding not to risk the descent, retraced their route, circled round by Lake Heron, and camped at the foot of the pass on February 2nd. The next day they crossed the saddle and descended some distance down the Pass River, 'till we were hemmed in by bush on both sides and found there was no chance of finding open country.'[4]

They duly reported their discovery to the Lands and Survey Office. In 1863, Henry Whitcombe and Jacob Louper managed to cross to the west, though they suffered great hardship, and Whitcombe was drowned in a river crossing after reaching the coast.

Ten years later, Butler drew on these experiences for the opening of his novel *Erewhon*. In the description of his hero Higgs's journey into the unknown country, he reconstructed the landscape in his imagination, yet never departed very far from reality. Through the eyes of his narrator, Higgs, one can sense the impact that the mountains made on Butler at a time when his inner life, as well as his physical existence, was at a turning point. After a steady climb of between three and four hours, Higgs reaches a tableland, close to a glacier that marked the summit of the pass:

> Above it towered a succession of rugged precipices and snowy mountain sides. The solitude was greater than I could bear; the mountain upon my master's sheep-run was a crowded thoroughfare in comparison with this sombre sullen place. The air, moreover, was dark and heavy, which made the loneliness even more oppressive. There was an inky gloom over all that was not covered with snow and ice. Grass there was none.
>
> Each moment I felt increasing upon me that dreadful doubt as to my own identity – as to the continuity of my past and present existence – which is the first sign of that distraction which comes to those who have lost themselves in the bush. I had fought against this feeling hitherto, and had conquered it; but the intense silence and gloom of this rocky wilderness were too much for me, and I felt that my power of collecting myself was beginning to be impaired. (E65)

In these early months Butler returned from his mountain journeys to the practical tasks of developing his station and expanding the Mesopotamia homestead. He built a 'cob' hut; cob is a mixture of clay and chopped up tussock, sun-baked but not fired, and is good building material so long as it is kept dry. Butler's inexperience – or the inexperience of his workmen – is witnessed by the story that the original thatch was put on the wrong way round – from the ridge to the eaves instead of from the eaves to the ridge – so that the rain ran into the roof. A friend and neighbour, John Enys, remembered being taken by Butler to 'see the place he had chosen for a pig sty, which he said he thought a good one; but when I said I thought it a perfect place as the whole drainage went into the drinking water, he remarked that I was dreadfully practical'.[5] In spite of these blunders Mesopotamia became a place of moderate comfort. Within a year Butler acquired a considerable team, with Cook as overseer, together with a shepherd, bullock-driver, hut-keeper, and two station hands to work on the fencing.

Meeting Robert Booth in Christchurch, whom he had already known up-country, he offered him a post as manager at a salary of £60 a year. Booth recorded that Butler's snug sitting-room 'was fitted with books and easy chairs – a piano also, upon which he was no mean performer ...

'At daybreak we all assembled in the common kitchen for breakfast, after which we separated for our different employments.

'At 12 noon we met again for dinner, and again about 7 p.m. for supper, which meal being over, Butler, Cook, and I would repair to the sitting room, and round a glorious fire smoked or read or listened to Butler's piano.'[6] Butler had taken out pictures that used to hang in his Cambridge rooms, including two watercolours, one of Langar Rectory and a seascape of Budleigh Salterton, in Devon.[7]

Another visitor to Mesopotamia was Haast, the Provincial Geologist, who used it as his headquarters for surveying the district. While attempting to cross the Rangitata to join Haast at Mesopotamia Dr Sinclair, his botanist friend, was drowned: Butler was away at the time, and no prayer book could be found on the station, so Haast read the service from the Mass Book belonging to Butler's bullock-driver.[8] Haast remained on friendly terms with Butler throughout his life, as did so many of his New Zealand acquaintances. A note of Butler's records the Mesopotamia routine at this period:

April 1861. – It is Sunday. We rose later than usual. There are five men sleeping in the hut. (This is before the building of the cob hut.) I sleep in a bunk on one side of the fire; Mr Haast, a German who is making a geological survey of the province, sleeps upon the opposite one; my bullock-driver and hut-keeper have two bunks at the far end of the hut, along the wall; while my shepherd lies in the loft among the tea and sugar and flour. It was a fine morning and we turned out about seven o'clock.

The usual mutton and bread for breakfast with a pudding made of flour and water baked in the camp oven after a joint of meat – Yorkshire pudding, but without eggs. While we were at breakfast a robin perched on the table and sat there a good while pecking at the sugar. We went on breakfasting with little heed to the robin and the robin went on pecking with little heed to us. After breakfast Pey, my bullock-driver, went to fetch the horses up from a spot about two miles down the river where they often run; we wanted to go pig-hunting.

I go into the garden and gather a few peascods for seed till the horses should come up. Then Cook, the shepherd, says that a fire has sprung up on the other side of the river. Who could have lit it? Probably some one who had intended coming to my place on the preceding evening and has missed his way, for there is no track of any sort between here and Phillips's . . . (N70–1)

By September, 1861, Butler's second hut was complete, and he could describe both his achievements, and his sense of what was lacking. For the only time in his life, he talked about marriage as a half-serious prospect, as he told his aunt, Mrs Worsley:

I hope that Phil is by this time happily married. I am seriously beginning to think of following his example. I want a wife dreadfully up here. What will you say if I marry a Maori? Unfortunately there are no nice ones in this island. They all smoke, and carry eels, and are not in any way the charming simple-minded innocent creatures which one might have hoped. Can you not imagine that a nice quiet wife – a good stay-at-home helpmate – would be a very great boon to anyone situated as I am? I hardly dare commission you to pick me one out and send her on spec., but I wish one would drop down from somewhere.

After cataloguing the contents of his vegetable garden, the fruit trees

The interior of Butler's second cottage at Mesopotamia, about 1868.
Watercolour by William Packe

and bushes and the flowers he has planted, he goes on to analyse his financial position, and, more pertinently, his state of mind:

> I am in a state of great affluence, and great poverty – that is to say, that it is all I can do to make the two ends meet with my wool money; that is the poverty – the affluence is that I am netting my lambs, which is a very handsome return for my outlay and is all that any man can expect for his first two or three years. I am perfectly satisfied. I have plenty to eat and drink, fresh air of the purest kind, good health and spirits, nice quiet steady and industrious servants, than whom I shall never have better, nor do I wish for better – what more can a mortal desire? I have a piano-forte at which I practise very regularly, and fancy I am improving. My sitting-room is hung with the pictures I had at Cambridge, and I have more books than I can read. The only thing I really do want is the intellectual society of clever men. From that I am totally debarred and feel that I am in great danger of getting far behindhand in consequence. I sometimes fancy that for all my excellent prospects and not-withstanding the good success I have met hitherto, I may have made a *mauvais pas*, and forfeited more than I have gained. On the other hand, I have entirely recovered my health, my constitution is more robust and my eyes completely recovered; and moreover I felt an immense intellectual growth shortly after leaving England – a growth which has left me a much happier and more liberal-minded man.

This kind of personal and intellectual balance sheet, prelude to the meticulous double entry book-keeping of later years, reveals the ambivalence Butler already felt about New Zealand. He was enjoying the climate, the out of doors life, the sense of adventure and enterprise, the freedom; he knew that his financial prospects, though far from secure, held much greater promise than any comparable situation in England; and he had escaped from the confines of religious prejudice. Now he was meticulously thinking everything out for himself, working his way through the New Testament: 'the worst of it is that in the total wreck of my own past orthodoxy I fear I may be as much too sceptical as then too orthodox. I try to avoid the subject, contenting myself with an endeavour to follow out the main practical points on which we shall all agree; but I might as well try to leave off thinking of music.' He was at work on St Paul's First Epistle to the Corinthians. 'I find so much in it that is entirely unsuited to the present age, and much that must have been wrong in theory (as far as I can test it alone, but such are the times when I want a sound-headed companion) even at the time it was written, that I wonder more and more at the blind deference that is usually paid to the letter of Scripture.' (FL102–6)

His inner wrestlings, parallel to those of countless Victorians, were accompanied in his case by an acute sense of personal betrayal. No one had prepared him for unbelief. He felt that he had been betrayed by his family, and especially by his clergyman father; by his education, and especially by Kennedy; by all those whom he had blindly trusted and believed. Scepticism about the efficacy of infant baptism was simply a milestone on the road; loss of faith in the Resurrection an apparently final destination. Butler continued to turn these questions over and over in his mind all his life; they never ceased to matter to him profoundly, nor did he easily find a position that gave him comfort or satisfaction. At Mesopotamia, the process of relentless intellectual enquiry began to quicken.

While he scrutinised and sifted the New Testament, his other major study was Darwin's *The Origin of Species*. Throughout his life he tended to share his preoccupations with anyone who would listen, and, eventually, to avoid the company of those who did not share them. He never found the 'intellectual society of clever men' particularly easy to come by even in London, at least in the terms in which he defined it. There were clever, well-educated men and women in New Zealand; but few who shared his somewhat unorthodox point of view. He would ride over to Mount Somers to visit his neighbours, the Tripps: his music and conversation were welcomed, but his opinions caused alarm. Mrs Tripp, a daughter of Bishop Harper, recorded in her diary that Butler was a constant visitor during their life at Mount Peel, and afterwards at Mount Somers: 'His was a peculiar nature, and full of wild theories. My husband enjoyed talking to him, but I thought his views very upsetting, and we did not like it when he tried to convert our maid to his ideas. He played the piano beautifully and would do so for hours . . .'[9] After a Butler visit, Mrs Tripp is reported to have taken a shovelful of burning coals from the fire and fumigated the room to disperse the evil spirits he might have invoked.[10]

Another contemporary diarist, E.R.Chudleigh, gives some insight into Butler's attitude: 'He is one of the cleverest men in New Zealand. He is a little man and nearly as dark as a Mouray. And is at present very nearly if not quite an infidel and yet I believe would not do a dishonourable thing to save his life.'[11]

In the absence of sympathetic friends nearby, Butler corresponded with his Cambridge contemporaries: 'I do not mean half the arrogance which I express. Hoare gave me rather a sharp wigging for a letter I wrote him not long since – just a few days before I came to see that the death of Jesus Christ was not real . . . For the present I renounce Christianity altogether.' (N193) Some eighteen months later, Chudleigh commented on a long talk he had had with Butler: 'I think he has gone as far as man can go now. He is an ultra Darwinian . . .'[12]

One thing he did not do at Mesopotamia, rather surprisingly in view of his later career, was to draw or paint. 'I don't draw at all,' he wrote to his aunt. 'For one reason there is nothing to draw and, for another, I find very little time – for another, it is almost always blowing from some quarter or another, and there is no shade or shelter.' (FL105) The points about time, wind, and lack of shade or shelter were true; but when Butler saw Haast's drawings in an exhibition at the Geographical Society in 1865, he commented, 'I wish I had drawn more myself when I was out there.'[13] At the time, he found that the loneliness, the lack of 'any traces of human handiwork and habitation' (FL106), detracted from the natural beauty, so that he never thought about it when he was out looking for sheep; while at home he was thinking of music, of his 'pretty considerable' studies, or of the garden.

In the midst of all this activity he found time for a typical dispute with his father, though purely on financial matters. In 1860, when Canon Butler surprised his son by sending him £2000, he promised a further £3000, an offer that Butler somewhat rashly declined. He later changed his mind, after his successful discovery of the Mesopotamia runs; but by the time this reappraisal reached Langar, Canon Butler had had second thoughts. A densely argued, prickly letter was despatched from Christchurch; the transactions would be frustrating to both sides since an exchange of letters might take six months. But Canon Butler, innately cautious, was impervious to his son's wish to pour further investment into his sheep run: 'I have no doubt that the better sheds and pits and stock you have the better your work will be, but your improvements must come as you have the means of making them.' £2000 of the £3000 held in reserve had already been sent out in instalments; now a final £600 was promised, as a loan, with the remaining £400 invested to help towards its repayment. The initial gift had taken Butler by surprise; he was now disappointed by his father's new approach: 'You have gone out with advantages far greater than you will find most of your neighbours have enjoyed and must be content to let time be one of the elements of success,' his father wrote on August 22nd, 1861, ending on a faintly ominous Old Testament note, 'I will keep a regular account.' (FL101–2)

Even without the full sum, Butler prospered. By the end of March, 1861 his holdings extended to around 40,000 acres, and the various runs were all declared stocked, which gave him a minimum of 2000 sheep. His own 'candlestick' brand had been registered on November 26th, 1860. He also owned the freehold of 40 acres. It had been a remarkably energetic fifteen months. Over the next year the station continued to thrive; perhaps as a consequence of his father's decision, he seems to have taken a friend, John Brabazon, into a quarter partnership in March, 1862, and the next month Hoel Pattisson came to Mesopotamia as a cadet. A letter to Acland in July comments that he is shorthanded, and cannot leave the run, having been obliged to sack his bullock-driver; and another letter of October thanks Acland for some marrow seed, and discusses other domestic matters: it is too late in the season to transplant gooseberry or currant trees, his cherry trees have buds on them, a milk cow has a broken hind leg – 'we are all in mourning about it.'[14] He seemed to be on the verge of a settled way of life.

Today the Mesopotamia homestead is sheltered by bands of trees, and surrounded by well-kept gardens. Next to the plaque that marks the site of Butler's cob house is a school, with its playing field where Butler once planted his vegetables and fruit trees. It takes an effort of the imagination, or an early photograph, to appreciate the bareness of the landscape that the early settlers had to transform.

Butler's drawing shows Mesopotamia about 1862, confirming the layout of the homestead and providing, in its mock-archaic language

Sod cottage, Caton's hut and Butler's cottage, Mesopotamia, about 1862.
Pen and ink sketch by Samuel Butler

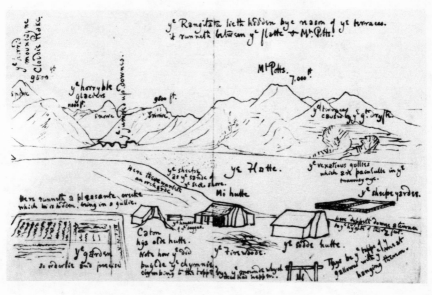

View from Mesopotamia, looking across the Rangitata, about 1862. Pen
and ink sketch by Samuel Butler

and lettering, a comically distancing effect, as though he was placing himself at one remove from it. Butler liked to give names to the features around him; some of the names he used at the time – Mesopotamia, the Two Thumb Range – have been retained, while others, Butler Saddle, Butler Range, Chowbok Col, commemorate his journeys and the world of Erewhon. One note on the map, 'Here there wanteth an orcharde', shows his awareness of the way he might have developed Mesopotamia. His neighours, the Aclands and Tripps, planted orchards, and families, at Peel Forest and Orari Gorge. Butler, 'that bloody entrepreneur',[15] was soon to withdraw from the role of settler, to concentrate on the questions surging through his mind.

CHAPTER 8

Christchurch and Pauli

That August, Butler had been revising the proofs of *A First Year in Canterbury Settlement*. His intellectual concerns took up more and more of his attention as the months went by, and he had sufficient confidence in Brabazon and Pattisson to leave them in charge at Mesopotamia and move his base to Christchurch.

Christchurch was expanding rapidly. The original settlement at Port Lyttelton, cut off by the volcanic hills, was soon overtaken in size and importance, a process accelerated by the building of a short stretch of railway between the town and the estuary, and later by a tunnel – opened in 1867 – connecting Christchurch to the port. Butler had influential friends in the town, notably William Sefton Moorhouse, the second superintendent of the Province, and his predecessor James Fitzgerald, who had returned to Canterbury and was the owner of the leading newspaper, the Christchurch *Press*, which first appeared on May 25th, 1861.

Butler wrote many articles for the Christchurch *Press*, and it is difficult now to identify them all indisputably. The first, published on December 20th 1862, was entitled: 'Darwin on the Origin of Species, A Dialogue'. (FY155–64) It takes the form of a dialogue in which F is the apologist for Darwin and C the unmoved traditionalist. F attempts to elucidate some of the Darwinian principles of competition, or perpetual warfare in Nature, with examples drawn from New Zealand life: 'Take cats, for instance; see with what rapidity they breed on the different runs in this province where there is little or nothing to check them; or even take the more slowly breeding sheep . . . Remember the quail; how plentiful they were until the cats came with the settlers from Europe. Why were they so abundant? Simply because they had plenty to eat, and could get sufficient shelter from the hawks to multiply freely. The cats came, and tussocks stood the poor little creatures in but poor stead.' C is forced to admit the truth of the propositions, though signalling distaste from time to time: 'It is very horrid'. F's retort, 'No more horrid than that you should eat roast mutton or boiled beef', springs the underlying objection: 'But it is utterly subversive of Christianity; for if this theory is true the fall of man is entirely fabulous; and if the fall, then the redemption, these two being inseparably bound together.' This 'objection' may have coincided with Butler's current thinking, but F replied more circumspectly: 'My dear friend, there I am not bound to follow you. I believe in Christianity, and I believe in Darwin. The two appear irreconcilable. My answer to those who accuse me of inconsistency is, that both being undoubtedly true, the one must be reconcilable with the other, and that the impossibility of reconciling them must be only apparent and temporary, not real . . . The true course is to use the freest candour in the acknowledgment of the difficulty; to estimate precisely its real value, and obtain a correct knowledge of its precise form.'

The dialogue is a clear and candid response, the first fruit of Butler's close reading of *The Origin*, which had invaded his mind so insistently during the previous months. Darwin himself, obtaining a copy, forwarded the dialogue to a journal with the following commendation: it was 'remarkable from its spirit and from giving so clear and accurate a view of Mr D [sic] theory. It is also remarkable from being published in a colony exactly 12 years old, in which it might have been thought only material interests would have been regarded.'

The context of public opinion in Anglican Canterbury made the circumspect 'I believe in Christianity, and I believe in Darwin' sufficiently outspoken. The *Press* published a rejoinder, 'Barrel-Organs' (FY164–7), on January 17th, which Butler thought was the work of the Bishop of Wellington. The Barrel-Organ analogy is a reference to old tunes coming round again and again, and, interestingly in view of Butler's later argument, relates Darwinian theory to 'the old story that his namesake, Dr Darwin, served up in the end of the last century'. The final sentence even anticipates the nub of the future Butler–Darwin controversy: 'All his fantasias, as we saw in a late article, are made to come round at last to religious questions, with which really and truly they have nothing to do, but were it not for their supposed effect upon religion, no one would waste his time in reading about the possibility of Polar bears swimming about and catching flies so long that they at last get the fins they wish for.'

This was just the kind of argument Butler relished. Masked as another contributor to the debate, 'A.M.' – because, as he later explained a little ingenuously to Darwin, 'my dialogue was in my hearing very severely criticized by two or three whose opinion I thought worth having' – he purported to comment on both the previous articles, but while admonishing the writer of the first – 'He is rash, evidently well satisfied with himself, very possibly mistaken' – he castigates the second in rounder terms: 'I cannot sit quietly by and see "Darwin" misrepresented in such a scandalously slovenly manner.'[1] The debate continued briskly with two further contributions apiece. Although Butler had reason on his side, there is a certain recklessness and inattention to detail in his argument. The correspondence tailed off when it became apparent that the two combatants were disputing quotations drawn from different editions.

Another notable Darwinian article was the satirical 'Darwin Among the Machines',[2] which envisages a future in which 'man will have become to the machine what the horse and the dog are to man':

Day by day, however, the machines are gaining ground upon us; day by day we are becoming more subservient to them; more men are daily bound down as slaves to tend them, more men are daily devoting the energies of their whole lives to the development of mechanical life. The upshot is simply a question of time, but that the time will come when the machines will hold the real supremacy over the world and its inhabitants is what no person of a truly philosophic mind can for a moment question.

Our opinion is that war to the death should be instantly proclaimed against them. Every machine of every sort should be destroyed by the well-wisher of his species. Let there be no exceptions made, no quarter shown; let us at once go back to the primeval condition of the race.

The article was later to form the nucleus of 'The Book of the Machines' in *Erewhon*, and so may be seen as the first published nucleus of that work. Attacks on the dominance of the machine are scarcely original in post-industrial English writing – *Hard Times* was a recent fictional treatment – but Butler pursues his theme with a directness inspired, perhaps, by the pastoral society of New Zealand.

In January, 1863, *A First Year in Canterbury Settlement* was published in England. Butler's attitude to his first major work was characteristically ambivalent. In later life he distanced himself from it, suggesting that it had been produced without his involvement and knowledge. This is only partially true. His father edited it, but he did send the proofs out to New Zealand for correction and amendment. The ship that was bringing them back to England, the *Colombo*, was wrecked in the Indian Ocean, and the proofs so badly water damaged that they could only be deciphered in places with the help of a mirror. The book is now recognized as one of the most valuable and vivid accounts of life on an early New Zealand sheep station. But it is easy to understand that, in retrospect, Butler may have felt irritated at having letters tailored for an orthodox Langar audience, and edited letters at that, masquerading as his own authentic voice. 'My people edited my letters home,' Butler confessed to Alfred Marks years later. 'I did not write freely to them, of course, because they were my people; if I was at all freer anywhere they cut it out before printing it – besides I had not shed my Cambridge skin, and its trail is everywhere I am afraid perceptible. I dipped into a few pages when they sent it to me in New Zealand, but saw "prig" written upon them so plainly that I read no more and never have and never mean to.' (M2.70)

At least one copy found its way to Canterbury in 1863 and on October 28th a curious review appeared in the *Press*. 'We have received a copy of a little work entitled "A First Year in Canterbury Settlement," by one Samuel Butler. Who Mr Butler may be we have not the remotest conception; but we should in a friendly manner advise him henceforward to keep his first impressions in M.S. until they become more matured and better worth presenting to the public. The preface (which, to do Mr Butler justice, is not written by him, nor apparently with his knowledge) informs us that the "unbiased impressions of colonial life as they fall freshly on a young mind may not be wholly devoid of interest." ' Surely the author could not be the same Mr Butler, certainly no youngster, tolerably well known as a sheep farmer, though the coincidence in the Christian name and the frequent references to the Rangitata district were suspicious:

> ... though we have no personal acquaintance with Mr Butler himself, we confess to having expected better things than those

with which he has furnished us in the book before us. The fact is that the work is one which ought never to have been published. It is crude and wholly destitute of method, the faults in style are numerous, and there is an abundance of those details which, though interesting enough to the family circle of the writer, and therefore well enough adapted for a M.S. letter, are excruciatingly tedious to the general reader . . .

A number of features suggest that this review may have been written by Butler himself. The criticisms are those that he upheld at a later date. He takes time to criticise the preface, and seems to separate the book from any possible responsibility of the Mr Butler of the Rangitata district, while simultaneously cementing the connection, a device he used when speaking on behalf of the *Press* at the opening of the Christchurch railway, when he claimed he was 'in no way connected with Mr Butler of the Rangitata Forks'. The only passage quoted is drawn from his description of his arrival in Port Lyttelton, consistent with someone dipping into a few pages. He may have been trying to forestall possible criticism; though to review his own work belongs to a pattern of anonymity and masks that characterised much of Butler's early writing.

During 1863 the prospects of returning to England, never completely absent from his mind, became more defined. Canon Butler had been in correspondence with Haast, who had sent him a collection of New Zealand plants in return for an extensive collection of British plants destined for the New Zealand museum. (Canon Butler was elected an honorary member of the Philosophical Institute of Canterbury in recognition of his services.) 'Your mention of my son is most gratifying to us,' he wrote on January 23rd, 1863. 'I have no doubt with health and prudence he will do well and prosper in such manner as to enable him to return here at no very distant period.' A letter of September 21st is more cautious: 'I fear you overestimate my sons success. I trust however he is reaping the fruit of his active life.'[3]

By September much of Butler's activity was centred on Christchurch. He had made at least one more exploratory journey, this time with Brabazon, in April,[4] and as late as November bought a section of freehold land in Tent Creek, but he was already thinking of selling up. At the end of December William Parkerson rode to

Mesopotamia to inspect the station; and in March, 1864, the partnership with Brabazon was formally dissolved, as a preliminary to Parkerson taking delivery of the run in May. Disposing of his assets, and various financial and legal arrangements, took some time to finalise, but it is reasonable to assume that from the beginning of 1864, Mesopotamia, at least, did not feature strongly in Butler's long-term plans.

Apart from his occasional writings for the *Press*, Butler busied himself in a variety of Christchurch affairs. He may simply have been filling in time while his business affairs were resolved; he may, on the other hand, have been contemplating a somewhat longer stay in New Zealand than he later admitted. For example, in October he was proposed for a committee investigating founding a School of Art in Canterbury; in December he was examining the boys of Christchurch school;[5] in February, 1864, he attended a cricket match between Canterbury and a visiting team from England, and celebrated the event in verse;[6] in March he played a Bach fugue at a concert to raise funds for an orphan asylum, and contributed a short piece on *The Tempest* to a volume of 'Literary Foundlings' sold in aid of the same charity.[7] He had, too, as much company as he ever enjoyed. He had been a member of the Christchurch Club since soon after his arrival, and an active one, judging by the entries in the complaints book.[8] There were other friends besides Fitzgerald and Moorhouse, such as Alexander Lean, an architect who acted as music critic for the *Press*, and Colborne Veel, the editor. This was a life very different to the isolation of Mesopotamia.

His most significant new friendship, one that was to cramp his life for over thirty years, was with Charles Paine Pauli. They had met at the Club, at the Fitzgeralds', and through dealings with the *Press*, but Butler dated the birth of their closer friendship to an occasion when Pauli visited him at the Carlton Hotel in September, 1863. Pauli was the youngest son of a German businessman who had settled in England; some two and a half years younger than Butler, he had been educated at Winchester and Oxford, and he had the easy charm, good taste and handsome appearance that Butler both lacked and admired. 'We Johnians looked on Oxford men as being a good deal above ourselves, at any rate in outward appearance and address . . . Pauli's clothes must have cost at least twice as much as mine did. Everything that he had was good, and he was such a fine handsome fellow, with such an attractive manner, that to me he seemed everything I should like myself to be, but knew very well that I was not. I knew myself to be plebeian in appearance and believed myself to be more plebeian in tastes than I probably in reality was; at any rate I knew that I was far from being all that I should wish myself either in body or mind . . .' Butler was writing in 1897, with hindsight sharpened by disillusion.[9] He recalled dryly his friend Moorhouse's judgment: 'Very handsome, well-dressed men are seldom very good men.'

That evening, Pauli stayed till midnight: 'His visit was unexpected; I had not called on him and had no intention of doing so: I was surprised at his calling on me, but he was doing his best to please, and when he left I was aware that I had become suddenly intimate with a personality quite different to that of anyone whom I had ever known.'

There have been many attempts to analyse the nature of this strange relationship. A.C. Brassington has pointed out how his biographer Festing Jones made slight changes to the account above, transposing 'suddenly' from its original position to precede 'aware', in an attempt to preclude any hint of homosexuality; he even argues that Pauli's overtures were homosexual.[10] This seems, in the light of Butler's future complex relationships with men and women, too straightforward an explanation, and inherently improbable. Butler observed a traditional and rigid social code, to which he adhered the more punctiliously because it was removed from any religious context. He paid for sex with women. The habits of his London life, and Jones's comments about Butler already knowing who was or was not a 'respectable' girl, make him a likely customer for a Christchurch brothel. There is no hint of physical homosexuality in any of his notes or letters. E.R. Chudleigh records a conversation with him about this time: 'Here he said "My dear boy you are quite right to maintain your own opinion but you cannot blame me for doing as I do, holding such opinions I shall not do *it* (a thing I had been talking to him about) because I do not think it right. I do right because I think it wrong to do otherwise. *Right* is that which agrees with the interest and law of man. And I suppose human instinct is to tell one right from wrong." '[11] Such a comment merely indicates Butler's general frame of mind; but knowing how painstakingly he formed his opinions and moral attitudes, he does not seem a likely candidate for a casual initiation. He was, by his own admission, younger than his years. His main desire was to 'conceal how severely I had been wounded, and to get beyond the reach of those arrows that from time to time still reached me'.[12] Naively, Butler admired Pauli's good looks and confident manners. Pauli was a great favourite with the Fitzgeralds' children, and was expected to marry the elder daughter, Amy; 'it was hard to say whether he was more devoted to the mother or to the daughter', was Butler's later sour comment. Pauli was a schoolboy fiction swell, a tall, handsome hero of the cricket scene with a reputation as a fearsome fast bowler. Butler, short and dark, had been emotionally starved during his childhood and youth and had never yet found the affection he craved. The sudden and flattering offer of intimate friendship took Butler by surprise. He was devoted to him 'much as a dog to his master', and in his gratitude he was eager to make some gesture in return.

Butler himself had been linked romantically with a Christchurch girl. There is no direct evidence, but a family tradition has persisted that he was a rival with William Rolleston for the hand of Mary Brittan: 'it is said that whenever William Rolleston and Samuel Butler came to Christchurch they put aside their prejudice against church-going and made a point of attending matins at the Avonside church solely for the pleasure of watching Mary singing in the choir.'[13] A burlesque poem by L.J. Kenneway, 'A Peculiar Dream',[14] about three men attempting to make a rendezvous with a loved one, lends support to the story; one of the three is 'Cotton Roley' (Rolleston), and another is 'Cutler', 'an explorer, who had seen some very hard times, and who, inside a sunburnt and wrinkled forehead, possessed far-thinking and acute brains, and for whom all sorts of forms of deeper modern thought had much attraction.'

> 'Gad zooks!' said I, 'not at the Club?
>   Or safe at home with your sheep pens, O?'
> 'No!' he replied, 'I took a stroll
>   To clear my brains of that Colenso.'

> He's mad, I thought.

The poem offers an amusing glimpse of how the eccentric Butler was viewed in Canterbury, suggesting a certain popularity and notoriety. It also supplies a vivid portrait:

> And one is burnt like black pine wood
> Bronzed in a bushman's fire;
> His forehead, when he frowns, is like
> A coil of fencing wire.
>
> His beard is black, and black his hair;
> His hat I used to carry;
> It was sometimes, I recollect,
> A very small Glengarry.

William Rolleston married Mary Brittan on May 24th, 1865. Instead of a wife, Butler found, as he thought, an ideal friend.

Pauli took Butler into his confidence. He had come out to New Zealand to stay with his elder brother, the resident magistrate at Kaiapoi. He disliked up-country life, and had moved to Christchurch, where he worked for the *Press* during 1862 and 1863 as book-keeper and accountant. He longed to leave New Zealand. He was in poor health and wanted to return to England, first to consult medical specialists, and secondly to be called to the Bar. He persuaded Butler that he had no money (in spite of a substantial salary from the *Press*), but would come into four or five thousand pounds on the death of his parents. This was a scenario with which Butler could warmly sympathise: a young man thwarted in an ambition which could easily be satisfied by an act of generosity. Butler himself had found generous friends in New Zealand who had loaned him money without security when he was waiting for funds to arrive from England. His own initial capital of £4800 was now worth over £8000, once he could realise it, and he intended to keep it in New Zealand for the immediate future, where the rate of interest was 10%. With such a level of projected income, it seemed a simple matter to pay the £100 for Pauli's passage, and to advance him £200 or so a year while he read for the Bar. He felt sure it would not be long before someone so able as Pauli would earn enough to be independent, and in any event the loan could eventually be repaid out of the reversion.

It is not clear at what point Butler made his generous offer. The meeting with Pauli was in September, 1863, and Butler spent another nine months in Canterbury, winding up his affairs and taking part in a variety of social activities. On 9 June he said farewell to Haast, inscribing a copy of *A First Year in Canterbury Settlement* with 'very kind regards'.[15] He placed his capital in the hands of Moorhouse, wrote a last letter to his neighbour Acland, and sailed with Pauli from Port Lyttelton on June 15th, 1864. It was midwinter, and the ship ran into a hurricane; when the main yard broke, they were almost driven on to the coast of North Island. The voyage remained full of incident: an earthquake in Callao, a yellow fever epidemic in Panama, an influx of refugees from the American Civil War at St Thomas. They arrived in Southampton on August 29th. (M1.109–10) Pauli was extremely ill during the voyage, with an infected tongue and throat, though he would not let anyone apart from Butler know. The private knowledge, and Pauli's brave public front, bound Butler closer to him.

Butler was twenty-eight. He had achieved, as he supposed, financial independence, and was free to pursue his wish to train as an artist. He had experienced an immense intellectual growth, though as yet he had no clear idea in what direction it would take him. In terms of confidence, and physical energy and well-being, he was unrecognisable.

CHAPTER 9

Homecoming

There is something both paradoxical and sad about Butler's home-coming. Here was a man who had ridden into the mountains and built a hut (almost) with his own hands, who had wrestled, seemingly successfully, with the demons of family and religion, who was eager to follow his thwarted desire to become a painter, and who had travelled right round the world to establish an independent life in London. But the autonomy that he had achieved was severely quali-fied. He had loosened some kinds of bonds only to replace them with others in his friendship for Pauli.

By September, 1864, Pauli had found two neighbouring sets of chambers in Clifford's Inn, off Fleet Street. Butler's was No. 15, a second floor set with a sitting-room and pantry that faced west over the garden, and a bedroom and painting-room facing east over Fetter Lane, for a rent of £23 a year. Clifford's Inn was to be Butler's home for the rest of his life: Pauli stayed there no more than a year. Initially, he breakfasted with Butler and spent the evening in his company. Gradually, he distanced himself, moving in 1865 to lodg-ings in the West End which, he maintained, were better suited to his health. He never told Butler his new addresses, and Butler did not like to ask, reasoning that Pauli would have surely told him had he wished him to know. However, when Pauli fell ill with typhoid in February, 1866, he moved into Butler's chambers, and Butler nursed him back to health. They went to Dieppe that autumn, so that Pauli could convalesce. The holiday was not a success. 'I am in a state of profound dejection about art – having done very badly at Dieppe,' Butler wrote to May, his most regular Langar correspondent. The return crossing to Newhaven was rough, and 'poor old Pauli was an awful sufferer'.[1] At the end of the trip Pauli informed his friend that, while he believed Butler had been pretty happy, he had never been so miserable in his life. They never went on holiday together again, and Pauli's contacts with Butler were gradually reduced to his lunching with him regularly three times a week. Every quarter, at one of these lunches, he would collect a cheque for £50.

Of all Butler's complex, intense and enigmatic relationships, this friendship is the hardest to understand. There is little to lay hold of: there are entries in Butler's notebooks, in which he records Pauli's mundane and often malevolent comments as though they are exceptionally witty or profound; there is the selective testimony of Butler's later friend, Festing Jones, and the long tortured account that Butler wrote in 1898 after Pauli's death, when the facts, or some of them, about Pauli's duplicity were revealed. None of these indicate anything extraordinary or admirable, rather the reverse. Yet for thirty-odd years Pauli, or the image of Pauli, remained a constant element in Butler's emotional life – he described his feelings as 'the white heat of devotion' – sustained by the pattern of lunches and cheques: he even made a will in Pauli's favour (later revoked) which was found among Pauli's papers on his death.

The features that attracted Butler to Pauli were superficial. He was good-looking – at least, according to Butler and a San Francisco barman:

> A S. Francisco barman always used to press Pauli to have something whenever he saw Pauli coming into the bar-room. 'Come, come,' he used to say, 'you must have something. You're the handsomest man God ever sent into San Francisco, so help me God you are.' Having known Pauli for nearly 30 years I should like to say that I believe the barman to have been right. (N78)

It was the external that captivated Butler: the fashionable dresser, who wore his clothes well, the man about town, confident, smart, sociable and fond of society. But once he had acknowledged his admiration, and put his confidence in Pauli, he resolutely refused to withdraw it, even when experience revealed to him the one-sided nature of the intimacy.

Butler's fascination with Pauli's elegance and style was accompanied by a belief in his superiority of mind; habitually, once he had given someone his friendship, he ascribed to him unusual powers. He found Pauli's mockery of religion particularly congenial:

'He was very ill one Passion week; he said he should go to bed on Good Friday and like a celebrated historical personage, rise again on the third day' (N84); 'Pauli said Christ's sayings were like quack pills intended to be swallowed whole without chewing, or knowing what they were made of, and they poisoned one.' (N69) Butler recorded similar comments from many sources, both wittier and lamer. They do not tell us much more about Pauli than that his iconoclastic perspective struck a chord with Butler; but an anecdote about the Salvation Army is more demeaning:

> He met the Salvation Army and eyed them with disgust. A prig of a young high church curate stood near, and seeing Pauli look very well done all round as he always does, vented a few ejaculations about its being 'awful' &c. Pauli hated him nearly as much as he hated the Salvation Army, and woman-like wanted to tease him. His quick wit suggested a two-edged blow, and he smiled pleasantly as he said, 'They do look bloody fools, don't they?' (N234)

It remains something of a shock to read Butler's claim: 'Pauli has done more to shape me than any other man. I have often cribbed from his good sayings; several of them are in *Erewhon*, and indeed in every book that I have written there is something of his.' (N243) At the end of his life, Butler reviewed the relationship:

> I had felt from the very beginning that my intimacy with Pauli was only superficial, and I also perceived more and more that I bored him. I have not the least doubt that I did so, and I am afraid he is not the only one of my friends who has had to put up with much from me on the same score. He cared little for literature and nothing for philosophy, music, or the arts. I studied art and he law. Law interested him whereas it was nothing to me. He liked society and I hated it. Moreover, he was at times very irritable and would find continual fault with me, often, I have no doubt, justly, but often, as it seemed to me, unreasonably. Devoted to him as I continued to be for many years, those years were very unhappy as well as very happy ones.
> I set down a great deal to his ill-health, no doubt truly; a

great deal more, I was sure, was my own fault – and I am so still; I excused much on the score of his poverty and his dependence on myself – for his father and mother, when it came to the point, could do nothing for him; I was his host and was bound to forbear on that ground if no other. I always hoped that, as time went on, and he saw how absolutely devoted to him I was, and what unbounded confidence I had in him, and how I forgave him over and over again for treatment that I should not have stood for a moment from any one else – I always hoped that he would soften and deal as frankly and unreservedly with me as I with him; but, though for some fifteen years I hoped this, in the end I gave it up, and settled down into a resolve from which I never departed – to do all I could for him, to avoid friction of any kind, and to make the best of things for him and for myself that circumstances would allow. For the last fifteen years or so not an angry or an unkind word has ever passed between us.[2]

Butler was unfortunate in his friends' ill health – Pauli's successor, Jones, was a professional invalid – but he only vented his impatience in *Erewhon*, where sickness is treated as a crime. The argument that Butler was Pauli's 'host' is tortuous; he must have known that Pauli would not have starved without the lunches, or even the pension. The one resolve in which he proved steadfast was that he would not behave to Pauli as his father, he believed, had behaved to him. However badly he felt himself treated, he refused to do anything that might cause Pauli to reproach him, at whatever cost to himself.

The relationship, so heavily circumscribed as to be almost invisible at times – for Pauli kept Butler in a watertight compartment, almost completely segregated from the rest of his life, and the lunches scarcely impinged on Butler's other routines and friendships – nevertheless pressed heavily upon Butler's financial and emotional resources in the years to come. There is a photograph of Pauli, in morning coat with prominent watch chains and handkerchief in breast pocket, and on the table beside him a tall black hat. P.N. Furbank noted that in Butler's painting of the interior of 15 Clifford's Inn

One detail, a tall black hat, dominates the whole scene. The hat stands upon a shelf in the angle of two walls; this shelf one imagines to have been built specially for the hat; and the hat itself seems to be sitting for its portrait.

So many of the domestic possessions that once filled the bachelor rooms at Clifford's Inn have found their way into collections: ordinary, humdrum, slightly pathetic objects – toothbrush, kettleholder, leather (or sham leather) cigarette case from Palermo. 'Their very dullness is characteristic of Butler, and has a meaning which may easily be overlooked ... And a meaning may equally be extracted from the tall hat that so dominated the rooms in Clifford's Inn. Worn, or merely exhibited on a shelf, the tall black hat was still the permanent symbol of normality.'[3] From this ambiance shared at first with Pauli, an ambiance of tall black hats, of acquaintance with the best people, of the easy sneer at Salvation Army and High Church curate alike, he walked each morning to the different world of the art school.

Butler studied at the South Kensington Museum and at two art schools: Cary's, Streatham Street, Bloomsbury, and then, from 1867, at Heatherley's in Newman Street. He approached the business of becoming a painter with great seriousness, and allowed himself to be persuaded that meticulous practice and concentrated industry were the major ingredients for success. It was a challenge that at first he thoroughly enjoyed. 'You cannot tell how greatly I prefer England,' he wrote to Haast in February, 1865. 'I have been taking lessons in painting here since I arrived, I was always very fond of it and mean to stick to it: it suits me and I am not without hopes that I shall do well at it. I live almost the life of a recluse seeing very few people and going no where that I can help – I mean in the way of parties and so forth: if my friends had their way they would fritter away my time without any remorse: but I made a regular stand against it from the beginning and so, having my time pretty much in my own hands, work hard: I find, as I am sure you must find, that it is next to impossible to combine what is commonly called society and work.'[4]

He was only as much of a recluse as he chose to make out. 'I have dropped into my old place among college friends in a way that would surprise you – this lot has stuck together wonderfully,'[5] he wrote to Veel, enclosing an article for possible publication in the Christchurch

Press. But the programme he set himself was a demanding one, since he continued with his music, and was proceeding with his New Testament studies, in addition to his painting. 'I mean beginning chiefly with portraits, but feeling my way on to historical subjects as soon as I find the ground pretty firm beneath my feet . . . I will say this much, that if my hopes are founded on a good basis and I do ultimately succeed, I shall be the very first painter that ever owned a sheep run in the Upper Rangitata district.'[6]

Success in his chosen field was something Butler desperately wanted, and he sensed it was at least within his grasp. 'Sometimes I find myself painting almost very well, and then I make horrid failures . . . I work without interruption and very hard: my average is fully 7 hours a day at painting independently of music – and writing.'[7] The progress he felt he was making even led him to risk exposure to his father's judgment, inviting him the next time he was in London to call and ask old Heatherley what he thought of him. Heatherley never flattered: 'he looks very absurd and at first I thought him very affected in his manner and dress – his get up being dishevelled and what he thinks "artistic", but the more I see of him the better I like him; it is a funny place too and would amuse you.' (FL 116)

It seems unlikely that Canon Butler would have been much amused. The studio was crammed with objects – 'old tapestries, casts from the antique, weapons, curious pots and pans, queer specimens of draperies' – all of which featured relentlessly in the typical Heatherley subjects that could be recognised at exhibitions. Heatherley presided, pipe in mouth, 'a quaint figure in a long black velveteen coat; his auburn hair, divided in the centre, fell on his shoulders; the face was extremely refined; the features were small, and so like the portrait of Jesus Christ that his sobriquet amongst the students was "The Creeping Jesus" – creeping, because he wore soft felt slippers, so that nobody ever heard him approach.'[8]

If Heatherley seemed at first affected and 'artistic' to Butler, Butler in his turn struck his fellow students as alien: his stiffness and conventional background set him apart from most of them. Heatherley's is the oldest independent fine art school in England. It was founded by a group who wanted life studies to be central to their study, and was the first art school in England to enrol women. John Butler Yeats was a younger fellow pupil, and has left a revealing account[9] of the impact Butler made on the atmosphere of the school:

'We were art students and tried to be Bohemian, or would have done so had not Butler been one of us. A Scotch friend of mine and his, whom Butler loved because of his knowledge of music, would sometimes say, "Yes, Mr Butler, you are a dominie" – and he would chuckle slowly in his Scotch manner. Like a dominie he kept us all in order. We called each other briefly by our surnames without the prefix of the Mr – Butler was always *Mr* Butler.' A London student once dared to ask, 'Have you been to the Alhambra, Butler?' pronouncing it 'Al'ambra': 'Is there an aitch in the word?' asked Butler, crushing any further attempt at intimacy.

Yet the man who was so set apart by his class and his superior manner was, as Yeats perceived, intellectually free. His 'emancipated intellect had won for his soul and senses a freedom that he wished to share with others; he had as it were acquired a freedom to be on good terms with himself . . . Butler wanted people to be on good terms with their senses and appetites and everything else that goes into our make-up as men . . . He found us, as he thought, enslaved by this or that convention or illusion and by his mockeries and his wit worked for our liberation.' One form that Butler's method of liberation took was to lend a student the book of books, *The Origin of Species*, which had, as he told Yeats, completely destroyed his belief in a personal God. In fact, he might ask a student if he believed in God as an alternative to asking if he had read *the book*. He once, in the deep silence of the class, asked the nude model, 'Moseley, do you believe in God?'

> Without allowing a muscle of a change of expression, Moseley replied, 'No, sir, don't believe in old Bogey.' The form of the answer was unexpected; its cheerful cockney impudence was beyond even Butler's reach of courage. He retired in confusion, and we laughed.

Yeats learned, or would have learned, from Butler. He sensed the slow-burning, deeply buried core that fuelled Butler's relentless enquiries. 'Slowly I have come to feel that affection for human nature which is at the root of all poetry and art, whether the poet be pessimist or optimist. Had I stayed much with Butler I should have learned my lesson almost at once . . . With tenderness of humour and a most real poetry he touched, healingly, all the sores of ailing humanity . . . Sam Butler's desire for truth and his stripping away from life and belief all the veils of illusion was the characteristic of a man truly poetic.' For Yeats, Butler was a man of poetic and artistic temperament who was labouring in the wrong field.

Yeats considered that Butler had little talent, and was trapped within a vain ambition to paint like Bellini. At Heatherley's, he always occupied a place 'chosen so that he could be as close as possible to the model and might paint with small brushes his kind of John Bellini art. There he would stand very intent and mostly quite silent, intent also on our casual conversation, watchful for the moment when he could make some sally of wit that would crush his victim. He had thick eyebrows and grey eyes, – or were they light hazel? These eyes would sometimes look tired as he plied his hopeless task of learning how to paint.' It is typical of Butler that he should make his ambition to become a painter almost unachievable by taking as his model Bellini; just as he restricted his aspirations in music by dismissing all composers but Handel as worthy of consideration. It was, however, the sense of affectionate delight in Bellini's paintings that most appealed to him, and to which he strove to be true.

Another student who coincided with Butler for a short time at Heatherley's was the future actor Johnston Forbes-Robertson, who went there to draw from the Antique and send in work to earn acceptance at the Royal Academy. According to him, Butler too was anxious to become an Academy student; he submitted his drawings several times, but they were never passed. Forbes-Robertson, who was only sixteen when he first went to Heatherley's, remembers Butler as a shy man who hated social gatherings. 'He always wore rough homespun and thick boots, and his hair and beard were cut quite close, the face was short and the complexion ruddy. The eyes could snap and sparkle and they could beam with sympathy. His voice was sweet and low, his laugh quite infectious, and those few who knew him loved the man.'[10] Forbes-Robertson recalls going off to a midday meal at an ordinary over a public house, the Horse Shoe, on the corner of Oxford Street and Tottenham Court Road; and the occasion when Butler photographed him in a suit of armour kept by Heatherley in his back room. There was some dispute over a suggestion that the breastplate should be fixed over the gorget, which Butler and Forbes-Robertson knew to be wrong: 'Slowly he got a hearing, and with great deliberation and softly smiling all the while, he gave them a lecture, full of biting sarcasm, proving that he knew more about armour and the proper wearing of it, than all of them put together.' This was one of Butler's first photographs, a kind of serious joke like those he would take at Varallo, juxtaposing the old and the modern, art and life.

Butler did have some talent as an artist, but it did not lie in the sphere or style that he mapped out minutely for himself, the grand design which would enable him to progress from portraits to historical subjects. In the year of his return from New Zealand when the academicism of the art school had had little opportunity to influence him, he painted 'Family Prayers'. Years later, he added a note in pencil: 'I did this in 1864 and if I had gone on doing things out of my own head instead of making copies I should have been all right.'

This painting has been described by Graham Reynolds as 'one of the comparatively few worthy naive paintings of the English school' – 'a pictorial expression of Butler's unending warfare against the narrow and cruel hypocrisy of Victorian family life'[11] – one might add, of Victorian society, expressed in the rigid postures, the expressionless faces, the unseeing eyes, with each individual, so stiflingly close to each other, locked within a private world. The servants, ranged against the wall, form a captive congregation: the women's bonnets are like mock halos. The patriarch, with lowered, spectacled eyes that make him appear blind, reads the Word from the Bible placed on the red tablecloth of the domestic altar. The stiff-backed matriarch facing in his direction serves as a framing device, stern and redolent of uncomfortable duty. At the far right hand edge of the picture is the softer figure of a younger woman, clearly part of the family, and in the background, by the window, a younger man, who seems half removed from the event, a withdrawn observer.

The picture has another dimension: it explores the same central image as that of Chapter 23 of *The Way of All Flesh*, and shares its unnerving clarity of traumatic experience. In the novel the father, red-handed after beating his young son, rings the bell for prayers, and the narrator describes how the manservant, William, set the chairs for the maids, 'and presently they filed in. First Christina's maid, then the cook, then the housemaid, then William, and then the coachman. I sat opposite them, and watched their faces as Theobald read a chapter from the Bible. They were nice people, but more absolute vacancy I never saw upon the countenances of human beings.' (WF125)

There is one major difference between the picture and the literary exploration of 'Family Prayers', and that is the figure of the woman on the right. One possible reading might see her as Butler's sister May, still living at Langar, and the withdrawn observer as Butler himself on one of his awkward visits, finding that nothing had changed in his absence, and that he was still haunted by his memories. The picture usually hangs in the Senior Combination Room at St John's, a position that would have appealed to Butler.

The paintings with most vitality are those closest to Butler's own experience, and those that reflect his satirical attitude and eye for the odd or absurd: the portraits, 'Family Prayers', 'The Christening at Fobello', 'Mr Heatherley's Holiday'; or the smaller-scale sketches and watercolours of Italy and Switzerland, which are infused with Butler's delight in line and detail. In his notebooks is a list of 'Pictures that I Never Painted':

> Priest lighting his pipe from the fire of an itinerant tinker – Burial of Fidele (or Snowdrop) [Snowdrop was one of his many cats] – Nostradamus – Seven Sleepers of Ephesus – A sack race – Priest superintending alterations in the village fountain – Cat's meat man followed by cats – Archway of my staircase (I did this but got tired and never finished it) – A puppy having a row with a large cock, (both afraid) – *Minga scuola* (Father carrying his truant son to school at Angera) – An important industrial centre in the flint period – A fine horse in love with an ugly little old donkey – The unanswered challenge (a cock crowing at early morning to a wooden cock on a crucifix) – Women on trees at Fobello – Pigs sleeping in Piazza Gaudenzio Ferrari at Varallo. (N100)

Most of these subjects are small in scale, anecdotal, mildly grotesque or bizarre, like many of Butler's notes or his observations in letters; some were subjects of future photographs. Apart from 'Mr Heatherley's Holiday', these unpainted pictures seem more interesting than some of the arid titles that were eventually hung in the Royal Academy: 'Miss Acheson' (1869); 'A Reverie' (1871); 'A child's head', (1874); 'Don Quixote', 'A girl's head' (1876).

Butler remained true to his artist's vocation all his life, through painting or photography, or as enthusiast, critic and art historian. As with so many of his projects, the positive habitually contained, or was balanced by, the negative: action was inhibited by inaction, inaction qualified by 'if only'. 'If I had sold "Heatherley's Holiday", I should I feel pretty sure have stuck to painting': 'A man should have a painting room not less than a mile from his living rooms. It was the not having this that choked me off – I mean the incessant interruptions, and temptation to go on with other work. But I suppose there was something more than this – and yet I do not know.'(N107)

One frustration arose from the way his insight as a critic was at odds with his own practice. He could formulate an ideal approach, for instance, 'When in doubt do as nearly nothing as you can' (N92), or, more challengingly, 'After having spent years in striving to be accurate, we must spend as many more in discovering when and how to be inaccurate.' (N241) But all the evidence suggests that Butler did too much to his paintings, and too slowly, and never felt confident enough to reach the stage of willed inaccuracy. He knew the kind of art that stirred him, and which he strove to emulate: an art of feeling. 'Art has no end in view save the emphasising and recording in the most effective way some strongly felt interest or affection. Where either interest, or desire to record with good effect is wanting, there is but sham art, or none at all: where both these are fully present, no matter how rudely and inarticulately, there is great art.' (N104–5) The impulse to feeling beat strongly in him; but his hand was governed by rigidly orthodox principles of accuracy and discipline. His iconoclastic instincts were countered by an inherited desire to succeed on the Establishment's terms. So he laboured away at Heatherley's, sent in his drawings, and worked up conventional pictures for the Royal Academy; and minded very much whether they were accepted or rejected. His portraits were more successful, both the strong self-portraits, and the studies of New Zealand friends who were passing through London, such as Thomas Cass and John Marshman. Marshman invited him to a séance, which Alfred Wallace also attended: 'Transparent humbug,' commented Butler.[12] If ever a spirit-form took to coming near him, he told Wallace, he would not content himself with trying to grasp it: 'in the interests of science, *I will shoot it!*' (M1.317)

Butler made many friends during the years at Heatherley's: the

Heatherleys themselves, and artists such as Lionel Smythe, Gaetano
Meo, Thomas Ballard and Charles Gogin; and his circle widened to
include many who were studying at the Slade, like Tom Gotch,
Benwell Clark, Henry Paget and Henry Scott Tuke. Gogin, according to Festing Jones, was one of the few men who really understood
Butler. He remained a life-long friend, the relationship surviving his
marriage in 1894 to another Heatherley student, Alma Broadbridge.
On his Christmas or Easter breaks Butler would often go abroad
with him to Boulogne. Gogin, who exhibited only rarely, painted the
portrait of Butler in the National Portrait Gallery. He was also a
cartoonist, and his independence of mind and dark humour matched,
rather than echoed, Butler's.

The person at Heatherley's who had the deepest influence on
Butler was a woman, Miss Eliza Mary Ann Savage. Known at art
school as the Incarnate Bachelor, Butler, according to Yeats 'liked
women but disapproved of marriage'. 'He liked women because, as
I heard him say, they are so good natured. They would laugh with
him but never at him . . . The charming women of those backward
days were still in the Middle Ages, apologetic, almost penitential, as
if they asked pardon for being so beautiful or so merry and engaging,
and did not a bit mind if Butler regarded them as inferior, especially
as towards them he was always kindly and fatherly and innocent.'
Miss Savage was a student at Heatherley's, not very young, and lame:
'She was fair, with a roundish face and light blue eyes that were very
sensitive and full of light; a small head, her features charmingly
mobile and harmonious. She radiated goodness and sense. She kept
herself very much to herself, yet all liked her, even though we never
spoke to her.' Butler consulted Yeats as to 'whether he could with
safety ask her a schoolboy riddle he had picked up somewhere, a
schoolboy riddle in that, though quite innocent, it was not altogether
nice. I don't remember how I advised, only that they became fast
friends.'[13]

The incident that cemented the friendship is described by Miss
Savage in one of her letters, prompted by reading the manuscript of
Alps and Sanctuaries years later:

I liked the cherry-eating scene too because it reminded me of
your eating cherries when first I knew you. One day when I
was going to the gallery, a very hot day, I remember, I met you

on the shady side of Berners Street, eating cherries out of a basket. Like your Italian friends you were perfectly silent with content, and you handed the basket to me as I was passing, without saying a word. I pulled out a handful, and went on my way rejoicing without saying a word either. I had not before perceived you to be different from anybody else. I was like Peter Bell and the primrose with the yellow brim. As I went away to France a day or two after that, and did not see you again for months, the recollection of you as you were eating cherries in Berners Street abode with me, and pleased me greatly, and now it pleases me greatly to have that incident brought to my recollection again.

Butler, on copying out the letter, added the following note:

I hope no one will imagine that I could have written the foregoing passage without emotion far deeper and more varied than
so trivial an incident on the face of it appears to warrant. How
I wish I could say this to Miss Savage herself. (S255)

Miss Savage was a year younger than Butler, and was the daughter of an architect. From 1862 to 1866 she worked as a resident govern-ess in Kent for a son of the Archbishop of Canterbury, and then continued to act as governess when the family were in London, though living with her parents. She studied drawing at Heatherley's, wrote articles and reviews, and became involved in the affairs of a women's club in Berners Street and in the Society of Lady Artists. The extant correspondence with Butler, which begins in 1871, reveals a penetrating intelligence, mordant wit, and a rare capacity for sympathy. She acted, in time, as Butler's literary editor, and he could not have found a shrewder or more perceptive judgment in which to place his trust. To his own eventual sadness, he himself seems to have misread the nature of their relationship as it developed into intimacy.

On his return from New Zealand, family relationships were guarded but calm. As his parents were abroad at Mentone in the winter of 1864, he went to stay with his Aunt Anna at Kenilworth, and then on to his uncle Sam Worsley at Clifton. He was at Langar on three occasions during 1865, including ten days at Christmas.[14]

May suffered some sort of personal crisis in 1866; she may have turned down a proposal of marriage. She was afraid her brother would be angry: 'I was very sorry for your last –' he replied, 'but angry! The idea is preposterous – no one has any right to be angry with any one – on such matters.' May, dangerously timid, must do whatever she thought fit about her own future happiness. Butler advised her to go up and bite the next six people she met, 'and take it quite as a matter of course that you have a right to bite them'. The thought of May's being crossed, either forced to do something against her will or made to feel guilty for not doing it, brought out his latent sympathy, and he ended his letter with his 'very best love'.[15] As well as his visits to Langar, he went several times to Wales to stay with his brother Tom and his wife Henrietta.

Tom, who had left St John's in mysterious circumstances without taking a degree, had married a Welsh girl, Henrietta (Etta) Rigby, while Butler was in New Zealand. They lived in Wales initially, where Tom worked for a time in forestry, and had four children in quick succession: Charles, Elizabeth (Elsie), Henry (Harry) and Mary (Maysie). It was not a good marriage. Tom drank heavily, and was consistently unfaithful: and they were always short of money. Butler found it easier to be an affectionate uncle than a son or a brother, and he became fond of Etta, sympathising with her increasingly difficult circumstances. The children were often at Langar, where Canon and Mrs Butler provided a happy second home for their grandchildren with May's support, in contrast to Samuel's own harsh childhood.

Butler also called regularly at his uncle Philip Worsley's house in Bloomsbury, especially on his Sunday evening 'At Homes', when he had the chance to meet artists and architects and writers like Crabb Robinson. Reginald Worsley, Philip's youngest son and a fellow student at Heatherley's, was Butler's favourite cousin.

After an accountancy job in Whitbread's brewery, Reggie became an architect, and partnered Butler in his later property ventures. He was also an accomplished violinist. In 1867 he sought Butler's confidence about a love affair. Reggie was in evident distress, having placed himself under some undefined obligation, and Butler's equally clear and characteristic advice was not to marry the woman. For this, he was reproved by the Worsleys, while Reggie went and secretly did the decent thing. 'I believe however that they are very fond of one another,' Butler wrote to his father, 'and that the affair may end less badly than one has the slightest right to expect.' (FL116) The brief marriage produced two children, Edward and Amy, and ended in divorce, after which Butler's close friendship could be resumed. These anguished relationships convinced Butler that sex was better catered for by regular visits to a bawdy house.

The factor which drove a wedge between Butler and most of his family was his concept of God and his rejection of traditional religion. His godmother Anna Russell, a Unitarian like most of the Worsleys, was brave enough to tackle him head on:

My dear Sam,

I have long been screwing up my courage to write you a disagreeable letter, and at last I think I am really going to do so, and you must do your best to forgive me, and to look at the matter from my point of view, rather than from your own.

I have been from time to time so pained by what has come round to me, of the influence you are exerting on others, younger, and less skilled in argument than yourself – leading them, it may be, to make the same shipwreck of faith and hope that you have made, that I have felt as if I must utter some remonstrance, and that if I did not, I should be a cowardly traitor to my own conviction of duty. It is of little use I fear to speak to you of the wrongness of what I refer to, because I imagine our standards of right and wrong are perfectly different, and that you admit no rule of duty beyond your own will and feeling; – but I *may* speak of its cruelty. You have lost all yourself, and you would have others lose all; – gain there can be none . . . It is as if a blind man were not content to bear his blindness alone, but must do his utmost to put out the sight of those about him . . . Do not think you must reply to this – I do not think I wish an answer, and having uttered my protest I shall be silent in future. So if you can dear Sam, still feel love and charity towards your affectionate Aunt and godmother . . . (FL114–15)

The letter, for all its strength of purpose, reveals how little the family understood, could understand, Samuel's views; and also how much they were afraid of him. It was as well they did not know that he had already published his pamphlet, *The Evidence for the Resurrection of Jesus Christ as given by the Four Evangelists critically examined*. Butler's replies to his aunt, though uncompromising, were received sympathetically. He felt she had been unjust, to which she responded: 'you do not know as I do the bitter tears of which you have already been the cause – not *less* the cause because not deliberately and intentionally so. I thank you dear Sam from my heart, for your tender forbearance and for your concluding paragraph. They are like yourself.'[16] Encouraged by this response, Butler enlarged upon his concept of God. His aunt replied:

> I confess myself utterly unable to understand such a conception of God as you have worked out for yourself . . . still, that you believe in some sort of God, is a comfort to me, albeit I gather that God is not the foundation on which you rest your notions of Right and Wrong.
>
> I could *almost* find it in my heart to wish that Langar could see some such statement – I think after the first shock, it would be less painful to *both* parties – certainly to you, than the present footing you are on there . . .[17]

But even his kindly Aunt Anna could go no further than '*almost*'. On this matter the breach between Butler and Langar was absolute, and permanent. There were, unfortunately, few neutral subjects through which Butler could reach his father. One, notably, was botany. Haast had sent more 'cargo' to Canon Butler from the Southern Alps, which was enthusiastically received. 'Nay,' Butler wrote to Haast, 'I will do anything you may command (in tolerable reason) if you will only send the old boy some more plants: if you will pay anyone (say) £10 to make a collection – any shepherd you may know of – I would gladly reimburse you giving you a cheque on my agent.'[18]

Butler may have been ready to part with £10 to give pleasure to his father; but the disagreements and tensions about money continued to sour the atmosphere. First, there was the business of the £600, advanced reluctantly by Canon Butler as part of the investment in Mesopotamia. Butler was receiving interest from New Zealand, but his capital there was tied up, and he could not repay so much out of income. He offered to insure his life or borrow against his eventual inheritance, commenting that he knew his father would not like such a scheme, 'and neither do I': 'I would repay it out of my allowance, but I was short my first year – still shorter owing to unexpected circumstances, and after repaying what I borrowed to make up deficiencies up to date, shall not have for the quarter more than enough to take me economically to the continent ... Believe me I am as anxious to repay it as though I had the most inexorable creditor in the world.' The 'unexpected circumstances' must refer to Pauli, about whose financial dependency Butler kept silent. Whatever the misunderstanding about the £600, Canon Butler had reason to be puzzled and eventually suspicious about his son's lack of money.

There was, too, the delicate matter of the Whitehall property. Butler grew increasingly sensitive about this, believing that it was responsible for all his difficulties:

> As the subject of the Whitehall property has turned up, I will ask a question concerning it which I should never probably have asked otherwise for I dislike the subject. I should like to know the exact nature of my interest in it. If ever it comes to me is it mine absolutely or no? Can I do what I like with it if ever I own it at all? I rather gather that I can, inasmuch as Tom's and W. Lloyd's consent was not attached to the sale of the Whitehall – but I cannot quite make out. Of course the nature of my interest is very different in the one case and the other, and a man really *ought* to know what he has. (FL112–14)

Butler's full feelings would erupt in time. Meanwhile, he could pursue the minutiae of his account with his father with tart irony:

> I hardly know how to answer yours received this morning, for I confess I had thought that at the time you gave me an allowance and ceased to retain the proceeds of my scholarships, the college account caution money and all was transferred from you to me, and have never imagined that you expected the caution money to be returned to you when I took my name off the books; of course however seeing I was mistaken on this point I send a P.O. for £4.15.0, the sum you have paid on my behalf. (FL117)

He wrote of money, one among many references: 'The last friend that shall not be subdued.' (N 106).

Butler spent very little money on himself. His one regular expense was his annual trip abroad, a habit that served almost as a life-line for him. Some kind of holiday was a necessary relief from the long hours he spent painting or writing, preserving him from eye-strain and 'brain-fag'. The journeys to Europe, and in particular to the north of Italy, became in time as much part of the rhythm of his life as the art studio or the Reading Room of the British Museum, offering the stimulus of different landscapes, architecture, languages and friends. In November, 1869 he set off on a longer journey than usual. His health had been troubling him: a tumour on the back of his neck had grown, and he was conscious of loud noises in his head, usually just as he was about to go to sleep. He called them his storm-signals: 'When they show signs of returning I know it to be time for me to slacken off work. Neither symptoms became materially better until the death of my father . . .' (M1.130) He went to consult Dr Dudgeon, a homoeopathic doctor, who recommended four or five months' change. Butler made his way by gradual stages to Mentone, and stayed there painting until March, though he did not like the landscape so well as that of north Italy: too many olives and not enough grass. Then he travelled east, via Turin, Parma, Modena, Florence and Padua, seeing and re-seeing pictures. At the Hotel La Luna in Venice, he found himself all alone and unsettled. It was too cold to paint. There was no one in the hotel – no English, that is, only French and German. If he stayed longer than three or four days, he intended to shift. He did, however, meet an elderly Russian baroness.

> She was plain, quiet, and not, at first sight, attractive; but she took a fancy to me, and we went about together more than once. When I was going away she said to me:
>
> 'Et maintenant, Monsieur, vous allez créer,' meaning that I had been looking long enough at other people's work and should now do something of my own.
>
> This sank into me and pained me; for I knew I had done nothing as yet, nor had I any definite notion of what I wanted to do. All was vague aspiration, admiration, and despair; nor did I yet know, though I was fully 34 years old, that the study

of other men's works – except by the way – is the surest manner of killing the power to do things for oneself.

'Vous allez créer.' Yes, but how to create? and what? I had not yet, for all my education, got to know that doing is the sole parent of doing, and creating a little the only way of learning how to create more; . . . I have often wished I could thank the Baroness (if she was a Baroness) Von Bülow (if her name was Von Bülow). Anyhow she was a Russian. (M1.132–3)

He returned to London resolved to do something in literature, if not in painting, and began to tinker with the articles he had written for the Christchurch *Press*. It was the first step in the direction of *Erewhon*.

CHAPTER 10

Erewhon

Butler had a strong sense of the uniqueness of his personal vision, and an ambition to make his mark in the world, but he had no idea that he could become a writer. The Russian baroness's comments had been aimed at his art; in the summer of 1870 a New Zealand friend, Frederick Napier Broome, called on Butler and suggested he might rework some of his Christchurch *Press* articles into a book: the book would be sure to sell, which his pictures seemed hardly likely to do.[1] Butler had already revised some of the essays for publication in *The Reasoner*. With these materials already to hand, he began to construct a framework, writing initially only at weekends and in the evenings, when his relentless painting schedule had been fulfilled. He wrote *Erewhon* with reluctance; he wanted 'to go on painting and found it an abominable nuisance being dragged willy-nilly into writing it'. (N106) But like all his books, it insisted on being written.

By the end of February 1871 he had completed a draft, and was in the process of rewriting and correcting. His first extant letter to Miss Savage indicates the trust that Butler would now place in her: 'will you read the MS. by small instalments, each about the size of a good long letter, at a time? If so I will send you some at once. It is meant to be entertaining, and is not more than 200 printed pages. I am not at all sure that I shall publish it, and you may save me from committing a grave indiscretion.' (S2) The invitation was accepted. A few days later, Butler increased the size of the instalments. 'I send a lot of the MS. to save the trouble of sending it in smaller pieces; you need only read a little at a time. Make a cross, please, in pencil, wherever you disapprove, and I shall know what you mean. If not you can tell me when we meet...' (S17) Butler, sensitive in every area of his life, was acutely so about his writing; it is a testimony to Miss Savage's tact and judgment, and to the personal warmth and reassurance she managed to convey while acting as critic, that Butler submitted so readily, even eagerly, to her suggestions:

> Can you name a time and place when and where I can trespass on your good nature further? And yet I cannot call it trespassing, for one can only trespass on things that have bounds, and your good-nature has none.
>
> I have condensed, cut out, transposed, amended, emended, and otherwise improved the MS., but there are a few points about which I am still in doubt, and should be very thankful for a little further advice . . .

That spring, Butler had substantial hopes that his period of creation had begun. A second picture of his, 'A Reverie', was accepted at the Academy: 'it does not look well but that is not their fault. I was there all yesterday; it is a capital exhibition.' (S17–18) In May he went abroad for four months, staying for the most part at Arona on Lake Maggiore, and making his first visit to Varallo, drawn by accounts of the Sacro Monte. This was to prove an initiation into many visits and friendships, and would provide him with the stimulus for two future books, *Alps and Sanctuaries* and *Ex Voto*. *Erewhon*, meanwhile, was sent to Chapman and Hall for a publisher's opinion.

Butler enjoyed an extended holiday. He travelled via Antwerp, Cologne, Basel and Bellinzona to Arona, on Lake Maggiore, where he stayed at the Hotel d'Italia. Day after day he would sketch the castle, or be rowed across the lake to Angera. One of the daughters of the family who ran the hotel, Isabella, was extraordinarily beautiful.

> I have never seen any woman comparable to her, and kept out of her way on purpose after leaving Arona as the only thing to be done, for we had become thick. I kept away from Arona for years . . . (M1.284)

From Arona, he visited Fobello. 'I liked Fobello,' he wrote to Miss Savage – that summer he liked everything. 'Ask me about the offertory when I come back, and the selling the wax arms and legs; and the pictures (votive) of the women in leggings and short blue petticoats trimmed with scarlet, falling from the tops of high ash trees when gathering leaves for the cattle, and the saints with very large gridirons who appeared underneath them and broke their fall; and the woman who was tossed by a cow, and the outrushing of the whole family to see what the matter was. . . .' (S18–19)

Back in London he embarked on an oil painting, 'The Christening at Fobello', which exists also as an unfinished watercolour. It shows a father holding his baby up to the priest for a blessing; the angle allows the priest's house to be seen through the porch columns, and behind are the sloping fields and 'the trees which are stripped by the women who wear the leggings and short petticoats and fall off the trees and get put in the votive pictures' (M1.147); the people are in their country costume, and the grouping has a delightful informality, and yet the atmosphere is one of reverence. The painting makes an interesting contrast to 'Family Prayers': there, each person was separate, eyes sightless, rigid; here, there is a strong sense of unity, the attitudes of prayer lending dignity to the central action, which is given additional emphasis by the two small boys, one with a candle, in front of the priest, and the golden light on the fields behind. (Butler later added a caustic note, like Beckett's Krapp, perhaps sensing what he might have done in art had he persevered: 'I forget whether this picture ever got finished – yes, it did – I sent it to the Academy, and it was rejected, quite rightly. I know I gave it to somebody, but I forget who. I wish I had destroyed it.') (S21)

On his return to London, he was met with the news that *Erewhon* had been rejected by Chapman and Hall's reader, George Meredith. 'This is not strange,' Butler noted later, 'for I should probably have condemned his *Diana of the Crossways*, or indeed any other of his books, had it been submitted to myself. No wonder if his work repels me that mine should repel him.' (M1.148) The rejection set the pattern for Butler's future dealings with publishers. He revised the manuscript once more, and it went next to Trübner and Co.: 'They never so much as looked at it before, and said they supposed it was something to do with the Contagious Diseases Act. Now I am to pay their reader a guinea for reading it and giving an opinion; I shall then have the right to bully him and tell him he is a fool if he does not like it.' (S22)

The report was, in fact, favourable; but Trübner would not take the risk himself, only offering to publish it at the author's expense. Henry Hoare, the banker, and one of Butler's old college friends, lent him the money, a loan that contributed to Butler's looming financial crisis. The proofs reassured him: 'It reads very well and the type is excellent, even Pauli who has been the most freezing critic hitherto (in so far as he could be got to listen to a passage here and there) thawed a little as he read: the fact is he is frightened out of his wits about it, and expects my father to cut me off with a shilling, but he dares not say this because he knows I should fly at him if he advised me to let my father's will enter in the matter at all.' (S23) On March 29th he was able to tell Miss Savage: '*Erewhon* is out, and will be advertised tomorrow: I have your copy: the sample copy, i.e. the first issued: I have written your name in it to make sure . . .' (S24)

Erewhon, or Over the Range, was published anonymously. In 1871 a Utopian novel, *The Coming Race*, also anonymous, had attracted some attention. It was widely believed (quite correctly) to be by Lord Lytton, and there were enough small points of similarity to suggest that *Erewhon* might be a sequel. Butler, though his sales were inflated by the error, was understandably prickly about the false attribution. He had already changed one name, from Zelora to Zulora, on dis-covering that the heroine of *The Coming Race* was 'Zee', and he explained in the preface to the second edition that *Erewhon* had been virtually finished before *The Coming Race* was even advertised. As he was in an out of the way part of Italy, he 'never saw a single review of *The Coming Race*, nor a copy of the work. On my return, I purposely avoided looking into it until I had sent back my last revises to the printer.' One of Butler's grounds for disliking his uncle, Philip Worsley, was that he would tell him that *Erewhon* only sold well because the critics thought it might be written by someone famous. As if to confirm the force of the insult, the sales fell off sharply once Butler's authorship was announced.

Butler's anonymity was always a complex business, stemming partly from insecurity, partly from a mischievous delight in wrong-footing people, substantially, in this instance, from anxiety about the reaction from Langar. *Erewhon* is, demonstrably, autobiographical: leaving aside the finer implications of any such statement, it is written in the first person and describes the adventures of a young man living on a sheep run in a colony very much like New Zealand; among the targets of its more blatant satire are Christianity and the Church. More particularly, as far as Langar was concerned, it included two mischievous misquotations from old school essays of Canon Butler's.

In the manuscript, there was also a potentially explosive allusion to a youth who was charged 'with having been swindled out of large property during his minority by his guardian, who was also one of his nearest relations ... "Young man," said the judge sternly, "do not talk nonsense. People have no right to be young, inexperienced, greatly in awe of their guardians, and without independent professional advice. If by such indiscretions they outrage the moral sense of their friends, they must expect to suffer accordingly." ' Butler omitted this, perhaps on Pauli's advice, and it appeared only in the expanded edition of 1901. The possibility of being 'cut off with a shilling' may have been a realistic apprehension; at the same time, Butler genuinely wished to remain close to his family, however much he disliked everything he thought they stood for, and longed somehow to win their approval.

Whether Butler himself took the decision to acknowledge his authorship, or whether it was taken for him, is not clear. A number of favourable reviews and a consequent steady, if modest, sale may have encouraged the revelation, as did the praise of those to whom he presented copies.

> I have heard nothing more about the book except the verdict of one or two friends' friends; on the whole I think their reports sound well, but am always sceptical about what my friends say unless it is by way of scolding. Mr Heatherley said it did not drag and that it interested him throughout. I lay great stress on Gogin's liking it; he would not stand being bored beyond reasonable limits. – A friend of Pauli's, one of the proctors this year, read it and satisfied Pauli of his approval – handsomely. (S24–5)

He even gave Forbes-Robertson a copy to pass on to his father: 'Sam, my people say you are a great writer!'.[2] The fact of Butler's authorship was announced on May 25th in *The Athenaeum* and *The Drawing-Room Gazette*. Three days later, Butler wrote to his father, saying how well the book had been received – 'this was injudicious,' he noted – and asking whether his father objected to his putting his name to it. Any hopes that the publication of *Erewhon* might reconcile him with his parents were brusquely dispelled. His father wrote:

I shall take your advice and not read the book. It would probably pain me and not benefit you. I do not the least object to your putting your name to it tho' I may not value the éclat. The grief is that our views should be so wide asunder.

Perhaps the book might pain me less than your letter leads me to infer. I gladly give it the benefit of the doubt. (FL118)

His mother's response was softer in tone but equally negative; she was not surprised that success pleased him, but wished it had been gained in some way in which she could rejoice. 'Everything that confirms me in the knowledge of how far apart we are in views – and feelings – and hopes is a blow to me; – but I have no right to be surprised – for I had little hope that it was otherwise with you. I am very glad we have heard of it all from yourself – and I am very glad too that you don't mean to forsake painting. I don't know what Papa feels, but to me, the adding of your name to the book, would make no difference to me whatever.' Having heard of a visit to Darwin, she was glad he had had 'such a pleasant variety'. (FL119)

That painting could be viewed as preferable to writing is a measure of the hurt the publication of *Erewhon* caused. Harriet Bridges, in receipt of a 'sad and disturbed' letter from May giving the Langar view, wrote to her brother from Ventnor to make him realise the pain he was giving. She urged him to let his parents see that he at least cared about what they must be feeling. Butler accordingly wrote what he intended to be 'a conciliatory and apologetic' letter. As so often, his letter had the reverse effect, stirring up a swarm of intense feelings: anger, hurt, resentment, incomprehension, sorrow:

If one holds one's religious beliefs with any reality, don't you think it natural that one should feel something a great deal stronger than a mere 'passing regret' that those dear to us do not feel with us. If there is anything whatever in it there is everything in it.

As for expecting us to feel any vanity or triumph in your success it is wholly impossible. We should heartily rejoice to find it as ephemeral as I am disposed to hope and believe it may be. (He was quite right here, but at the same time he was only wanting to say something unpleasant. S.B.) . . .

I don't greatly care whether you put your name to the book

or not. I quite believe you withheld it for our sakes, but the pain is in your having written it, not in its being found out. But it is quite out of the question that such success can be anything but pain to us. It will probably prove an injury to yourself in many ways. Partly in diverting your attention from such degree of drawing as you have attained to. (I had already, as he knew, exhibited more than once at the Academy. S.B. June 16, 1901) And if you fancy that your name will be found in the 'front rank of the writers of your time and country' is not that a little strong? (This is just enough. S.B.)

At present your visits could be nothing but pain to us all and therefore painful to yourself. I do not therefore wish you to come down. (I had not talked of doing so.) But I believe your letter was written as one of conciliation and so have answered it at length that you might understand what our feelings are. But anything like an argument I should decline as it could do nothing but embitter

Your affectionate father if you will still let me be so,

T. Butler.   (FL121–2)

The father's disclaimer that the exchange of letters constituted an argument and the son's annotations nearly thirty years later mark the Aeschylean persistence of their conflict. One further accusation was still to come, the most wounding of all: that Butler's writing of *Erewhon* hastened his mother's death. To his family the book was an explicit and public confirmation of everything they had suspected and feared since his refusal to be ordained in 1859. For his parents and sisters, Butler was among the damned.

Erewhon, which Butler named as his opus 1 (disclaiming, for reasons already discussed, *A First Year in Canterbury Settlement*), is a startlingly original work, a major source for much of his serious later writing. It haunted him in later life, as his notes testify: Trübner told him he was a 'homo unius libri', and, recording an enquiry as to why he did not write another *Erewhon*, he commented: 'They say these things to me continually to plague me, and make out that I could do one good book, but never any more.' (N181) Yet at the end of his life, with many disclaimers, he returned to revise and enlarge it, asserting all the while that this was simply to extend the copyright;

and drew further attention to it by writing its sequel, *Erewhon Revisited*.

One attribute of *Erewhon*, as a friend explained to Butler, was that it brought the sound of a new voice. It is a kind of sport, stimulating, elusive, difficult to classify, deliberately or fortuitously inconsistent. It invites comparison to *Gulliver's Travels* (inevitably to its disadvantage). It has narrative deficiencies, and much of the characterisation is perfunctory, as Butler pointed out with relish in 1901. He also said that there was no central idea, which is overstating the case. But the apparent failures of art give the book a freshness that the more experienced and fluent writer Butler became found it hard to emulate.

The book is narrated by a young man who does not even have a name (he becomes Thomas Higgs in *Erewhon Revisited*). The opening sequence is based on Butler's own experiences in Mesopotamia, and the journey Higgs undertakes with the native Chowbok echoes the explorations Butler made with Baker in the Southern Alps. The style is spare and direct, and the developing sense of danger, of physical and spiritual solitude, is strongly conveyed. The motif of a young man's journey into an unknown land is traditional enough; what gives this example such force is the air of complete conviction supplied by the practical details. Against the factual texture of daily life – last night's tea leaves frozen at the bottom of the pannikins, the comfort derived from the sound of a watch ticking – is juxtaposed the terrible image of the ten stone statues through whose hollowed heads the wind moans Handelian chords, and who guard the pass into Erewhon.

One of Butler's most successful techniques was to take the ordinary, or at least the actual, and extend or distort it with some leap of the imagination or shift of perspective. He had an artist's eye for landscape, and had become accustomed to describing his travels. He made detailed use of his pioneering explorations: he transposed one or two geographical features, adding another section of gorge to the Rangitata; and whereas he and Baker doubled back and approached the Whitcombe Pass from the east, Higgs descends 'over the edge of horrible precipices on to the river, which roared some four or five thousand feet below' (E58); but he wrote out of hard won, first-hand knowledge. Even the topography of Erewhon gains authenticity from its relationship to reality, inviting an attempt to superimpose an

Erewhonian map on that of New Zealand, just as later Butler would transpose or trace the *Odyssey* on to the geography of Sicily.

Butler's experience of New Zealand not only supplied the physical setting of *Erewhon*, but also furnished many of its ideas. The concept of Utopia, or Arcadia, arises naturally in a new country. The founders of Canterbury conceived it as a Church of England colony, with a funding arrangement intended to endow religious and educational purposes and institutions. Many early settlers had idealistic views about the potential of their society, and did not see New Zealand as, necessarily, a distant reflection of England. The Pacific has always been a rich hunting-ground for Utopias, and for the reverse, from the images of paradisal tropical islands to the horrors of the penal colonies. Squatting in his Forest Creek hut and hauling timber from the bush, Butler may have pictured himself as Ferdinand; certainly, he imposed a back-country overlay on *The Tempest* in his note: 'Ferdinand is for the present a sort of cadet, a youth of good family, without cash and unaccustomed to manual labour; his unlucky stars have landed him on the island, and now it seems that he "must remove some thousands of these logs and pile them up, upon a sore injunction." ' Caliban, he wrote, was 'like the man cook on a back-country run'. (FY195–7)

The use of names in *Erewhon* is inconsistent: Butler claimed that he failed to appreciate the importance of names because of inexperience. One or two have a Maori ring about them, notably Arowhena; the real name of the old native whom the shearers had nicknamed Chowbok is Kahabuka, 'Cabbage-head' (near enough) in Maori. Butler did not have much contact with Maoris, since there were so few in his part of Canterbury. One he did know was Abner Clough, a half-caste Maori who worked at Mount Peel: 'Abner is the son of a Maori Princess and is, as Butler says, a prince by nature and if he had had a good education would have been a polished gentleman'[3] – the antitype of Chowbok. There was also an Australian aboriginal at Mount Peel, Black Andy, who had come to New Zealand with Sir George Grey when the latter was appointed Governor of New Zealand in 1845. Black Andy's interest in rum is one feature he has in common with Chowbok.

Understandably, since so much of *Erewhon* relates to actuality, there have been attempts to identify the source for the statues that guard the pass. 'They show a lot of stones on the Hokitika Pass . . .

which they call mine, and say I intended them in *Erewhon*. I never
saw them and knew nothing about them,' noted Butler in 1884.
(M1.151-2) Other attributions have included the statues on Easter
Island, and some clay and shingle pillars in the Forest Creek area.
Butler could scarcely complain at such speculation. The image recurs
three times, dominating the early chapters of the book, and providing
a ritual passage between the two worlds. Butler criticised *Erewhon*
for having no central idea, but the story's impetus comes from Higgs's
speculation:

> But over and above these thoughts came that of the great range
> itself. What was beyond it? Ah! Who could say? There was no
> one in the whole world who had the smallest idea, save those
> who were themselves on the other side of it – if, indeed, there
> was any one at all. (E43-4)

Seeking an answer to those questions, Higgs catechises Chowbok in
the woolshed. Chowbok rolls bales of wool into a pile, jumps up on
the highest, and sits bolt upright, as stiff as stone, with a fiendish
expression: 'Then there came from his lips a low moaning like the
wind, rising and falling by infinitely small gradations till it became
almost a shriek, from which it descended and died away . . .' (E47)
    In Chapter 4, when Chowbok has turned back and Higgs, wet and
lost in the chasm, dreams of Handel at the organ, he wakes to hear
'a faint and extremely distinct sound of music, like that of an Æolian
harp, borne upon the wind which was blowing fresh and chill from
the opposite mountains'. (E60) Finally, at the very summit of the
pass, he encounters the statues themselves:

> A few steps brought me nearer, and a shudder of unutterable
> horror ran through me when I saw a circle of gigantic forms,
> many times higher than myself, upstanding grim and grey
> through the veil of cloud before me.
>   I suppose I must have fainted, for I found myself some time
> afterwards sitting upon the ground, sick and deadly cold. There
> were the figures, quite still and silent, seen vaguely through the
> thick gloom, but in human shape indisputably. (E66)

Higgs advances timidly and inspects the statues – which are barbarous, malevolent, terrible; looking at them from behind, he sees that their heads had been hollowed.

> Then came a gust of howling wind, accompanied with a moan from one of the statues above me. I clasped my hands in fear . . . The wildness of the wind increased, the moans grew shriller, coming from several statues, and swelling into a chorus . . . It was horrible. However brave a man might be, he could not stand such a concert, from such lips, and in such a place. I heaped every invective upon them that my tongue could utter as I rushed away from them into the mist, and even after I had lost sight of them, and turning my head round could see nothing but the storm-wraiths driving behind me, I heard their ghostly chanting, and felt as though one of them would rush after me and grip me in his hand and throttle me. (E67–8)

On his return to England, so the narrator relates, he heard a friend playing chords on the organ that reminded him of the music of the Erewhonian statues, and learned they were by Handel. Butler wrote of Handel's big chords, 'one feels them in the diaphragm. They are, as it were, the groaning and labouring of all creation travailing together until now.' (N263) Within the novel, Higgs is on the brink of experiencing a new creation. He follows a track down into the sunlight, and sees 'such an expanse as was revealed to Moses when he stood upon the summit of Mount Sinai, and beheld that promised land which it was not to be his to enter. The beautiful sunset sky was crimson and gold; blue, silver, and purple; exquisite and tranquillising; fading away therein were plains, on which I could see many a town and city, with buildings that had lofty steeples and rounded domes.' (E70) Tired out, he falls into a profound sleep. When he wakes, like Ferdinand, to this brave new world, after the storm and stress of the mountain pass, it is to the sound of tinkling bells and the chattering and laughter of two lovely girls.

The description of the statues, and the dreams and visions associated with them, form one of Butler's few poetic sequences. In constructing his first work of fiction, he created a representation of the dreadful gods that man has set to guard received tradition and convention; in terms of the fable, they protect the Erewhonians from the outside world, but in terms of Butler's own intellectual and emotional journey, they present a challenge, like the challenge to his father, which has to be taken up at the risk of death.

The promised land that Higgs wakes to is a new creation of Butler's making: on the other side of the great divide, he superimposes on the Southern Alps the geography of Lombardy and the Ticino. The people he meets are of his ideal type, Italian mountain peasants: 'They were of the most magnificent presence, being no less strong and handsome than the women were beautiful . . .' (E71); 'their manners also were eminently Italian, in their entire unconsciousness of self.' (E74) The village to which they lead him is 'like one of those that one comes upon in descending the less known passes over the Alps into Lombardy'. The language, however, is incomprehensible; and one or two of Higgs's actions seem to arouse unease, for instance, the striking of a match. Higgs is eventually escorted to a neighbouring town and taken before a magistrate for a thorough examination. His perfect health, general robustness and, above all, his fair hair and blue eyes are clearly points in his favour: in his pockets, however, is a watch, and this evokes grave displeasure.

From this point, the nature of the book changes, in so far as the narrative drive is largely superseded by philosophical and satirical commentary. The story does continue, but in a somewhat perfunctory manner: Higgs serves a prison sentence, for possession of the watch, during which he is taught the Erewhonian language partly by an interpreter, but more effectively by the jailor's beautiful daughter, Yram. Sent to the metropolis, he stays with a leading merchant, Mr Nosnibor, and duly falls in love with his younger daughter, Arowhena. He is presented at court, interviewed by the King and Queen, and visits a number of public institutions. Finally, when he learns that the warmth of his welcome is beginning to cool, he persuades the Queen to grant him permission to construct a balloon, and escapes with Arowhena. With the exception of the last episode, the events are sketched in the simplest of outlines.

The power of the book lies less in the story than in the descriptions and comments on the laws and customs of the Erewhonians. Erewhon is variously presented as a development of Western civilisation, a reversal of it, and an aberration from it: it is as though one is viewing Victorian England through a series of distorting mirrors, and mirrors that distort in different ways. The business of the watch, for example, is explained by a revolution some five hundred years previously, when civil war was waged between the machinists and the anti-machinists, resulting in victory for the latter and the destruction of all machines, engineers' workshops and treatises on mechanics. Butler 'translates' the theoretical work which prompted the revolution in the three chapters, 'The Book of the Machines'. Some readers saw this as an attack on Darwin's *The Origin of Species*, although Butler hastened to assure Darwin that his intended target was Bishop Butler's *The Analogy of Religion*. Another reference point was Paley's *Natural Theology*. Both Butler and Darwin would have studied these in preparation for ordination; and Butler took obvious pleasure in turning Paley's classic argument for the existence of God on its head, by Higgs's commentary of the Erewhonians' reactions when they find his watch:

> I remember that when they first found it I had thought of Paley, and how he tells us that a savage on seeing a watch would at once conclude that it was designed. True, these people were not savages, but I none the less felt sure that this was the conclusion they would arrive at; and I was thinking what a wonderfully wise man Archbishop Paley must have been, when I was aroused by a look of horror and dismay upon the face of the magistrate, a look which conveyed to me the impression that he regarded my watch not as having been designed, but rather as the designer of himself and of the universe; or as at any rate one of the great first causes of all things. (E82)

While Butler was probably laying one of his own troublesome ghosts in this passage, his extended application of the theory of evolution to the development of machines begins to bear critically on the theory of evolution itself. By demonstrating its only marginally absurd logic as metaphor, Butler introduces the suspicion that the theory of evolution may be more metaphorical than scientific.

Some of Butler's targets are solid, monolithic: the Law, the Church, the Universities are relatively contained objects of satire, vulnerable to a method that relies strongly on reversal, the Universities as Colleges of Unreason, for example. But Butler's treatment is double-edged and ambiguous. The gravest crimes in Erewhon are ill health and ill luck, whereas embezzlement or violence are carefully treated either in hospital or by men trained in 'soul-craft', called 'straighteners'. For 'Some Erewhonian Trials', in which a man is found guilty of pulmonary consumption, Butler used a Victorian judge's summing-up from a crime report 'with scarcely more alteration than the name of the offence'. By the time one has been subjected to the full force of this trenchant address, one can almost believe in a society that accepts the original premise. The treatment of disease as crime (and crime as disease) becomes significant and valid.

The same kind of process operates in other targets of satire, such as the Musical Banks, Butler's equivalent for the Church. The Erewhonians appear to have two entirely distinct currencies, each under the control of its own banks and mercantile codes. The musical bank code is supposed to be *the* system, and all who wish to be considered respectable keep a certain amount of this currency at these banks, but it is a very small part of their possessions. Higgs decides that they take the money, put it into the bank, and then draw it out again, repeating the process day by day, while they pay the expenses of the bank with the other coinage. The novel extends the analogy with the Church; the clergy are cashiers, 'all at their desks ready to pay cheques'. Apart from a few women and children, Higgs notices hardly any customers, though he has been told almost everyone in the city deals with the establishment. But Butler's vehement dislike of the Church as a purveyor of cant and hypocrisy is tempered by his recognition of its value as symbol; and this implicit respect is strengthened in his 1901 revision:

> Some Erewhonian opinions concerning the intelligence of the unborn embryo, that I regret my space will not permit me to lay before the reader, have led me to conclude that the Erewhonian Musical Banks, and perhaps the religious systems of all countries, are now more or less of an attempt to uphold the unfathomable and unconscious instinctive wisdom of millions of past generations, against the comparatively shallow, consciously reasoning, and ephemeral conclusions drawn from that of the last thirty or forty. (E146–7)

The saving feature of the Erewhonian Musical Bank system was that while it bore witness to a kingdom not of this world, it made no attempt to pierce the veil that hid it from human eyes.

The general air of ambiguity, the impulse to qualify and revise, is inherent in Butler's cast of mind. In *Erewhon* it is seen again in his treatment of the Colleges of Unreason, where, after preparatory courses in Inconsistency and Evasion, the Erewhonian youths progress to a study of 'hypothetics'. The absurd curriculum is given a strictly logical justification: the importance assigned to hypothetics rests on their being 'a preparation for the extraordinary', while studying Unreason develops 'those faculties which are required for the daily conduct of affairs'. (E187) This intellectual malleability and flexibility is different in kind from the more traditional varieties of Utopian or dystopian satire, nearer, perhaps, to the farcical surrealism of *The Importance of Being Earnest* than to *The Soul of Man Under Socialism*, and close in spirit to the absurdist world of Ionesco or Beckett. One can imagine Butler enjoying *The Bald Primadonna*.

In *Erewhon* Butler does supply one central point of stability to anchor his erratic speculations. This is the worship of Ydgrun, goddess of public pragmatism and common sense, as epitomised by Mrs Grundy. In describing the 'high Ydgrunites', Butler came close to defining his ideal: 'They were gentlemen in the full sense of the word; and what has one not said in saying this? Their physique is superlative and appearance most prepossessing, as might be expected in a country where bodily disease has been stamped upon for so many generations. Most had a smattering of the hypothetical language; they were strong, handsome, and kindly nurtured; living fearlessly under the eye of their peers, among whom there exists a high standard of courage, generosity, honour, and every good and manly quality, what wonder that they should have become, so to speak, a law unto themselves; and, while taking an elevated view of the goddess Ydgrun, they should have gradually lost all faith in the recognised deities of the country?' (E157–8)

Butler, inelegant and maladroit in the ways of the world, could mock his own aspirations in the handsome, successful Ydgrunites, and at the same time elevate them more than half seriously as the new race. These paragons resembled Pauli, or at least a Pauli who did not suffer from ill health: 'In other respects they were more like Englishmen who had been educated at such a school as Winchester (if there be such another) and sent thence to one of the best colleges at Oxford or Cambridge.' The idealisation is related to the cult of the dandy, as epitomised by Lord Darlington in *An Ideal Husband*.

Higgs proposes persuading half a dozen to come over to England and go on the stage: 'such a man upon the stage, becomes a potent humanising influence, an Ideal which all may look upon for a shilling.' (E158) In a later note Butler (thinking of Pauli as well as the Ydgrunites) promotes the 'swell' as nature's finest achievement:

> People ask complainingly what swells have done or do for society that they should be able to live without working. The good swell is the creature towards which all nature has been groaning and travailing together until now. He is an ideal. He shows what may be done in the way of good breeding, health, looks, temper and fortune. He realises men's dreams of themselves at any rate vicariously; he preaches the gospel of grace. The world is like a spoilt child; it has this good thing given it at great expense and then says it is useless. (N79)

For a brief golden time, Butler/Higgs/Ferdinand enjoys the life of a swell, before his good looks begin to fail him, and he contrives to be spirited away with Arowhena in a balloon.

If the elevation of the Ydgrunites and their values was offensive to Langar, and those who thought in the Langar way, Butler's concept of the Unborn was even more subversive. The Unborn are souls, pure and simple, the most foolish of whom make the mistake of choosing to be born, and are allotted by chance to two people 'whom it is their business to find and pester until they adopt them'. They are lectured to severely by wiser heads about the dangers of being born to wicked or silly parents, who might regard them as their own property: 'Again, you may draw utterly unsympathetic parents, who will never be able to understand you, and who will do their best to thwart you (as a hen when she has hatched a duckling), and then call you ungrateful because you do not love them; or, again, you may draw parents who look upon you as a thing to be cowed while it is still young, lest it should give them trouble hereafter by having wishes and feelings of its own.' This onslaught on parenthood per se, however whimsical, struck at the heart of Victorian beliefs about the family.

Butler spent a long time, and much effort, in releasing *Erewhon* from the World of the Unborn. Its ending reflects his own uncertainty when he began his life again in Europe. As their balloon sinks into the sea, Higgs and Arowhena 'sat in the car of the balloon with the waters up to our middle, and still smiled with a ghastly hopefulness to one other'. (E251) Significantly, they are rescued by a ship bound from Callao to Genoa; Butler had passed through Callao on his way home from New Zealand, and the captain of the ship who rescues them, Giovanni Gianni, bears the name of the Italian Butler sailed with in 1865. The dream journey brings the traveller back through the looking-glass to his own life; although he duly reports the marriage to Arowhena in the last chapter, her presence fades, and the hero is left 'desolate and disconsolated in the world', like Robinson Crusoe. For all the book's energy and ebullience, the conclusion is deliberately deflating. The argument, and the narrative, simply come to rest.

The modest success that *Erewhon* received was short-lived. The 750 copies of the first edition were sold by the end of May. Trübner had not taken moulds, so the book was reset, with a new preface and some minor changes (Butler was an avid reviser), and re-issued in July. But sales dwindled: by 1898, Butler records, he had sold 3842 copies for a cash profit of £62–10–10, with stock valued at £6–13s.

Other Ydgrunite gains were few. Butler was too defensive and awkward in company to become a literary figure. The eminent men with whom the reputation of *Erewhon* brought him into contact were found wanting. People said too little, or too much, or the wrong thing. 'I have since found that this silence trick is common with people who would get reputation cheaply. Rossetti, the painter, played it when I met him in Wallis's rooms shortly after *Erewhon* appeared; he sat still, moody, impenetrable . . .' He disliked his face, and his manner, and his work, he told Miss Savage, and hated his poetry and friends. Marriott gave a dinner so that Butler could meet John Morley.

'Marriott gave a splendid feed, which I regret to say I have never to this day returned, and Morley and I were put to sit in the middle of the table side by side, and there was to be a feast of reason and a flow of soul – a part of the programme which did not come off. Morley talked a great deal, and so, I have no doubt, did I; but I cannot, happily, remember one syllable that was said by either of us; all I remember is that I disliked and distrusted Morley.' (M1.153–5) Part of Butler's isolation arose from his persistent refusal, or incapacity, to meet people on their own terms. Also, he shrank from anything in the nature of competition. He sensed, too, that society would distract him from his writing. Miss Savage wanted him to sit down and write a novel. He was, however, already at work on his next book, *The Fair Haven*: 'a genuine thing done not because some one wants me to do it,' he wrote to her, 'but because I am bursting with it'. (S29)

CHAPTER 11

The Fair Haven

After the unexpected, if qualified, success of *Erewhon*, Butler was in a mood of intellectual ferment and unprecedented confidence. In *Erewhon* he had fired off a salvo at long-range in the general direction of Victorian values and institutions. Now he planned a more insidious and concentrated attack on the very heart of the age as he perceived it: the doctrines of the Established Church. This was a task for which he had been preparing himself assiduously ever since he had recoiled from ordination in 1859. The first fruit of his solitary study was the pamphlet, *The Evidence for the Resurrection of Jesus Christ as given by the Four Evangelists critically examined*, which he had published in 1865. In this, broadly, Butler analysed the accounts of the Crucifixion of Jesus, his burial and the Resurrection, and concluded that Jesus had not in fact been dead when his body was handed over to Joseph of Arimathea, but later recovered consciousness. From the Apostles' sincere belief in the supposed miracle of the Resurrection, everything else in orthodox Christian doctrine followed.

Butler made a characteristic disclaimer in his Preface:

> I have no doubt that the line of argument taken in the following pages is a very old one, and familiar to all who have extended their reading on the subject of Christianity beyond the common English books . . .

Although certainly not original, Butler's theory was still relatively uncommon in England, as was his scrutiny of the variations in the Gospel accounts, though standard practice in Germany. The most widely disseminated discussion was in Strauss's *The Life of Jesus Critically Examined*, which had been published in England in George Eliot's translation in 1846; this caused a stir, but the book was too long and dense to appeal to the general public as much as Renan's

more accessible *Vie de Jésus*. Butler's approach was independent
and bold. The controversy over the mildly liberal religious attitudes
expressed by the seven contributors to *Essays and Reviews* in 1860 is
an indication of the current climate of opinion: eleven thousand
Anglican clergy signed a Declaration in 1864 affirming the Church's
faith in the authority of the Bible, while Convocation formally condemned the book. This was just the kind of cause that Butler
relished.

Much to his disappointment, no one took much notice of his
pamphlet. He sent a copy to Charles Darwin, who responded kindly:
'It seems to me written with much force, vigour, and clearness: and
the main argument is to me quite new . . . I do not know whether
you intend to return to New Zealand, and if you are inclined to
write. I should much like to know what your future plans are.'
M1.123) Encouraged by Darwin's interest, Butler replied at some
length; and it was on this occasion that he sent him a copy of his
Christchurch Press article. Darwin's approval was no doubt flattering,
but it did not compensate for the general indifference. For the issue,
Butler believed, was of over-riding urgency. In his own mind, what
happened at the Resurrection was the overwhelming question, and
he had wrestled day and night in his attempts to answer it, while his
response had affected his entire network of family relationships. It
must surely, he argued a little naively, be equally important to the
whole age. 'It's all very well but I cannot settle down to writing a
novel and trying to amuse people when there is work wants doing
which I believe I am just the man to do, and which it seems to me
is crying out to be done. I shall never be quiet till I have carried out
the scheme that is in my head.' (S28)

Butler had already sent an idea for a novel to Miss Savage, but
remained doubtful about the project.

So that is what you want me to do. 'To sit down with the
foregone conclusion to write a novel, etc.' with oddity rather
than originality for the result. No. If I have talent it may be
safely let alone to work its own way out: if I have not, it does
not matter two straws what I do – only the best thing would be
for me to do nothing.

If I do write a novel after what I have got on hand now, I
shall write two or three bad ones first, and then a better one,

or two, but I must be allowed two failures first. What I am doing now is a genuine thing done not because some one wants me to do it, but because I am bursting with it. (S28–9)

Perhaps because of Miss Savage's advice, Butler gave *The Fair Haven* something of the form and structure of a novel. He invented a pair of brothers, the eldest of whom he finally named John Pickard Owen. The younger, William Bickersteth Owen, presents *The Fair Haven* as the magnum opus of his deceased elder brother, prefacing it with a memoir, and assuming the role of editor, with occasional interpolations and annotations. The subtlety of Butler's method lies in the persona he has constructed for John Pickard Owen, and the nature of the apologia he undertakes as his life's work: 'to show to Rationalists that Christians are right upon Rationalistic principles in all the more important of their allegations; that is to say, to establish the Resurrection and Ascension of the Redeemer upon a basis which should satisfy the most imperious demands of modern criticism.' (FH 58) To accomplish this task, Owen first presents the Rationalist arguments, and then proceeds to refute them, Butler's true intention being to promote a rational approach, and to satirise the specious arguments with which objections to Christianity were customarily met.

At the core of *The Fair Haven* stand two 'alternative' interpretations. The first is that of Strauss, who refuted both supernaturalist and naturalist explanations in favour of the mythological. Strauss held that Jesus died on the cross, and that belief in his Resurrection developed on the basis of the visions experienced by the women and Apostles who visited the tomb. The second is a restatement of Butler's own thesis that Jesus did not in fact die on the cross but merely lost consciousness. Butler places this theory towards the close of his book, and treats it as a much more formidable proposition than Strauss's 'hallucination' approach. He is, however, less concerned to establish a particular point of view than to insist on the importance of the evidence being thoroughly sifted, and to expose the weaknesses of the orthodox doctrine and its justifications.

The book reveals more about Butler than his theological position alone. The Memoir, for instance, contains in its first few pages two brief but disturbing portraits of a father and mother: the father a reverse (reverse, that is, in the author's view) image of Canon Butler, 'a singularly gentle and humorous playmate who doted upon us both and never spoke unkindly' (FH1); the mother, on the other hand, shares several features with Fanny Butler, for she is pious, narrow and literal: 'Her plans of Heaven and solution of life's enigmas were direct and forcible, but they could only be reconciled with certain obvious facts – such as the omnipotence and all-goodness of God – by leaving many things absolutely out of sight.' (FH4)

The book also includes a story supplied by Miss Savage, of a lady visitor who shares a bedroom with the young Owens, and who says her prayers when she thinks the two boys are awake and may observe her but never prays when she thinks they are asleep. Like his creator, Samuel Butler, John Pickard Owen teaches in Sunday School and is shocked when he realises that baptism appears to have no measurable effect on conduct. This leads him to undertake a series of rapid experiments: he joins the Baptists, and is immersed in a pond near Dorking, only to quarrel with his instructors over predestination; he is received into the Church of Rome, but rebels against the stifling of free enquiry; he falls in with a Deist, and is shorn of every shred of dogma; and finally he makes his way back to the Christian faith as the broadest of Broad Churchmen (a position that Butler would at a much later date quite seriously claim for himself).

The first part of the Memoir moves with purpose and often pungent satire. However, as the book proceeds, Butler becomes more and more immersed in a slightly arcane ironic mode. He takes obvious pleasure in imitating the tone and style of religious apologists, both through the dual personae of the brothers Owen, and in his use of quotations from other commentators.

Butler's Nabokovian delight in aping and undermining religious language and attitudes overwhelms the actual arguments. But so successful was the imitation that on the publication of *The Fair Haven* in 1873, some readers took the book as a straightforward defence of the Christian faith. 'Mr Ainger, the reader of the Temple, sent it to a friend of a friend of mine, whom he wished to convert,' (S56) reported Miss Savage with delight; the Reverend Archer Gurney wrote to Butler expressing warm sympathy with the writer's views: 'He wrote so nicely and kindly that for fear I should show the letter about, I tore it up as soon as I had got it back from Miss Savage.' (S55) *The Rock*, fervently evangelical, devoted two long reviews to a work that was extraordinary 'whether regarded as a biographical record or a theological treatise': 'To the sincerely inquiring doubter, the striking way in which the truth of the Resurrection is exhibited must be most beneficial, but such a character we are compelled to believe is rare among those of the schools of neology.'[1] *The Scotsman* also reviewed the book seriously. Butler was able to make cutting use of these and other references in his Preface to the second edition of October, 1873 when he declared his authorship and at the same time refused responsibility for the interpretations of his readers.

Unfortunately, both for the immediate success of the book and for his future reputation, Butler had covered his tracks too thoroughly. The façade of irony was too delicate, the joke inherently private. He could share it with Miss Savage, and with a few intimate friends, who rejoiced with him in the credulousness of old ladies and earnest clergymen. But the satire was, by its very nature, lost on the orthodox, and only a particular kind of mind would appreciate John Pickard Owen in full flow. The serious purpose behind Butler's mockery was largely ignored. Darwin thanked him for his 'extremely curious' book but observed shrewdly, to Butler's irritation:

> If I had not known that you had written it I should not ever have suspected that the author was not orthodox, within the wide stated limits ... It will be a curious problem whether the orthodox will have so good a scent as to detect your heresy. ... What has struck me much in your book is your dramatic power – that is to [say] the way in which you earnestly and thoroughly assume the character and think the thoughts of the man you pretend to be. Hence I conclude that you could write a really good novel.

'Very nice and kind,' commented Butler in 1880. 'He told me he thought I should do well to turn my attention to novel-writing. All scientific people recommend me to do this.' (M1.186–7)

He received Darwin's letter at Mentone. His father and May had accompanied his mother there in an attempt to restore her health, and he finally joined them at the beginning of April, 1873. His emotions were highly charged. He had spent the last few months preparing *The Fair Haven* for publication, knowing full well the hurt and bitterness it would create within his family should they ever connect him with it: the reaction to *Erewhon* gave ample warning.

He had also spent several frustrating weeks cooped up in Clifford's Inn after falling down the stairs of a horse-drawn omnibus, the kind of self-inflicted injury that he found especially exasperating. Unable to paint, he made use of the enforced leisure by reading novels. On Miss Savage's recommendation he tackled *Middlemarch*, which he found a 'long-winded piece of studied brag' (S40), clever enough but singularly unattractive. Much more to his taste was *Ready-Money Mortiboy*, which he found 'very powerful and clever', he informed May, 'but I don't think you would much like it'.[2] Its hero was a ruthless and unrepentant prodigal son, which matched his mood. His father wrote to him on March 21st, 1873 in terms which could not fail to distress:

> You will I know be sorry to hear that I can give but a sad account of your mother. She has for some time suffered a great deal of pain and it is only kept under by Morphia . . .
>
> She consistently mentions you. If I say with anxiety and distress I must also say with the deepest affection and love. May is an unspeakable comfort to us . . .
>
> I think she would like you to know that she finds prayer an inexpressible comfort and that her faith is able to support her in the suffering which she endures. (FL128)

Although the letter held out a faint hope that it might prove possible to move her, Butler read the signs correctly.

'My mother is ill – very ill,' he wrote to Miss Savage. 'It is not likely that she will recover –
> 'I had rather
> 'It had been my father.'
I am pained about it – she is at Mentone, and though my father writes as if he had no hope, they clearly do not want me to come. . . .What pains me is that I cannot begin to regain the affection now which Alas! I have long since ceased to feel.' (S41–2)

Yet for all the strain he believed his presence would cause, he was acutely conscious that he ought to be, and wished to be, with his mother.

Butler was also in touch with May, and asked her to let him know the moment there seemed any immediate danger:

'I could not think of myself as going about my daily affairs and my mother lying perhaps at the point of death, without a sight of the one whom I am very sure that she loves not the least of her children. It would be intolerable to me to think of this, yet I know and deeply regret that my presence could not be without its embarrassments.'[2] Why, then, had he written *Erewhon*? 'The mistake was in not keeping it more quiet, and then in thinking that the very great success which the book has met with would make my father and mother proud of my having written it ... But had I known that my mother's health was failing at the time, I would have kept it back. Whatever else I do, I will do my utmost to do without it reaching the ears of those whom it will pain; but I cannot hold my tongue.'[3] *The Way of All Flesh* was already forming in his mind.

At the beginning of April the summons came, and he travelled out to Mentone. Fanny Butler died on April 9th, 1873, and was buried in the cemetery at Mentone the following afternoon. It was then that Canon Butler told his son that the shock of *Erewhon*'s publication, which had barred him from Langar, had been directly responsible for his mother's death. As Butler commented, the doctors gave the cause as cancer of the stomach. He left for London the next morning. In May his father forwarded to him a letter that he had found among Fanny Butler's papers, together with a seal in the form of an owl, and a locket. The letter had been written by Fanny to Sam and Tom when she was in poor health and low spirits before the birth of May, and had been gathering emotional force for over thirty years. Strangely released by his mother's death, and provoked by his father's accusation, he channelled his feelings into the novel that Miss Savage had been urging him to write.

Although in later life Butler regretted the anxieties which, he claimed, prevented him from working to his full capacity, the tension of these months seems to have roused his creativity. He continued to paint, and made an energetic start on *The Way of All Flesh*. He also acquired a new distraction: the investment of the capital that he had recently recalled from New Zealand. A financial crisis, never far away until his father's death, was imminent. There were two major factors: first, the drain on his resources caused by his £200 a year 'loan' to Pauli, a drain made more severe by his inability to earn anything substantial by writing or painting; second, his lightly-buried resentment about the handling of the Whitehall estate.

At this time Shrewsbury school was looking for a new location, and the land surrounding the Whitehall was one potential site. As Butler stood to inherit the estate, after his aunt's and his father's life interest, it was necessary to obtain his consent to any sale. He consulted a Shrewsbury solicitor, an old school friend, who told him that he had been poorly advised over the 1857 transaction, when the Whitehall house was bought by Thomas Lloyd, and might even be legally entitled to have it overturned. However, he decided to ask for the redress of what he saw as an injustice by insisting that the entail should be lifted as the price of his consent to any arrangement with the school. This would have given Butler an absolute interest in the estate, and allowed him to borrow money against its security.

He had written long and detailed letters to his father in January, 1873. Canon Butler replied, somewhat optimistically: 'I am much comforted by your letter. I now see your standpoint, though I don't think you quite see mine.' He continued, less happily: 'I can however only imagine one motive for your caring about the present power over it or the power of willing it otherwise than it would naturally fall and that is that you may be either married, which I do not think, or wishing to marry. If this is the case and you will deal openly with us, there is another method by which I could facilitate the making settlements if as I have no reason to suppose the lady is such as we can fairly approve.' (FL126)

Once again, Canon Butler's *rapprochement* had the reverse effect to the one he had intended. Butler suffered multiple irritations: he was not married; because of his commitment to Pauli, he could not afford to marry, had he wished to; he was disinclined to make an unequal marriage. This may be the reason he had kept away from Arona and the beautiful Isabella, feeling that any sexual relationship with her would have to lead to marriage. He was horrified by the predicaments of his cousin Reggie and his brother Tom, and he recalled the advice of an old sailor he had met on the train to Bangor, en route to stay with Tom and Etta and their four children: 'It's cheaper to buy the milk than to keep a cow.'

Butterfield, an elderly bachelor who lived in the rooms above Butler's in Clifford's Inn, received a weekly visit from a buxom woman known by the laundresses as 'Mr Butterfield's nurse'. Butler had made a regular arrangement with a dark, fine-looking young Frenchwoman, Lucie Dumas, whom he had come across near the Angel, Islington. She had had predecessors, according to Jones, but

no rivals during the next twenty years. It was fifteen years before
Butler revealed his name and address. They spoke in French, and
he visited her regularly, paying her a pound a week, including holidays: she called this her *douceur*. A strict Catholic, she kept the
church's fasts, imposing them on her cat Marquis, who had a hot
cross bun sopped in milk on Good Friday, and fish instead of meat.
'Oh, bother, Alfred,' he would say to his man-servant (in later years),
'it's Wednesday today, and I've got to go to Handel Street.' He
would leave at about two-thirty and be back by five, walking both
ways.[4]

The existence of this liaison, and the complexities surrounding
Pauli, fuelled Butler's indignation.

> I am neither married nor (most unfortunately) likely to be
> married at present. When I *am* you may be quite easy that the
> lady will be one whom you can approve. I have a *horror* of
> unequal marriages and mésalliances of all kinds.
>
> I do not understand your writing 'if this is the case *and you
> will deal openly by us*'. . . . If you imagine that I am in any money
> straights or jeopardy or anxiety of any sort whatever, you are
> simply disquieting yourselves in vain; all that I ever had I have
> now – and *very* securely placed. Still every additional power
> with regard to money is a valuable thing – and appears more
> so to me the older I grow. Of course I *might* use my power
> foolishly – play ducks and drakes with the money before inherit-
> ing and so Tom would take nothing. (FL126–8)

He shifted his demands to a request for £1000 in cash from the
Shrewsbury governing body as the price of his consent. However,
the plan was dropped, and the governors found another site.

The phrase about 'ducks and drakes' is ironic in view of what
Butler proceeded to do. His description of his money being 'very
securely placed' may have been strictly true when he wrote the letter,
but not for much longer. Since he needed capital, and was in any
event uneasy about some aspects of its handling in New Zealand –
the distance and delay were inconvenient – he decided to call his
money in. His friend Moorhouse was his mortgagee, and Butler later
suffered much remorse that he might have embarrassed someone
who had shown him 'infinite kindness' by giving him such short

notice. However, Moorhouse made no difficulty, and the £8000 was transferred to London.

Butler was now seeing a good deal of Henry Hoare, the banker, who had married the sister of another Cambridge friend, Paley. Butler felt under some obligation to Hoare, who had lent him money to publish *Erewhon* and was encouraging him to be more sociable. On Hoare's advice he began to invest his capital in a range of speculative business ventures to earn high rates of interest. Miss Savage enjoyed teasing him about his new occupation. He might be ruined, but experience could not be bought too dearly, and he might even be drawn to Christianity in the hour of his affliction. 'But then you may become rich, very rich, a millionaire, a great capitalist and be knighted for having made a gigantic fortune with your patent steam-engine. Well! I have no objection. I should like to know a Rich Man, but then while you are making yourself rich you will be doing nothing for me – I mean you will not be writing books that delight me more than anything else. So on the whole I think I had rather you were not rich . . . Goodbye, Dives, and good luck to your companies.' (S51–3)

Confident that he had found a solution to his financial anxieties, Butler took up his painting with renewed enthusiasm. He was working on an important picture: 'A man mending old Heatherley's skeleton and a child looking on – background, all the pots and pans and knick-knacks in the corner opposite the washing-stand, with the Discobolus and half the Ilyssus. I think it will come very well, but I am only just beginning it. Old Tom can't make it out.' (M1.201) The picture was at first to be called 'Tinkering a Skeleton'; the man, old Tom, was an assistant at the art school. Various anecdotes lie behind the subject matter: according to Festing Jones, 'The school skeleton was always getting knocked about, and no wonder; the students used to dress it up in the costumes and dance with it.' By the time the painting was finished and exhibited at the Royal Academy, old Tom had been replaced by the school Principal, and the title became 'Mr Heatherley's Holiday: an incident in studio life', the private joke being that Heatherley reputedly never went on holiday.

The central image of the painting, the skeleton, suggests Butler's preoccupation with his mother's death; and although the treatment leans towards the comic and grotesque, there is a hint, too, of the *danse macabre*. (The Discobolus, and the stuffed owl, would feature in Butler's poem on a Montreal lumber room, 'A Psalm of Montreal', in 1878.) The combination of statuary and the human figure, and the relationship between the two, is a subject that Butler returned to during his investigations at Varallo; and the composition has similarities with the interiors of several chapels on the Sacro Monte. As Elinor Shaffer comments, 'The classical and the popular-gothic are in dialogue in this painting.'[5]

But there was yet another sense in which 'Mr Heatherley's Holiday' proved 'important' to Butler: it did not sell, a fact that he listed as one of his reasons for abandoning painting to concentrate on writing. He was becoming increasingly involved in his novel, sending extracts to Miss Savage and revising them on her advice: 'I send you the first 15 pp of the novel and will send as many more in about a week,' he told her on 16 August in the same letter as he described his picture. He could not have found a more receptive reader. ' "Never have I been so calm, so soothed, so happy, so filled with a blessed Peace &c." as this morning when the first instalment of your novel came. I was delighted to have it, and still more delighted to read it, and I am delighted that you should have done it, and not anybody else. If it goes on as it begins it will be a perfect novel, or as nearly so as may be.' (S63–4) She pressed him for more: 'When am I to have more MS.? You said in about a week, and it is now a fortnight. I read what you sent me two more times – once to try to find fault and once for complete enjoyment.' (S65) She mixed criticism with praise, and offered detailed comments: 'You must *soigner* the composition a little more – near about the middle there is quite a constellation of sentences beginning 'but' and 'yet', which coming one after the other are not pretty . . .'

Miss Savage's technical criticism was penetrating, especially on the role of Butler's narrator, Overton. 'Is the narrator of the story to be an impartial historian or a special pleader? The inconvenience of special pleading in a story is that one's sympathies are apt to go over to the other side. One's sympathies do not go over to Pontifex as yet, but there might be danger further on.' (S66–8) Through the autumn her letters trace the gradual development of the story, including the difficult task, for her, of commenting on Alethea, for whom she herself was in part the model – 'I do not mind Alethea having blue eyes much, as she is not the heroine, but I like people with dark eyes best.' (S76–7) In November, after a long critique, she voiced a personal note of anxiety: 'Do you know I don't think the last time or two when I have seen you that you looked so happy as you used to be. I am afraid your relations with your family trouble you more than you choose to allow – or what is it?' Butler commented, 'No doubt by this time I was waking up to the fact that Hoare's companies which were to make our fortunes would be more likely to do what they did in fact do.' (S73–5) Finally, in March, 1874 the bubble burst.

'I have had a very great shock,' he confessed. Hoare had been speculating wildly, and had come to grief. Pauli and he ought to have realised, but they had such confidence that they suspected nothing, even when asked to take up shares on Hoare's behalf. 'Of course we ought to have asked him why he did not take up the shares himself – but there! And then our companies! I still believe and hope that the one of which I am a director will turn out right, and I see no flaw yet in the others, but the source from which they have come is tainted, and both Pauli and I are very anxious.' The bank reassured them about their liabilities, and turned Hoare out: 'He thought he could treble his income; fancy wanting to treble £40,000 a year! Don't show this letter to anyone.' (S85–6),

Miss Savage wrote to say how sorry she was. 'I am afraid the worry and overwork will do you harm,' she added, 'but you will let Mr Pauli do the hardest of the work. He is stronger than you are.' (S86–7) Her warning was not heeded. Butler, as she feared, was quite unable to go on with his novel. No more sections passed between them. She tried not to complain: '*I* am very good too. I have never once thought of the Pontifexes till this minute. I am the most unselfish woman in the world.' (S87–8) But she could not help letting Butler know how much she missed the frequent contacts and their literary relationship:

I have been very unhappy lately. I have not slept for two nights, and Thursday and to-day I have had no appetite, and you know how *gourmande* I am. Yesterday I saw you at your window and felt dreadfully inclined to rush in and ask your advice, but common sense prevailed and I went on my way. I wish I had not common sense, for then I should have told you all about the matter, and that would have relieved me very much . . .

This is a weary world, I think I shall go into a convent – that is the only place for such bunglers as I. At all events the mischief one does is kept within four walls. Goodbye, and don't forget that I want to know how you are. (S88–9)

Butler was impervious to such appeals. Not only Pauli, but other friends – such as Heatherley, and Jason Smith – had invested in the companies on his recommendation. His highly developed sense of responsibility became something close to paranoia where money was concerned. He was also furious with himself for having been so gullible; as early as August, 1873 he had enquired about using his father's brokers, rather than Hoare's, but foolishly had not wished to offend his old friend. Now he became over-confident in his grasp of business – after all, he had made a success of sheep farming and his New Zealand land deals – and accepted a proposal from the other directors that he should go out to Canada and investigate the affairs of the Canada Tanning Extract Company, the one business out of all his investments that looked salvable. Before he left he had the pleasure of seeing 'Mr Heatherley's Holiday' hung in the Academy. On June 10th, 1874 he sailed for Montreal.

CHAPTER 12

O God! O Montreal!

Butler sailed to Canada to try to salvage his New Zealand fortune. The fact that Pauli was also involved increased the pressure. So confident had he been about Hoare's financial skill that he encouraged Pauli to borrow against the reversion due to him on his parents' death: ostensibly, this was already pledged to him as security for the quarterly 'loans', and he released Pauli from this obligation. As he noted years later, 'We did not know that Hoare had been plunging for some time, and we did not know that old family bankers ought to be and generally are the very last people in the world who should be able to advise on commercial undertakings. They and we were all fools together . . .' On Hoare's advice, Butler had invested in the Grand Trunk and Erie Railways; the Foreign Patent Steam Engine company; a patent gas meter company; and (this time on Jason Smith's advice) a company for pressing jute in India. He lost money on all these ventures. But his largest investment was in the Canada Tanning Extract Company; he later calculated his loss at £3600.

He left England strained and unwell. But, as so often, a sea voyage and change of scenery helped to invigorate him. A passenger recalled Butler gazing over the Atlantic on a lovely moonlit evening, then turning to his neighbour after a long silence and saying: 'Yes, Beale – yes, an honest God's the noblest work of man.' (M1.212) This was more in his old vein. 'We have had a delightful passage,' he wrote to May, 'no rough weather, no fog, pleasant fellow passengers and no misadventures of any kind. I was not sea sick for a moment, and in fact have enjoyed the voyage extremely. It has already done me infinite good, far more than a trip to Switzerland or Italy would have done in the same time . . .'[1]

He was surprised to find himself in a French, rather than English, country. He soon travelled out of Montreal to inspect the company's headquarters. 'I am to stay with a "habitant" to-morrow,' he informed

Miss Savage, 'in order that I may go to mass on Sunday and inspire the village with confidence in the company. Madame Vigneau has had so many lodgers since we started, that she has become quite rich, and out of gratitude has had a four-dollar mass said for the company. This is the best mass that money can buy in these parts; the cheapest is 25 cents or one shilling; the average is about half a dollar. I have instructed our agent to have an occasional mass said on our account, about 6 two-dollar masses a year for each set of weeks. This I am told will be about the right thing. There are bears and wolves and great cariboo deer in our woods – as big as oxen but I have not seen any.' (S92)

After inspecting the company's plant and processing, and scrutinising the books in the Montreal office, Butler returned to London to report to the board of directors.[2] He was then given wider powers – 'I am to take complete control over the whole thing' – and by the end of August he was back in Montreal, with a salaried position, and a firm resolve to save the company and his investment.

He stayed in Montreal until the end of 1875, with one more intervening visit to England in midsummer, and worked long and vigorously in an attempt to turn the company round. Probably it was a hopeless task, since the product had a basic flaw that made it hard to sell. The company had been set up to manufacture a tanning extract from bark; the extract was cheap and effective, but turned leather an unpleasant colour. Butler did not at first concern himself with selling the end-product, but with the day-to-day manufacturing. He dismissed the manager, Foley, who had patented the process, and found himself locked into a complex series of law suits.

This had one interesting side effect: Butler had to give evidence about his concept of God in the Canadian courts. Foley's counsel sought to have Butler's evidence set aside on the grounds that he did not believe in God, and so was an unreliable witness. In answer to the question 'Do you believe in the existence of God?' Butler stated in a deposition that was read out in court: 'In a way, certainly, and in a way certainly not. I believe in a great first cause from which springs the Universe, and "God" is my expression for that omnipotent cause, but the subject is so enormous that I cannot answer it in three lines. When I say I do not believe, I mean I do not believe in the Deity with a turban and a flowing beard, and great drapery, as represented in picture books.' Butler interrupted the reading at this point to say, 'It should be flowing drapery.' 'Do you believe in the existence of God, as revealed in the scriptures?' 'As revealed in some parts of them, certainly.' 'Will you state what parts of Scripture you do not accept as revealing the existence of a God?' 'I reject the part in which we are told that God put his hand over Moses's face, and showed him His back; I accept the part in which it is said God is a Spirit, and they that worship Him must worship Him in spirit and in truth.'[3] Butler's credibility as a witness was confirmed, the courts eventually found in his favour in every case, and awarded him judgment with costs against Foley.

One unexpected result of the Canada venture was a reconciliation between Butler and his father. The fact that, for the first time in his life, he was earning a salary helped; each director was entitled to a hundred guineas a year, as well as expenses incurred on company business abroad. He may, too, have made a conscious effort to improve relations, suspecting that he might need his father's help in the near future. The wounds of *Erewhon* had healed sufficiently for him to visit Langar during the summer of 1875.

Apart from his father and May and Miss Savage, there were few people he could write to frankly; other friends were involved, and much of the information was confidential. Pauli was little help. 'It was at this time,' Butler wrote later, 'that I first learned that Pauli had no backbone.'[4] His own efforts brought minimal results. 'If my advice had been taken we should have saved a brand or two from the burning, but as it was, do what I might, I could not persuade the London board. In the autumn of 1875 they again issued contracts for some £30,000 of bark, and that was the *coup de grâce*.'[5] Back in London in December, 1875, as he found that the Board continued to ignore his advice, he resigned; the company folded shortly after. Even the debenture-holders lost their investment.

Butler had not really enjoyed Canada: Montreal itself was agreeable enough, but he found the food, and the culture, insipid. Poking around one day in the Museum of Natural History, Butler found a plaster cast of the Discobolus, banished to a back room among a collection of skins, plants, snakes and insects, where an old man was stuffing an owl. He might have imagined himself momentarily back at Heatherley's.

'Ah,' said I, 'so you have some antiques here; why don't you put them where people can see them?'

'Well, sir,' answered the custodian, 'you see they are rather vulgar.'

He then talked a great deal, and said his brother did all Mr Spurgeon's printing.[6]

Out of this incident came his response to Canada, 'A Psalm of Montreal':

Stowed away in a Montreal lumber room
The Discobolus standeth and turneth his face to the wall;
Dusty, cobweb-covered, maimed and set at naught,
Beauty crieth in an attic and no man regardeth:
                              O God! O Montreal!

.   .   .   .

And I turned to the man of skins and said unto him, 'O thou man of skins,
Wherefore hast thou done thus to shame the beauty of the Discobolus?'
But the Lord had hardened the heart of the man of skins,
And he answered, 'My brother-in-law is haberdasher to Mr Spurgeon.'
                              O God! O Montreal!

.   .   .   .

'The Discobolus is put here because he is vulgar,
He has neither vest nor pants with which to cover his limbs;
I, Sir, am a person of most respectable connections –
My brother-in-law is haberdasher to Mr Spurgeon.'
                              O God! O Montreal!

.   .   .   .

Then I said, 'O brother-in-law to Mr Spurgeon's haberdasher,
Who seasonest also the skins of Canadian owls,
Thou callest trousers "pants", whereas I call them "trousers",
Therefore, thou art in hell-fire and may the Lord pity thee!'
                              O God! O Montreal!

.   .   .   .

Although Butler's business preoccupations left him little time to write, he was thinking continually of the ideas that inform his next

book, *Life and Habit*. He escaped from the city whenever he could:
'There is a good high hill behind the town, some 700 or 800 feet
high with rocky ground and native forest. I never saw so good a
natural pleasure ground to any city – and the views over the St
Lawrence and far away to the Adirondack mountains are delightful.
And the colour is splendid. I can get to the best parts in an easy
hour's walk, and go to them almost every day as soon as the office
is closed.' (S95) This was in September, 1874. Butler always carried
a small notebook with him, and would jot down his ideas and
impressions. The very first time he was on Montreal Mountain, one
magnificent summer's evening, he began making notes for his book.
He had written the first few lines of a passage 'when the bells of
Notre Dame in Montreal began to ring, and their sound was carried
to and fro in a remarkably beautiful manner'. He immediately
inserted the incident into his train of thought:

It is one against legion when a creature tries to differ from his
own past selves ... His past selves are living in him at this
moment with the accumulated life of centuries. 'Do this, this,
this, which we too have done, and found our profit in it,' cry
the souls of his forefathers within him. Faint are the far ones,
coming and going as the sound of bells wafted on to a high
mountain; loud and clear are the near ones, urgent as an alarm
of fire. 'Withhold,' cry some. 'Go on boldly,' cry others. 'Me,
me, me, revert hitherward, my descendant,' shouts one as it
were from some high vantage-ground over the heads of the
clamorous multitude. 'Nay, but me, me, me,' echoes another;
and our former selves fight within us and wrangle for our
possession.[7]

The vision encapsulates Butler's notion about the role of memory in
evolution. *Life and Habit* marks a substantial shift in Butler's thought.
Its long gestation period heralded a fresh subject that was to absorb
him for more than a decade; and while he strove to clarify his own
theory of evolution, he was made acutely aware of his personal destiny
and the forces wrangling within him for possession. The first casualty
was his relationship with Miss Savage. She had grown used to a
pattern of frequent exchanges, with new pages of *The Way of All
Flesh* as the *raison d'être*, but even before his second trip to Canada

he had sounded a warning: 'I shall write in America, if I find I have any spare time, and prepare for a rainy day. Yes my novel will at last go ahead; but it must be quite innocent, for I am now reconciled to my father, and must be careful not to go beyond scepticism of the mildest kind.' (S92–3) That letter signalled a gentle disengagement from the previous intimacy. Butler did send her notes on his reading – *Wilhelm Meister* was the very worst book he had ever read – and at first kept her up to date with the financial saga. But his letters became intermittent, and instead of a spontaneous sharing of thoughts, they read like dutiful responses to hers – at least that is how she interpreted them. Butler heard nothing from her between August and December, 1875. 'Knowing how much she had been piqued and pained by my silence in the spring I wrote three times in the autumn without eliciting an answer. Then I was forgiven. I never was placed in a much more difficult position. To write was to encourage false hopes – not to write was to be grossly unkind – so I wrote, and I suppose this was right.' (S102)

When Butler was finally reinstalled in Clifford's Inn in December, 1875, he wrote at once to Miss Savage: 'I came back last night – very well but exceedingly anxious about the Company . . . How is it that I have never heard from you? Pray let me do so at once.' (S110) A meeting was arranged, but when Butler called Miss Savage was out:

Did I tell you Wednesday? How stupid of me. I have so many things on my mind just now that I forget those which are the most important. My wits are beautiful to look at, but not much good for use. I send you a ticket and a programme. My dear little Gabrielle Vaillant (!S.B.) plays exquisitely – some night you must come and hear her. She shall play Beethoven's romance in F for you (!!S.B.). Is there anything else you would like?

I have got such a delicious cake, it was only given me half an hour ago. I wish you could have had some of it. How stupid of me to go out. The fact is Wednesday is a day of reception here [at *The Woman's Gazette*] and by a very curious coincidence, I generally have an important engagement on that day. The older I grow the less I care for company, unless it is exactly the company I like. I don't care about the company being good, but I like it to my taste. Alas! I remember the time when if two or three (no matter who) were gathered together I liked to be there in the midst of them. (S110–11)

Most of Miss Savage's letters are witty, controlled, astringent; this one, and several others from the first months of Butler's return, strike one as waspish and coy by turns, as though she intended either to punish Butler in some way, or to shift the grounds of the relationship. The sentence 'I don't care about the company being good, but I like it to my taste' was the sort of thing to set alarm bells ringing in his mind. She bombarded him with suggestions – he could write for Mr Voysey's new magazine; her friend Mr Lewis had opened a gallery in Pall Mall, and might sell some pictures for him; was he going to paint some decorative panels for Gillow's? Here was the address in Dulwich of an admirer, Miss Wilson, and an invitation to visit her on Sunday. She wrote again the following day:

I have had another letter from the lady who admires you. She wants you and me to go on Monday to meet Mr Voysey, who it seems is also an admirer of yours . . . *There is one thing*, though, that I must tell you – and that is that if you become surrounded by a circle of adoring spinsters (of which I see symptoms) I shall drop your acquaintance. Have you not taught me that there is nothing so contemptible as a boree? And a boree I shall be when you are worshipped by your spins. (S113–14)

The adoring spinsters were her own acquaintances. She may have been executing an elaborate tease, but the small shreds of evidence accumulated and alarmed Butler. 'Mind you let me know as soon as it is quite dead,' she wrote in April 1876 about the Tanning Company, then *in extremis*, ' . . . I wish you did not know right from wrong.' (S122) Butler chose to interpret this last phrase as one more allusion to suppressed love, and sexual passion, on his part. Of the earlier letter he commented:

' . . . I have no recollection either of Miss Wilson, or of going to see Miss Wilson. Still I may have gone. As for my being surrounded with a circle of adoring spinsters – who, I wonder, was it that was doing her utmost to surround me, and boring me almost beyond endurance in spite of all my admiration, respect, gratitude, and compunction at my own utter inability to requite her affection for me in the only way that would have satisfied her? If ever man gave woman her answer unequivocally and at the beginning, I gave mine to Miss Savage – but it was no use. She would not be checked and I had not either the heart to check her – or – well, never mind. I would if I could, but I could not, and to this day she daily haunts me in that I could not.' (S112)

Undoubtedly, Butler's return to London initiated some kind of crisis between two fiercely independent and unusual personalities. It may be that Miss Savage held out hopes that, once the business venture was over, their relationship might go on as it was before, and even develop; but there is little more evidence than the kind of ambiguity quoted above to suggest she really expected a proposal: she seems too clear-sighted for that. Butler, on the other hand, his antennae over-tuned, felt that she was edging him towards a marriage of more than true minds. Towards the end of his life and long after her death, while editing their correspondence, he reproached himself for his treatment of her, and wrote three sonnets whose cruelty points to his own vulnerability:

> She was too kind, wooed too persistently,
> Wrote moving letters to me day by day;
> The more she wrote, the more unmoved was I,
> The more she gave, the less could I repay.
> Therefore I grieve, not that I was not loved,
> But that, being loved, I could not love again.
> I liked, but like and love are far removed;
> Hard though I tried to love I tried in vain.
> For she was plain and lame and fat and short,
> Forty and over-kind. Hence it befell
> That though I loved her in a certain sort,
> Yet did I love too wisely but not well.
> > Ah! had she been more beauteous or less kind
> > She might have found me of another mind.

The second sonnet picks up that possibly innocent phrase about not knowing right from wrong:

And now, though twenty years are come and gone,
That little lame lady's face is with me still;
Never a day but what, on every one,
She dwells with me, as dwell she ever will.
She said she wished I knew not wrong from right;
It was not that; I knew, and would have chosen
Wrong if I could, but, in my own despite,
Power to choose wrong in my chilled veins was frozen.
'Tis said that if a woman woo, no man
Should leave her till she have prevailed; and, true,
A man will yield for pity, if he can,
But if the flesh rebels what can he do?
    I could not. Hence I grieve my whole life long
    The wrong I did, in that I did no wrong.

In 1901, when he wrote these sonnets, his state of mind was very different. But even in 1876 guilt was already troubling him; he actually proposed that they should write a book together, an offer that was tactfully declined. Butler's recoil from marriage, or any long-term intimate relationship with a woman, was probably a lucky instinct, both for his own sake and for any partner's. In his third, and most vicious, sonnet –

Had I been some young sailor, continent
Perforce three weeks, and then well plied with wine . . .

he concluded:

And here, alas! at any rate to me
She was an all too, too impossible she. (S372–4)

By some Butlerian process of selection, the women he encountered were all, one way or another, impossible: the too beautiful Italian Isabella of Arona, with whom he could not trust himself; the little lame Eliza Savage, who understood him only too well, and whose intimacy he restricted to the intellectual. Just as he admired good-looking men, so he insisted on beauty in his ideal woman; and marriage, for all but the fortunate few driven by irresistible forces, was something to avoid and mock. Reporting acidly on some Panto-

155

mime of Conjugal Felicity – 'He takes her hand affectionately, and placing it on his knee he strokes it caressingly from the wrist towards the tip' – was one of Miss Savage's staples. Partners in irony, and equally jealous of their independence, they could not draw closer without sacrificing too many principles. Instead he made his regular visits to Madame. Desmond MacCarthy, who first met Butler when a boy on holiday in Switzerland, commented in a memoir on Butler's sexuality:

> Butler was a man to whom continence was impossible. But he never fell in love with a woman; women represented a necessity for which he paid. This must be known if he is to be understood; and happily nowadays such things may be mentioned. The sex impulse was unusually strong in him from boyhood to old age, and he canalized it in that prosaic way which some men adopt who dread emotional disturbance in their lives. To the woman, who figures as 'Madam' [sic] in his biography, whom he used to visit twice a week, he did not even tell his name until he had known her for more than ten years; so great was his caution, so entirely had he disassociated intimacy from such relationships. When he was an old man he told me that now they had become impossible, unless he had 'a kindly feeling for the woman', but that it had not been so when he was younger.[8]

One example of Butler's sexual appetite comes in an incident he recorded of an early visit to Varallo. There was no bawdy house; everyone complained, the ostler at the Hotel d'Italia informed Butler, but the municipality had refused his offer to set one up. 'I had the greatest difficulty in getting a woman,' complained Butler, 'but at last was taken to the house of an old lady who kept a half idiot loathsome creature whom I had to put up with as the only thing that was to be got.' The next day, he was surprised to spot both women in a procession in the church at the Sanctuary on the Sacro Monte.[9] It may have been Butler's frankness and coarseness about his sexual behaviour that offended the young Robert Bridges; Butler, he told his sister Carrie, one day 'revealed to me a side of his nature with which I had no sympathy, but rather a strong disgust for it, and from that day I avoided him'.[10]

As far as marriage was concerned, Butler shunned any relationship undertaken out of duty or convention, for that broke his first law that a man's first duty was to himself: if he failed in that, he would fail in duty towards the very people he was trying to serve. Some years later, believing that Henry Scott Tuke was being forced into an engagement, he offered this advice: 'Don't marry any woman without being so much in love with her that you feel you would rather be made into mincemeat than not marry her. Even though you may have proposed, break the match off (it is the kindest thing to do, in the long run) rather than this . . .'[11] Butler was well aware that he risked offence by writing so bluntly – he did not know Tuke particularly well – but he was wholly sincere in his belief that a loveless marriage was a crime, one of the gravest of which a man could be guilty.

Butler reserved emotion, for the most part, for his relationships with men. When he returned from Montreal in 1875 he decided to speak to Pauli 'with the utmost affection', and told him he ought to let him know more fully how he was doing at the Bar, and what chance there was of his releasing Butler from his obligations:

> I said: 'You ought to tell me, good or bad, that I may know better how I stand; I have kept nothing from you; I am sharing everything with you, and you ought to use like frankness with myself, whereas, in point of fact, I do not even certainly know whether you make enough to pay the expenses of your clerk and chambers.' I told him that he was estranging me and implored him not to do so.
>
> Again he burst into a passionate flood of tears, but do what I might I could get nothing out of him, except a general impression that he was just covering his expenses, and a promise that in the course of the ensuing year he would be more explicit. I believed his distress to be due to his conviction of the gravity of our difficulties and of his utter inability to do anything towards lightening them.[12]

(Pauli, the polished man of the world, had previously burst into tears when Fitzgerald had urged him to return to New Zealand, and Butler had advised him to go.)

At Christmas, 1876, with Butler even more straitened, he put the question again, to be answered with more tears and a promise of greater openness, and at Christmas, 1877, the same question, the same passionate flood of tears. On one of these emotional end-of-year accountings Pauli confessed 'he knew he ought to have said more by way of thanks than he ever had said, but that his pride forbade him to do so. On this I said the only bitter thing that I believe I ever said to him. I said: "Pauli, that is not well said. Your pride never hinders you from receiving an obligation and if it were of the right sort it would not hinder you from acknowledging it." He said nothing, but presently he said: "I know I shall die without ever having said what I ought to have said, and if I do I shall suffer the agonies of the damned." '

Butler, reserved and shy, was far from being a recluse. He shrank from formal entertainment, did not like being lionised, and shunned the company of writers or artists who were part of the Establishment. But he was a member for some years of the Century Club, along with Walter Bagehot, Leslie Stephen, John Tyndall and Edward Tylor; and he had a wide acquaintance with people who shared his interest in art and music. He would play the piano on request, mostly Handel, but once forgot his guests and improvised for hours. Nobody wished to interrupt, so they slipped out one by one, while Butler, transported, did not notice he was alone till the clock struck four in the morning.[13]

He went regularly to the theatre, but avoided serious pieces: melo-drama, burlesque, farce, pantomime and music hall delighted him. In *Champagne, A Question of Phiz*, William Penley came on as a lugubrious knight in armour with a great coat and umbrella, and Butler turned instinctively to Reginald Worsley to say, 'What muck *Hamlet* is after this.' (N221) (He noted that you could buy a sugar figure of Hamlet for twopence in Exmouth Street, complete with skull.) In the same piece, Claude Marius sang:

> Some girls do and some girls don't,
> Some girls will, but this girl won't,
> I tried very often to see if she would,
> But she said she really couldn't, and I don't think she
> could.

Butler introduced this into *Life and Habit* as 'Some breeds do, and some breeds don't'. In *The Way of All Flesh* Overton, who makes a living writing for the theatre, takes Ernest to a burlesque of *Macbeth* to celebrate his release from prison: 'Macbeth had said he could not kill Duncan when he saw his boots upon the landing. Lady Macbeth put a stop to her husband's hesitation by whipping him up under her arm, and carrying him off the stage, kicking and screaming.' (WF331) Butler thought little of Henry Irving, and much preferred Sophy Larkin as Lucretia Tickleby, or the annual pleasures of the pantomime playbill, where Queen Elizabeth's reign was summed up as: Mary Queen of Scots, Sir Walter Raleigh, potatoes, tobacco, Shakespeare. (N220)

Desmond MacCarthy described him as 'the one man among Victorian men of letters who chose his friends most regardlessly of class',[14] and, one might add, of age. He had already met the young man who would take Pauli's place in his affections. This was Henry Festing Jones, a solicitor. Jones had been at Trinity Hall, Cambridge, with Edward Hall, whose family lived near Langar. Jones remembered seeing page-proofs of *Erewhon* in Hall's rooms at Cambridge, but they first met in Hall's lodgings in London, after one of the Monday Popular Concerts at St James's Hall, when Butler had not entirely abandoned modern music for Handel. Butler 'would sit on the sofa in Hall's rooms with a piece of newspaper spread on his knees, eating his supper of bacon and bread, which had been in his pocket all through the concert, and talking about painting, as became an artist; but his mind was full of his writing'. (M1.232)

Jones called on him at Clifford's Inn, at first with another friend, John Elder, and then one evening towards the end of March, 1876 he dropped in alone on his way back from the city. Butler took him into the painting-room, which looked out on Fetter Lane, to show him the pictures he was working on for the Academy. 'The more important one was in oils; he called it "Don Quixote", but admitted that it was only a study from a costume model at Heatherley's, and no more like one's notion of Don Quixote than it was like any other man in armour; but he was obliged to give it a title, otherwise, he said, the Academy would not look at it.' (M1.235)

That year Butler had two 'things (I cannot call them pictures)' in the Academy, he told Miss Savage, 'Don Quixote' and a water-colour of a girl. He took comfort that this triumph would at least annoy his 'country friends' at Langar. (S124) The 'Don Quixote' was bought for fifteen guineas: 'I never liked the picture till now, but now I like it very much.' (S129) Miss Savage advised him that if the picture of the girl did not sell, he should call it 'Mignon' and send her to a provincial exhibition.

Butler had reached an important turning point in his life. Although he did not yet know it, Jones would soon become the close friend he so badly needed, with less scope for the kind of misunderstandings he dreaded. In August he went to stay at Langar for the last time. His father was retiring, and moved that autumn to Shrewsbury, to a house with the mocking name of Wilderhope. The Canadian diversion was over; his personal losses were £3560. Most importantly, his writing found a new impetus and direction. He had begun to record his observations in a series of notebooks, which he would edit and revise over the years to come. In spite of the double success at the Royal Academy, painting was beginning to slip in his order of priorities. Released by Miss Savage from the joint writing project, he took up his notes on *Life and Habit*, and completed the first two chapters.

CHAPTER 13

Butler vs Darwin

Life and Habit was the first of Butler's books on evolution.[1] His argument with Darwin's theory, and his growing quarrel with the man himself, preoccupied him for the next decade, and most intensely between 1877 and 1880. He began from a position of gratitude and even awe. Reading *The Origin of Species* in the physical and intellectual isolation of New Zealand had provided him with a philosophical framework at a time of desperate insecurity, while speculation about the notion of machines provided the germ of *Erewhon*. From Darwin himself Butler received praise, kindly interest, encouragement and hospitality; and Darwin's son Francis became a friend.

Unfortunately, Butler positively enjoyed being crossed, especially by someone of his father's generation and authority. He slid imperceptibly into challenging Darwin; once there, he relished the exposure and the conflict. *The Origin of Species* was the Victorian's scientific bible; Butler used to refer to it as The Book and in his eyes it was just as fallible. As with every problem he tackled, Butler assumed that if he thought long and hard enough, the solution would be revealed almost as a matter of course.

While Darwin was the supreme example of a methodical scientist, Butler operated quite differently as a speculative philosopher or theologian. Darwin deliberately did not pursue the implications of his theory, beyond the laconic 'Much light will be thrown on the origin of man and his history.' Butler, on the other hand, having disposed of the miracle of the Resurrection and hence the rest of orthodox Christian doctrine, now needed to satisfy himself about the fundamental principles of life. He came to see that Darwin's theory raised almost as many questions as it answered, and with courage and obstinacy he set himself to solve them.

He invested a great deal of emotional and intellectual energy in

Life and Habit. He described it to Miss Savage as 'a very dry, but exceedingly (to me) interesting subject . . . At any rate it has the merit of not being aimed directly or indirectly at Christianity, and not being satirical save incidentally. It is on the force of habit.' (S115) All through 1876 and 1877, it occupied his mind: 'The theory frightens me – it is so far reaching and subversive – it oppresses me, and I take panic that there cannot really be any solid truth in it; but I have been putting down everything that it seems to me can be urged against it, with as much force as if I were a hostile reviewer, and I really cannot see that I have a leg to stand upon when I pose as an objector. Still, do what I can, I am oppressed and frightened.' (S136) The effort of writing prevented him from painting: he blamed his absorption with the book for the failure of his last serious picture, 'The last days of Carey Street', which was rejected by the Academy in 1877. He discovered the pleasures of the British Museum Reading Room. To start with, he went there on Mondays, Wednesdays and Fridays from ten till one, sitting at letter B whenever possible. By September, he was going there every day, instead of spending the mornings in his painting-room or at Heatherley's; he never returned to Heatherley's on a regular basis, but his mornings in the Museum became part of his routine.

Butler left a detailed account of the development of *Life and Habit* in Chapter 2 of his third evolution book, *Unconscious Memory*. After cataloguing its genesis, with supporting evidence about dates of various sections and drafts, he comments: 'At this time I had not been able to find that anything like what I was advancing had been said already. I asked many friends, but not one of them knew anything more than I did . . .' This is revealing both about the intermittent, hit-or-miss nature of Butler's researches, and about the restricted knowledge of his closed circle of friends. However, other acquaintances began to provide more relevant criticisms. Francis Darwin informed him that Professor Lankester had written in *Nature* about a lecture by Hering, referring all life to memory. Butler's attitude to this pre-publication of 'his' idea was extremely defensive: (1) he was on holiday in Italy when the letter was published; (2) he never saw *Nature* at that time; (3) it was too late to alter his text; (4) if he read the letter, he might wish to rewrite his book, and he did not feel equal to making any radical alterations, etc., etc. (Oddly, he wrote later to Francis Darwin for details of the particular issue of *Nature*, but never found it, and the matter rested.)

Worse was to follow. Another friend had recommended Butler to read Mivart's *Genesis of Species*, as offering an alternative view on 'natural selection'. This sent Butler back to the latest edition of *The Origin of Species*: 'I had lost my original copy . . . and had not read the book for some years.' When he read it he was horrified to read this categoric statement: 'It can be clearly shown that the most wonderful instinct with which we are acquainted, namely, those of the hive-bee and of many ants, could not possibly have been acquired by habit.' The chapter's concluding words were 'positively awful': 'I am surprised that no one has hitherto advanced this demonstrative case of neuter insects against the well-known doctrine of inherited habit as advanced by Lamarck.' 'This,' commented Butler, 'was the first I had heard of any doctrine of inherited habit as having been propounded by Lamarck.'

There were two possibilities. Either Butler had been hopelessly deluded, busying himself with the 'stale theory' of a 'long-since exploded charlatan', or Darwin's theory was seriously flawed. A more sceptical re-reading of *The Origin of Species* convinced Butler that the latter was the correct interpretation. Instead of providing a philosophical adjunct to Darwinism, Butler saw himself as offering radical opposition. He went through the earlier part of his text, removing any expressions that were inconsistent with a teleological view. There was no reluctance now to reshape and extend. He wrote the last five chapters, about a third of the book, during October and November, 1877, rapidly, combatively, and, since *Life and Habit* was with the binder on December 4th, with no opportunity for reflection and reconsideration.

There is little reason to doubt Butler's version of the evolution of *Life and Habit*; he was scrupulous to the point of pedantry about such things. A less honest, or more politic, man would have suppressed at least part of the account, since it makes him appear more misinformed, unmethodical and amateur than he was. As a description of the way ideas germinate and grow, it is entirely convincing. It explains both the book's strange mixture of laborious speculation and aggressive polemic, and why, when it was finally published, it was so easily dismissed or ignored.

By the end of November, 1877 Butler was able to tell Francis

Darwin that he had arranged for two copies to be sent to him, 'one of which, if you think fit after reading it, you will perhaps be kind enough to give to your father'. Butler explained his misgivings: 'it has resolved itself into a downright attack upon your father's view of evolution, and a defence of what I conceive to be Lamarck's. I neither intended nor wished this, but I was simply driven into it.' There follows a lengthy account of the way in which Butler's ideas had developed, at a late stage in the book's formation, leading him to look on natural selection as a 'rope of sand'. 'Nothing would surprise me less than to see something sprung upon me in reviews and answers which cuts the ground completely from under me; and, of course, I neither expect nor give quarter in a philosophical argument. We want to get on to the right side; and neither your father, I take it, nor I care two straws *how we get on to the right side* so long as we get there . . . we want to come to an understanding as to what is true and what false as soon as possible . . .'

Finally, Butler launched into an apology of Byzantine tortuousness:

> Please excuse this erasure. Its purport was to say how sorry I was that your father should have been at school under my grandfather, inasmuch as I myself should dislike an attack from a son or grandson of Kennedy's, when I should not care twopence about it from any one else. (M1.257–60)

In dragging in the family, and two other generations, Butler was already beginning to exhibit symptoms of the paranoia that would infect all his dealings with Darwin and the scientists. As to not caring twopence about attacks and criticism, nothing could be further from the truth. Francis Darwin sent a tactful and restrained response:

> Many thanks for your interesting letter; I am very glad to hear a history of the evolution of your book, and I shall be very eager to see it. It will, at least, differ from Mivart, and, I imagine, from Lamarck, in having some fun in it!
>
> I confess to feeling lost in astonishment at your saying that you have cut out all support to natural selection, and also that you consider it a rope of sand. I suppose from this that you deny any effect to natural selection? If so, you must find it rather a hard position to hold, I should guess. Because, of

course, you have to deny that such a thing as variations occur . . .
Anyhow, I am sure I shall enjoy your book very much; even
if you are severe it will be sure to be a pleasant severity.
(M1.261–2)

Life and Habit is a stimulating, uneven, idiosyncratic, mischievous
and irritating book. At last, Butler was confident enough to publish
under his own name and to avoid the distancing framework he had
constructed for *Erewhon* and *The Fair Haven*, but he remained as
sensitive as ever about its reception. 'Friends have complained to me
that they can never tell whether I am in jest or earnest . . . I am not
aware of a single argument put forward which is not a *bonâ fide*
argument, although, perhaps, sometimes admitting of a humorous
side . . . I have, therefore, endeavoured, for a third time, to furnish
the public with a book whose fault should lie rather in the direction
of seeming less serious than it is, than of being less so than it seems.'
(LH305–6)

Clearly, *Life and Habit* was in earnest. But its readers had a
problem deciding how to respond. Was it scientific, philosophical or
imaginative? Was it original or derivative? Here Butler made a tactical
error, by adopting the pose of an average, intelligent, feet-on-the-
ground enquirer: 'I would wish most distinctly to disclaim for these
pages the smallest pretension to scientific value, originality, or even
the accuracy of more than a very rough and ready kind . . . I have
no wish to instruct, and not much to be instructed; my aim is simply
to entertain and interest the numerous class of people who, like
myself, know nothing of science, but who enjoy speculating and
reflecting (not too deeply) upon the phenomena around them . . . It
is plain therefore that my book cannot be intended for the perusal
of scientific people.' (LH1–2A) Perhaps he wrote this opening before
the great leap forward of the closing chapters, and was not able to
revise them; but they were not calculated to reassure either scientist
or philosopher. This mask of the common-sense speculator was one
of Butler's more confusing poses: he believed it, and yet he was
constantly dismayed when anyone – especially reviewers, or the educated, or prominent contemporaries – accepted it at face value.

The early chapters of *Life and Habit* do, in fact, emphasise this
stance, as Butler builds up his analogies, like some popularising
journalist, from everyday acts like piano playing, writing and reading.

By the conclusion, Butler is quoting wholesale, both from *The Origin of Species by means of Natural Selection* and *Variations of Animals and Plants under Domestication* (referring to them, incidentally, by inaccurate titles), and criticising Darwin over detail: 'I do not, however, think that Mr Darwin is clear about his own meaning.' Inexorably, he arrives at a position that endorses evolution, and congratulates Darwin *en passant* for having made evolution generally acceptable, but he then advances a radically opposed theory of the mechanism that, he believes, generates the process, again bolstering his theory with an appeal to the 'fairly intelligent and observant' man. He rejects the idea that life-forms have developed through the 'accumulation of small, divergent, indefinite, and perfectly unintelligent variations' in favour of the sense of need aided by memory:

> Our own progress – or variation – is due not to small, fortuitous inventions or modifications which have enabled their fortunate possessors to survive in times of difficulty, not, in fact, to strokes of luck (though these, of course, have had some effect – but not more, probably, than strokes of ill luck have counteracted) but to strokes of cunning – to a sense of need, and to study of the past and present which have given shrewd people a key with which to unlock the chambers of the future. (LH248–9)

It is difficult to calculate how much naivety, and how much cunning, was involved in the scenario Butler constructed. At first he poses as the representative of common sense, aiming to entertain the general public, before establishing his credentials as a historian of ideas. He then patronises Darwin, concludes that he is massively in error, and finally admits that the theory that has transformed his view is not original, but belongs properly to Lamarck:

> Then came one who told me that the stone was not mine, but that it had been dropped by Lamarck, to whom it belonged rightfully, but who had lost it; whereon I said I cared not who was the owner, if only I might use it and enjoy it.

The mock-archaic, semi-Biblical style marks Butler's unease and he ends with a self-conscious mystical flourish:

Will the reader bid me wake with him to a world of chance and blindness? Or can I persuade him to dream with me of a more living faith than either he or I had as yet conceived as possible? As I have said, reason points remorselessly to an awakening, but faith and hope still beckon to the dream. (LH306–7)

In spite of his disclaimers, Butler confidently expected to be taken seriously by Darwin and the scientific and intellectual establishment. Francis Darwin thanked him for his copy in a friendly letter – 'if I have pitched into you it isn't that I don't like your book, because I do, very much' – but he challenged him directly on the weakest part of his argument: 'I don't see how intelligent variation will help you, for instance, to make the beginnings of limbs grow out of a limbless animal.' Two comments in particular worried Butler. In his postscript, Francis Darwin asked, 'Why do you call *Animals and Plants*, *Plants and Animals*? and the *Origin*, *Natural Selection*?' He also added, 'My father hasn't read it yet.' (M1.263–4) Butler replied by return of post: 'Of course, when I wrote, I knew that much of what I was writing was crude, and would require alteration, but I did not see my way further then; and felt that, such as the book was, it must stand or fall for the present.' (Butler noted in 1901, 'I wrote this because F.D.'s letter had fogged and frightened me, and I did not know what else might not be coming. I was oppressed and scared by the far-reachingness and daring of what I had done . . .') He apologised for the extraordinary error in mistaking the titles of Darwin's books: 'It was very stupid; I will look out for the place and correct it. I hope I have not misquoted any passage.' (M1.264–5)

The book was reviewed respectfully, but without great enthusiasm, and sold modestly. One reviewer voiced the major difficulty: the book was a production 'for which I do not anticipate much popular success, and for the reason that the general public will not know what to make of it. The writer has the gift of humour, to an extent exceedingly rare in the present day, and, as he exercises his subtle and delicate satire upon subjects very seldom approached in the sarcastic vein, he is liable to misapprehension on the part of the majority, and is either mistaken for an apologist of that which he desires to destroy, or is tabooed as an audacious and revolutionary thinker . . .'[2] Butler sent this and another notice to Shrewsbury, thinking, ever hopeful, that they would please his father. The response was predictable: 'I return the papers, which must no doubt be very gratifying to you. I have purposefully refrained from reading any of your books except *Canterbury* and could feel more sympathy in any artistic success you might attain than in this.' (FL140–1) As Butler explained ingenuously to May, his intention was not to force differences upon his father, but 'to show him that disinterested third parties considered us in more substantial agreement than he was perhaps aware of'. (FL141–2)

The general indifference hurt him deeply, and he spent much time during the next decade underpinning and extending his theory in an attempt to promote his views and provoke an appropriate response. As it happened, Butler's critique of Darwinism had much to offer. There were many possible objections and difficulties, as Darwin freely admitted, and Butler, by luck or cunning, put his finger on several. Because so little was known about genetics, there was no way of demonstrating how species might develop by means of variation within the grand design laid down by Darwin; and it was not until the application of Mendelian theory and, recently, the discovery of DNA and RNA that the general tenor of Darwin's theory could be firmly substantiated. The debate continues, as the activities of the creationists, or books like Richard Dawkins's *The Blind Watchmaker*, demonstrate. Dawkins's last chapter, 'Doomed Rivals', elegantly disposes of Lamarckian theory; it is significant that it still requires disposal. Shaw, pre-eminently, and Koestler followed the broad path carved out by Butler. Karl Popper, who was unimpressed by most of the evolutionary philosophers 'with the one great exception' of Samuel Butler, placed his originality in perspective: 'Thus men like Butler and Bergson, though I suppose utterly wrong in their theories, were right in their intuition. Vital force ("cunning") does, of course, exist – but it is in its turn a product of life, *of selection*, rather than anything like the "essence" of life. It is indeed the preferences *which lead the way*. Yet the way is not Lamarckian but Darwinian.'[3]

Temperamentally, Butler was an old-fashioned eighteenth-century deist. He had, partly through the influence of *The Origin of Species*, his book of books, lost faith in received Christianity, but, on finding himself in a world from which Christ had been removed, he reverted to a belief in vitalism. He was still, like Paley, in wonder at the intricacy of design when you opened up the watch, but unable to accept a pre-ordained plan. So he substituted for the exploded idea of instant, once-for-all creation a belief in the essential unity of life, life with a sense of will, purpose and progress. The mechanical alternative, as he saw it, blind, random, soulless, was too awful to contemplate.

Throughout 1878, Butler was immersed in his writing. He was revising his Pontifex novel, and, as before, sending sections to Miss Savage for her comments. But his main task was his second book on evolution: 'I cannot part with any Darwin MS., it is going ahead fast, and will be done by the middle or end of January,' he told her at the end of May. 'It gets more and more telling and I shall get it quieter also. A friend accused me the other day of liking a row. I am afraid he is right, but I only like it when I am quite sure that I have the right end of the stick.' (S184) Early in July he broke off for an extended solitary holiday in Switzerland and Italy. The stress of confronting Darwin affected his health as badly as rowing with his father, though the symptoms were different. He was suffering from breathlessness: 'Writing *Life and Habit*, literally took my breath away,' he noted, 'I kept wanting to take a long breath, and quite unable to do so.' (S190) The break restored him, though the breathing problem remained for a full year. This second book was finally published on May 1st, 1879. Its full title describes its scope: *Evolution, old and new; or, the theories of Buffon, Dr Erasmus Darwin, and Lamarck, as compared with that of Mr Charles Darwin.*

Evolution Old and New carried the dispute with Darwin, initiated in *Life and Habit*, to a new level of vehemence. To some extent the argument was a reiteration of Butler's former position. But to this was added a historical survey of the theory of evolution and of modification by descent, intended to lend weight to Butler's own position, by suggesting that he was extending and developing a theory that had some philosophical and scientific history; at the same time it would weaken Darwin's by arguing that Darwin had muddied and confused a long-standing teleological theory of evolution by an irrelevant and illogical addition, namely, natural selection.

He also rashly implied that Darwin, with a reputation for frankness and candour, was guilty of plagiarism: citing the variations between different editions of *The Origin of Species*, Butler tried to demonstrate that Darwin had been extremely reluctant to acknowledge that any natural philosopher before him had contributed significantly to the development of his theory. In the first edition, for instance, Darwin had made only two passing references to Lamarck; while in the 'brief but imperfect' historical survey that Darwin later inserted (Butler enjoyed himself with that phrase) there were innumerable misrepresentations, including the slightest imaginable reference to Darwin's own grandfather Erasmus. Butler spent a substantial section of his book rehabilitating Dr Erasmus Darwin, claiming that his theory of evolution was more developed even than Lamarck's (suggesting, even, that Lamarck had read and been influenced by him), and implying that in all respects except the one crucial step of natural selection, Charles Darwin had been anticipated by his grandfather. The major step of natural selection was, he argued, an aberration.

All this was rough enough, even by the relaxed standards of Victorian polemic. Darwin was the acknowledged great man of science, honoured throughout the world; he was elderly, frail, and of a retiring and consistently courteous nature. There was, admittedly, a little justification in some of what Butler wrote: Darwin seldom gave much acknowledgement to predecessors or contemporaries (in contrast to Alfred Wallace, who was invariably generous to the man who expounded the theory he himself had independently formulated). But to present this as deception, or suppression, on Darwin's part, was unfair and improbable. It did Darwin no harm, and demeaned Butler. Darwin's theory was logical, modern, radical, uncomfortable. Its very radicalism was one reason why he refrained from elaborating on its implications for mankind. So when Butler buzzed excitedly about on the fringe of his life with teleological theories, which even incorporated a concept of God, Darwin chose not to respond directly either to the arguments or to the accompanying insults.

However, he did not ignore Butler completely, and a dispute arose that inflamed the controversy into a personal quarrel, upsetting to Darwin, and extremely damaging to Butler. The relevant dates are these: *Evolution Old and New* was announced on February 22nd, 1879, with some indication of the ground it would cover, but was not published until May. Meanwhile, a German scientist, Dr Krause, had published an account of Erasmus Darwin's life, entitled a 'Contribution to the History of the Descent Theory', in the February number of a German periodical, *Kosmos*, in honour of Darwin's seventieth birthday. Krause gave permission for a translation, and Charles Darwin published this in November, 1879 with an introductory Memoir of his grandfather Erasmus. The preface indicates clearly that the translation is of an article that appeared in February, and on the second page there is a note to the effect that *Evolution Old and New* had appeared since the article's publication. In other words, there would seem to be no connection between *Evolution Old and New* and the Krause article other than the coincidence of two people writing about the same subject at much the same time.

When Butler got hold of a copy in November, he turned first (characteristically) to the last page, and found this:

> Erasmus Darwin's system was in itself a most significant first step in the path of knowledge which his grandson has opened up for us, but to wish to revive it at the present day, as has actually been seriously attempted, shows a weakness of thought and a mental anachronism which no one can envy.

Butler recorded his reaction in *Unconscious Memory*:[4] ' "That's me,", said I to myself promptly.' The more he read, the more puzzled and angry he became, since he discovered what appeared to be direct references to his own work, quotations from Buffon line for line as he had quoted him, and in the same form, in addition to the kind of indirect allusion outlined above. Butler sent to Germany for a copy of the February *Kosmos*, began to learn German in the fortnight's interval before its arrival, and systematically compared the translation with the original. He found there were major discrepancies: the English version contained both omissions and additions; and the last six pages of the English text were new matter. As he stated, 'I could no longer doubt that the article had been altered by the light of and with a view to *Evolution Old and New*.' Butler not unnaturally assumed that Krause had revised his article in the light of *Evolution Old and New*, as indeed to some extent he had. In support of his interpretation, he tracked down two notices in the *Popular Science Review* for January, 1880, one of which quoted the passage about mental anachronism and added: 'This anachronism has been committed by Mr Samuel Butler in a . . . little volume now before us, and it is doubtless to this, *which appeared while his own work was in progress* [Butler's italics], that Dr Krause alludes in the foregoing passage.' The editor of the *Popular Science Review* was Dallas, the translator of Krause's article.

Butler accordingly wrote to Darwin, asking for the edition of *Kosmos* that contained the revised text of Dr Krause's article; he drew Darwin's attention to the discrepancies, quoted the most offensive paragraph, and pointed out that, from the statements in the preface about *Evolution Old and New* and the 'accuracy of the translation', readers would naturally suppose that 'all they read in the translation appeared in February last, and therefore before *Evolution Old and New* was written'.

'I do not doubt that this was actually the case,' he wrote, 'but have failed to obtain the edition which contains the passage above referred to, and several others which appear in the translation.

I have a personal interest in this matter, and venture, therefore, to ask for the explanation, which I do not doubt you will readily give me.'[5]

Butler's letter was unmistakably tart. Across it, Darwin has written, 'To be returned as it means war we think.'[6] Unfortunately, Darwin did not at this stage confer with family or friends, but replied by return of post:

Dr Krause, soon after the appearance of his article in *Kosmos*, told me that he intended to publish it separately and to alter it considerably, and the altered MS. was sent to Mr Dallas for translation. This is so common a practice that it never occurred to me to state that the article had been modified; but now I much regret that I did not do so. The original will soon appear in German, and I believe will be a much larger book than the English one; for, with Dr Krause's consent, many long extracts from Miss Seward were omitted (as well as much other matter), from being in my opinion superfluous for the English reader. I believe that the omitted parts will appear as notes in the German edition. Should there be a reprint of the English Life, I will state that the original as it appeared in *Kosmos* was modified by Dr Krause before it was translated. I may add that I had obtained Dr Krause's consent for a translation, and had arranged with Mr Dallas before your book was announced. I remember this because Mr Dallas wrote to tell me of the advertisement.[7]

Butler was outraged. Darwin's 'regret' constituted an apology of sorts, but it was essentially private; he may, too, have felt insulted by the reference to 'common practice', as though he was ignorant of academic convention. The promise of an additional note should a second edition of Darwin's book be called for he regarded as wholly inadequate. The sort of reparation Butler wanted, he claimed in *Unconscious Memory*, was a letter to *The Times* or *The Athenaeum*, and a printed erratum in all unsold copies. On the other hand, he believed that he had found Darwin to be inaccurate and in error. Instead of writing again, asking perhaps for some public acknowledgement of the omission, he chose to pursue the disagreement in as public a manner as possible, with a detailed letter in *The Athenaeum* on January 31st, 1880.

Darwin was extremely distressed. For someone of his age and reputation for candour to be publicly called a liar was deeply wounding. He had answered the complaint privately as best he could, though, as will appear shortly, not as fully as he might with hindsight have done; to do so in public risked prolonging the quarrel. He drafted one letter, and circulated it for advice; he drafted another. Leslie Stephen and T.H. Huxley were called in: each counselled silence. In the end Darwin was convinced by Huxley, though Francis Darwin and some of his brothers thought their father should have written publicly. 'Oh Lord', Darwin told Huxley, 'what a relief your letter has been to me. I feel like a man condemned to be hung who has just got a reprieve. I saw in the future no end of trouble, but I feared that I was bound in honour to answer. If you were here I would show you exactly how the omission arose.'[8]

The 'omission' is the key to the whole business. Krause had indeed, quite normally, revised his article, and Darwin had drafted a note to that effect for inclusion in the preface:

> Dr Krause has taken great pains, and has added largely to his essay as it appeared in *Kosmos*; and my preliminary notice, having been written before I had seen the additions, unfortunately contains much repetition of what Dr Krause has said . . .

It was later agreed to omit Krause's additions about Erasmus Darwin's life, and the whole paragraph was struck out of the proofs, including the statement that the article had been altered since its original publication. The far-fetched conspiracy theory that Butler had engendered vanishes, and in its place there is a simple oversight.

But if Butler was absurdly quick to take offence and assume duplicity, it is unfortunate that the straightforward explanation was never given to him, either immediately in Darwin's first letter or later. It remains puzzling, too, that Darwin did include a reference to *Evolution Old and New* in a footnote to his preface, but advised Krause to delete overt criticisms of the book in his revised article. For Krause and Darwin conducted a frequent and detailed correspondence throughout the summer of 1879, with many references to Butler's book. Krause quickly obtained a copy, and Darwin was fully aware that he was contemplating some discussion of it, for he wrote to him on June 9th: 'I hope that you will not expend much powder and shot on Mr Butler, for he really is not worthy of it.'[9] In fact, Butler's dispute should properly have been with Krause. Krause's reply in *Nature*[10] makes his and Darwin's respective roles clear:

> Mr Darwin advised me decidedly against taking any notice of Butler's book but I could not possibly deny myself the pleasure of at least hinting in a concluding sentence and without naming any names that there were people of this day who looked upon Erasmus Darwin's conception of the living world as the only soul saving one.

The episode left Butler with a profound sense of injury at the hands of what he saw as the scientific establishment, in the person of Darwin and his followers, Huxley and Romanes. He pursued the vendetta remorselessly, penning lengthy and obsessive letters whenever the matter resurfaced in the public domain, in, for example, reviews of his next book, *Unconscious Memory*, or references in Francis Darwin's Life of his father. The pity was that his largely imagined wrongs served to convince him that his theory of evolution was correct. He became locked within it, fruitlessly refining and extending it; he also became absurdly jealous, scouring the writings of others for signs that they had used something of his without acknowledgement, or defending his prior originality against the claims of thinkers such as Herbert Spencer. Each successive volume rehearsed the course of the controversy in wearisome detail, until the death of

Darwin brought a kind of peace, in the preface to the second edition of *Evolution Old and New* in 1882.

Meanwhile, he aired the whole matter in *Unconscious Memory*, which was published in November, 1880. The book adds little to the thesis advanced in *Life and Habit*, but merely translates a lecture by Dr Ewald Hering, 'On Memory as a Universal Function of Organised Matter', and the chapter on Instinct in von Hartmann's *Philosophy of the Unconscious*: this was a holier than thou act on Butler's part, demonstrating the correct way for a thinker to acknowledge previous or parallel expositions of his ideas. Years later, he reflected on the whole question of publication:

> . . . I cannot help wondering whether or not *Unconscious Memory* was or was not a wise move as regards the getting a hearing for *Life and Habit* – the thing about which I was, and still am, most anxious. I do not know. But policy or no policy, Mr Darwin having done what he did, and having made no amends when his attention was called to it in the *Athenaeum*, *Unconscious Memory* was inevitable. Such an attempt to ride roughshod over me by a man who was by way of being such a preux cavalier as Mr Darwin set my back up, and I determined to place the whole story on record. I do not think it added much to the odium in which I already was; nothing could well do this; to have written *Life and Habit* at all was an unforgivable offence, and *Evolution Old and New*, though it could hardly make things worse, assuredly did not mend them . . . At any rate, whether *Unconscious Memory* has helped *Life and Habit* or no, there can be no doubt that it and my other books on evolution have had a large share in making Huxley execute a volte-face, to use his own words. (N127)

Butler made one further major foray into the Darwinian controversy. In December, 1883 (by which time Darwin had died, while his own father was dangerously ill), he began to prepare materials for a volume of *Selections from Previous Work*. However, he was roused to fury by George Romanes's *Mental Evolution in Animals*, in which Romanes claimed that Charles Kingsley had used the phrase 'hereditary memory' in an issue of *Nature* in 1867. Romanes was an arch-demon for Butler; he had reviewed *Unconscious Memory* in the most condescending and sarcastic terms, accusing Butler of inordinate vanity and suggesting he seek a hearing among the homoeopathists. Since *Nature* did not begin publication until 1869, Butler considered he had ample fuel, and he was further encouraged by a review of Romanes's book in *The Athenaeum* that ascribed the phrase to himself. He wrote, first, a long essay that was included in *Selections*, and then set to work on the volume originally intended as a sequel to *Life and Habit*, but which evolved, by November, 1886, into *Luck or Cunning?*

This, the most combative of his books, lashed out at all his enemies and rivals: Herbert Spencer, Romanes, Darwin, Grant Allen, Ray Lankester. His argument had advanced little further. Darwin, Wallace 'and their supporters' are 'the apostles of luck'; Erasmus Darwin, Lamarck, and Butler the apostles of cunning. The book's essence is 'to insist on the omnipresence of a mind and intelligence throughout the universe to which no name can be so fittingly applied as God'. It did no better, in terms of sales, than its two predecessors, though Shaw, an arch puncturer of reputations, reviewed it enthusiastically, under the heading 'Darwin Denounced'.[11] The index is a reliable guide to Butler's method. There are over two hundred entries under Darwin. Some are neutral and factual, some – 'cannot be denied rare greatness' – seem positive. But there is a pervasive sprinkling of pejorative, petty categories such as: 'heir to discredited truth'; 'intended his change of front to escape us'; 'ostrich-like and pitiable'; 'suave, but singularly fraudulent'; 'not especially great as an observer'; 'gave his esoteric doctrine to the world'. After a while, one begins to lose sight of Butler's theories, and to speculate instead about the source of his vehement dislike of Darwin. He had imagined him as a prophet and saviour, sympathetic, charismatic even, but when he went to stay at Down, he found someone superficially rather like his father; and, just like his father, someone who did not take him very seriously. So he decided Darwin was yet another false god, an icon elevated by the establishment, and convinced himself that he was striking a blow for truth in attacking 'a muddle-headed old fool'.

His antagonism towards Darwin spread outwards to embrace a mythical 'Darwin literary and scientific clique', whom he blamed for his public neglect. Even attempts by friends like Edward Clodd, who introduced him to Grant Allen on a Sunday evening at his home, failed to shift his suspicions – Clodd commented that Butler 'nursed the delusion that every man of science if he defended Darwin was in conspiracy against himself and this made that freedom which is the charm of intercourse very difficult'.[12] Alfred Wallace, who reviewed both *Life and Habit* and *Evolution Old and New* for *Nature*, and thought the former wonderfully ingenious and witty, had tried to reason with him, courteously, by letter: 'In your admiration of Lamarck you do not seem to observe that his views are all pure conjecture, utterly unsupported by a single fact.' 'Spontaneous variability', on the other hand, was a fact.[13] Butler did not reply; and Wallace too was entered in the ranks of his private demonology. Butler's habitual strength lay in opposing the unthinking acceptance of received ideas; but here the originality of his voice was lost in the stridency of his personal feud.

CHAPTER 14

Friends and Relations

Butler felt particularly exposed and vulnerable during the years of his quarrel with Darwin. He needed some stable source of affection and approval. He would never find this among his relations; Pauli, to whom he had dedicated *Life and Habit*, and whom he was still subsidising, was a legacy from the past, the shadow of a friend; and Miss Savage had to be kept outside the reach of intimacy. The most promising candidate was Jones, whose evening and Saturday afternoon visits were becoming more frequent. In 1878 the acquaintance moved on to a new level, not without some trepidation on Jones's part.

'Something had been said during the summer about our meeting in the Canton Ticino if it should be convenient; but nothing definite was settled, and in the middle of August I went for my holiday to the Black Forest. I soon began to feel solitary, walking alone with a knapsack.' (M1.281) After some hesitation, he sent Butler a telegram asking whether he might join him. Butler replied from Faido that he was just off to the Sacro Monte, above Varese, and would be staying at the Albergo Riposo. Each was uneasy about the prospect: 'if he bores me,' thought Butler, 'I will shunt him.'[1] Jones reflected that, if anything went wrong, they ought to be able to separate without much harm being done.

He accordingly made his way to Varese, arriving too late for the hotel dinner. After some supper, he sat on the terrace with Butler, 'smoking in the moonlight, and watching the lamps down in Varese, and the lightning that played incessantly over the plain below'. After a while, to make conversation, he pointed out a star and asked if Butler knew its name. Butler replied, with some asperity, 'I do not know anything about astronomy.' Jones, rebuked, was silent. After a pause, Butler said 'in a conciliatory tone, as though he had, perhaps,

gone too far: "I know the moon." And there the matter dropped.'
(M1.282) The critical moment was over.

Butler showed Jones the Sacro Monte at Varese, and explained
the chapels to him; and Jones observed: 'I soon perceived that he
enjoyed showing me these things as much as I enjoyed seeing them.'
Butler then took him to the castle of Angera, where S. Carlo Borro-
meo was born; and from there they were rowed across Lake Maggiore
to Arona to see Isabella. Butler later noted significantly:

I kept away from Arona for years; but at last returned with
Jones, for I wanted to show her to him and to see her again,
which I might now safely do. She was at the hotel door, leaning
against the side of the house, as we came up from the quay,
looking much older, and, as usual, very sad, when her face was
in repose. It made me feel unhappy; but I went on, and she woke
up from her dreaming when she saw strangers approaching.
(M1.284)

Jones takes up the story:

She recognised him, and he began his apologies as soon as we
were near enough for her to hear:
  'I do not know what to say to you; I have been behaving very
badly; I ought to have been to see you before; every year I have
intended to come, and this –'
  'And this year,' she interrupted, 'you have come, and I am
very glad to see you.'
  She smiled as she held out her hand and came down the
steps to meet him, like Elizabeth greeting Mary in the Salutation
Chapel on the Sacro Monte. Of course I fell in love with
Isabella on the spot.

They went on by steamer to Locarno, then by post to Bignasco, and
up the Maggi valley to the mountain village of Fusio, and the ideal
upland valley of Sambuco; from there they walked over the mountains
and into the Ticino Valley, to stay at Faido, a base for short
expeditions to see Butler's favourite sketching places, and especially
the porch of Rossura church.

Jones was rather disappointed by the porch. It was so very plain, 'and could not well have been otherwise, as it seemed to me. Even admitting that it was pleasing, the architect deserved no credit for what could have cost him no labour or thought.' Butler took the opportunity to continue Jones's education. He told Jones he was 'like Mr Darwin, who could see no design in the organic kingdom, and thought it all rested on accident. There could be no doubt that the architect had made the porch, and made it as he wanted it to be; accident was present, if you like, but it was accident of which the architect had designedly taken advantage . . .The impression that the porch could not be otherwise, that feeling of inevitableness, was just one of its charms.' It was like Handel's music; it was a background for Giovanni Bellini, not for Michael Angelo. Having put Jones on the right track about architecture, music and painting, Butler gave him some paper and a pencil and set him to draw a chalet before he left for Zurich. 'We were together only a week,' comments Jones; 'but we had seen enough of one another to be sure that nothing need ever go wrong between us.' (M1.286) Jones was struck by Butler's kindness, courtesy, consideration; by his uncompromising sincerity, and by his gaiety. Butler was determined to enjoy himself on holiday – he used to say that 'A man's holiday is his garden' – and to make sure that all about him enjoyed themselves too.

Jones became his companion and collaborator. At times, as with Pauli, Butler's estimate of his new friend's gifts and capacities seems distinctly inflated. In the Note-Books, for example, his name litters the pages: 'Jones says', 'Jones on Dickens', 'Jones and My Books', often attached to comments scarcely worth recording from any source: 'The First Good Friday', 'Jones said there was a crucifixion on that night.' (N274) Butler may have overvalued his intellectual powers: in terms of worldly success, he proved a remarkably unsuccessful solicitor, and ended up as salaried companion to Butler, though his later literary output was considerable. But he was the ideal foil to Butler: admiring, unaffected, interested (unlike Pauli) in music, painting and literature, and infinitely malleable. Butler soon sorted out Jones's conventional tastes, weaning him from his attempts at writing poetry, putting him straight about Charlotte Brontë, gently ridiculing his efforts to educate himself: 'You've been reading that damned *Republic* again.' (M1.345) He found him 'easily pleased, very patient, more free than anyone I have ever met from affectation or bounce of any kind, very gentle in all his ways, and, in fact, in all

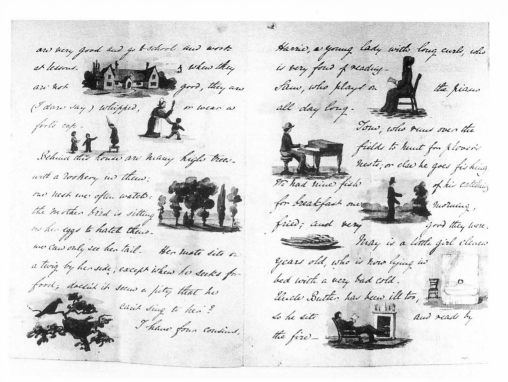

are very good and go to school and work at lessons ... when they are not (I dare say) whipped, or wear a fools cap.

Behind this house are many high trees with a rookery in them; one nest we often watch: the mother bird is sitting on her eggs to hatch them. we can only see her tail— Her mate sits on a twig by her side, except when to seeks for food; doesn't it seem a pity that he can't sing to her?

I have four cousins,

Harrio, a young lady with long curls, who is very fond of reading—

Sam, who plays on the piano all day long.

Tom, who runs over the field to hunt for plover's nests; or else he goes fishing. We had nine fish of his catching for breakfast one morning, fried; and very good they were.

May is a little girl eleven years old, who is now lying in bed with a very bad cold.

Uncle Butler has been ill too, so he sits and reads by the fire—

1 Illustrated letter by Alice Worsley: Sam playing the piano.

2 Langar Rectory. (This watercolour, previously assumed to be by Butler, is inscribed on the back 'October 14th, 1844, F.R. to S.B.': possibly Frederick Russell, who married Anna Worsley, Butler's aunt and godmother, in 1844.)

3 Samuel Butler's family, about 1865. Left to right: Samuel, Harriet, Henrietta (Tom's wife), Mrs Butler, Tom, May, Canon Butler.

4 *Family Prayers*, 1864.

5 Samuel in 1862, wearing the glengarry noted by Kenneway in 'A Peculiar Dream'.

6 The headwaters of the Rangitata, 'that torrent pathway of desolation'.

7 Charles Paine Pauli, and his tall black hat.

8 *Self-portrait*, about 1873.

9 Butler at the piano in Clifford's Inn.

10 Eliza Anne Savage, 1863, aged 27.

11 *The Christening at Fobello*, 1871.
12 *Mr Heatherley's Holiday*, 1873.

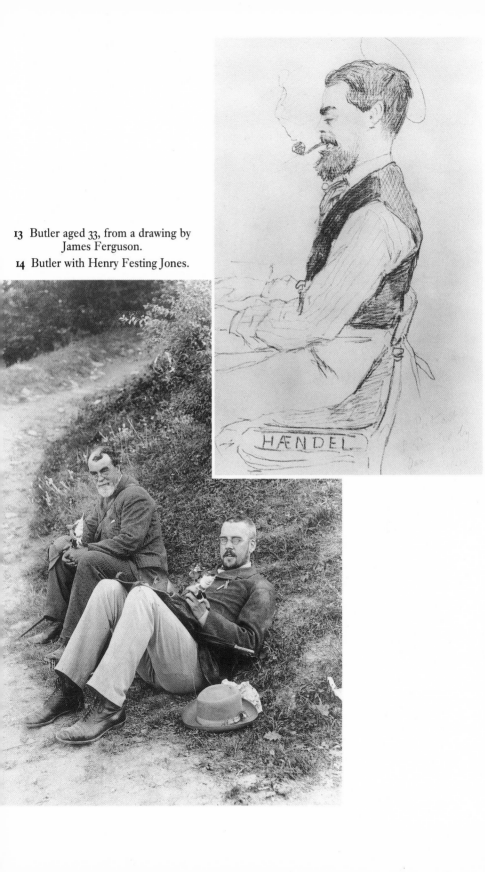

13 Butler aged 33, from a drawing by
    James Ferguson.

14 Butler with Henry Festing Jones.

HÆNDEL

15 Charles Gogin and blocks of ice on the quay, Boulogne, 1891.

16 Butler and Hans Faesch in the garden of the 'Falstaff', Gad's Hill, 1894.

The D. George Inn Edgeware
Oct. 2. 1880.

18 The Old George Inn, Edgeware, 1880.
17 Butler on a stile, Abbey Wood, 1891.
19 Butler on an avalanche, 1894.

20 Chapel XIX, The Triumphal Entry into Jerusalem, Sacro Monte, Varallo.
21 Mycenae, Tomb of Atreus, 1895.
22 Fleet Street and 'the ineffable St Pauls'.

23 Blind Man with Children, Greenwich, 1892.

24 Account book in Butler's hand, 1899.

25 Account book in Alfred's hand, 1902 – note Alfred's indignation about Dr Gairdner's guinea.

26 Alfred Cathie, Higham Station 1893.
27 Butler in 1898, aged 62, from a photograph by Alfred Cathie.

respects singularly amiable.' One of his chief attributes was that he did not pose any kind of threat. True, he professed to like his mother and to speak no ill of his elder sister, but this would change. Butler set to work to mould Jones in his own image, so that at times he seems to be a fictional invention, a younger, naive straight man to Butler's more volatile and mischievous comic persona.

Jones had passed the test of the holiday. Back in London, he began to visit Butler at Clifford's Inn three or four times a week – 'I know of no one else,' wrote Butler, 'from whom I could have stood such frequent visits.'[2] In the autumn of 1878, Jones received a further accolade: he was invited, together with Reginald Worsley, to go on one of Butler's Sunday outings, on this first occasion from Westerham to Redhill. These walks had been a regular feature of Butler's life since the publication of *Erewhon*. With his cousin Reginald Worsley, or the painter Charles Gogin, and now with Jones, or Jones's brother Edward, he would take a train and explore some stretch of country within thirty miles or so of London, marking the route in red ink on an ordnance map. They would take sandwiches, drink beer in a public house, collect eggs from a farmer's wife, and entertain each other with sarcastic comments at the expense of God, women and their own relatives, and with the sayings of Mrs Boss, Worsley's laundress.

Mrs Boss, the model for Mrs Jupp in *The Way of All Flesh*, provided a link for Butler with another world, and he noted her sayings with relish. A former whore – her notion of the highest thing of which the human race is capable was a young whore – she reminded him of Mistress Quickly, and her speeches might form a coda to the darker Eastcheap scenes in *Henry IV Part 2*: 'I do hate a wet Saturday night – poor women with their nice white stockings and their living to get.' She called children 'overtimes', the work a man did when the rest of his day's work was over, and would do the chores singing 'Farting Fan':

> 'Twas through a fart
> I lost my sweetheart,
> So the wind of your arse go with you.

One Saturday afternoon, half tight, she said, 'I shan't be here much longer. When I am dead and gone, and dear Mr Butler sees me in my coffin, he'll say, "Ah, poor old Boss, she'll never talk any more smut now." [3] Butler did not record only the smut. But he was drawn to the backstreets and brothels, and in Jones and Worsley he had friends with whom he found he need conceal nothing. 'Getting into a married woman', Worsley told him, was 'like fucking a loaded pistol.' He soon organised Jones's sex life: the arrangement with Madame was modified to include a visit from Jones each Tuesday, and their continental tours included visits to brothels. At Madama Castalda's in Turin, Butler was waiting for Jones to come down, when some 'very nice women' surrounded him. He explained that he had already been attended to. 'One asked me to stand her a cup of coffee. I offered coffee for the lot. They overhauled the contents of my bag, very quietly and nicely, and not at all as English or French women would have done.'[4] Down went the incident into the little black pocketbook that he took everywhere so that no experience should be wasted, part of the contents of the very bag through which the women had rummaged.

While he strove to establish himself as a serious writer, his relationships with his family, and especially with his father, became strained once more, largely because of financial difficulties. Since the Canadian fiasco, Butler had been a little more at ease with his father, particularly at Wilderhope House. True, sending the reviews of *Life and Habit* had been a signal failure, but he found a safer way of maintaining communications with offerings of dried plants collected on his holidays abroad. Now the personal obtruded once again.

Butler had 'loaned' Pauli between £3000 and £3500. In 1879, after running through all his capital, he told Pauli he could do no more. Pauli accepted the situation as calmly as he had accepted the loans, but Butler noticed that the coat in which he came to lunch was one he would have cast off long before if supplies had not failed; and his cough became worse.

Butler wrote to tell his father that he was 'without means'. (FL144) He shrank from telling him too much, for whatever he said would be passed on to May, and May might influence their father against him. However, he confessed that the only way he could extricate himself was by borrowing money against his eventual interest in the Whitehall estate. His father replied:

Your letter distresses me ... You say that the time approaches when you shall be absolutely without means. Will you write to me and tell me exactly what has happened and what your condition is. I might be able to help you. But what has failed or how?

Pray do not require me to conceal anything from May. I should be a bad hand at doing so and would rather know no more than be bound to silence.

I can promise nothing till I know the circumstances and what would set you free, whether it is a temporary or a permanent difficulty and how deep.

Pray let no false shame hinder you from making a clean breast of it and reply at once. (FL145)

Inevitably, Butler took exception to two expressions in particular. 'What would *set you free*' was one. 'I am perfectly free,' he wrote, 'and under no sort of obligation to any one except to one near relation and that to no great extent.' The other was, 'Pray let no false shame hinder you from making a clean breast of it.' 'I have done nothing which I am ashamed of and have nothing to make a clean breast of.' (FL146) Once again he laid the chief blame on Henry Hoare, 'head of Hoare's bank on Fleet Street', he added, as though this made him less culpable. The truth lay somewhere between this position and his father's suspicions of some indiscreet liaison. He was technically free, but his moral obligation to Pauli had effectively deprived him of economic independence. His father found Butler's initial explanation about Pauli incredible. How could the '£9500' which Butler brought back from New Zealand have vanished, even with the £3600 loss from the Tanning débâcle: there should still have been £5900, and the interest would amount to £240 a year. Was it conceivable that Butler had been drawing on *capital* to eke out his and Pauli's income? How could Pauli, if he was a man of any integrity, agree to such an arrangement? '. . . from 1866 or 1867 he has been living upon you at the rate of £300 a year and since the Tanning business at £105 more . . . It would appear that he must have known that your supplies were run out at least as early as Midsummer because he was to repay the 360 borrowed from Reginald Worsley which shews that he knew you had to borrow it. But still he lives upon you and though perhaps not earning so largely as I supposed still he is earning something and more I imagine than yourself.' (FL150)

Canon Butler, while understandably making some misinterpret-ations, nevertheless assessed the situation shrewdly and fairly. In the end, after much advice from his solicitor friend Creswell Peele, Butler laid out the details of his finances, and of his relationship with Pauli, in an immensely long letter to his father, headed 'Private and Confidential'. (FL152–62) He admitted the foolishness of his investments, which had lost him something in the region of £6000. He justified his 'Quixotic' insistence on making himself responsible for Pauli's – and others' – losses in Hoare's companies. On his continued subsidy of Pauli, he was less convincing:

> He is a man universally liked and universally respected, who will yet I believe weather this storm and do well ... less than what I have done I did not feel that I could do, under all the circumstances, without laying up myself matter for regret more profound than I now feel for any action of my life, and which would pain me more than any subsequent loss of income over and above what was absolutely necessary for my reasonable maintenance.

Now that most of the facts were at last out in the open, Canon Butler delivered his judgments. They were not designed to please his son. He accepted the explanation about Pauli's conduct, though in terms that showed his poor opinion of his son's behaviour: 'I thought it highly probable that you had pressed the money upon him and can readily excuse a man at his extremity from receiving it. I do not quite understand his continuing to accept it knowing that you were now without funds and with the purpose not merely of enabling him to live but to make such appearance as might impress others with the notion that he was doing more than he really was.' He refused to disentail the Whitehall estate and rejected Butler's request, sent through the solicitor, of £1060 in the current year and £405 per annum afterwards; instead, he offered to give him £664 immediately, and £300 a year as an allowance. But Butler's behaviour, above all the spending of capital, gravest of Victorian sins, shocked him deeply: 'I felt this reckless spending of capital so wrong that in the first interview I had with Mr How upon the subject I told him I saw it necessary to protect you from your own romance and to tie up the greater part of your expectancy on your children first, and in default of them on Tom's children, and I mention it now because I do not wish it to come upon you as a surprise.' (FL163–5)

Butler's reaction to this unwelcome news was more restrained at the age of forty-four than it would have been in the past, and he remembered that he was as effectively his father's pensioner as Pauli was his. Nevertheless it bristles with hurt and indignation: 'It is impossible for me to pretend that I am indifferent to your decision to give me only a life interest in the greater part of what you had intended to leave me; on the contrary I regard it as almost the heaviest and most far-reaching blow which a father can inflict upon a son and feel it accordingly. Nor yet can you expect me to acquiesce in the sufficiency of the reason you have given for your decision. At the same time, the matter is one which is so entirely within your own control that it is impossible for me to disagree with you concerning it.' (FL165)

November was a bad month for Butler. At the very same time, he was combing through *Erasmus Darwin* to compare it with Krause's *Kosmos* article, and building up for his confrontation with Darwin, whom he wrongly assumed to be acting as unjustly and patriarchally as his own father. The two sources of resentment mingled and fed each other.

With his sisters, Butler was in a permanent state of armed truce. Harriet, the widow of George Bridges, now lived in the Isle of Wight. She frequently invited Samuel to stay, but when he made one of his rare visits in October, 1878 it was the first time he had seen her for over two years, and he only stayed one day. Harriet had a strong, unbending personality; she spoke her mind, and was fiercely orthodox in her Christian beliefs. Even before she moved to Shrewsbury in 1884 to make her home with her father and sister, she exerted a powerful influence. According to her niece, the goading hand of Harriet lay behind Canon Butler's harsh letters, making reconciliation impossible: 'She suffered from a diseased conscience, so over-scrupulous that she feared to do good for fear of doing evil.'[5]

May, the peacemaker, was a more sympathetic personality; and Samuel maintained a wide-ranging and regular correspondence with her. She never gave up with her brother, and happily exchanged notes about books, music and painting with him. But if Harriet was too stern, May's very sweetness galled. Everything with her was 'nice' and 'bright', words that irritated Samuel and which he deliberately used in his letters to her. In 1882 she founded a home in Shrewsbury for ruined children, presumably child prostitutes or the daughters of prostitutes, an act of charity peculiarly appropriate in view of her two brothers' knowledge of brothels and bawdy houses. She even went to London to inspect similar institutions, and trudged the streets of Stepney from morning to night.

With his sisters, Butler maintained at least the pretence of civility. This was not the case with his brother Tom, who was living in Brussels, with a wife, four children and, it transpired, two mistresses to support. To Butler it often seemed that Tom was treated more generously by his father than he was himself.

Canon Butler's anxieties about his younger son also sharpened his suspiciousness and irritability. Like Samuel, Tom was running into financial problems. When Canon Butler travelled over to Brussels in the autumn of 1880, he reported that he 'did not like to find the hours Tom kept but there was nothing tangible'. (FL177) Butler, piecing the story together afterwards, learned that Tom had visited Shrewsbury at the turn of the year. While Tom was in the drawing-room at Wilderhope House, Barbe Kuster, the Belgian woman who had secretly accompanied him, stood outside in the garden in the snow – 'her footsteps were noticed next morning' – and tapped quietly on the window to attract Tom's attention, perhaps even to deliver a forged telegram, summoning Tom back to Brussels because his son Harry was dangerously ill. Certainly a telegram was sent, because it was through the later enquiries about Harry's health that the truth emerged, when Henrietta finally told her father-in-law the whole story and asked for his protection.

Barbe Kuster, it transpired, was only the last of a series of women with whom Tom had become involved, in her case to the tune of 70,000 francs and near-bankruptcy. Butler wondered if the bizarre events at Shrewsbury, echoing the melodramas he was so fond of, might have formed part of an elaborate system of blackmail: 'What follows is conjecture. There had been recently a Belgo-Anglian cause célèbre in which a Belgian woman of the Barbe Kuster class had proposed to a young Englishman that they should murder his father. The woman never meant that the father should be murdered, but only desired to get compromising evidence against the son, which she could use as a means of extorting money, certainly from the son, and possibly from the father. I imagine that Barbe Kuster had laid some hardly less nefarious scheme before my brother – and not intending that it should ever be carried out had prepared the telegram which she had arranged should be sent, as soon as she considered that my brother had been sufficiently compromised.' (FL179–80)

Whatever the true motive, Barbe Kuster was highly resourceful, employing lawyers, announcing that she intended to seek interviews in England, and sending letters to the Shrewsbury chief constable and postmaster. Canon Butler was in his element in this kind of situation and composed a pastoral letter to Tom: 'I think God is giving you a new start and another trial. How you will use it I cannot tell. To any one even of strong will and mental power the habit of eleven years of sin and falsehood is a terrible thing to strive against, and with your weak and feeble nature more terrible and but for one thing insurmountable. But it will and must be hard, an uphill fight and one of long continuance and if you fall again I cannot conceive a hope of your recovery.' (FL175–6) The 'one thing' was God's help and the power of prayer, though Canon Butler clearly did not put much faith in either where Tom was concerned.

On receipt of this scarcely consoling advice, Tom, according to his wife Henrietta, said, 'Come, I'll soon answer that; give me ink and pen,' and wrote three or four pages beginning, 'Father, I have sinned, and am no more worthy to be called thy son. I cannot hope that you will forgive me but I trust God can and will,' laughing all the while. May thought the letter 'had the true Christian ring', but Canon Butler did not believe a word. (FL176–7)

Meanwhile, he set about appointing himself as guardian, and securing as much financial provision for Henrietta and his grand-children as he could. The negotiations dragged on throughout 1881, and eventually the family were settled in a house in Liverpool, with Canon Butler undertaking to provide for them. Tom's last letter to Samuel began 'Sir' and ended 'yours obediently': he had declared 'war to the bitter death'.[6] He sent Forget-me-not cards to his wife and daughters, and vanished out of all their lives. Tom, so Butler declared with a distinct note of triumph, was a disgrace to them all, and no words were to be bandied with him. On this matter, at least, he saw eye to eye with Harriet; May's sympathies ran towards Tom, even after she learned that he had actually settled money – family money – on one of Barbe Kuster's predecessors, Miss Adams. Butler believed, with some justification, that Tom's example stiffened his father's attitude towards himself.

In the middle of all this, Samuel and his father had one of their fiercest rows. Tom's disgrace had brought about what Butler had long been hoping for, the disentailment of the Whitehall estate. Canon Butler saw the sense in altering the terms of succession, so that Henrietta and her children should benefit rather than Tom, in the event of Samuel's dying before his father; at the same time How, the family solicitor, suggested the disentailment, as an 'act of justice' to Butler. At last Butler was free to raise capital on the security of the estate.

One might suppose that, knowing the full extent of his father's commitments towards Tom's family, he would now assume responsibility for his own affairs, and release his father from the promise of an allowance. Certainly he wished to be independent. But his sense of old wrongs remained undimmed. As he frankly admitted, 'Another reason why I did not strike instantly on the cutting off the entail was that I was at the end of my half year's allowance, and wished to have the half year due June 1st in hand before I took a step the effect which I could not foresee.' (FL184–7) His father wrote outlining the reduced allowance he could expect in future in view of his commitments to the rest of the family: 'You will not therefore be surprised that I shall expect you to do something for your own maintenance.' (FL182)

This eminently reasonable, if tactlessly expressed, hope was seized on by Butler:

> I have been endeavouring to answer your letter of the 31st May in a way agreeable on the one hand to my own sense of self respect, and on the other to what is expected from a son towards his father. On the whole I conclude I shall best succeed in this by confining myself to the acknowledgement of your letter and to saying that I have noted its contents and taken steps accordingly.
>
> The only way in which I believe I can increase my income at once is by entering business. I propose therefore to take advantage of an opening which I declined a few days ago ... I have written to Mr How asking him to find me a lender for the money I require.

Will you give me a lease during your life of the Whitehall
land at the same rent as the present tenant has it on? This
would help me materially as it seems ripe for development as
a building estate. (FL182–3)

The posts were rapid enough to allow Canon Butler a day to wonder
at his son's letter, and still reply on 3 June. What did Samuel suppose
his income to be? He had allowed him £300 – 'a very serious sum'
– out of it, and though he was now compelled to reduce this allowance, he had at least given him fair notice: 'I have never had a sign
of gratitude for all I have done for you and you talk magnificently of
what is due to yourself as if you were treating me with the greatest
generosity in not using hard language. This is simply absurd . . .'
Samuel's proposal was unjust to the present tenants, and besides, he
had no intention of leasing the land to him: the fewer money transactions between them the better. 'I think,' he concluded, 'if you had
an offer of entering business it was your duty to have accepted it
rather than live in idleness on me. I gather you will now do this.'
(FL183–4)

Butler now used the family solicitor as intermediary to enquire
whether he was still welcome at Wilderhope, an overture to which
his father responded:[7] 'I am *quite* willing to see you and should be
glad if you would come down at once and sleep here. I am most
anxious that we should live the little time I have to live on really
amicable terms. There is no reason on my part why it should be
otherwise.' (FL187)

On June 10th, after seeing How, Butler arrived at the house and
after supper a punishing quarrel began. Canon Butler wished to
continue the allowance. Butler replied that he could not agree: he
had been accused of idleness and ingratitude and had made up his
mind the allowance must cease. For between ten and fifteen minutes
each gored the other, until, as Butler bowed and turned at the door,
he said, 'It is not likely that you and I shall meet again.' Canon
Butler replied 'probably not' in a tone which said distinctly 'and so
much the better for me'; and so they parted. Once again, however,
the family solicitor acted as conciliator: Canon Butler would still be
glad to see him. On June 18th tempers had recovered sufficiently
for Butler to write and offer to go to Shrewsbury in the autumn –
'unless I hear you would be glad that I should do so earlier'.

The row has the air of a necessary ritual, a squaring up of two combatants in which each knows how far the other will go. Butler, though not yet free of financial anxiety, felt himself to be finally independent, at the age of forty-five. He managed to overlook, or rationalise, the fact that he had already achieved this independence once, and squandered it through his own imprudence. He never quarrelled seriously with his father again, though he waited with often unconcealed impatience for him to die and complete his release.

CHAPTER 15

Alps and Sanctuaries

Butler, as he tells us in the Introduction to *Alps and Sanctuaries*, chose Italy as his second country, and dedicated his first Italian book to her 'as a thank offering for the happiness she has afforded me'. (AS21)[1] He had been drawn to Italy, to the people, the landscape, the art and the language, since his two boyhood visits; and the student tour he had made with 'Guiseppe Verdi' during the summer vacation of 1857 had ended on the plains of Lombardy. On his return from New Zealand, he had travelled whenever he could to Switzerland and Italy more than to France and Germany, and over the years had come to love, in particular, that area of northern Italy between the lakes and the Alps, and the Italian-speaking cantons of Switzerland.

Places like Faido, in the Val Leventina, Fusio, in the Val Maggi, and Varallo, in the Val Sesia, featured year after year on his itinerary. He looked on the hotel keepers as his intimate friends, he came to know the residents, especially in Varallo, and the Italians and their way of life brought out his innate warmth and generosity, which in England he sometimes concealed. In that same Introduction, Butler prefaces his descriptions of Italy with praise of London: 'I know of nothing in any foreign city equal to the view down Fleet Street, walking along the north side from the corner of Fetter Lane.' Had Dickens written that, the irony of 'Fetter Lane' would have been intentional; but every familiar, homely step of Fetter Lane was sacred territory, even though the butcher was called Darwin and Butler was robbed of his watch in broad daylight. He goes on to invoke Waterloo Bridge, 'and the huge wide-opened jaws of those two Behemoths, the Cannon Street and Charing Cross railway stations', and to wonder whether the prospect may not be even finer than in Fleet Street: 'See how they belch forth puffing trains as the breath of their nostrils, gorging and disgorging incessantly those human atoms whose movement is the life of the city'. (AS19–20) Butler seems half attracted, half repelled, by the idea of the city as a machine, and of the human atoms as parts of it. He needed the contrast between his normal habitat in the smoky, fog-bound, overcrowded streets of London and the calm spaces of Italy.

Foreign travel was Butler's one luxury, a luxury, that is, judged by his own thrifty standards. Even in years of extreme financial constraint, he managed to cross the Channel to Le Havre or Boulogne and spend a few days or weeks in France. But his proper holidays always included a period near the Alps. Train travel was inexpensive, and he stayed in the simplest hotels and inns. He noted, but was not particularly interested in, food and wine. His pleasures were to absorb the art and architecture, and to observe the way of life; to draw and paint; and to be out in the open air, walking in the upland valleys and over the mountain passes, appreciating the landscape, the flowers and wild life, but seldom romanticising it. Predictably, he was not drawn to the spectacular or to the established picturesque: 'As for knowing whether or not one likes a picture . . . I once heard a man say the only test was to ask one's self whether one would care to look at it if one was quite sure that one was alone; I have never been able to get beyond this test with the St Gothard scenery, and applying it to the Devil's Bridge, I should say a stay of about thirty seconds would be enough for me. I daresay Mendelssohn would have stayed at least two hours at the Devil's Bridge, but then he did stay such a long while before things.' (AS23–4) Butler liked nature to be humanised and inhabited, rather than sublime; and if he does not quite reduce Piedmont and the Ticino to the scale of Surrey and Sussex, he had reached an age when he no longer sought the isolation and severe physical challenge of the glaciers and high peaks, as he had in New Zealand.

Over the years he developed different inventories for his various 'outings': 'Boulogne', 'Shrewsbury', or 'Foreign'. This was the final shape of his 'Foreign Outing' list:

Handle Half of Gladstone Bag. – MS. Music Book. Copying paper. Driers. Oil sheets. Spare drawing-paper. Best Coat & Vest. Flannel Shirt. Rulers. Case for paint-brushes and pencils. Japaned Tray. Slippers. Strop. Medicine Chest. Looking-glass. Hat & Clothes-brush. 2 pr. of Socks. 12 Handkfs. W.C. paint-box and bottle. Top of Camp-stool.

The other Half. – best trousers. Collar-box, contg. Collars; Horn Cup; Bootlaces; Ties; Cotton-wool. Towel. *Erewhon* and *E. Revisited.*

Sandwich-box, contg. Menthol; Bread-box; Toothpicks; Scissors; Water-colours; Sponges; India-rubber; Cork of drawing-pins; Sticking-plaster; Elastic bands; Mouthpieces; 2 Note-Books; Studs; Corks; Corkscrew; Spare knife; Stiletto; Paper-fasteners; Waverley pens; Red Chalk; Pencil; Caustic; Compasses; Diarrhoea pills; Magnifying-glass.

Night-shirt. Sponge and case. Hair-brushes. Tooth-brush. Soap. Tooth-powder. Vaseline. Spare specs.

In the Flap. – Lint. Diachylon plasters. Powders. Paint rags. Visiting Cards. Newspaper Wrappers. Curlpapers.

Sling Bag. – A/c Book. Passport. Ticket. Small Sketch-book. Sketching Portfolio charged. Writing Portfolio charged. Paper-knife. Cap. Copying-ink. Telescope.

In Overcoat Pocket. – Cigarettes. Mouthpieces. Gloves.

Roll. – Umbrella. Under Vest. Drawers. Camp tripod. Foreign money. Linen Bag. (M2.472–3)

The inclusion of *Erewhon Revisited* dates this list as 1901 or 1902. Holidays were seldom used for extensive reading, unless he needed to revise or correct proofs for a deadline. The painting kit, and the bits and pieces of the Victorian toilette, did not leave him much room for socks and shirts, but even so, he contrived to take a fair amount of the Clifford's Inn clutter with him. He did not like to change his habits and routines. 'You may also bring a quill toothpick or two from the club,' he suggested to Jones, who was due to join him in Italy, 'you can steal two or three; I have had mine some months now and my teeth pick it as much as it picks my teeth.'[2]

Initially, Butler went on holiday by himself. This helped him to become fluent in Italian, since he was often dependent on the company of the hotel keepers, the waiters, local people and other visitors. 'He finds his words as easily as we do,' an Italian friend informed Jones. (M2.56) After Jones had joined him for that first holiday in 1878, the pattern was repeated year after year, though Butler still normally spent some period on his own. He derived enormous pleasure from showing Jones, or anyone else, the places and buildings he loved; and from this there developed the idea for a book on Italy. David Bogue, the publisher, offered him £100 for an illustrated book, a promise that he rashly boasted about to his father. In the event, Bogue withdrew his offer, and Butler had to publish once more at his own expense. The book's subject matter was, at least, relatively safe, though Canon Butler grumbled that he should have finished it sooner. Butler sent him copies of the illustrations, and there may have been an element of teasing as he related to his Protestant father discussions about the Madonnas, or accounts of a dinner with the Rosinian fathers, the English representatives of the S. Michele sanctuary.

There was another claimant to the origin of *Alps and Sanctuaries*. Miss Savage wrote:

> I admire your coolness in trying to pass off the idea of the Italian Book as your own . . . Why I suggested it to you years ago. It may be a poor thing, but it is *not* your own. I should have written to you *much* sooner, but I have had hard work, writing poetry, and inspiration comes quickly, but the finishing and polishing take long – however, here are the verses, they are for a preface, to your Italian Book – I present them to you.

> When Jones was tired of trampling on his mother
> (Occupation so congenial to a son)
> 'Devolve', I said, 'that duty on another
> Or her lot will be a much too easy one; Easy one.'
> I too am tired, of goading Darwin into madness,
> So we two innocents abroad will gaily go,
> Bribed to intensify the public sadness
> By the writing of a volume for a hundred pounds or so.[3]

> However, seriously, the scheme is a delightful one. We shall have a delightful book, and you will have a nice little sum of money . . .' (S223–4)

In 1901 Butler noted he was still £110 to the bad with the book, and in all those years had only sold 344 copies.

Alps and Sanctuaries of Piedmont and the Canton Ticino was published in November, 1881. It is fully and attractively illustrated; most of the work is Butler's, although Charles Gogin was responsible for the frontispiece and title-page illustrations, as well as two views of Angera, and for adding figures to some of Butler's illustrations. Jones, Gaetano Meo, and (with familiar idiosyncrasy) 'an Italian gentleman whose name I have unfortunately lost', also contributed. In the preface to the first edition, Butler acknowledged 'the great obligations I am under to Mr. H.F. Jones as regards the letterpress no less than the illustrations; I might almost say that the book is nearly as much his as mine . . .' The 'Alps' of the title are not the mountains, but the high pastures grazed for two or three months in summer, while the 'Sanctuaries' are the collections of chapels illustrating aspects of the life of Christ or of some saint which are peculiar to the region, and which had become local places of pilgrimage and celebration for festivals. These are not the exclusive subject matter of this discursive book, but they give it a sense of focus and structure. The one notable, and deliberate, omission is the sanctuary, and Sacro Monte, of Varallo, which Butler reserved for his second Italian book, *Ex Voto*.

Alps and Sanctuaries, Butler's 'opus 6', was largely ignored when it was first published. Once again, Butler wrong-footed his public by producing, after a series of increasingly polemical philosophical works, this easily accessible, warmly appreciative guide to what is still a little known region. It is a travel book; but it belongs within that English tradition in which the personal quirks of the writers, their enthusiasms and prejudices and past experiences, their anecdotes and chance encounters are as integral as the information and description. Butler synthesised the minor events of many holidays into one narrative; and when he found words inadequate, he expressed his sense of the essence of a place or mood by a musical quotation from Handel, or by a sketch.

An unexpected dimension of the book is Butler's sympathy towards the Roman Catholic Church, or, rather, towards the broadmindedness of many of the country priests and the relaxed, cheerful atmosphere of religious observance. He describes the Sacro Monte at Varese as a 'kind of ecclesiastical Rosherville Gardens, eminently the place to spend a happy day'.

We happened by good luck to be there during one of the great *feste* of the year, and saw I am afraid to say how many thousands of pilgrims go up and down. They were admirably behaved, and not one of them tipsy. There was an old English gentleman at the Hotel Riposo who told us that there had been another such *festa* not many weeks previously, and that he had seen one drunken man there – an Englishman – who kept abusing all he saw and crying out, 'Manchester's the place for me.' (The old English gentleman was Edward Lear.)

The processions were best at the last part of the ascent; there were pilgrims, all decked out with coloured feathers, and priests and banners and music and crimson and gold and white and glittering brass against the cloudless blue sky. The old priest sat at his open window to receive the offerings of the devout as they passed; but he did not seem to get more than a few *bambini* modelled in wax. Perhaps he was used to it. And the band played the *barocco* music on the *barocco* little piazza and we were all *barocco* together. It was as though the clergy man at Ladywell had given out that, instead of having service as usual, the congregation would go in procession to the Crystal Palace with all their traps, and that the band had been practising 'Wait till the clouds roll by' for some time, and on Sunday as a great treat they should have it . . .

Then the pilgrims went into the shadow of a great rock behind the sanctuary, spread themselves out over the grass and dined. (AS256–7)

Butler never lost his religious inclination; it was false dogma, as he saw it, and the deadening, joyless imprint of Protestant 'morality' that he detested.

'The Roman Catholic religion', he comments, 'if left to itself and not compelled to be introspective, is more kindly and less given to taking offence than outsiders generally believe. At the Sacro Monte of Varese they sell little round tin boxes that look like medals, and contain pictures of all the chapels. In the lid of the box there is a short printed account of the Sacro Monte, which winds up with the words, "La religione *e lo stupendo panorama* tirano numerosi ed allegri visatori." (Religion and the magnificent panorama attract numerous and merry visitors.)

'Our people are much too earnest to allow that a view could have anything to do with taking people up to the top of a hill where there was a cathedral, or that people could be "merry" while on an errand connected with religion.' (AS125–6)

It was the casual, happy yet reverent approach to religion which appealed to Butler, as depicted in the christening at Fobello, or in this image of the porch of Rossura church:

One lovely summer Sunday morning, passing the church betimes, I saw the people kneeling upon these steps, the church within being crammed. In the darker light of the porch, they told out against the sky that showed through the open arch beyond them; far away the eye rested on the mountains – deep blue save where the snow lingered. I never saw anything more beautiful – and these forsooth are the people whom so many of us think to better by distributing tracts about Protestantism among them! (AS51)

The religious atmosphere, which seemed so natural an element to Butler, forms an important strand within the book. To his surprise, some of the more favourable of the notices of *Alps and Sanctuaries* came in Catholic publications, such as *The Weekly Register* and *The Tablet*. He had, too, on this occasion, suppressed some of his more barbed thrusts, most notably the full line-up of his Seven Humbugs of Christendom: Raffaele, Plato, Marcus Aurelius Antoninus, Dante and Goethe were named, but Beethoven and Christ were referred to simply as 'two others, neither of them Englishmen'. This restraint, however, did not make him any more popular. As usual, most of Butler's readers would be drawn from future generations, though *Alps and Sanctuaries* brought him some unexpected friends, notably Mandell Creighton, Bishop of Peterborough and later of London.

Even as Butler wrote, the St Gothard tunnel and the railway were altering the Valle Leventina 'almost beyond recognition'. That apart, following Butler's tracks today brings a succession of pleasures. The Sacro Monte at Orta remains, as E.M. Forster found it in 1911, 'the scene for a Decameron'.[4] At the Sanctuary of Oropa, the community's rules still match Butler's description, with visitors permitted to stay no less than three and no more than nine days. To reach the

Rossura Church Porch

The Terrace at the Castle of Angera

castle of Angera, one can walk through a vineyard, pass under the old gateway, and find oneself practically alone on the terrace Butler liked so much: 'I know nothing like this terrace. On a summer's afternoon and evening it is fully shaded, the sun being behind the castle. The lake and town below are still in sunlight.' (AS262) He knew of no place so pathetic, and yet so impressive in its decay.

Up in the mountains, the villages remain outwardly little changed. At Fusio in the Val Maggi, the view from the cemetery reveals much the same roof line and cluster of buildings as in Butler's sketch. Above the town, the Sambuco valley has been dammed, and you now have to walk – or drive – some way beyond it to reach one of his ideal places:

An upland valley should first of all be in an Italian-speaking country; then it should have a smooth, grassy, perfectly level floor of say neither much more nor less than a hundred and fifty yards in breadth and half-a-mile in length. A small river should go babbling through it with occasional smooth parts, so as to take the reflections of the surrounding mountains. It should have three or four fine larches or pines scattered about it here and there, but not more. It should be completely land-locked, and there should be nothing in the way of human handiwork save a few chalets, or a small chapel and a bridge, but no tilled land whatever. Here even in summer the evening air will be crisp, and the dew will form as soon as the sun goes off; but the mountains at one end of it will keep the last rays of the sun. It is then the valley is at its best, especially if the goats and cattle are coming together to be milked. (AS281–2)

Considering it 'hopeless' as regards painting, Butler expressed the valley of Sambuco by an extract from a Handel organ concerto. The flowers are still as profuse as Butler recorded: slopes 'gay with tiger and Turk's-cap lilies, and the flaunting arnica, and every flower that likes mountain company'. (AS285) Over the years, Butler explored the three main passes into the Valle Leventina: the Sassello Grande to Airolo, the Alpe di Campolungo to Dalpe, and the longer pass by the Lago di Naret to Bedretto, sending his luggage round by road to Faido. These passes, approaching 8000 feet high, should not, Butler commented, be attempted by strangers without a guide, though presenting not the smallest difficulty. They are rough walking, with steep slopes and marmots whistling at you from the rocks: 'The descent from the top of the pass to Faido is about 5300 feet, while to Fusio it is only 3400. The reader, therefore, will see that he had better go from Fusio to Faido, and not *vice versa*, unless he is a good walker.' (AS286) Butler never lost the stamina acquired in the Southern Alps of New Zealand.

Miss Savage remarked, when she read the manuscript, that she liked the scenery descriptions – 'just what they ought to be, not elaborate but complete – a delightful contrast to the interminable "word pictures", that have been the fashion lately'. (S254) Butler, the most puncturing critic of inflated writing, did in places allow himself more freedom to soar than in any other of his books until *Erewhon Revisited*. In his chapter on Piora, for example, he recounts his apocalyptic dream, which takes its place in the book as the expression of the heightened emotions that the landscape, above all the peopled landscape, aroused in him. He walked up the valley in the moonlight, and came upon a man in a cave before a furnace, burning lime; he was a quiet, moody man, polite but not communicat-

Fusio from the cemetery

ive. Moving on and upwards, he found himself on the Lago di Cadagno: 'Here I heard that there were people, and the people were not so much asleep as the simple peasantry of these upland valleys are expected to be by nine o'clock in the evening.' These were the young people who moved up to the chalets for two or three weeks to cut the hay; and the pagan nature of their celebration is hinted at by Butler. Reflecting on this dream of youth, he found himself slipping off into a doze, and imagined that the lime-burner came and laid his hand upon his shoulder: the green slopes were suddenly much higher, and, recalling the scale of the Southern Alps, he saw two glaciers that 'came down in streams that ended in a precipice of ice, falling sheer into the lake'. The edges of the mountains 'were rugged and full of clefts, through which I saw thick clouds of dust being blown by the wind as though from the other side of the mountains'. The dust became crowds of people, the amphitheatre a huge orchestra, the glaciers two armies of women singers:

When I turned my telescope upon them I saw they were

The Chapel of S. Carlo, Piora

crowded up to the extreme edge of the mountains, so that I could see underneath the soles of their boots as their legs dangled in the air. In the midst of all, a precipice that rose from out of the glaciers shaped itself suddenly into an organ, and there was one whose face I well knew sitting at the keyboard, smiling and pluming himself like a bird as he thundered forth a giant fugue by way of overture. I heard the great pedal notes in the bass stalk majestically up and down, like the rays of the aurora that go about upon the face of the heavens off the coast of Labrador. Then presently the people rose and sang the chorus 'Venus laughing from the skies'; but ere the sound had well died away, I awoke, and all was changed; a light fleecy cloud had filled the whole basin, but I still thought I heard a sound of music, and a scampering-off of great crowds from the part where the precipices should be.

The Handelian vision of heaven faded; the voices of the young haymakers singing in the chalets died away; as Butler neared his hotel, he passed 'the man at the mouth of the furnace with the moon still gleaming upon his back, and the fire upon his face, and he was very grave and quiet'. (AS80–5) The chapter, too, dissolves into a laconic series of facts and figures. These dream-like glimpses of the inner world, echoing the vision in *Erewhon*, recall passages in Stevenson's *Travels with a Donkey*; Stevenson's experience in the Trappist monastery of Our Lady of the Snows,[5] however, suggests a tension with the culture and religion he is describing that is absent from *Alps and Sanctuaries*. Stevenson, too, writes more consciously about his own feelings and concerns. Butler tries to re-create the life around him, but is always aware that he cannot properly become part of it, except in his imagination; so that his descriptions, his sketches, even his visions are infused with a sense of the temporary and the partial, and in places the absurd, like being able to see underneath the soles of the chorus-singers' boots as their legs dangled in the air. His sense of the ridiculous and grasp of reality keep his flights of imagination in check. Though he praises the landscape, he notes the privations of the climate and the way of life, nowhere more vividly than in the chapter Jones later compiled from Butler's notes, 'Fusio Revisited'.

In this chapter, as the tourists walk with their guide over the Sassello Grande, they meet a peasant woman and her daughter, climbing 4000 feet in the wind and rain without shoes and stockings, carrying two hundred eggs and a few fowls to Airolo to earn an additional twenty francs. Butler notes the dreadful living conditions in the damp summer huts. He says that for picturesqueness, he knows no subalpine village so good; but reports that few of the houses are 'even tolerably wholesome', and wonders what it must be like to live there after the middle of October.

> How chill and damp, with reeking clouds that search into every corner. What, again, must it be a little later, when snow has fallen that lies till the middle of May? The men go about all day in great boots, working in the snow at whatever they can find to do; they come in at night tired and with their legs and feet half frozen. The main room of the house may have a *stufa* in it, but how about the bedrooms? With single windows and the thermometer outside down to zero, if the room is warm enough to thaw and keep things damp it is as much as can be

expected. Fancy an elderly man after a day's work in snow climbing up, like David, step by step to a bed in such a room as this. (AS299)

Sympathising with the poor, Butler characteristically blames the Church for the missed opportunity: 'If the Church would only use her means and leisure to teach people how to make themselves as healthy and happy in this life as their case admits!' For to Butler all the people in Fusio were good. He once asked his guide, Gugliel-moni, what happened when anyone did something wrong. 'He seemed bewildered. The case had not arisen within his recollection.' (AS292-3)

These valleys were the places where Butler approached nearest to happiness. He was able to shed his English cultivation and education and see the landscape, the art and the people with freshness and simplicity. He and Jones could enact, temporarily, the role of inno-cents abroad in Piedmont and the Ticino. Each year he returned home with a note of melancholy, carrying with him seeds of the Fusio tiger-lily to scatter in Epping Forest: 'We looked at nothing between the top of the St Gothard Pass and Boulogne, nor did we again begin to take any interest in life till we saw the science-ridden, art-ridden, culture-ridden, afternoon-tea-ridden cliffs of old England rise upon the horizon.' (AS303-4)

CHAPTER 16

Deaths and Inheritance

Lacking the stimulus of a single book after *Alps and Sanctuaries*, Butler plunged into a range of projects. In 1882 he wrote an extra chapter for the second edition of *Evolution Old and New*; he edited a volume of selections from his previous works; and he continued compiling his notebooks. He also settled down once more to revise and refine his novel, a job that always both vitalised and disturbed him. The business offer he had mentioned to his father was put into action: with borrowed money, he began to buy cheap leasehold houses for renting, employing Reginald Worsley as consultant architect and Jones as his lawyer.

One way or another Jones took up a great deal of Butler's time and attention in these years. Miss Savage was particularly conscious of the change. 'You know I don't *always* write to Mr Jones', she added to one letter, on which Butler noted, 'I suppose I must have told her that Jones always enjoyed her letters.' (S, 246) In November 1881 Butler was laid up with a cracked rib, and Jones had scarlet fever. Butler's accident was of the banana-skin variety, the kind of incident he might have invented (and which, in a sense, he did). It happened on a Sunday walk between Long Reach Tavern and Northfleet: 'I had a small bottle (a homoeopathic round bottle) of Worcestershire Sauce in my pocket to eat with my lunch which I had in my pocket with me. Getting over a stile on a wet slippery day & with an umbrella in my hand I slipped & fell with all my weight on the top rail but so that all the weight bore on the homeopathic bottle; this did not break the bottle but it cracked the rib.'[1] In spite of his injury, Butler sat up with Jones on several nights. 'I am very much afraid you will knock yourself up with your attendance on Mr Jones,' remonstrated Miss Savage. 'Please write to me very soon to tell me how you are, as I shall be very anxious about you. Poor Mr Jones I am very sorry for him too, but please do take care of yourself, and if you sit up at night, be sure you rest by day. I dare say you won't though, broken rib or not.' She returned to the theme at some length and concluded astringently: 'Nature abhors an impatient . . . Perhaps by the time I come you will have got some peacock's feathers, and a lily. I should think a cracked rib would be favourable to aesthetic attitudes.' (S244–6)

In the last three years of her correspondence with Butler there are longer gaps between letters, and a higher proportion of neutral subjects. Miss Savage's tone is more even, cool and taut, although there are coded messages in many of the exchanges, private jokes and shared confessions. Her deliberately conventional enquiries – 'This mild weather must be favourable to your father, is it not?' – clearly indicate Butler's covert wish for his father's death. They enquired after the health of each other's cats with affection, avoiding more personal matters.

Butler liked cats. The health and habits of Madame's two, Marquise and Victor, were faithfully chronicled. When his beloved cat finally disappeared, he replaced it with one he found abandoned inside the railings of Clifford's Inn, where people came to 'lose' their animals. 'I have already selected a dirty little drunken wretch of a kitten to be successor to my poor old cat,' he informed May, parodying her children's home. 'I don't suppose it drinks anything stronger than milk & water but then you know so much milk & water must be very bad for a kitten that age – at any rate it looks as if it drank . . . I believe if it had a home it wd become more respectable, at any rate I will see how it works.' He had already presented Miss Savage with another stray kitten. She called it Purdoe, after the original pseudonymous author of *The Fair Haven*, Richard Purdoe Davies; she told Butler she had baptised it with ink.

Butler, editing the letters in 1901, defends himself repeatedly for his neglect:

The only excuse I can make for myself for neglecting Miss Savage so long, is that she very well knew she had only got to whip me up with a scrap of any kind, when she thought I had been too long without writing, and also that if I answered her letters at once I should be written to again immediately; and these years from 1881 till the death of my father, were the most harassing and arduous of my whole life. I cannot unfold the tale here, but I was in a very bad way as regards Pauli, my houses, the failure of my books, and my relations with my people. I often wonder how I got through it all as well as I did. Moreover, I had not the faintest idea that Miss Savage was stricken with mortal disease, as by this time she certainly must have been. (S281)

The one role in which she was wholly secure was as Butler's editor. He had returned to *The Way of All Flesh* in the spring of 1882, and submitted his revisions to her: 'Thank you very much for sending the last part. The bit about the smoking and St Paul and the cup of tea is lovely, and there are many other bits in it equally delightful. I give in to the aunt, almost, and if I read it over a third time I should accept her altogether. The last part is rather *risqué*, is it not?' (S276) In July, 1883 he used the novel as a peace offering, one which he knew she would accept. He was rewriting the greater part of the third volume, having completed the first and second and shown them to Richard Garnett at the British Museum. Working on the material stirred too many ghosts, and his head throbbed dangerously. 'I am afraid you are not well or rather very ill yourself. I growl and complain about nothing. You have ten times as much to growl about, but don't complain as I do.' As a substitute for meeting her, he paid Miss Savage the private compliment of giving one more of her sayings to Alethea: 'Instead of making Miss Pontifex say that Ernest's father and mother would make him put a pinch of salt on the tails of all the cardinal virtues I have said "of the seven deadly virtues".' (S289–90)

Miss Savage, the perfect reader – 'WHEN AM I TO HAVE SOME MORE?' – was the best sort of critic, able to be truthful because she had convinced Butler of her belief in him and in the novel:

Your Townley, too, must be toned down. A coarse creature with vicious propensities which he indulges in a slum such as you describe, Ashpit Place! You see I am in a dreadful temper, so I may as well tell you that Ernest gets *tant soit peu* priggish – in fact very much so towards the end, and especially in the treatment of his children which is ultra-priggish. There is no end of delightful little bits, but you must not convey the idea that Ernest is only a peg on which to hang your theories and fancies. In his marrying and unmarrying he is perfectly natural and life-like, and now, my spleen being over, I have nothing more to say at present, except that I greatly enjoyed my first reading, and am going to read it again for greater pleasure. It is a very great treat to have it to read, and I quite forgive you for keeping me awake till 4.45 a.m. (S301–2)

The manuscript passed backwards and forwards between Clifford's Inn and Miss Savage's home in Marylebone. The man in charge of the umbrellas at the British Museum Reading Room acted as *poste restante*. 'I always leave my things there in preference to mounting up to the ladies' room,' Miss Savage informed Butler. 'A lady I knew was quite shocked when she saw me one day getting my umbrella there, and said the authorities would not like my doing so. I told her that although no doubt the indiscriminate association of male and female umbrellas might in a general way be productive of evil, yet my umbrella having become imbued with my personal qualities, she might be trusted to conduct herself with the most perfect propriety. At all events I should wait for the authorities or the male umbrellas to complain before altering my ways. Perhaps if they hear of my basket eloping with your MS. I may receive a reprimand, but I do not think it likely.' (S300)

Though lying dormant for almost twenty more years, the novel was practically complete. Constantly intending to revise it, Butler always found some other more pressing task. The story has the deceptive simplicity of domestic melodrama, or, perhaps, of a subtle parody. Ernest, destined for the Church, suffers a moral fall and is imprisoned for indecent assault. This proves his salvation but he is rescued through a combination of luck and cunning rather than by repentance. He marries Ellen, his parents' disgraced kitchen maid, has two children, absorbs the economic facts of life running a second-hand clothes shop in the backstreets of London, and learns that Ellen is an alcoholic. Then his luck changes. Ellen, he discovers, is already married, which releases him from his obligations. The children are entrusted to a jolly bargee family, to be brought up in the fresh air untainted by middle-class humbug; and Ernest comes into a fat legacy from his Aunt Alethea, delightfully increased by prudent investment. He ends up as an idealised Butler, living in bachelor rooms and writing books 'in which he insisted on saying things which no one else would say even if they could, or even if they would'.

Parallel to the autobiographical framework, the book illustrates Butler's theory of evolution. Ernest is an example of the power of the unconscious, half-suppressed memories urging him towards the light of a new life. Yet even while the narrative expresses optimism, the blatant, mechanical contrivances of the plot mock the conclusion, so that the novel leaves a bitter taste, partly because of a cruel element in the dissection of the first, rejected life, and partly because of the hollow nature of the 'comic' rebirth. Butler was one of the first Victorian novelists to embrace the negative, and exploited his awareness that nothing is funnier than unhappiness.

Miss Savage, though conceivably hurt by Butler (yet probably not sexually rejected in the way he imagined), remained the truest of friends. She understood his temperament, and the way his mind worked, and the early volumes of *The Way of All Flesh* are a testament to her perception. After she returned the revised manuscript in January, 1884, Butler scarcely looked at it again. There was always another more pressing matter. Writing to her from Shrewsbury, where his father was gravely ill, he commented sardonically: 'If you don't hear again soon please conclude that my father is making all the progress his many well wishers can desire. I won't wish you a Merry Xmas and a Happy New Year because then perhaps you may get a better one than you would do if I were to wish you one, but I will go as near to wishing it as I think prudent on your behalf.' (S315–16)

Butler's qualified wish was distressingly accurate. Canon Butler recovered; without telling Butler, Miss Savage became increasingly ill. During 1884 the letters are more perfunctory, the rare visits even more infrequent. 'I have been ill,' she wrote more objectively than usual in October, 1884; 'I was ill when I went to see you, and I am ill still.' Her self-mockery quickly reasserts itself: 'I have had a bad attack of influenza; I am told, however, that I could not have had influenza, as no other cases have occurred. I can only say if it is so the whole epidemic must have concentrated itself in me, and I wish it would go and attack a great many other people.' She had less opportunity to help Butler with his work, although she went to hear Romanes lecture, and reported back, and sent Butler notes about Diderot and his theories on evolution. But Butler was occupied with

Jones on their cantata, *Narcissus*. She then offered a different kind of present:

'I have lately developed an extraordinary talent for knitting stockings, and was so enchanted with the first *one* I made, that I immediately began to wear it, regardless of the fact that it was of a lightish blue colour while the other was black. You should be thankful that I have not required you to do likewise. I can knit much better now, and I mean *always* to make your stockings for the future.' If they did not fit, she suggested he might give them to Jones with her kind regards, or even to his father. 'You can tell him (your father) that they are a tribute of respect from an admirer of your literary genius – which is exactly the truth. Popular authors, curates, etc., are always receiving little attentions. I am told that Mr Irving is deluged with knitted knee caps from his female adorers – it being only too evident which of his articulations stands specially in need of comfort. You will be pleased to hear that the socks were made entirely on the Sabbath. Sunday afternoons I retired in my closet, and shut the door (as we are told to do in the Bible) and knitted. So that they represent a religious service, and are sanctified. I think you had better let me have an old sock that fits you, as a pattern to do the next by.' (S335–7)

Butler was tested severely by the socks. He sent a short preliminary note of thanks, while he searched for words adequate 'to express my gratitude'. By the evening post, he had recovered his aplomb. After thanking her, he added: 'As for doing me any more, I flatly forbid it; I believe you don't like my books, and want to make me say I won't give you any more if you make me any more socks, and then you will make me some more, in order not to get the books. No, I will let you read my stupid books in MS. and help me that way. If you like to make me a kettle holder you may, for I have only one just now, and I like to have two because I always mislay one, but I won't have people working their fingers out to make me stockings.' (S337–8) Back came the kettleholder: 'I can only say that a man who is equal to the control of two kettleholders fills me with awe ...' (S339) Butler, uncertain of his role in this elaborate game, decided that the kettleholder was a hoax, and suggested that Miss Savage had bought it at a bazaar: 'and that little touch about the affixing a fetter to it is just like one of my own lies ...' He covered himself with a postscript: 'If you did knit that kettleholder I shall think you even cleverer than I did before. If you did not knit it, I shall think you are just as clever as I have always thought you.' (S341–2).

Miss Savage had outwitted him. 'No doubt your powers of lying are great, but when you assert that my TRUTH is like your lies, you considerably overestimate their value and some day you will get into a scrape from your over-confidence.' (S342) The kettle holder tease ran on, and the kettleholder still hung on its fetter by the fire, when the last postcard she wrote to Butler arrived: 'I am *not* vindictive, but I wish you to know that I have made 12 Xtian kettleholders to be cast loose on society like the 12 apostles.' (S352) Butler's last letter to her – he had no idea she was ill, let alone how ill – was full of death: he told her of the deaths of his brother Tom, and of his friend Mr Tylor, and of his father's delicate state: 'I don't write on black-edged paper because you would think I had become an orphan – but next time I write you will know, so I shall use black-edged paper.' (S353) On February 19th, 1885, Butler heard from a friend of Miss Savage that she had undergone a painful operation. On 22 February she died. He felt it so deeply that he even unburdened himself to Harriet Bridges, the sister with whom he had perhaps least in common of all the members of his family:

> I received such a shock last night that I hardly know how to write. I have lost my friend Miss Savage whom you have often heard me speak of, and no words of mine can express how great this loss is . . .
>
> When I first came to know her, nearly twenty years ago, she was lame and suffering from what I supposed to be hip-disease; the lameness constantly increased and of late I had seen that she walked with great difficulty. I have no doubt that the operation was in connection with this. I never knew any woman to approach her at once for brilliancy and goodness. She was the most heroically uncomplaining sufferer I ever met, and the most unselfish. It is not that I saw much of her – this I did not – but we were in constant communication and, happily, for the last ten years I have preserved everything that she wrote – and she wrote nothing that was not worth preserving. It is out of the question that I can ever replace her. I have it in my power, and am thankful to think of this, to leave a memorial of her, traced chiefly by her own hand, which will show what manner of

woman she was; but it is one which cannot possibly be made public till I have long followed her.

I had rather that you none of you alluded to this letter. When I come down next I shall probably speak of her, if I do so at all, much as I have always done. But you none of you probably had any idea, and indeed cannot possibly have had any idea, how much I valued her. For the moment I am incapable of thinking of any other subject. (FL258–9)

Butler went uninvited to the funeral on Saturday, February 28th, 1885. It was a lovely soft spring afternoon, he recalled; during the whole time of the funeral birds were singing, and the sun was shining: 'As for me I felt that I was attending the funeral of incomparably the best and most brilliant woman that I had ever known.' Miss Savage haunted Butler: because she had been a better and kinder friend to him than he to her; because of his neglect and impatience; because of her goodness and brilliance, oppressive though he found the latter; because he thought that he would have been doing what she wanted by offering to marry her. 'I should have married her in cold blood, not because I wanted to marry her, but because she wanted me to marry her.' (S362–4)

The least he could do now was to construct a memorial, by collecting and editing her letters. When he eventually came to do this, at the very end of his life, he suffered further remorse, and continually redefined his feelings: 'It may almost appear as though I had been in love with her, but I never was and never pretended to be. I valued her, but she perfectly understood that I could do no more. I can never think of her without pain.' (M1.443) As a more immediate memorial, Butler wished to associate her name with the album of musical pieces which was on the point of being published. As nothing of his had the appropriate feeling of sadness, Jones's 'miserable fugue' in C was chosen to be prefaced 'In Memoriam E.M.A.S.' Butler, for once, seems unaware of the irony.

He spent much more time at Shrewsbury during the last five years of his father's life. The disentailing of the Whitehall estate, and the consequent easing of his financial predicament, removed the major cause of open conflict. A state of undeclared truce was reached; and the letters between them became more equable, with only occasional outbreaks of impatience and asperity. Butler was deft at conjuring up uncontroversial topics, and there are signs of reconciliation in the enquiries and responses about family history, or (a guaranteed peace offering) Canon Butler's brushes with the Darwins. Butler would usually take the initiative in their correspondence: he would ask after the health of everyone in the house, chart his travels or his literary and musical progress, fill out his pages with anecdotes of cats or owls or parrots, or send a specimen of woodsia or some seeds of everlasting.

His father's memories of Darwin were especially pleasing to Butler:

> I spent a summer at Barmouth with him on a reading party before taking my degree and walked over all the neighbourhood with him and others, diversifying the way in catching moths, butterflies and beetles. I remember his killing the two largest vipers I ever saw. They were the length of my walking stick. But we saw little of him except on these expeditions and he and I were not very thick.
>
> Lady Powis was staying at Barmouth and used to ask me to dinner every now and then and the Darwins hated that kith and kin because Lord Powis was almost the only great man of the neighborhood who employed Du Gard, so Darwin used to jeer me about going to Lady Powis, and I took offence not seeing why I should not go when she made her little dinners pleasant. I never saw him again after that summer till he came back wasted to a shadow on his return from the Beagle expedition, when I travelled with him and Southey in a stage coach from Birmingham to Shrewsbury . . . (FL208–9)

'It is curious that he should have trodden upon your toes as well as mine,' replied Butler. 'I knew he did not like my grandfather for I heard him and his brother Erasmus talking about Shrewsbury and my grandfather. Erasmus evidently liked both well enough. Charles was frigid and said as much against these as he decently could, considering that I was present and joining in the discussion. I had no idea, however, that there had been any little passage of arms between yourself and him.' (FL209–10)

Dislike of a mutual foe brought some measure of understanding. Interest in Dr Butler provided further common ground. In May,

1883 Butler read some of his grandfather's journal, relating to an Italian tour in 1822. Dr Butler was delayed when about to embark at Lerici, and thus saved, accidentally or providentially, from sailing into a hurricane. Butler wondered whether this was the same storm in which Shelley drowned, and puzzled out the dates with the help of an almanac at the British Museum.

There is a gentler tone to the letters of these last years. On his father's seventy-eighth birthday he wrote to wish him many happy returns:

> I met a man who has taken a house in Salisbury Close, and noticed on quiet nights a curious kind of sighing sound come from the tops of some tall elm trees in the close. He often noticed it and could not make it out till one night he spoke about it to the close porter and asked him what it was. 'Oh Sir' was the answer – 'that's the rooks snoring' – and it was so. (No doubt it was owls really.) P.S. It will be 40 years tomorrow since we all went up to the top of St Peter's at Rome, except my mother whom we saw from the gallery inside the church standing under the dome. (FL226)

His father replied:

> Your rooks amused me . . . but I have heard owls do the same thing in the day time. My father kept a pair when he was a boy. When they had had their meat breakfast they retired into an old barrel at the back of their cage and slept to digest it. (FL227)

These shared memories created an appearance of affection. Butler's visits home, though brief, were regular; and he was quick to take the train to Shrewsbury whenever his father's health gave cause for serious concern. If the family letters from these years alone survived, he would seem the model of a dutiful son.

The death of Tom, too, brought the rest of the family together, as though the ill will and shame had been exorcised. Tom had travelled to Corsica in the summer of 1884, and was not heard from again: at least, no request came to his brother for payment of his dividends (Butler was a trustee of Tom's marriage settlement). Speculation, tempered with discretion, rose: Henrietta divulged that

Tom had been given a maximum of seven years to live by a doctor who had diagnosed venereal disease. Jeffes, the consul in Brussels, reported that Tom was 'on a botanical mission'; but this information was swiftly seconded by a message from the acting British Consul in Ajaccio to say that Tom had died on November 30th. There were three books in his possession: a bible, a botany book, and a copy of *Erewhon*. Canon Butler found it an 'inexpressible comfort that he should have wished reconciliation with his family and have desired all his Corsican collection of plants' should be sent to him: 'This touches me much because I always thought that his cruelty in leaving his family penniless was chiefly aimed not at them but at me.' (FL257) This was probably true. As with Samuel, so with Tom, emotions between father and son were negotiated in financial terms. Samuel was not impressed: 'As for Tom's being softened etc.,' he wrote to Henrietta, 'I don't believe a word of it.'[2]

Writing appropriate letters was relatively simple for Butler; but he felt the strain of keeping up appearances during his visits to Shrewsbury. His 'storm signals' – the cyst at the back of his neck, and the noises in his head when he lay down to sleep – grew worse under the régime at Wilderhope House. Sleeping under the same roof as his two sisters – in the winter of 1883 Harriet moved from Ventnor to join her father and sister – was a double imposition. Butler was telegraphed for on December 6th, 1883, and arrived to find his father desperately ill with bronchitis. 'I have been caged here a fortnight with Charlotte,' he confided to Miss Savage ('Charlotte' was Ernest's sister in *The Way of All Flesh*, an 'amalgamation' of May and Harriet), 'or rather two Charlottes, and I am sure I must have an angelic temper to have avoided a row. Every time my father has rallied they have flown at me. Every time he has sunk they have toadied.' (S314)

Butler fought his father openly, on equal terms. His quarrels with May and Harriet, highly charged, were more suppressed and pettier in substance. He never forgave May for suddenly pressing the tumour on his neck to see if it was cancerous, or Harriet for her silent accusation that he had misappropriated £5 from a cheque he had cashed for his father. He despised them, mocking their values and expressions with his friends, and battle was done over the breakfast table and through the minutiae of daily life. They persistently called his painting 'drawing'. 'If I say I am painting such and such a picture they reply that they are glad I am "getting on with my drawing" . . . it is intended as a way of cheapening what I am doing.' If he played anything to Harriet on the piano, she would say, ' "Oh yes, yes, I can see that would be very nice" – meaning of course, "if it was properly played, but you play it so damned badly that I can only see it would be very nice." ' (N244) When he stayed at Wilderhope House, Harriet and May always forgot that he took tea, not coffee, for breakfast, and banished him to the top bedroom if he wanted to smoke a cigarette.

Once he had inherited, Butler was quicker to see the comical side of these manoeuvrings. With his father still living, he feared his sisters' influence. 'As for May,' he had written to Tom's wife, 'I can hardly say how much I distrust her and dislike her. I cannot go down to Wilderhope much. For years past they have never once asked me to come, or said when I went away that they had been glad to see me, and hoped I would come again as soon as I could. I have always had to write and say I should be glad to come: then I am allowed to do so – in the coldest terms that can be used with decency, and am let to go again without, as I said, any of those little civilities which people expect, even though they know they do not mean much.' May, he complained, did her best to keep him and his father apart, and if he was not anxious to avoid giving him cause for complaint he would not go near him. 'If I were to do this I should be accused of having cut my family, and perhaps have it said that my family had cut me. I believe May would like this very well, and for this reason if no other think it better not to notice things that of course I see and am hurt by. For the present I agree with you and avoid a rupture by all means in my power, but if I survive my father times will change. Harrie is *very* disagreeable; I dislike her very much, but I do not distrust her as I do May.'

It was a relief, he admitted, to 'blow off steam' by writing in this way, adding, with some insight, 'May has become a kind of stepmother to me and I dislike her for doing it.' (FL210–12) The unspoken, and unspeakable, question of inheritance lay uppermost in Butler's mind. Once it was settled, relations improved.

Parallel to the family skirmishes ran a dark narrative about them constructed for Jones's benefit. Butler's friendship with Jones was at its most intense during the 1880s, when they began to spend so much time together, drawn into even closer contact by their musical collaboration; and Butler depended especially heavily on Jones in the months after Miss Savage's death. Butler, so reserved and controlled in most of his letters, would thank Jones for his 'carissima lettera', and allow himself to say, from his solitary holiday, 'I miss you very much'. Jones in his turn had confessed, when on holiday alone in Switzerland and Italy in 1883 (this was the year when Butler's finances would stretch no further than Normandy), 'I miss you dreadfully partly because I don't see you every day and partly because I have not got you to talk to and I am accustomed to do both.'³ Butler, like an over-anxious parent or fussy husband, smothered him with advice: 'Be very careful what you do at Venice. It is a dangerous place and whatever you do leave valuables behind you all except 5 Francs.'⁴

Jones became a close ally and confidant in Butler's dealings with his family. With Gogin and Worsley, he formed an audience for choice anecdotes about the latest outrage, responding dutifully: 'I am so sorry for you. Your people are beasts. I am glad you had no row with them.'⁵ Such sympathy was to be expected, when they shared so much, but Jones, encouraged by Butler to dislike and challenge his own mother, outdid his mentor in constructing fantasies about parricide. In a letter of September 4th, 1885 he wrote: 'I should like to mix some people's salad for them and use . . .' The next two lines have been heavily overscored by Butler with a liberal application of Milton's *Paradise Lost*. Butler admitted a liking for the 'disgusting salad' and added: 'By the way – may I say somewhere "It is not 'whom the Gods love that die young', but the papas and mammas of those whom the gods love who die reasonably early." '⁶

Wishing people dead, common enough as a passing thought, is not often elevated into a running motif. Writing to Jones on September 28th, 1885, Butler quoted a letter from May: 'This will show you that he is well.' Jones's response does not need much decoding: 'We were afraid the account would be about what it was but I am sorry it was not more satisfactory. I hope you have found something at Clifford's Inn more hopeful.'⁷ Throughout 1886, the bulletins echo the same theme: 'I am sorry there was no news from Shrewsbury'; 'The weather is more like July than October and as long as it lasts there will be no news.' The subtext became increasingly macabre. Jones enquired from Baden-Baden as to how Victor, Madame's cat, met his end. Jones had imitated Butler's way of life to the extent of visiting Madame on a regular basis, Tuesday to

Butler's Wednesday. It seems as if Butler paid. When they were both abroad, his servant, Alfred, paid her: 'I took her out once or twice myself,' he told Muggeridge. By this time, Madame knew Butler's name and address, wrote him letters, and came occasionally to tea. Had Victor been despatched, like his predecessor, with a hammer? Butler could report that Victor had died of his own accord, supposed by Madame to have eaten poisoned flies. Two days later he informed Jones: 'Papa got wet through about a week ago & it has not given him cold – It shows he is taking as many liberties as ever & that is a good thing.'[8]

One diversion from his obsession during 1886 was Butler's candidature for the Slade Professorship of Fine Art at Cambridge, vacant on the resignation of Sidney Colvin. This was not such a bizarre initiative as it might at first appear – certainly, it seemed entirely logical to Butler, who was a practising artist as well as a critic, even if the majority of his copious notes in art criticism had not been published. Apart from his continuing researches based on Varallo, he had been pursuing two pet theories, one about a Holbein watercolour at Basel, and another about the attribution and subject matter of a painting at the Louvre, 'Portraits d'hommes', attributed to Cariani, which he argued was a portrait of Giovanni and Gentile Bellini by the latter. 'The post would exactly suit me,' he told his father, 'as residence is not required and 12 lectures a year is all that I should have to give. I don't see why I should not try for this – so I went down yesterday and interviewed Kennedy and one or two more.' (FL264–5) The pay was £360 a year. Butler busied himself collecting testimonials, including one from Kennedy, others from Garnett and Fortescue (of the British Museum), Marriott, Heatherley, and a number of artists. 'Considering my age, connection with Cambridge, and literary and artistic record, I think I have as good a claim as any of the men (none over 35) who are in, but I don't think I shall get it.' (FL271) His fellow candidates were Harry Quilter, the art critic for *The Times* and *The Spectator*, and J.H. Middleton, whose book *Ancient Rome* had been published in 1885. He was neither surprised nor especially disappointed when Middleton, later to become director of the Fitzwilliam and the South Kensington Museums, was elected. He concentrated his energies on his cantata, *Narcissus*, and on the preparation of his fourth evolution book, *Luck or Cunning?*, which was published at the end of the year.

Canon Butler's eightieth birthday was November 28th, 1886. The next day he had two severe falls, and Butler went down to Shrewsbury early in December. He planned to put up at the George, but was persuaded by his sisters to stay in the house. He returned to London after a while; but his father remained 'penned up' in his bedroom, and Harriet and May caught colds, so Butler's niece Maysie, one of Tom and Henrietta's children, was sent for to nurse and entertain. She wrote to her uncle Sam:

> Grandpapa is waiting for me to play backgammon with him so I have not time to write much. He is really improving slowly and the arm is decidedly better, but he is quite an invalid and sits in the armchair all day, he only walks from his room to aunt Mays while his is being done. Both the aunts are kept in bed with bad colds. I suppose you have seen my reports home which give a full account and there is no change to speak of. (FL285)

Butler, delighted to have an ally in the house, wanted Maysie to report on the Wilderhope reaction to a review of *Luck or Cunning?*

> I must compliment you upon your literary style. It is very good. Do you think you could manage to give a few lessons in the art of letter writing? because I think there must be some people in Shrewsbury who – well, say even in Bellevue as well – I wish your aunts would write a quarter as well – and you have not said one word about chrysanthemums – but have just told us what we wanted to know, and the finest letter writer that ever lived can do no more than this. I am sorry my father does not gain faster, but let us hope he will pick up now that his arm has left off troubling him, and on the whole he seems going on satisfactorily.
>
> Maysie – please see how my father and your aunts take the review of my book in the *Academy* and *do* tell me what they say – I mean what your aunts say. If you will do this I will tell you anything that I know.
>
> It occurs to me that perhaps you will be kind enough not to let this letter lie about. (FL286)

Maysie was fond of her grandfather, and played backgammon, or read to him. She was a resilient girl, in a house full of bottles, screens, champagne for the invalids, and daily visits from the doctors; she had to rely on Rogers, Canon Butler's manservant, until a nurse was found. The aunts could do little to help: 'Aunt May is rather bad with congestion of the left lung and is being poulticed. Aunt Harrie is also in bed with a cold so "we are a merry family" '. (FL286–7) She did her best for her uncle. 'I have been trying to pump the aunts about what they think of the review of Uncle Sam's book in the Academy,' she wrote to her mother, 'but they are so exceedingly cautious that all they will say is "In spite of the hard hits that review will get his book read." I suppose they are afraid he will question me when I get back to London.'9

On Christmas Eve Butler went down to Shrewsbury with Reginald Worsley, then travelled on to Church Stretton, and walked over the Long Mynd. A telegram summoned him to Wilderhope House. His father was nearing his end. He would say 'Amen' to the vicar's prayers, and told the nurse, 'No, I know I'm gradually dying,' but was scarcely conscious of who was in the room with him. He died about half past five in the evening of December 29th. 'I and Rogers and the nurse were alone present,' wrote Butler. 'I was supporting his head between my hands as he died – which he did almost without any kind of fight with death – but Rogers told me that shortly before I was called into the room, he had fought hard for life. He never knew me since I saw him early in December. Nor did he know anyone. Once my cousin, Archdeacon Lloyd, began in a loud pro-fessional tone to repeat some prayers for the dying. On this my father for a few seconds, not more, opened his eyes and obviously regained consciousness; but as he did so there came an expression over his face as though he were saying to himself – "oh, no, it is not the day of judgement, it is only that old fool archdeacon Lloyd," and he became comatose again.' (FL287–8)

Butler's letters to Jones contain no hint of emotion; he could only express one part of his reactions to him. His thoughts ran on property. He had already shown Worsley the Whitehall land, and found him 'a good deal impressed with it'. Much to his annoyance, he discovered that although he had not been named as an executor, that 'old fool', Tom Lloyd, had. He considered this 'more or less of a slur', but resolved not to show signs of thinking so. Jones, who, with candour, sent no condolences about the death, agreed that it was a slur, 'but it won't matter if you have enough & it will save you a lot of trouble and bother'.[11]

Canon Butler was buried in Shrewsbury cemetery on January 3rd, 1887. Harriet and May made the arrangements for the gravestone and inscription; they never asked Samuel for his opinion, and he never went to see what had been put. He wrote the obituaries for the Shrewsbury newspapers; and there were mentions in *The Times* and other newspapers. 'It was nowhere said that he was father of the present writer, and this shewed me (but I wanted no shewing) how very little my books were known. I said laughingly to Dr Burd that I considered one of the greatest feathers in my father's cap to have been that he was father to myself. Dr Burd did not like this and said very drily that he had never looked at the matter in this light.' (FL288) Butler had been writing his own private obituaries in his notebooks. His father was his 'most implacable enemy'.

He never liked me, nor I him: from my earliest recollections I can call to mind no time when I did not fear him and dislike him; over and over again I have relented towards him, and said to myself that he was a good fellow after all; but I had hardly done so when he would go for me in some way or other which soured me again. I have no doubt I have made myself very disagreeable: certainly I have done many very silly and many very wrong things; I am not at all sure that the fault is more his than mine; but no matter whose it is, the fact remains that for years and years I have never passed a day without thinking of him many times over as the man who was sure to be against me, and who would see the bad side rather than the good of everything I said and did. He used to say to his nurse, so my aunt, Mrs Bather, said, 'I'll keep you: you shan't leave; I'll keep you on purpose to torment you,' and I have felt that he has always looked upon me as something which he could badger with impunity or very like it, as he badgered his nurse. There can be no real peace and contentment for me until either he or I are there where the wicked cease from troubling. An unkind fate never threw two men together who were more naturally uncongenial than my father and myself. (N231)

CHAPTER 17

Ex Voto

Now that the long anticipated event had taken place, Butler, at the age of fifty-one, was able to organise his life to his own specifications. He was not just financially secure, but positively wealthy. He suffered some restrictions: his father had left him only a life interest in his will, so that he could not spend the capital he had inherited. But the Whitehall estate, through his grandfather's will, was now his absolutely. His income was substantial, and he was able to repay the debts he had accumulated over the past decade. The years of anxious calculations to see if he could afford to go to Italy, or compromise on Normandy, were over. The book balancing, which he had learned from Reginald Worsley, continued, in infinitesimal detail; but with the happy confidence that he could go where and when he pleased. Each day, he calculated his expenses to the last penny. His style of living remained modest: dinner and fish, 1 shilling and 11 pence; bus, 1d; haircut, 6d. When he went to Sicily in 1897, seventy-one days cost him only £73-13-0; and his living expenditure for that whole year was only £220. The other major outlay was his pensioners: in addition to Pauli's £200 a year, he was also giving Gogin £100; and he was a generous employer.

His material circumstances did not greatly alter. He was too firmly dug in to Clifford's Inn to think about moving; he did go so far as to buy a new wash-hand basin. The pension to Pauli could be continued, at last without difficulty. There were, however, two new outgoings, that had a profound effect on his way of life. First, he proposed that Jones should resign from Paine's, where he was managing clerk, and devote himself to helping him with his music and his writing; in return he would give him his current salary of £200 a year. Having thus benefited indirectly from one parent, Jones was resentful when his own mother promptly withdrew her allowance of £100 a year, though she relented in time. Secondly, on January

18th, 1887 Butler engaged Alfred Cathie, the son of a friend of his
laundress, Mrs Doncaster, as valet, clerk and general attendant. The
trial period proved so successful that on August 3rd Butler dismissed
Mrs Doncaster with a pension, 'for being full of vermin, and frequently dead drunk',[1] and Alfred became a permanent part of Butler's life.

The household was complete. Butler made sure that he preserved
his privacy, for Jones kept his own set of rooms in Barnard's Inn,
and Alfred went off home at 5.30 p.m., and did not arrive until 9.30
each morning. Alfred was, so Butler wrote later, 'almost from the
very day he came to me, at once servant and friend. I began to feel,
almost immediately, that I was like a basket that had been entrusted
to a dog . . . He liked to have some one who appreciated him and
whom he could run and keep straight. I was so much older that to
him I was a poor old thing, with one foot in the grave, who but for
his watchful eye and sustaining hand might tumble into it at any
moment.' (M2.345–7) Alfred was quick to establish his personality
and set the bounds of the relationship. Butler, who brushed his hair
with a hundred strokes each night, bought a new pair of hairbrushes
in the autumn, and remarked to Alfred that they would last his time:

'Yes, sir,' said he promptly.
I was a little piqued and determined to give him a locus
paenitentiae, so I said:
'Of course, I can never hope to see them out.'
'No, sir,' he replied with equal promptitude.

'I was exceedingly amused,' he wrote to Harriet. 'Of course one can
never tell from week to week, but I am not going to settle the matter
out of hand that I am not to survive my hairbrushes.' (M2.59)

Alfred's age – he was twenty-two when he began to work for
Butler – made him part son, as well as servant; in the course of time
he acted as secretary (he soon mastered the Columbia typewriter),
nurse, minder, and friend. The relationship triumphantly survived
Alfred's marriage, a comparative rarity with Butler, who was often
agitated when his friends threatened such a step (the supposed
attentions of Mlle Vaillant, Miss Savage's 'dear little violinist',
towards Jones deeply disturbed him). Alfred had wished to marry
soon after entering his employment. 'I was then only giving him 25/-

a week and he had nothing behind him, so I said that if he married now, he had better stay with me till some better place turned up and then take it. The lady, finding that Alfred could not marry at once, married some one else, and I am not sure that Alfred was altogether displeased. We immediately began putting by a fund at the Savings Bank and by the time he was 30 he and I between us had got it up to £150. He then broached the subject of marriage again and, there being no reason why he should not marry, I raised no objection.' (M2.345–7) It was like being a father by proxy.

Apart from his regular duties, Alfred accompanied Butler on his Thursday outings to the country, on many trips abroad, and to the music hall. He also kept him up to the mark about his appearance. ' "Here, Sir, is a reminder for you; you must keep it in your waistcoat pocket and keep on repeating it to yourself." And the reminder was slipped by him into my waistcoat pocket. It ran: "I am to buy a new hat, and a new pair of boots." ' Alfred nagged Butler to trim his beard or have his hair cut, advised him where to take his dinner, and left him instructions when to break off from his music and go for a walk on the Embankment. His turn of phrase and individual outlook were sources of delight. He stopped Butler from patting a dog in Fetter Lane: 'You had better be careful, sir, he's a business dog, and he may not like being spoken to.' He was usually present when friends came to call, and would accompany Butler to the station when he left London: 'You never looked out of the carriage window to see me standing on the platform as I always do,' he once complained. 'There was I standing in the rain, and you never looked at me.'[2]

Business matters inevitably occupied much of Butler's time in the first few months of 1887. Apart from his own housing projects, he had in mind the future development of the Whitehall estate for housing; then there was the management of his father's farm at Harnage, in addition to other holdings of land and property. This meant regular trips to Shrewsbury, and closer connection with the school. Some of the music for *Narcissus* was performed by the boys at the school concert, which got the music master, Hay, into trouble with the headmaster, who clearly felt that *Narcissus* was too comic to be suitable. Butler apologised: Moss was 'a very good fellow, but we cannot expect a University swell to know anything about art or music'. (M2.53)

Butler also treated himself to more frequent trips abroad. At Easter, he went to Belgium with Gogin, and in August he was happily established in his Varallo. Varallo and its Sacro Monte had been purposely omitted from *Alps and Sanctuaries* because, he wrote, 'Varallo requires a work to itself.' His friend Dionigi Negri did not allow him to forget the promise. Jones wrote to Gogin:

Butler told me yesterday that I might write to you so I am doing it. He is up the Sacro Monte writing. He calls it taking a holiday, but really he has been making great progress with a new Italian book which is to run this place and Gaudenzio Ferrari. He has got some lovely things in the book. There is another man who did statues up here, Tabachetti, who is also to be run. On the other hand Varallo is running Butler, for we are to go to a banquet given in his honour on Thursday at the Albergo on top of the mountain, and he says we shall probably be kissed. Tomorrow we are going with Dionigi Negri to the vineyards, and it will be like the day at the Cantine in *Alps and Sanctuaries* – at least we think so . . . Butler is very good and behaves like an angel. All the people are so pleased to see him and compliment him on his good looks and on keeping so young. Then he puts on an air of great sadness, lowers his voice, and tells them he has had the misfortune to lose his father. (M2.54–6)

Butler was truly revitalised by his father's death. He was in high spirits, attuned to a subject wholly sympathetic to him, among friends in a place where he felt at home. He was chief guest at a municipal banquet, held on the loggia of the Albergo on the Sacro Monte, which he referred to as the 'greatest honour that has ever been conferred upon me'. It was, according to Jones, a tremendous affair: 'altogether there were 26 people including the Procuratore del Re, the Sotto Prefetto, the Direttore del Sacro Monte, the Municipio and all the swells. Butler was put at the head of the table and we had a very good dinner. The Director of the Sacred Mountain proposed Butler's health in florid terms, and Butler replied in Italian.' (M2.56–8) Descending the slippery mountain path to Varallo afterwards, Butler acknowledged that the next thing he did must be his book about the Sacro Monte.

By December he had written some 200 pages. He also bought two new cameras, one for snapshots and one for time-exposures, and took some instruction. He had experimented with photography before during his art school days, and had later wasted much time with a *camera lucida* in the hope that it would help him with his painting. He now wanted to take photographs to use as illustrations in place of his own drawings.

After spending Christmas at Boulogne with Gogin, he took the train to Basel.

It was bitterly cold and, between Chalons and the Swiss frontier, the snow drifted in from each window and piled itself up on the seats near the windows, so that I could only sit in the very middle of the carriage. Fortunately I was the only occupant.

I was very thickly clad, but was wearing a sling bag outside my greatcoat, so that the warmth of my body would hardly affect the thermometer that I had within it – still no doubt the temperature inside the bag would be warmer than that outside. About 2 a.m. I took the thermometer out and found it at 26°.

At Basel everything was warm. I crossed Switzerland to Luino on a brilliant cloudless day – everything was deep in snow. I never saw Switzerland look more beautiful, but I suppose it was chiefly the strangeness that made it fascinate me so strongly. After Luino there was very little snow, but all the little waterfalls were locked in frost. The carriages were now no longer warmed and I was half starved when I reached Varallo about 10 p.m.

It was bitterly cold all the time I was at Varallo – about 4 weeks – but it was quite clear; all day long great masses of ice were being brought in from the Mastallone to store in the ice-houses, and I did not see a waterfall that was not locked and turned to icy stalagmites. (M2.60–1)

Negri had arranged for him to be able to go inside the chapels; but the light was poor at that time of year, and even with the assistance of magnesium wire he had to expose the plates for half an hour or more. This gave him plenty of opportunity to observe and meditate on the statues. He spent the evenings with his landlord, Carlo Topini, or Dionigi Negri would take him to the house of his uncle Zio Paolo, a baker, where Butler would join the family circle around the kitchen fire.

Ex Voto was published in May, 1888, and was dedicated to the people of Varallo. It is, like *Alps and Sanctuaries*, one of Butler's most relaxed books. As he wrote in the Conclusion, he found his labour 'a very light and pleasant one'; everyone he encountered at Varallo helped him, and he felt himself in partnership, rather than in competition, with other scholars and researchers, all committed to discovering more about the origins and development of the Sacro Monte and to contributing to the public knowledge and appreciation of it. But whereas *Alps and Sanctuaries* was inherently, for all its breadth of reference, a traveller's book, *Ex Voto* is a serious work of art history, part of an enquiry that continued for years, as the various postscripts and addenda testify.

The link between the two Italian books is made clear in the chapter in *Alps and Sanctuaries*, 'Considerations on the Decline of Italian Art', where he wrote: 'As regards painting, the last rays of the sunset of genuine art are to be found in the votive pictures at Locarno or Oropa, and in many a wayside chapel. In these, religious art still lingers as a living language, however rudely spoken. In these alone is the story told, not as in the Latin and Greek verses of the scholar, who thinks he has succeeded best when he has most concealed his natural manner of expressing himself, but by one who knows what he wants to say, and says it in his mother-tongue, shortly, and without caring whether or not his words are in accordance with academic rules.' (AS145) Butler's ideal was the artist who expressed himself naturally, simply, even naively, because he had affection for his subject and wished to convey that affection to others. On Varallo's Sacro Monte he found an original, organic and, in the widest sense, popular work of art, in which he identified two crucial contributions: that of Gaudenzio Ferrari, whose artistic independence he seeks to emphasise, as representing an early, native tradition unsullied by the Renaissance; and that of Tabachetti, whom he traced as 'Jean de Wespin' to his Flemish origins in Dinant, and whom he saw as contributing the intense realism of a sculptor of northern Europe.

Butler's introduction mauls the received tradition by ridiculing Sir Henry Layard's comments on Varallo in Kugler's *Handbook of Painting*: 'a work which our leading journals of culture have received with acclamation'. 'Sir Henry Layard,' he announces, 'has evidently either never been to Varallo, or has so completely forgotten what he saw there that his visit no longer counts. He thinks, for example, that the chapels, or, as he also calls them, "stations" (which in itself should show that he has not seen them), are on the way up to the Sacro Monte, whereas all that need be considered are on the top. He thinks that the statues generally in these supposed chapels "on the ascent of the Sacro Monte" are attributed to Gaudenzio Ferrari, whereas it is only in two or three out of some five-and-forty that any statues are believed to be by Gaudenzio. He thinks the famous sculptor Tabachetti – for famous he is in North Italy, where he is known – was a painter, and speaks of him as "a local imitator" of Gaudenzio, who "decorated" other chapels, and "whose works only show how rapidly Gaudenzio's influence declined and his school deteriorated." As a matter of fact, Tabachetti was a Fleming and his name was De Wespin; but this is a detail . . .' (EV3–4) After more examples of Layard's ineptitude, Butler quotes a sentence 'which caught my eye in passing' – a typical Butler tactic – 'which I believe to be as fundamentally unsound as any I ever saw written, even by a professional art critic or by a director of a national collection'. Layard comments in his chapter on Leonardo da Vinci:

> One thing prominently taught us by the works of Leonardo and Raffaelle, of Michael Angelo and Titian, is distinctly this – that purity of morals, freedom of institutions, and sincerity of faith have nothing to do with excellence in art. (EV6–7)

This viewpoint provides the thesis that allows Butler to state his contrary doctrine: that it is 'agape, or the spirit, and not gnosis, or the letter, which is the soul of all true art. This, it should go without saying, applies to music, literature, and to whatever can be done at all. If it has been done "to the Lord" – that is to say, with sincerity and freedom from affectation – whether with conscious effusion, as by Gaudenzio, or with perhaps robust unconsciousness, as by Tabachetti, a halo will gather round it that will illumine it though it pass through the valley of the shadow of death itself.' After this, for Butler, relatively mild clearing of the ground, the book proceeds to unfold in clear, informative and generous appreciation. Butler naturally questions the accepted canon of taste, by elevating the later work of Tabachetti, 'the strongest and most robust of all the great men who have left their mark' there. Of his 'Journey to Calvary', he went so far as to claim, 'if I could have my choice whether to have created Michael Angelo's chapel or Tabachetti's, I should not for a moment hesitate about choosing Tabachetti's . . .' (EV74) This is Butler's way; and the crucial element is not the expression of the value judgment, or the denigration of the accepted masterpiece, which often seems perversely eccentric, but the revaluation of something overlooked, neglected or misinterpreted.

Butler chose wisely in retaining the subject for a book in its own right. The Sacro Monte is a hilltop commanding the town of Varallo. It was founded by a Franciscan, Bernardino Caimi, who conceived the idea of creating a New Jerusalem for the people of northern Italy, so that they could see with their own eyes replicas of the sites of Christ's life and Passion. Varallo's was the first of a series of Sacro Montes in the region, a result of the Counter-Reformation, but also an expression of simple faith. Building began in 1491 with the chapel of the Holy Sepulchre. Gaudenzio Ferrari was the first great artist to work on the chapels, creating both sculptures and frescoes, and he is now credited with an involvement in the overall architectural and spatial planning. At the end of the sixteenth century, the plan was considerably enlarged, with notable sculpture by Giovanni d'Enrico and Tabachetti, and the site continued to be developed into the eighteenth century. When Butler first visited it, many of the chapels, and particularly the frescoes, were in a state of serious disrepair; but there has been much restoration since, partly as a result of the renewed interest that his book and researches inspired.

The white chapels are dotted about on the hillside, some in the full glare of the sun, others in the deep shade of pine and beech trees. They are of all shapes and styles – round, square, octagonal, plain, baroque – and linked by paths and balustrades and flights of steps. You begin with the Fall, a powerful tableau with figures largely by Tabachetti, and then follows the story of Christ, from the Annunciation to the Holy Sepulchre. There are many parallels with the subjects of the Corpus Christi mystery cycles; and the experience is rather like seeing a series of dramatic scenes. At each of the chapels, you look through a grill or screen at a tableau, focused essentially upon one moment. But the frescoes, which provide a background to each group of figures, are in many cases symbolic as well as representational, providing a sense of context and continuity. Also, many of the chapels contain numerous figures; for example, the Road to Calvary is arranged with such wealth of detail that it suggests a complex narrative sequence.

The spectator, or pilgrim, is drawn into the experience partly by the beauty of the setting, and partly because of the way the chapels are placed on the mountain. At Varallo, you leave the town on a steep climb, a short journey that in Butler's day could be undertaken only on foot. The first chapel, the Fall, is the only representation of the Old Testament, and is separated physically from the rest of the cycle, to give time for meditation. There are, at appropriate points, sequences of chapels grouped together: those depicting the Annunciation, and those related to the Nativity, are examples; and the scenes involving Pilate are all housed in an ornate building, Pilate's Palace. Other mimetic examples include the cave-like, dimly lit stable of the adoration of the Shepherds, the climb to Calvary, and the low entrance underneath which you stoop to enter the Sepulchre. The style and quality of the statues and frescoes varies, as isolated works of art. But the combination of architectural and natural setting, of frescoes and statues, has a strength and unity that overrides any inconsistencies or roughness of execution.

Ex Voto sold even fewer copies than *Alps and Sanctuaries* during Butler's lifetime, but over the years he must have inspired thousands of people to go to Varallo. Cecil Lewis went there with the Shaws in 1926. 'The mountain itself is delicious,' he wrote to Charles Ricketts. 'The figures stand in little chapels, with frescoes on the walls – the whole closed with a glass front through which there are spy-holes – rather like a peep-show!' He thought Tabachetti beat 'all the others off the map – particularly the "Fall"; the naive Eve, and the ridiculous animals – an elephant with intelligent eyes like a retriever, and a splendid serpent with a mouth like a collie dog'. But at the thirty-third chapel Shaw remarked, 'Tis a rare work; would 'twere over.' And on seeing 'Christ with the Woman of Samaria' he remarked, 'Ah! Christ's first meeting with Constance Collier!'[3] Shaw's impatience emphasises that the Sacro Monte is not designed for a rapid tour. Butler, waiting in freezing January for his photographic exposures and contemplating each composite image for up to half an hour, returning year after year to continue his researches, appreciated its proper rhythm.

Butler researched its history and development and scrutinised the contents of each chapel, establishing the contributions of each artist within the complex and composite whole, and relating the work of Gaudenzio and Tabachetti to other examples of their art in the district. As late as February, 1902, he wrote to the publisher Grant Richards proposing a new edition of *Ex Voto*, and, when that found no favour, a short book entirely devoted to Tabachetti. It was one of his happiest and least contentious discoveries. To the question why there was no chapel of the Descent of the Holy Spirit at Varallo, he answered that 'the work of Gaudenzio Ferrari, Tabachetti, and Paracca was a more potent witness to, and fitter temple for, the Holy Spirit than any that the hands of even these men could have made for it expressly.' (EV254) Butler also approved of the fact that the 'Ex Votos and images in wax and silver with which each chapel formerly abounded' had long disappeared, 'and the sacred drama is told with almost as close an adherence to the facts recorded in the Gospels, as though the whole had been done by Protestant workmen'. (EV256)

The Conclusion of *Ex Voto* shifts the book temporarily from a work of art history and instead places it within the debate begun in *The Fair Haven* and continued through the evolution series. This was yet another kind of response to his Victorian bugbears, the uncritical doctrines and superstitions of the Church and the mechanical materialism of the new science. This extension, he commented, was 'trenching on somewhat dangerous ground', and he returned 'to the note struck at the beginning of my work – namely, that I have endeavoured to stimulate study of the great works on the Sacro Monte rather than to write the full account of them which their importance merits'. (EV258-9) For once, Butler's stated aim had been fulfilled.

It did him no good in England. 'Do you know how many copies of *Ex Voto* I have sold? I have sold 117,' he informed an Italian, Professor Preda. 'I mention this that you may see how cheaply people think of me in England. With one exception there is no journal of importance that would take an article by me. Every book that I write falls dead before it is so much as born – every book that I write costs me about £100 sterling; this is pure loss; and over *Ex Voto* I shall lose at least £150. I have not the ear of any publisher; I never invite a critic to dinner; I do my work as accurately as I can; I say what, after sufficient consideration, appears to me to be true and useful, and I leave everything else on one side.' (M2.84-5) But the work on

Varallo continued. In August, 1888 he was at Dinant, hunting out the family origins of Tabachetti. He returned to Varallo, and discovered what he thought to be a self-portrait of Tabachetti in the Ecce Homo chapel. These findings were published in an article for *The Universal Review* – the 'one journal of importance' referred to above – in November.[4]

Butler's next major subject had already been provided. The Shrewsbury Archaeological Society invited him to write a Memoir of his grandfather for their quarterly journal, some forty or eighty pages. His sisters, to help him, gave him Dr Butler's correspondence, which was a revelation. 'Everything from first to last, beginning (as yet, so far as I have dipped into earlier correspondence) with a correspondence in 1804 which would melt the heart of a stone, is good, straightforward, generous, forbearing and all that an anxious grandson would desire his grandfather to be. More I cannot say; less would wholly fail to convey an idea of the respect and admiration with which the character now first known to me impresses me. But – I must make my work into a full-sized book and publish it as my next volume. Of course it won't sell, but that is part of the game: I have got to do it.' (M2.71–2) Butler entered into a voluminous correspondence with those who had known Dr Butler, and tracked him doggedly through England and Europe. His 'straightforwardness, robustness, generous placability, kindness of heart, laboriousness, and a hundred other good qualities, have made me fairly lose my heart to him'. (M2.73) The more he discovered, the more he realised that the 'portrait' of him as George Pontifex in *The Way of All Flesh* was a gross distortion, but although he wished to right the libel, he never revised that part of the novel. His biographical study grew and grew, suffering many setbacks before it appeared in 1896.

In June, 1888, however, his cantata *Narcissus* was published, the first step in Butler's complicated act of homage towards Handel.[5] Searching for a theme, he had settled instinctively on his staples: the importance of money, the subordination of love to wealth, and the *dea ex machina* of a fairy aunt or godmother. He collaborated with Jones on the plan, wrote most of the words himself, and divided responsibility for the music. He called it a *jeu d'esprit*. It was an affectionate pastiche that sprang from detailed knowledge of Handel's music and adulation towards the composer.

Narcissus, a simple shepherd, and Amaryllis, a prudent shepherdess, 'have abandoned pastoral pursuits and embarked in a course of speculation upon the Stock Exchange'. They lose the £100 they planned to marry on. The obedient Amaryllis is adamant:

> Give but your hundred pounds again
> And I'll give back my heart;
> Till then your words are all in vain,
> And you and I must part.

In the interval, Narcissus's aunt and godmother, like Alethea, conveniently dies and leaves him £100. The couple are swiftly married. Then comes the crucial question: how to invest the fortune – in Egypt's dusky bonds or Columbia's flattering field? Happily, Amaryllis offers sound advice, and the Chorus celebrates the epitome of Victorian stability:

> How blest the prudent man, the maiden pure,
> Whose income is both ample and secure,
> Arising from Consolidated Three
> Per Cent. Annuities, paid quarterly.

Butler had thought of calling the work an 'Oratorio Buffo', but decided this might seem disrespectful. The music was composed in what Shaw described as 'a ridiculously complete command of the Handelian manner and technique'[6]: it was the most orthodox of his enthusiasms. When it was finished, Butler and Jones decided on a successor, *Ulysses*. Because Butler was so busy with his grandfather's life, Jones began work on his own, and after a while Butler decided to join him in taking lessons in counterpoint with Rockstro.[7] His initial reluctance was soon overcome, once he realised Rockstro's devotion to Handel. They became friends, and partly through the association Butler's circle widened to include Fuller-Maitland, the music critic of *The Times*, and Mrs Alfred Bovill, whom Butler decided was 'a human Easter Monday or some other Bank Holiday' (by the same scale, his sister May was a kind of human Good Friday). He often visited the Fuller-Maitlands on Sunday afternoons; Fuller-Maitland suggested he liked them because they never lionised him or invited people specially to meet him. As he had a rule never to smoke until ten to four, they would put on the clock's hands, and 'he would take his cigarette with a twinkle in his eye, as one who was well aware of the cheat but not unwilling to profit by shrouding his knowledge'. He noted his puckish love of mischief, and irresistible charm. Mrs Bovill gives a good picture of Butler at his most relaxed and approachable. He invited her and her two sons to tea at Clifford's Inn:

> . . . it was one of many such delightful tea-parties and I, as well as the boys, felt like a child going out to tea with a 'grown-up' – one in a thousand – for he never talked as if he was coming down to one's level, indeed he had the great gift of making one bring out some good things occasionally; I was never *quite* sure they were not things he had himself said, dressed up in one's own somewhat meagre clothing, but, if so, he never reminded one of that fact.
>
> His rooms and the stairway to them dated from before the great fire of London, I believe; at any rate if they did not I know I shall always think they did. The balustrade was lovely; the whole of one's hand rested upon it, it was much too wide to be clasped. Then the double doors opened and there he stood on the threshold beaming; beaming is what I mean and I will not alter that word; his glasses were very thick but they could not hide either the bright blue colour of his eyes or the delicious twinkle in them when he gave forth some rather more naughty and humorous speech than usual. Alfred was always there and Mr Jones sometimes – generally I think. Then there was the room itself and all his treasures and his dear little piano on which I used to play, and I was always to sing 'something that Alfred will like and understand, please.' The tea was lovely and we all ate too much always and were all the better for it. The floor of the room was not level, and even that was a delight and is a delight now.

She persuaded Butler to give a lecture at her house on 'The Whitewashing of Penelope'; as a result, Mrs Fuller-Maitland sent him a card for one of her musical evenings. He consulted Mrs Bovill as to whether he should go:

I think he had made up his mind to do so, although it was for

10 p.m. and he said: 'But there's my bally old body to be considered.' Finally he said he would go if I would promise to be there by 10 punctually. We both arrived at that hour, and I was very proud to walk into the room with him. He wore a shirt with a little frill down the front which looked old-worldish and delightfully like what he ought to wear. Several of my acquaintance asked me: 'Who is that charming old gentleman?' and those I introduced to him felt that, after all, I was not quite such a Bohemian as they had thought.

At 11.30 he asked me, 'May I go now?' and 'Must I say good-bye?' I said, 'Yes' and 'No' and he beamed and twinkled and began to feel in his pockets. As he did so his face became first serious then sad and long, and, when all the pockets had been searched, he bent towards me and said:

'And now I've lost my bloody ticket.'

I did so wish some of the quite Nice people who were there could have heard him.[8]

Butler could be more relaxed with married women. He asked Mrs Bovill for the loan of a prayer book when he went to stay with Mandell Creighton.

Another memory of Butler at this time comes from Desmond MacCarthy, then a boy at Eton, who was staying at the same hotel at Saas Fee.

Opposite us at *table d'hôte* sat an elderly man with very bushy black eyebrows, and with him, from time to time, they interchanged a few cheerful polite remarks. A day or two later I happened to feel an extreme reluctance to notice the bell which announced the midday meal, and instead of going in I continued to clamber about the valley rocks. After a short interval I saw what I knew I should see next, my mother appearing at the door of the hotel frantically waving her parasol. This was a signal which could not be ignored like the bell. She had evidently waited until lunch had well begun, and then, losing patience, come out to fetch me. I was not surprised. What did surprise me was that she was presently followed by the old gentleman with the thick eyebrows. As we all three entered the hotel together he whispered: 'I thought I'd better come, with a stranger Mama could not be quite so angry.' It was only long afterwards that I realized that it was kind of an elderly gentleman to jump up from his midday meal and hurry out into the blazing sun to prevent a small boy from getting a scolding; but when I did, I realized also that it was thoroughly characteristic of him to suppose that *every* child was likely to be bullied by its parents.[9]

MacCarthy used to go off sketching with Butler, and remembered that on Sunday mornings at breakfast he used to say: ' "Do you think Mr Selwyn would mind (Mr Selwyn was the chaplain, and in those days every hotel haunted by the British had its chaplain), do you think Mr Selwyn would forgive us if we did not go to church?" (He had been pleased to find that my favourite text was "And now to God the Father, God the Son, etc.") And off we would go together.' Later, as MacCarthy grew older, he would go to see Butler in London, at first with his father and later on his own, to receive advice of which he could make nothing at the time, such as: 'As long as you tell no lies to yourself and are kind, you may lie and lie and lie and yet not be untrue to any man.' He even gave up the last two hours of the Eton and Harrow match to listen to his talk, 'one of the greatest compliments ever paid to a philosopher in England. I must have been seventeen then, I was beginning to understand him.'

Butler may have seemed old to MacCarthy, and to Mrs Bovill's friends, but he was only in his mid-fifties. He had, however, become notably more mellow and patient since the death of his father and the end of his Darwin decade. The subject matter of *Ex Voto*, and the long imaginative exposure to the character of his grandfather, assisted the healing process. There was, too, the soothing presence of Alfred, who removed many minor, and some major, causes of stress.

Photography was an added source of interest and pleasure.[10] It was an ideal form for Butler, whose mind and eye were so fast moving, yet whose drawing and painting techniques were laborious. It was cheap, and a skill he could master in all its stages, and he soon trained Alfred to help him in the printing. The immediacy of photography appealed to him, and he used it to illustrate his books and pamphlets from *Ex Voto* onwards, and to record monuments and sites. But it was also a medium for expressing his unique vision of the world. Elinor Shaffer, in her study of Butler, suggests that 'in photography he at last found his true medium as a visual artist'. His photographs became an extension of his pictures and of his written notes about the oddities and 'sports' of human behaviour and appearance, and a record of his Hogarthian response to contemporary urban life. A study like 'Blind Man with Children, Greenwich' is clearly related to 'Family Prayers'.

Photography and music were also attractive because they were essentially private and could be kept away from critics and the establishment. But when *Ulysses* took the place of *Narcissus*, Butler began to reread the *Odyssey* in the original, just to make sure that Jones, who was relying on Lamb's *The Adventures of Ulysses*, had not been misled.

> Fascinated, however, as I was by its amazing interest and beauty, I had an ever-present sense of a something that was eluding me and of a riddle which I could not read. The more I reflected upon the words, so luminous and so transparent, the more I felt a darkness behind them that I must pierce before I could see the heart of the writer – and this was what I wanted . . .[11]

In an attempt to solve the riddle, he began to translate the poem into prose. By the summer of 1891 he was working fast and enthusiastically; he found it wonderful, he told May, 'but nothing can well be more *franchement bourgeois* & unheroic', and Ulysses was a 'servant's hall hero'.[12] In July, he made a note on a letter: 'It was during the few days that I was at Chiavenna (at the Hotel Grotta Crimee) that I hit upon the feminine authorship of the *Odyssey*. I did not find out its having been written at Trapani till January, 1892.' (M2.106) Butler had discovered his next subject and obsession.

CHAPTER 18

Sicily

The reading of the Homeric riddle became a major intellectual preoccupation for Butler until the end of his life. This interest produced a series of publications, including 'The Humour of Homer', first delivered as a lecture in 1892; a preliminary essay, 'On the Trapanese Origin of the Odyssey'; his full-length book, *The Authoress of the Odyssey*, eventually published in 1897; and his translations of *The Iliad* (1898) and *The Odyssey* (1900).[1] The last three were actually written in the reverse order to which they were published, and Butler compiled *The Authoress of the Odyssey* as a kind of teaser to the translations after these had been rejected by a sequence of publishers. The puzzle led to numerous expeditions to Sicily, and visits to Greece and Turkey, for Butler always wished to see things for himself, on the ground, and would not be satisfied until he had personally inspected the walls of Troy or the supposed site of Cyclops's cave. His circle of friends and correspondents widened, especially in Italy, for the Sicilians were delighted by the interest he showed, and were eager to claim the *Odyssey* for themselves. But the theory did little for his reputation in Britain. As so often, he ruffled the feathers of the orthodox and failed to convince the more radical.

The authorship of the *Odyssey* seems a less controversial subject today than the historicity of the Crucifixion or the mechanism of evolution. Yet Homer was imbued by the Victorians with a mystique that elevated him to near-religious status. As Richard Jenkyns has pointed out, on that part of the Albert Memorial frieze devoted to poetry, 'Shakespeare and Dante recline modestly, like attendant angels, at the foot of the central throne, while Virgil and Milton lurk still more diffidently behind them. Enthroned in the place of highest honour is Homer.'[2] In Froude's phrase, 'Whether one or two, the authors of the *Iliad* and the *Odyssey* stand alone with Shakespeare far away above mankind.' The Victorian public school boy, and the

Oxford and Cambridge undergraduate, were fed a rich diet of Homer; and for those who did not know Greek, a steady stream of Victorian translators (Francis Newman, Butcher and Lang, William Morris) offered access to this 'secular Bible of mankind'. Homer provided models and instruction in war and politics, religion and morals for the country's youth. The most prolific Homeric commentator was Gladstone, some of whose wilder theories make Butler seem the epitome of restraint, though Gladstone, because of the high moral and religious tone he adopted, avoided the disrepute that Butler's irreverence drew down upon him.

The interpretation of Homer formed a secular safety valve to the religious controversies of the age. The problem of Homeric authorship was first highlighted by Wolff, and ran in parallel to the biblical criticism that also flowed from Germany. The Victorians were active in re-examining Greek civilisation, both Homeric and later, in the light of new methodologies in literary and historical criticism, and in the developing disciplines of anthropology and archaeology; but they were also expressing and exploring their own preoccupations through art and literature. The *Iliad* and the *Odyssey* furnished the nucleus of this interest, for from Homeric pre-classical civilisation it was possible to extract and construct an ideal society to serve as a model for the complex, fallen modern age. There were almost as many models as critics: for Gladstone, Homer signified virtue, even Christian virtue; for Arnold, nobility and good taste; for Symonds, less prescriptively, the heroic. None of these approaches was designed to appeal to Butler; and he had personal motives for countering the first two, since he saw Gladstone as a symbol of cant and hypocrisy of almost Darwinian proportions, while he felt Arnold's father had stolen his own grandfather's rightful place as a great reforming headmaster and educator.

The literary and historical interest in the Homeric age was echoed in Victorian classical painting by artists such as Leighton, Alma Tadema, Poynter and Waterhouse.[3] Their paintings, large in scale, formed a developing visual commentary on the quest for Homer, and were even less to Butler's taste than the work of the Pre-Raphaelites. In Alma Tadema's 'A Reading from Homer' the listeners have their eyes fixed on the reciter as they lie or lean on uncomfortable-looking marble. Leighton (1878) and Poynter (1879) both exhibited paintings of Nausicaa; and G. D. Leslie had shown another Nausicaa in 1871, a year when Butler was also hung at the Royal Academy. Leighton's female figures tend to be wholesome, athletic types: his 'Greek Girls Playing at Ball', apart from their costume, might be St Leonard's girls practising cricket on the playing fields of St Andrews. Later in the century, artists chose more psychologically resonant subjects: Draper's 'The Sirens', Waterhouse's 'Circe Offering the Cup to Ulysses', and his startling image of Circe poisoning the sea in 'Circe Invidiosa' (1892), are explorations of darker contemporary neuroses made respectable by the ostensible Homeric subject.

There are three major elements, or stages, in Butler's approach to Homer and the riddle of the *Odyssey*. The first concerned the nature of the poet's style and tone. Butler had no inclination either to elevate or to distance Homer. For him, greatness always lay in simplicity, and his concept of Homer was of a poet who was accessible, domestic, realistic, and robust. Francis Newman, whose 1856 translation of the *Iliad* into unrhymed English metre had been attacked by Arnold, described Homeric verse as 'direct, popular, friendly, quaint, flowing, garrulous'; Butler might have agreed with the first three adjectives, but he thought that Newman's attempts to reflect the archaic quaintness of Homer's language and rhetoric obscured the simplicity and directness. Butcher and Lang's version, according to Butler, was 'Wardour Street' English: theatrical, decorated, artificial, falsely archaic. He himself set about translating the *Odyssey* and the *Iliad* into 'Tottenham Court Road' English: plain, vigorous, contemporary. He carried the texts in his overcoat pocket, and learned a book at a time by heart on rail journeys.

The second and most revolutionary stage in his Homeric exploration happened in Chiavenna that summer of 1891. He had reached Book X and the Circe episode when he decided he was reading 'the work, not of an old man, but of a young woman – and of one who knew not much more about what men can and cannot do than I had found her know about the milking of ewes in the cave of Polyphemus'. (AO8)

The third discovery occurred while he was revising his translation. In Book XIII, Neptune turns the Phaeacian ship, which is bringing Ulysses back to Ithaca, into a rock at the entrance of the Scherian harbour. Butler felt sure that an actual feature was being described. Guided partly by tradition and partly by previous authorities, he went to the fount of human knowledge, the British Museum, and sent for the Admiralty Chart of the west coast of Sicily. Hardly was it in his hand than he found the combination he wanted for Scheria lying right under Mount Eryx: 'the land's end jutting out into the sea – the two harbours one on either side of it – the narrow entrance between two marshes – the high mountain hard by – the rock at the entrance of one of the harbours – the absence of any river...' (AO164) The solution is fully in keeping with Butler's general approach: a little luck, a good measure of common sense, and the answer conveniently to hand under one's nose. The *Odyssey* was for him no longer a mystery, an imaginative *tour de force*, a compendium, a synthesis of oral sources: it was a straightforward voyage from Troy to Sicily, followed by a sail round the island, beginning and ending at Trapani. The 'Ionian' islands were islands off the coast of Sicily, and both Scheria and Ithaca were based on Trapani and its immediate neighbourhood.

Butler began to make his discoveries known at the end of January, 1892. He published a letter in *The Athenaeum*, and the same evening gave a lecture at the Working Men's College in Great Ormond Street, entitled 'The Humour of Homer'. His tone may be judged from this description of the *Odyssey*: 'its interest centres mainly in the fact of a bald elderly gentleman, whose little remaining hair is red, being eaten out of house and home during his absence by a number of young men who are courting his supposed widow – a widow who, if she be fair and fat, can hardly be less than forty.'[4] This kind of knockabout debunking illustrates Butler's problem in defining his audience. He longed to challenge the classical establishment, hence his letter in *The Athenaeum*. Equally, he wished to achieve a popular hearing. But while he was doing his 'little feeble best to amuse as well as interest'[5] the working men, he was also highly conscious that Dr Garnett, the Miss Butchers and Miss Jane Harrison were present, scowling the whole lecture through, or so he was informed. He then published the lecture and distributed it widely among scholars and journals, and was furious, though he can scarcely have been surprised, when it was savaged by reviewers. With a touch of paranoia, he even assumed that either Gladstone himelf, or more probably Jane Harrison,[6] had written the acid review which appeared in *The Spectator* of April 23rd, 'How to Vulgarise Homer'. 'We think Miss Harrison more likely. I think most people will see that it is by an angry woman who is determined to see nothing but bad and she will not even deign to notice the topographical suggestions which she cannot contradict.'[7] This kind of gnawing, fruitless speculation, a mixture of aggression and lack of confidence, too often distracted Butler from the work in hand.

The article in *The Spectator* at least showed how successful he had been in challenging the established view. 'Mr Samuel Butler, the able author of 'Erewhon', has been trying to explain to the members of the Working Men's College in Great Ormond Street, how full of humour is Homer. We agree as heartily with his contention, as we dislike, and, we may even say, are sickened by, his mode of demonstrating it. If Homer were what Mr Butler represents him to be, he would be, not a great epic poet who commands all the springs of irony, humour, tenderness, and pathos alike, but a proficient in nauseous burlesque and the chaff of the nineteenth century club-man.'[8] As for the translation, extracts of which were included in the lecture, it was in 'atrociously bad taste'; Butler's language was 'of the very essence of slip-shod familiarity, and the slouching, untidy pertness of conceited self-satisfaction'. Finally, the reviewer condemned his 'disastrous attempt to assimilate the humour of Homer to the humour of Dickens', an accusation very far from Butler's intentions.

Butler treated the *Odyssey* as a superior form of novel. He turned Ulysses into an antihero and gave the action and background a sense of authenticity. In his novels he drew closely on his own experience of people and places, incidents and conversations, transforming, transposing and occasionally guessing or inventing. He assumed that Homer would have done the same, and would therefore have written, wherever possible, out of personal knowledge. From this premise, it was a short step to imagining an author in a specific time and place, who made use of local knowledge and topography: 'No artist can reach an ideal higher than his own best actual environment' (AO208); and the more Butler thought himself into the text and subtext of the *Odyssey*, the more he became convinced that the author was a woman. His method was very much in tune with some of his earlier 'discoveries': he liked to inhabit and give new life to the dead, as he had attempted to do with Tabachetti, or, in a different way, to Lamarck. Predictable, too, was his instinctive wish to identify a self-portrait within a work of art, as he had done with Tabachetti and the Louvre

Bellini. In the *Odyssey*, he speculated that the authoress was none other than Nausicaa, the daughter of King Alcinoüs, who was on the beach with her maidens when she met the naked, shipwrecked Ulysses.

Butler was, of course, by no means the first critic to draw attention to the contrast between the *Iliad* and the *Odyssey*. Bentley, as he noted in his argument, had commented that the '*Iliad* was written for men, and the *Odyssey* for women'. (AO4) To state that 'if an anonymous book strikes so able a critic as having been written for women, a *prima facie* case is established for thinking that it was written by a woman' merely emphasises the weak logical grounds on which Butler bases his argument. Some of his arguments for female authorship – categorised by him as 'A Woman's Natural Mistakes', such as believing that a ship has a rudder at both ends – are both illogical and ludicrous: Jane Harrison would have quickly put him straight even then, had Butler allowed her the privilege of debate. But that a woman was capable of writing the *Odyssey*, and conceivably could have done so, was a radical proposition. Whatever its merits as argument, the promotion of the woman's point of view invites the reader to approach the *Odyssey* from a fresh perspective. The bald, elderly gentleman becomes peripheral; and in the centre of the story, told from within a precise social context, are Minerva, Penelope, Euryclea, Helen, Idothea, Calypso, Circe, Queen Arete, and Nausicaa herself. The women are more sharply depicted than the men, and their relationships with Ulysses form the structure of the narrative and provide the imaginative centre. The speculative theory opens the way to a challenging and radical reading of the poem.

For Butler, who had known Miss Savage, and admired Jane Austen, there was nothing improbable in suggesting a woman author. His theory may have been an unconscious tribute, even an act of reparation, to Miss Savage. By identifying the authoress with Nausicaa, he created an image of an ideal woman to complement his other perfect woman from Italy, Isabella:

> We have to find a woman of Trapani, young, fearless, self-willed, and exceedingly jealous of the honour of her sex. She seems to have moved in the best society of her age and country, for we can imagine none more polished on the West coast of Sicily in Odyssean times than the one with which the writer

243

shews herself familiar. She must have had leisure, or she could not have carried through so great a work. She puts up with men when they are necessary or illustrious, but she is never enthusiastic about them, and likes them best when she is laughing at them; but she is cordially interested in fair and famous women. (AO205)

Butler argued she must belong to the household of King Alcinous, noting the careful way the royal pedigree was explained and the affectionate treatment of Queen Arete; 'moreover, she must be a sufficiently intimate member of the household to be able to laugh at its head as much as she chose . . .' The house and garden are described with unique zest, 'and the evident pleasure which the writer takes in it is more like that of a person drawing her own home, than either describing some one else's or creating an imaginary scene.' Finally, no one apart from Nausicaa was drawn with such livingness and enthusiasm, 'and no other episode is written with the same, or nearly the same, buoyancy of spirits and resiliency of pulse and movement, or brings the scene before us with anything approaching the same freshness, as that in which Nausicaä takes the family linen to the washing cisterns. The whole of Book vi can only have been written by one who was throwing herself into it heart and soul.' (AO201)

Butler even annexed a portrait for her, and used it as a frontispiece for his book, while admitting that he thought it highly probable the authoress of the *Odyssey* was both short and plain (like Miss Savage), and was laughing at herself, and intending to make her audience laugh also, by describing herself as tall and beautiful (like Isabella).

The idea of Nausicaa, and the Sicilian origin of the *Odyssey*, possessed Butler. He would have understood Cavafy's poem, 'Ithaca':

> When you start on your journey to Ithaca,
> then pray that the road is long,
> full of adventure, full of knowledge.[9]

As usual, no one in England paid much attention. But when he lectured to the Fabian Society on 'Was the *Odyssey* written by a Woman?', George Bernard Shaw got up at the end and said that he had been entirely sceptical when he first heard of Butler's proposed title, 'but that on turning to the *Odyssey* to see what could have induced him to take it up he had not read a hundred lines before he found himself saying: "Why, of course it was!" '

The authoress of the *Odyssey* is a typically Shavian concept; and it would probably have been far more acceptable if it had been presented in dramatic or semidramatic form, like many of Shaw's or Wilde's more subversive ideas. There is a strong element of burlesque in his manner in this particular work. It is the Butler of the Note-Books, Butler apparently on holiday, as in *Alps and Sanctuaries*; just as in his Handelian cantatas he could not easily keep the serious and the comic apart. It was intended to entertain as well as to convince, and so create a 'market' (wishful thinking) for the translations. Yet there was also a wholly serious intention behind his attack on the Victorian myth of Homer, patriarchal, blind and bearded like some false image of God, and his replacement by the imagined portrait of a young girl. In the mid-twentieth century, Butler might have created a more obviously fictional form for his exploration. *The Authoress of the Odyssey* is a suppressed novel, in which the psyche of the narrator is revealed in the form of a quest for an author, a forerunner of *Flaubert's Parrot*. Robert Graves, who shared something of Butler's imaginative empathy with people and places, completed the novel whose outline Butler had sketched when he wrote *Homer's Daughter*.[10]

'The Humour of Homer' was translated into Italian, and Butler was soon part of a network of Italian enthusiasts and correspondents. In May, 1892 he received a letter from Emanuele Biaggini, who shared his views about the Sicilian origin of the *Odyssey* and about the identity of its author. The letter also contained a warm invitation to visit Trapani. So in July Butler made his way to Sicily for the first time, a journey that he would repeat almost every year until his death. A hundred years before, Goethe had made a similar pilgrimage. He called at Varallo, and at Casale, to stay with his lawyer friend Negri and pursue a line of enquiry about Tabachetti. Then he continued south via Genoa, Pisa, and Rome to Naples, and finally by steamer to Palermo and Trapani. Biaggini, in whose house he stayed, took him up Monte San Giuliano, the Eryx of classical times. For Butler, always susceptible to visions from mountain heights, the topography of the *Odyssey* was complete: there, beyond the island of Levanza, concealed by it at sea level from Trapani, was Marettimo, and Butler decided that this must have served as Ithaca for his authoress; to the west (on a clear day) could be seen the island of Pantellaria, which he identified with Calypso's island. Now that his theory, born in the British Museum Map Room, was so strongly confirmed by every detail, large and small, Butler's critical faculties were disengaged, and he could indulge himself by retracing Ulysses's steps from the moment he landed in Scheria.

I suppose him to have ascended the steep, and then, doubtless, wooded slopes of Mt. Eryx and to have passed along its high and nearly level summit (δἰ ἄκριας, xiv.2) to the other end of the mountain, where the Norman castle stands now 2500 feet above the sea level. Here he descended some two or three hundred feet to the spot now called *i runzi*, where there is a spring near a precipice which is still called *il ruccazzu dei corvi*, i.e. 'the rock of the ravens', it being on this part of the mountain that these birds breed most freely. This walk would take him about two hours, more or less.

The site is seen from far and wide, it is bitterly cold in winter, and is connected with Trapani by a rough mountain path which Ulysses may well have been afraid to travel without a stick (xvii.195). The path passes close to the round-topped *Colle di Sta Anna* which answers perfectly to the Ἕρμαιος λόφος of xvi.471. The time it takes to walk from the *runzi* to Trapani corresponds with all the indications furnished us in the *Odyssey* concerning the distance between Eumaeus's hut and the town of Ithaca – which seems roughly to have been a winter's day walk there and back. (AO170–1)

Returning from the same walk, Butler slipped in the streets of Erice and dislocated his ankle. This kept him mewed up for longer than he intended, but as soon as he was sufficiently healed he was driven down to Trapani to visit the Grotta del Toro, where Ulysses hid his treasure, and Cyclops's cave.

He was in high spirits, surrounded by friends, as in Varallo, amused and delighted by the attention and homage: 'They treat me like a Royal Personage.' The *Odyssey* took new life before his eyes, and the image of Nausicaa became more and more distinct. His letters to Jones are full of anecdotes and rich in detail. The one-eyed black sea captain who had translated 'The Humour of Homer' into Italian was 'a scorcher': 'About ten years ago he got into some row which made him furious; so he went on to the upper deck of his ship, put a pistol into his mouth and pulled the trigger; but the ball came out at his eye and lodged in the bone immediately above the eye. Finding he had failed, he flung himself into the sea and, when fished out of that, had to be bound with cords or he would have killed himself with his hands. He was quieted in the end and recovered absolute health, with the exception that his eye, of course, was gone.' (M2. 140–1) Butler made light of his injuries: 'I can walk about the room without sticks and the doctor says I may; but, when the bandage was off, the leg from the toes to the knee, all along the left side, was such a mass of rainbow bruises I should have been ashamed to ask a dog to eat it.' (M2.141)

As Jones commented, Butler generally accomplished everything he had once fairly set his mind on doing; three weeks later he rode up Mount Etna on a ten hours' night expedition to see the lava stream. He travelled north through Rome and Florence to meet Jones at the Sacro Monte at Varese. He was especially pleased to hear from Biaggini that the name Nausicaa was becoming quite a household word. 'When people meet a pretty girl they say "Here comes a Nausicaa." And then they begin talking about the *Odyssey* and about you, and run on for hours about our famous picnics to the caves . . .' (M2.147) He had woven himself into the myth of the *Odyssey*.

However, though fêted in Italy, he found that the English establishment maintained their indifference. Meeting Jowett at Shrewsbury, after dinner at the headmaster's house, and realising that he meant nothing more to him than as the author of *Erewhon*, he reminded him that he had written a good many books since:

'How is it, then, that I have never heard of any of them?'
'I suppose, Sir,' I said, laughing, 'because they failed to attract attention; but a year ago I did myself the honour of sending you a pamphlet on the Humour of Homer, and another this spring on the Sicilian provenance of the *Odyssey*.'
'Ah, to be sure, I remember there was something of the kind, but I have so many of those things sent me that – well – to speak frankly, I never read either of them.'

'Why should you, Sir? It was proper of me to send them as a mark of respect which I should have been sorry to omit, but I had very little idea that you would read them.' (M2.152–3)

Jowett then turned the subject on to Dr Butler, and assured him that everyone interested in the classics would read his *Life*. The conversation confirmed Butler's opinion that *Erewhon* hung 'rather as a millstone' about his neck; and the discomfort of these public ordeals haunted him. Why, for instance, did he go to the Shrewsbury Dinner? 'Why should I, knowing that I do not like these people nor they me, why should I, who never liked my school nor got much good from it, go and pay a guinea for a bad dinner, and eat and drink what it takes me a whole day to recover from?' Taking his Ishmaelitish line, should he avoid venturing into the enemy's camp, or was it tactically useful to do the correctest of correct things occasionally? He never resolved the dilemma.

It was not surprising that he should feel somewhat disheartened. By December, 1894, nearly thirty publishers had refused his translation of the *Odyssey*; and his labour of love on Dr Butler was suffering a similar fate. Its rejection by the Syndics of the Cambridge University Press (his and his grandfather's own university), though expected, was particularly galling. He pressed on with the *Iliad*, hoping to interest a publisher in the two translations together.

CHAPTER 19

Hans and Homer

Butler's journey to Ithaca was long and unhurried. He left a detailed description of his daily routine in a letter of November, 1896 to a young Swiss friend of Jones who had rashly asked how he spent his day.[1] 'I get up about 7 and immediately, in my night-shirt, go into my sitting-room and light my fire. I put the kettle on and set some dry sticks under it so that it soon heats enough to give me warm water for my bath. At 8 I make my tea and cook my breakfast – eggs and bacon, sausages, a chop, a bit of fish or whatever it may be, and by 8.30 I have done my breakfast and cleared it all away.

'Then I read the *Times* newspaper which takes me about 40–45 minutes. At 9.15 I do whatever little bit of work I can till Alfred comes at 9.30 and tells me all about the babies and whatever else interests him.' They decided what Alfred should do – letters to be answered, music to be inked over. Then Alfred would pack his portfolio and odds and ends in a brown paper parcel and help him on with his overcoat, and Butler would trudge off to the British Museum. 'I am there always about 10.15–10.30, according as I have any marketing to do or no.' (He would stop in Fetter Lane and order some meat on the days Pauli came to lunch, or, if friends called unexpectedly, he went round to the cook-shop for hot roast pork and greens.)

'I work at the Museum till 1, still at my Homer which is done now, all but about eight days' work.' Then he would call in at the Horseshoe for his lunch, 'but I never have more than one plate of meat and vegetables and no soup or sweets. I find the less I eat the better for me. Alfred and I generally waste half an hour or so till about 2.30 or 3, settling this, that, or the other.' (Alfred looked after all Butler's affairs: his house property, money, accounts, bills.)

'From 3 till 5 or 5.30 I write letters or work at home while Alfred typewrites for me, either my Homer or notes for my commonplace book or whatever it may be, and at 4 we always have a cup of tea together.'

At 5.30 Alfred would pack up, shake hands, and say goodbye till the next morning. Then Butler had his 'real tea which consists generally of a bit of fish and bread and butter and after that I may smoke. I may smoke after 4, if anyone comes or if I have to go calling anywhere, but never otherwise.

'From 6–8 I am alone and quiet, and at present I still go on with my Homer, but in a little while I hope to be able to get on with my music again and finish my very difficult chorus which I have long put on one side . . .

'Very well. At 8 I almost always go to Jones's, unless he comes to me; or we go out to a concert or theatre together, unless either of us has to go out to dinner. At 9.30 I leave him, come home, have some bread and milk, play two games of patience, smoke a cigarette' (seven a day was his maximum) 'and go to bed about 11. In bed I always read a scene or two of one of Shakespeare's plays till I find myself dropping off to sleep and then good-night.'

On Sundays and Thursdays he still went out for the day. 'Before I go I fill the coal-scuttle and fetch up water and trim and fill the lamp, etc., because my laundress, the good old woman who makes my bed and cooks for me when I am dining at home, will not have Alfred to help her.' Jones went out with him most Sundays, and on Thursdays, weather permitting, he would say, 'Alfred, I think fresh air does us good,' and they would go walking at Edgware or Stanmore, getting home about six: 'business wasn't thought of,' recalled Alfred. On Sundays, he did not go to Clifford's Inn at all, and Butler did the chores: to the end of his life he fetched a daily can of water from the tap in the court.

There were exceptions when he had to waste his time paying afternoon calls, but that was his normal, happy day. 'Alfred is half son, half nurse, always very dear friend and play-mate rather than work-fellow – in fact he is and has been for the last ten years my right-hand.' In Jones, Butler told Rémi Faesch, he had a friend 'the like of whom I shall never see again if anything were to happen to him – which Heaven avert'.

One feature of his routine that had already dropped out of Butler's life was his weekly visit to Lucie Dumas. Madame died of consumption in 1892, and Butler arranged for her burial: 'A very heavy blow,' he noted, 'to Jones as well as myself.'[2] Jones quotes her shrewd comment on Butler: 'Il sait tout; il ne sait rien; il est poète.' (M2.130)

In the interviews he gave to biographers and journalists, Alfred added his own comments on Butler's strict routine and abstemious habits. Every night he had a pint of bitter with his dinner, and if a friend was with him, an extra half-pint. But, unlike Alfred, he was not a Bohemian.[3] 'He liked everything to be arranged in a routine. And the three things he didn't like were Drink, Late Hours, and Strange Company. I remember him saying to me, "Alfred, I ought to have been Bohemian when I was young, same as you are." ' He liked the company of his friends; 'But he couldn't bear late nights, and he couldn't bear being lionised. You see, Mr Butler never liked doing all the talking. He liked to take a share in the talk, not to do it all himself. And sometimes people wanted him to talk as if he was a lion.'

Once Butler had educated Alfred – not that Alfred appears to have needed much education, strenuously resisting attempts to teach him music and astronomy – he allowed him to take charge of all the practical details of his life. 'Often and often he would come to me and say, "Alfred, how do we stand at the bank? Have we any money? Or are we pretty low?" And I would say, "We've got about a hundred pounds, sir," and he would say, "Good. Then we can go to the pantomime tonight." ' Sometimes Alfred was sent to the theatre on his own; sometimes he suggested that Jones took Butler: 'I think the change would do him good. He is having rather a harassing time of it just now.'[4] On Thursdays there were long afternoon walks, or excursions on river steamers in the summer to Clacton or Southend or Margate. 'The Governor used to point out the sights to me. Of course, I knew them all before, but I never let on. He enjoyed telling me and so I just let him go on.'

In the early years Butler took Alfred abroad at Whitsun. They began with short trips to Boulogne, and gradually went further afield, to Rouen, Brussels, Paris and, in 1894, to Switzerland, visits recorded in numerous photographs. Butler took Alfred up the Rigi, and pointed out the various sights: the Bernese Oberland, the Lake of Lucerne and so on: 'And then over here – you must look this way now – those are the Glarnisch Alps, and if you look that way you will be looking up the valley we go through on our way to Italy in the S. Gottardo Railway. Aren't you glad I brought you?' Alfred, who at Wassen had been terrified that the mountains would fall on him and bury him, thanked Butler politely, lay down on the grass and took out a copy of *Tit-Bits*. (M2.208–10) In time, Butler realised that Alfred would be happier taking his wife and children to the seaside, and gave him money for an annual holiday. He was invariably generous and courteous to servants, and likely to give Jones's laundress a shilling because it was such a beastly foggy morning.

When Jones was writing Butler's biography, he read the passage to Alfred, who said, 'Yes, Sir, that's all quite true, and I think you've done it very nice.' In relating the saying and doings of Alfred, there is an undeniable sense of *de haut en bas* on the part of both Butler and Jones, of the recording of a comic character; but Butler felt a genuine and deep affection and respect for him, which was clearly reciprocated. About Jones, Alfred had more reservations: 'A nice old fellow, but a bit of a gas-bag. Always blowing his own trumpet. There was too much of Jones in his book and too little Butler.'[5] Interviewed on radio in 1939, Alfred was asked, 'You were very great friends with Mr Jones?' He became very quiet, replied simply 'oh yes', and became for the first time a little confused in his speech, before asserting of the 'poor old Governor', 'He will ever live in my memory as long as I am alive.'

A certain amount of privacy was crucial to Butler, and was built into his daily routine. In a letter to Gogin, Jones described a rare occasion when he had to share a double-bedded room, 'which we never like', at Alagna in the Val Sesia above Varallo. 'He is afraid his snoring will disturb me and says I am to wake him if he snores. The consequence is we neither of us go to sleep; he is afraid if he does he shall snore and disturb me, and I am afraid if I do he will snore and I shall not be able to wake him, and he won't like that. In the morning occurred the toothbrush riots. He accused me of using his toothbrush – said he could see the marks of my teeth upon it. It was only with the greatest difficulty I got him to believe he was mistaken by assuring him that I had not cleaned my teeth for a fortnight.' (M2.56–8)

Daily companionship and emotional intimacy were another matter. Particularly as he grew older, Butler became accustomed to sharing his simple pleasures, whether it was a favourite place, or a visit to the music hall. At Christmas, he might go to Lewes or East Grinstead with Jones and Worsley, or to the Hôtel de Paris at Boulogne with

Gogin. Gogin recorded one typical outing to Boulogne in 1893: the light, the air, the colour, fishing off the pier, walking ten miles a day, and visiting Lionel Smythe in his old château at Wimereux on Boxing Day, with its antique garden and woods and the three children 'a flight of wild sea-gulls'.[6] When Jones or Butler were on holiday alone, each would write to the other about the casual friendships which they formed as substitutes. Butler described a delightful Italian boy of eighteen: 'The Germans dote on Camillo and are as jealous when I take him as possible, but they can't paint and he likes seeing me paint, so I take him sometimes.' Butler liked the company of young people, and understood them, as Desmond MacCarthy's anecdotes indicate. Camillo was, he told Jones, 'like Amy and Teddy' – Reginald Worsley's children – 'in one'.[7]

Jones, following the pattern, would catalogue the more charming of the waiters he came across. Returning from holiday by train in 1893, he fell into conversation with a young Swiss boy, Hans Rudolph Faesch, who was on his way to London to learn English and find a post in commerce. He introduced him to Butler, and Hans quickly became part of the family circle, spending evenings in Clifford's or Barnard's Inn, and joining them on the Sunday excursions into the country. A favourite expedition was to take the train to Gravesend and walk from there to Gad's Hill, stopping off at the Falstaff Inn for a glass of beer to drink with their sandwiches. Hans, naive, gentle-natured, impressionable, was an ideal audience for the ritual jokes and elaborate, mildly improper, dialogues that Butler enjoyed with the farmers' wives and landladies. Butler had constructed a charade with the landlady of the Falstaff. The landlady 'was one of those who enjoy bad health', and Butler would enquire sympathetically about her symptoms:

'I trust, ma'am, you are feeling better?' inquired he one Sunday in what was almost the professional bed-side manner.
   'Oh, sir, I am a great sufferer,' replied the landlady.
   'Are you sleeping fairly well?'
   'Yes, thank you, sir.'
   'Is your appetite pretty good?'
   'Yes, thank you, sir.'
   'You do not suffer from palpitations?'
   'No, sir, thank you.'

'Are your – ?'

Here the inquiries became so particular and intimate that Hans, who already had nearly disgraced himself, had to be bundled out into the road as quickly as possible. (M2.165–6)

The idyll lasted until February, 1895, when Hans left London for his home in Basel, *en route* for a new job in Singapore. Butler and Jones went to Holborn Viaduct to say goodbye. It was a poignant farewell, with tears flowing freely from all three. The next day, Butler, convinced that he would never see Hans again, expressed his feelings in a long poem which he called 'In Memoriam HRF: 14 February 1895'.

Out, out, out into the night,
With the wind bitter north-east and the sea rough;
You have a racking cough and your lungs are weak,
But out, out into the night you go,
    So guide you and guard you, Heaven, and fare you well!

We have been three lights to one another, and now we are two,
For you go far and alone into the darkness;
But the light in you was clearer and stronger than ours,
For you came straighter from God, and, whereas we had
    learned,
You had never forgotten. Three minutes more and then –
Out, out into the night you go:
    So guide you and guard you, Heaven, and fare you well!

It concludes:

The minutes have flown and he whom we loved is gone,
The like of whom we never again shall see.
The wind is heavy with snow and the sea rough,
He has a racking cough and his lungs are weak.
Hand in hand we watch the train as it glides
Out, out, out into the night.
    So take him into thy holy keeping, O Lord,
    And guide him and guard him ever, and fare him well!
                                            (M2.201–2)

Whatever its merits as a poem – and one cannot avoid the suspicion that Butler might have handled the sentiment rather roughly had it come from someone else's pen – it is a remarkably transparent admission of the unity of affection that Butler and Jones believed they shared with Hans. Butler brought the poem to Jones the following day, and then sat down to put another version of his feelings into a letter to Hans, using a deliberately plain style and limited range of vocabulary:

> I never called you by your Christian name before, but I know I may do so now. We keep thinking of you all the time, and hoping that you got through your awful journey without the serious harm which such a terribly bleak night might very easily do you. I woke often in the night, and after one o'clock I said to myself, 'Thank heaven he is off the sea now.' I saw next morning that it had been rough. We fear you suffered much. What a beast I was for not taking you as far as Calais myself and helping you if you were ill; but it only occurred to me yesterday. Before I had done dressing I got out Bradshaw and noted your whereabouts, and glad indeed was I when it was half-past five and I could think of you as warm, and, I hope, being packed off straight to bed.
>
> In the evening I went up to Jones's, and we tried to talk of other things, but it was no use; we kept turning back to you again and again, and saying to each other that, as we had never seen anyone like you before, so we never expect to do so till, as we hope, we again one day see your own dear, kind face, looking well and strong and happy as you deserve to be. (M2.202–3)

Butler recognised that the intensity of his feelings needed explanation, both to Hans, and to Jones and himself:

> I should be ashamed of myself for having felt as keenly and spoken with as little reserve as I have if it were anyone but you; but I feel no shame at any length to which grief can take me when it is about you. I can call to mind no word that ever passed between us three which had been better unspoken; no syllable of irritation or unkindness; nothing but goodness and

kindness ever came out of you, and such as our best was we
gave it to you as you gave yours to us.

Butler defined his sense of grief: 'I feel as though I had lost an only
son with no hope of another.' That done, he could end his letter:
'And now with every loving and affectionate thought which one man
can think about another, Believe me always from the bottom of my
heart yours S. Butler.'

Hans, from his home in Basel, wrote to his friends with details
about his job in Singapore. Butler, while hoping that the climate
would do Hans good, and recognising that he would never be happy
till he had travelled, had one 'last, great favour' to ask of him. If he
found he had made a serious mistake when he got to Singapore,
'then, my dear Hans, let me beseech you in the name of all the
affection a dear father can bear to a very dear son, by the absurd,
idiotic tears that you have wrung from me, by those we wrung from
yourself, by the love which Jones bears you and which you bear
towards him – if these things will not prevail with you nothing will
– apply to me, and do so without delay in whatever way will ensure
your getting the answer quickest which you will immediately receive
– I mean *draw on me at once for your passage money and necessary
expenses* and come home.' (M2.203–4)

Tokens and letters passed to and fro. The poem was despatched,
and Butler asked Hans for a lock of his hair. He had taken some
photographs, which had not been successful, and he intended to
paint Hans's portrait from an enlargement, and wanted to get the
colour right. Hans, on the receiving end of this torrent of affection,
which seems to have been held in check while he was actually in
London, did his best to respond as his ship sailed east: 'I have to
thank quite especially for the last letter, also without this letter I did
know that I had found a true and real friend and I need not tell you
how I feel towards you . . . I feel I found a second father and I enjoy
this idea.'[8] Hans was clearly perplexed about the 'In Memoriam'
poem, and about the prospect of its being published, which was
Butler's current intention; the references to Heaven, and what
seemed like a prayer, from a man so sceptical about religion, were
most confusing. Butler did his best to explain about the poem: all
names would be concealed. 'I wanted to set you and Jones and myself
together, as it were, in a ring where we might stay and live together

in the hearts of the kind of people we should have loved had we
known them. Mrs Bovill, Jones, Gogin, and myself are the only ones
that know about it. No more will be told.' The lines were so obviously
true and simple that the 'best people' would like them; Jones and
Mrs Bovill agreed, so he decided to 'let the thing go'. 'You must not
think that I am becoming more a believer in prayer and all that
nonsense than I was. We think exactly the same, but I know no
words that express a very deeply felt hope so well as those I have
used, and the fact that others make money by prostituting them shall
not stop me from using them when I am in the humour for doing
so.' (M2.205)

Butler was overwhelmed by the affection he felt for Hans. All the
emotional warmth that had never found expression in his family
relationships, or his relations with women, and which had been so
trampled on in his strange friendship with Pauli, were now channelled
into the ring he had formed of a chosen few with himself, Jones and
their adopted son Hans in its centre. That the relationship was
shared with the younger Jones was both a comfort and a complication.
He could rehearse memories of Hans with Jones, but there was a
competitive element in the correspondence: 'I thought it *very* kind
of you to send me a postcard as well as to Jones.' He told Hans that
he and Jones had been out at dinner, where the lady of the house
said 'she did not begin to like people until they were about thirty
years old. Did not Jones and I flare up just as much as we dared!
and when we came away Jones said to me, "She would never have
said that if she had known Hans." '9

Jones and Butler exchanged letters with Madame Faesch. Butler,
travelling east that spring on his Homeric quests, broke his journey
at Basel in order to meet, in Jones's words, 'our Dear Little Man's
people'. The bereaved friends were desperate for more images of
Hans. There was a lovely photograph of him aged nineteen, which
Butler copied with his camera. Hans's brother Rémi was a potential
substitute: 'Rémi did not do anything special but I saw his face
working several times. He attracted me. At times his face is really
very beautiful, and then again directly he is plain – I never saw
anyone's face assume such an infinite variety of expressions. You
said the same of dear Hans, but I noticed it even more in Rémi.'10

The picture of Hans sailing further and further east through the
heat of the Red Sea towards Colombo and Singapore accompanied

Butler as he moved across Europe to inspect the site of the *Iliad*. Schliemann had recently excavated Troy, and Butler may have scented a fresh area of controversy. He called at Florence, where he found Isabella older, but just her old self; at Corfu, to eliminate it from the long list of Odyssean possibilities; and at Athens. There in the hotel he found Jane Harrison – 'odious woman', he noted elsewhere – whom he had suspected of attacking him about 'The Humour of Homer'.

> I went up and recalled myself to her. She was still sore about the lecture and I apologised, reminding her that I had had to keep a room full of working-men in good humour.
>
> 'Besides,' I added, 'you chastised me quite severely enough at the time.'
>
> 'Was I rude?'
>
> 'Yes,' said I, laughing, 'very rude.'
>
> So we made it up and smoked a couple of cigarettes. We dined together during the rest of my stay in Athens, and I tried to ingratiate myself with her, but it was rather up-hill work, and I shall never be genuinely forgiven.

Butler, hypersensitive as ever, could not accept that anyone who did not agree with him on certain key issues could be other than, at heart, unfriendly: 'We did not quarrel but we did not, I think, like one another.' (M2.212) Jane Harrison's more generous perspective is revealing: 'At Athens I met Samuel Butler. We were in the same hotel; he saw me dining alone and kindly crossed over to ask if he might join me. Of course I was delighted and looked forward to pleasant talks, but, alas! he wanted me only as a safety-valve for his theory on the woman-authorship of the Odyssey, and the buzzing of that crazy bee drowned all rational conversation.'[11] Butler was invariably courteous and thoughtful towards his fellow travellers; yet anyone who failed the *Odyssey* test – or the Darwin, or Handel, or Tabachetti tests – remained, for him, outside the circle of intimacy.

With the *Odyssey* and his feelings about Hans dominating his thoughts, Butler needed the distraction of Greece and the Troad. 'It is an enormous comfort to understand now all about the Areopagus, the Pnyx, and all that rubbish. When a man dines at Corinth, gets coffee at Megara and lights his last cigarette at Eleusis he remembers where the places are,' he told Jones. (M2.212) He went on an excursion to Mycenae and Argos, Tyryns and Nauplia, where he met five English ladies, 'very nice all of them' (M2.214): they thought the same of the 'oldish gentleman in a brown cap, like a tam-o'-shanter'. One of the five, Miss Aldrich, correctly identified Brown Cap as Butler, found him 'delightfully simple and childlike', and noted how he pronounced his classical Greek in the 'old' English style: 'Mr Butler, who is a great English Greek scholar, would have been understood everywhere if he had pronounced the vowels and accented the words as the Greeks do.' (M2.215–16)

Butler sailed from the Piraeus to Chios and Smyrna, and so on to the Dardanelles. The American and English consuls made suitable arrangements for him, and he set off on horseback with an interpreter, a mounted soldier, and a servant, through a landscape 'a good deal like Winchelsea and Rye', but inhabited by camels, tortoises and storks. Perched on an over-padded saddle and reaching the stirrups with difficulty, he soon found himself upside down among the horse's feet on a bank of soft sand. But the men picked him up, and he rode off again – the horse now christened Hans, because he was so sensible and good – for five hours to a farm near Troy. The farm belonged to Calvert, the American vice-consul: 'A large family party – all very kind and hospitable and like a first-class New Zealand sheep station.' (M2.217–18)

Next morning Mr Calvert's nephew took him to Troy and explained the latest excavations. The first impression was disappointing; the walls appeared to be poorly put together. But on seeing the parts that had been sheltered from exposure, he realised how beautifully built they were. More significantly, he established that Helen could 'perfectly well distinguish swells down below on the plain as in *Iliad* iii'. He described the scene to Jones: 'Then up comes the governor of the Dardanelles forts – coffee, cigarettes, compliments, etc. At last I get away and ride across the plains to the place where the Grecian fleet lay; get to understand how very substantially accurate it all is, bar occasional gross poetical licences – Hector's running round the city is out of the question. The two springs, sources of the Scamander, one hot and one cold, are really forty miles off or more. I am on my way now, with two soldiers, to see them . . . Not a line of Homer now. Nothing but a week on horseback. My horse is worthy of his name; he is a little beauty. Tell dear Alfred as much of this as is good for him with my best love.'

Butler convinced himself that the *Iliad* gave an accurate description of Troy, and he treated this as indirect confirmation of his approach to the *Odyssey*. He also enjoyed the novelty of his oriental expedition, in spite of the ordeal by horseback, and other discomforts: 'Bairemitch, or however it should be spelt, was not a nice place – a filthy earthen floor; cobwebs in every angle of the small square box I had to sleep in; a sour smelling sack or two of stale straw to lie on, covered, it is true, with a fair Turkish hearth-rug; nothing to wash in till I made them bring me an old tin petroleum box; neither table nor seat till Yakoub and I improvised one – need I go on? . . . There was a place where they went to discharge their natural functions but I would sooner marry Mrs Danvers than go near it a second time; indeed it reminded me of Mrs Danvers, again, need I say more? The food? Hard-boiled eggs, up-country bread, cheese, and a little lamb's liver – five pieces on a skewer like a cats'-meat skewer.' (M2.220–1)

This letter exaggerates the physical horrors for Jones's benefit, to emphasise what an unsuitable trip it would have been for him. Butler duly visited the hot and cold springs, and amused himself with the local official, who was extremely hospitable and who struck up an immediate friendship with his visitor. He was not married, and at the age of fifty was troubled as to whether he had done right or wrong; having fallen in with wisdom from the West, he asked for advice. Butler obliged by delivering one of his favourite aphorisms, that it is cheaper to buy the milk than to keep a cow, claiming that the advice came from the lips of the great English imam, the Archbishop of Canterbury. He continued to demythologise in his usual fashion. The Scamander reminded him of the valley of the Lesse near Dinant; the birds were almost as good as some of the bird-stuffers' windows in Oxford Street; he found 'lovely English scenery, with cattle standing up to their middles in the Scamander and swishing their tails, the flats on either side well grassed and studded with Vallonia oak trees, the grass growing right up to their trunks'. There was, however, no riddle to be solved or received tradition to contradict. He made a slow journey home. He stopped off in Sicily, to report to his friends about his findings in the Troad; lingered in Rome, where he wrote to Gladstone, urging him to visit Trapani and investigate the Sicilian theory on the ground; and visited Negri at

Casale, to inspect a contract he had discovered for Tabachetti's Road to Calvary chapel. He was back in London at the beginning of June.

There was the question of the indiscreet poem to settle. At the beginning of April, Jones had been to see *The Importance of Being Earnest* – 'a mad farce and something of a burlesque melodrama in the form of a modern comedy and made me laugh a good deal'[12] – and later in the month he told Butler about Wilde's trial. 'I note what you say about "being Oscared",' replied Butler. 'It is very funny, but if he were not such a swaggering conceited charlatan and coxcomb I could find it in me to pity the poor wretch.'[13] The possible implication of Wilde's predicament for his own reputation was not lost on him. He wrote to A.P. Watt, his agent, who had been circulating 'In Memoriam' to publications such as *The Spectator*, *Saturday Review*, *Academy*, and *Athenaeum*. Having heard nothing, he concluded that it had gone the rounds and not been accepted: 'kindly therefore return it to my address at Clifford's Inn.'[14] A few days later, he confessed to Jones that Hans was always in his head, but that he had an uneasy feeling that he might 'have written just a little more effusively than he may quite like', though he could not think of anything in particular.[15] As the trials proceeded, the decision about 'In Memoriam' became clear. 'About the poem,' he wrote to Hans, 'which I consider to be the best thing I ever wrote, things have happened in England which make Jones and me decide not to publish it even anonymously. So it will be left with my papers. At any other time it would have been perfectly right, but people are such fools.'[16] (A note on the letter reads: 'This means the trials of Oscar Wilde.') Butler was at pains to avoid misinterpretations, though his gloss to Hans, who had enquired about the lock of hair, may not have achieved that aim: 'No, my dear Hans I wanted it exactly for the reason I told you – when I have used the lock for painting I shall give half to Jones, & shall have the other half put into a little silver locket & wear it myself.'[17] Butler even envisaged a voyage to Singapore to visit him. But this idea slowly faded – an uncomfortable passage from Athens to Sicily reminded him of the disadvantages of a long, hot voyage – and the emotional temperature cooled with time and distance and the occasional request from Hans that his English friends should not send him quite so many letters so frequently. Butler eventually proposed that he and Jones should write each alternate fortnight. He sent Hans a camera, and a penny was entered into the accounts for the *Daily Graphic*s, which Alfred bought and forwarded to Singapore.

Work on the *Odyssey* was interrupted by *The Life and Letters of Dr Samuel Butler*. No publisher would accept it as it stood, and Butler was most unwilling to reduce it as drastically as was required. He arranged with John Murray to publish it at his own expense, after a certain amount of editing. This, and the proofs, kept him busy for the next year, and the work finally appeared in October, 1896. It was well received: at last, Butler had written something uncontroversial, and he received a gratifying amount of praise. The Queen desired that her best thanks be conveyed; the Master and Fellows of St John's passed a special vote of thanks; even Gladstone sent a postcard, which Butler treated 'somewhat in the spirit in which we used to read that the North American Indians treated scalps' (M2.225): he had it framed and hung in his rooms. Many of these commendations came, it is true, in response to Butler's presentation of the two volumes. But there were also many spontaneous expressions of appreciation, and the tone was uniformly warm: 'I think the book is a perfect model of delicacy and reticence,' wrote Mayor from Cambridge, thanking Butler for 'the honour you have done to the college and the dear old school'.[18] The biography won him golden opinions; but, as he told Hans Faesch, 'though every one speaks well of it very few buy it. I could hardly expect them to do so, for it is a scholastic academic book with little to interest any but schoolmasters, college dons and clerics.'[19]

For a few weeks, Butler was optimistic; John Murray was reading the Homer translations. By Christmas, however, he had decided against publishing them at his own risk; and, partly on his advice, Butler decided to write a 'popular' book about the poems, so as to have a better chance with the translations. This 'popular' book became *The Authoress of the Odyssey*, which, as it was largely a reworking of existing articles, did not take him very long. He left it with Murray in April, 1897, and set off for his annual visit to Sicily.

As in 1896 Jones accompanied him. Until that year, according to Jones, Butler had not wished to expose him to the attendant dangers and discomforts, which included bandits, the climate, the food, fleas and seasickness. Jones was becoming anxious about Butler's own health. Gout was taking hold, there were dizzy spells, and all the usual symptoms of 'brain-fag'. As always, Butler derived immense pleasure from sharing his knowledge with a receptive friend; and Jones was incorporated into *The Authoress of the Odyssey* as an illustration: 'Festing Jones Esq. (height 6 ft, 2 in.) in flute of column at Selinunte'. The pleasures of the 1897 tour were somewhat marred by Murray's rejection: he had enjoyed the book, but found the argument inconclusive; he had also 'received a very elaborate report from a well-known Homeric scholar'.[20] Alfred wrote to say that he was 'pulverized' by Murray's answer. Butler retreated to his fall-back position, to find Murray refusing even to publish at Butler's own cost; so did Bentley, and Bell. Eventually, somewhat to Butler's surprise, Longmans agreed, which gave him special satisfaction, for Longmans had brought out his grandfather's school text books. In due course the *Iliad* (1898) and the *Odyssey* (1900) followed, to complete Butler's Homeric voyage.

Butler's originality in relation to Homer lies less in the ingenuity of his theory than in his capacity to re-create the *Odyssey* and the *Iliad*. He paid a high price for tweaking the tails of the Hellenic establishment, which resulted in the depressing pile of polite rejections, and the long delay, while he became overpossessed by the beauty of his solution. Though highly entertaining, his book was deliberately provocative. The translations themselves, revised and remodelled, are a considerable accomplishment. That of the *Odyssey* properly belongs with his Sicilian researches, but there was only room for an abridged version of the poem in the text of *The Authoress of the Odyssey*. Butler's was 'the first translation to reflect the new view that Homer knew what he was talking about. Its plain prose is not simply of the surface; Butler's rule was to deduce the underlying fact, and then put that plainly.' He thought himself into the mind of the poet, and from there into the minds of the characters; and the action of his *Odyssey* unfolds in realistic settings, domestic or natural. The Homeric house was a crux of Hellenic scholarship; Butler prefaces his story of the *Odyssey* with a description and plan of the house of Ulysses which is practical, convincing, and could be realised as a working model or a stage set. He visualised the action minutely, answering the questions posed by the text. He established a position for the seat from which Ulysses shot through the axes, and from which he sprang when he began to shoot the suitors; for the spear-stand; and for the door to the tower in which Telemachus slept. Butler assumed that the poem was written by a real person in touch with reality, in the form of cooking utensils, and sleeping and washing arrangements; with pigs and horses, cups and spoons, axes and arrows. The poet, he argued, used her own home, Trapani, and the surrounding landscape and seascape, as the framework for her story; and when her factual knowledge fell short, she elaborated, guessed and invented, but always with an underpinning structure of first-hand experience.

Butler's translation is at its best when he descibes action, the strength and directness driving the narrative forward. Ulysses confronts the suitors:

> On this he aimed a deadly arrow at Antinous, who was about to take up a two-handled gold cup to drink his wine, and already had it in his hands. He had no thought of death – who amongst all the revellers would think that one man, however brave, would stand alone among so many and kill him? The arrow struck Antinous in the throat, and the point went clean through his neck, so that he fell over and the cup dropped from his hand, while a thick stream of blood gushed from his nostrils.

According to Stanislaus Joyce, Butler's was one of only two translations he recollected his Greekless brother using. Hugh Kenner,[21] drawing attention to Butler's placing of Telemachus 'in a lofty tower', wonders whether *The Authoress of the Odyssey* helped to suggest Joyce's whole enterprise, imagining the effect that Butler's concept of the epic sweep of the *Odyssey* would have on a man thinking about Ulysses in Dublin. If that speculation is correct, it would be entirely the kind of mental life Butler would have wished. He counted his readers in tens: *The Authoress of the Odyssey* had sold 176 copies by his death, the *Iliad* 177, the *Odyssey* 121. He minded, but learned not to mind, that his books were slow to appreciate in value. His tracking of Homer and Odysseus heralded a spate of modern adaptations and literary explorations. Kenner commented: 'that his most serious reader should have been James Joyce was, perhaps, more than he deserved to expect'; but Butler, for all his diffidence, nurtured the highest expectations.

CHAPTER 20

Pauli and Shakespeare

In 1898, Hans Faesch returned to Basel for a holiday, and to arrange for his marriage to his fiancée, Stéphanie Rabe. Jones was in Basel – he was a more frequent visitor to the Faesch household than Butler – and gave Stéphanie the locket with his share of Hans's hair. 'You did very prettily about the locket,' wrote Butler, 'I had better share mine with you month by month, turn and turn about.'[1] In August, 1900 Butler and Jones were in Switzerland for another of Hans's leaves; Butler moved on to Wassen to sketch while Jones made a short tour with Hans. That December, Hans was in London with a Norwegian, Peter Hauff, with whom he planned to deal in rubber in the Shan States. Butler gave them a farewell dinner, attended also by Jones, Gogin and Alfred. Then at Waterloo station he said his last goodbyes.

Butler's involvement with Hans has the air of an idealised, Arcadian idyll. For Butler, he was an adopted son, even grandson; he was a kind of foundling, found by Jones, if not in a railway cloakroom, at least on a train. He was not Italian, but, the next best thing, Swiss. One is reminded of other Victorians, such as John Addington Symonds, with his admiration for Davos peasants and his infatuation for Christian Buol. Hans was young and had everything to learn, including English. A true innocent abroad, with innate goodness and natural charm, he could be educated in the proper way; and once he had gone out into the night, Butler could give free rein to the affection restrained during the country outings and the evenings at Clifford's Inn.

So Butler, towards the end of his life, found a son: Hans, whose own father was dead, would address letters to his 'dearest Mr Butler' as 'father'. In keeping with the symmetrical pattern of his life, he also suffered a corresponding loss, the death of Pauli. Pauli, albatross-like, had shadowed him for over thirty years, the reticent, elusive partner in a relationship that Butler regretted but would not sever.

For ten years after Pauli had been called to the Bar, Butler had continued to 'loan' him money, to the tune of between £3000 and £3500, to enable him to become established. For that one brief period when he had been totally dependent on his father, Butler was free. Once the Whitehall entail had been cut off, he reverted to his previous role as benefactor, believing, presumably on the evidence of his shabby coat and racking cough, that Pauli was in great need of money. Butler's explanation of this curious step is ingenuous, and not wholly convincing: 'I forget whether or no he told me that this was so; I think it probable that he never said anything directly, but he certainly conveyed the impression to me that he was in great difficulties.'[2] Butler promised him £200 a year without any condition: 'I did what I did simply out of pity, and to avoid that self-reproach which I knew I should feel if Pauli had to leave the Bar while I had a shilling left. Had this happened, I know very well it would have haunted me as Moorhouse haunts me. I can forgive myself for having been the fool I was, and I can forgive Pauli for having let me indulge in such folly, but I could never have forgiven myself if he had been wrecked while I was able, at whatever cost, to help him.'

Butler paid Pauli another £3000 or so from 1880 onwards. It was decided to record the sums in a superintendence account, as though Pauli were managing the house properties. He never did any management. Over the next fifteen years the lunches were reduced to three a week; Pauli would arrive at 1.20 and leave about 2. Butler had by this time 'recognised that anything worthy of the name of friendship' was not to be. He always consulted Pauli on any matter about which he was in doubt, and to all outward appearances they were the best of friends; 'nevertheless I could see that it was an effort to him to be in my company at all, and knew perfectly well that the whole thing was a sham – on my part an endeavour to deny that my passionate devotion to him for so many years in times gone by was spent in force, and on his to satisfy himself that the intimacy between us was still so close as to warrant his taking money from me.' In 1883 or 1884, Butler has been obliged to cut Pauli down to £100 a year; he suggested that Pauli borrow the second £100 from his brother, and that he would repay the loan on Canon Butler's death.

Coincidentally, Butler's and Pauli's fathers died on consecutive days. Pauli, like Butler, came into his reversion. This was the long-awaited opportunity to repay his debts, but he told Butler that when all the other debts had been paid there would be nothing left. Butler heard no more about it. He repaid Captain Pauli the arrears of the allowance (with 5% interest) that he was supposed to have advanced with a cheque made out to Pauli, and reinstated the £200 a year. Butler was 'determined that nothing but death' should end the relationship, although he was afraid that Pauli might have a wife and children hidden away, and that after he had gone, Butler might find a family sprung upon him. Throughout these years, he never knew Pauli's home address, communicating with him only at his chambers; and seeing very little of him apart from the ritual lunches.

Each winter, Pauli suffered from bronchitis. Alfred thought him at death's door on several occasions. In the last few years, the other change that Butler and Alfred noted was that Pauli seemed a little better off. Just before Christmas, 1897, he gave Mrs Cathie, Butler's laundress, five shillings; he had never given so much as a sixpence before to Mrs Cathie or Mrs Doncaster during all the years of the lunches.

Pauli was especially sympathetic about the caustic reviews of *The Authoress of the Odyssey*, and lunched with Butler on December 15th, a Wednesday. The next day, he wrote to say that he had a heavy cold, which developed into bronchitis. More notes were exchanged; Butler's to say that he was going to Boulogne for Christmas, but leaving an address where he could be reached by telegraph, Pauli's dictated to a nurse. On December 30th, Butler read in *The Times* that Pauli had died the previous day. As had happened with Miss Savage, a close friend had died with Butler in ignorance of the circumstances. Butler immediately began to torture himself: 'I rather think I had better not enquire nor put myself into communication with his friends. If he had wished the communication to be established he would have ensured its being so. All I should have wished to do would be to attend the funeral to do away with the supposition that there was any estrangement between us and as the only fitting termination of so close an intimacy; but I feel convinced I shall be communicated with (in which case I shall certainly attend) unless it was Pauli's distinct wish that I should not be present, in which case of course I am better away.'[3] However, he was communicated with, by the undertaker, and invited to travel down to Brookwood Cemetery with the body.

He duly took his place wearing his black silk hat outside the Necropolis station in Westminster Bridge Road. He recognised two men only; Captain, now Colonel, Pauli, to whom he did not speak, and Lascelles, whom Pauli had once brought to lunch thirty years ago. There were some men whose looks did not please him, especially one who announced himself as Pauli's executor: 'this man struck me as one with whom Pauli should have had nothing whatever to do.' Butler introduced himself to Lascelles, and they got into a carriage with a most respectable looking man whom Butler took to be one of the undertaker's men but who turned out to be the valet of an old friend of Pauli named Swinburne.

Butler received a great deal of information during the journey to the cemetery, most of it disturbing and unwelcome. Lascelles told him that Pauli, at one stage of his career, had been earning £700 a year. (Butler learned later that the figure had even approached £900, though less of late because of Pauli's ill health, and recalled how he had flown at his father for suggesting that Pauli was making £1000 a year.) He also heard that Pauli had been living at Belgrave Mansions, Grosvenor Gardens, to be near Mr Swinburne; besides, explained Lascelles, the rooms were very cheap, only £120 a year, less than his previous address in Bruton Street. (Butler's rooms in Clifford's Inn cost him £28 in rent.) During Pauli's last illness, Mr Swinburne had seen that he wanted for nothing: 'he had two nurses, and his doctor, who was an old schoolfellow of his own at Winchester. Everything that he fancied he had, but for the last day or two he could take nothing but grapes and champagne.' Swinburne's valet sat by Pauli's bedside, and read the paper to him every afternoon.

After the service, read with an 'unctuous affectation' Butler had seldom heard exceeded, the mourners sat down to a luncheon that had been brought down on the train; and Butler reflected 'with a certain grim satisfaction' that for once in his life he was making a hearty meal at what was nearly Pauli's expense. It was the nearest thing to a dinner from him that he ever had. The shocks continued. He overheard the executor saying that Colonel Pauli had been left £1000 pounds, which was the first intimation that Pauli had any estate at all. Naturally, having given, or advanced, him between £6000 and £7000 over the years, Butler's curiosity was focused on the true state of his affairs. He was also deeply hurt that there was not even a message of any kind in the will. As he confessed to Gogin, for many years he was 'passionately attached' to Pauli, and he was relieved only that he did not 'break the thing off till death broke it off for him'.[4]

By writing to Swinburne, and meeting Pauli's solicitor, Ainslie, Butler put together some pieces of the puzzle. Swinburne, he deduced, had been helping Pauli in much the same way as he had, though neither was aware of the other's involvement. Ainslie said to him, so Butler reported, 'When you wrote to Swinburne that Pauli had been lunching with you three times a week up to the day he was taken ill, Swinburne was very much surprised, and said, "Butler? Butler? Why I have not heard of Butler for this twenty years past." ' Butler laughed and answered, 'Nor I of Swinburne.' Butler discovered that the gross estate was £9000, and had his own theory as to how he came by such a sum.

Butler's theory is revealing, not because there is any firm evidence to support it but because it points to hidden undercurrents in his relations with Pauli. Pauli had a friend, X, whom he would tell Butler about. X, Pauli felt sure, had been blackmailed for years, and was continually trying to evade income tax. In his last years, he became paralysed, and had two men to take charge of him and keep him away from drink. Pauli was X's executor, and was apparently left only £200 by him. Butler decided that X had gifted £10,000 to Pauli, to avoid paying legacy duty, and that Pauli as sole executor destroyed all traces of the transaction. Thus satisfied of the source of Pauli's money, and having placed him within the hidden Victorian agenda of fraud and blackmail, Butler could bring the 'squalid, miserable story' to an end. 'If I had withdrawn from him and said I should do no more for him, I firmly believed that he would say nothing, leave me and probably blow his brains out or drown himself,' he confessed, nudging the story towards melodrama, as he reconstructed it in Sicily and Rome the following spring, 1898, and recorded it in the third volume of his Note-Books.

> The thing is over: I am thankful that it is so. I can laugh at the way in which Pauli hoodwinked me; and, as I said to Ainslie, though he left me nothing in his will, he has, in effect, left me from £200–£210 a year, clear of all outgoings, for the luncheons

must be taken into the account. We both of us laughed heartily when I took in the luncheons.

As Butler emphasised, the story is his version of events. After reading Jones's account in the *Memoir*, Pauli's executor, Bircham, wrote to *The Times Literary Supplement* to record his 'belief and trust' in his 'dear old friend. There must be some explanation.'[5] Jones commented, 'if anything further is ever done about the relations between Butler and Pauli this Maxim of La Rochefoucauld must be used as a motto: *Il est plus honteux de se défier de ses amis que d'en être trompé.*'

Side by side with his analysis of his friendship with Pauli, Butler carried out a literary investigation. Shakespeare was as important to him as Homer. He kept the Temple edition in a special bookcase fixed above his bed, and read from the plays before going to sleep. In December, 1897 an article by William Archer in *The Fortnightly Review*, followed by one by Sidney Lee on the identity of Mr W.H., set him thinking about the Sonnets. Here was a literary problem closer to home, but no further from his heart, than the authorship of the *Odyssey*. He had solved the latter. He decided, once his translation of the *Iliad* was off his hands, to give the Sonnets the *Odyssey* treatment. His approach was much the same: to familiarise himself so closely with the work that it revealed its true nature to him. He achieved this, to his own satisfaction, by learning the Sonnets by heart. By September, 1898 he had them at his 'fingers' ends',[6] and daily from that time 'repeated twenty-five of them, to complete the process of saturation'.

The appearance of Archer's and Lee's articles coincided with the death of Pauli. There followed the revelations of the funeral, the probing enquiries, and the dissection of the relationship. There are parallels between Butler's view of his friendship, intimacy and love for Pauli, and his interpretation of Shakespeare's for Mr W.H. The tortuous self-analysis is echoed by his reading of the Sonnets, and the language he uses of the one is reflected in the other.

The main points of Butler's theory are these: that the Sonnets are early (he assigns dates to them between spring, 1585 and December, 1588); that Mr W.H. was the person to whom most of the Sonnets were addressed, who was certainly William and probably Hughes (or Hewes, or Hews), but that a small group was addressed to, or about,

Shakespeare's mistress; that the correct order of the Sonnets is, broadly, the same as in the original Quarto edition, with two crucial exceptions; and that, if you place one particular Sonnet much earlier in the sequence, the whole story falls into place.

This Sonnet (121 in the Quarto) Butler dates as '1585. Probably August', and prefaces with the following explanation: *To Mr W.H. Written by Shakespeare before he had calmed down after the catastrophe referred to in the previous note.*

> 'Tis better to be vile than vile esteem'd,
> When not to be receives reproach of being;
> And the just pleasure lost, which is so deem'd
> Not by our feeling, but by others' seeing:
> For why should others' false adulterate eyes
> Give salutation to my sportive blood?
> Or on my frailties why are frailer spies,
> Which in their wills count bad what I think good?
> No, I am that I am, and they that level
> At my abuses reckon up their own;
> I may be straight though they themselves be bevel;
> By their rank thoughts my deeds must not be shown,
>   Unless this general evil they maintain –
>   All men are bad and in their badness feign.

The catastrophe that Butler imagines is a sexual trap. Shakespeare has moved from admiration to a friendship better expressed as love, as in Sonnet 23:

> O, learn to read what silent love hath writ:
> To hear with eyes belongs to love's fine wit.

Mr W.H. lures Shakespeare to a rendezvous, with an invitation to a sexual act. The trap is

> a cruel and most disgusting practical joke, devised by Mr W.H. in concert with others, but certainly never intended, much less permitted, to go beyond the raising coarse laughter against Shakespeare. I do not suppose that the trap was laid from any deeper malice than wanton love of so-called sport, and a desire

to enjoy the confusion of any one who could be betrayed into being a victim; I cannot, however, doubt that Shakespeare was, to use his own words, made to 'travel forth without' that 'cloak,' which, if he had not been lured, we may be sure that he would not have discarded. Hardly had he laid the cloak aside before he was surprised according to a preconcerted scheme, and very probably roughly handled, for we find him lame soon afterwards (sonnet 37, lines 3 and 9) and apparently not fully recovered a twelvemonth later, cf 109 (89 Q), line 3.

The offence above indicated – a sin of very early youth – for which Shakespeare was bitterly penitent, and towards which not a trace of further tendency can be discerned in any subsequent sonnet or work during five and twenty years of later prolific literary activity – this single offence is the utmost that can be brought against Shakespeare with a shadow of evidence in its support. (SS91–2)

The 'incident' is part of a sequence that begins with Shakespeare's liaison with his mistress, the dark lady; Mr W.H.'s involvement with the mistress, and subsequent dismissal by her; and then a protracted and turbulent relationship between Shakespeare and his friend full of absences, estrangements, reconciliations and ruptures. The Sonnets can, then, be read like a story, 'a very squalid one', but one which should not be judged too harshly: 'all of us who read the Sonnets are as men who are looking over another's shoulder and reading a very private letter which was intended for the recipient's eye, and for no one else's.' If one considers only 'youth, the times, penitence, and amendment of life, I believe that those whose judgement we should respect will refuse to take Shakespeare's grave indiscretion more to heart than they do the story of Noah's drunkenness; they will neither blink it nor yet look at it more closely than is necessary in order to prevent men's rank thoughts from taking it to have been more grievous than it was.

'*Tout savoir, c'est tout comprendre* – and in this case surely we may add – *tout pardonner.*' (SS113–14)

That Butler was thinking of his own friendship with Pauli, as he annotated the 'cat and dog life', which, in spite of all Shakespeare's infinite sweetness and forbearance, he believed the two men had been leading, seems natural enough. Butler supposed that in his heart Shakespeare must have known that the friendship had been a one-sided affair from first to last; and he says of Mr W.H., 'He was vain, heartless, and I cannot think ever cared two straws for Shakespeare, who no doubt bored him . . .' (SS151) He could have been talking about himself and Pauli. There is no need, and no evidence, to suggest a parallel catastrophe. The similarities he seized on were psychological. Yet when Butler writes about homosexual acts, his language – 'cancer', 'gross', 'infamous' – seems stronger than his argument requires, as though he is deliberately protecting himself from possible criticism; and his last paragraph is an apologia for the concept of ideal friendship, however disillusioning the reality:

> One word more. Fresh from the study of the other great work in which the love that passeth the love of women is portrayed as nowhere else save in the Sonnets, I cannot but be struck with the fact that it is in the two greatest of all poets that we find this subject treated with the greatest intensity of feeling. The marvel, however, is this; that whereas the love of Achilles for Patroclus depicted by the Greek poet is purely English, absolutely without taint or alloy of any kind, the love of the English poet for Mr W.H. was, though only for a short time, more Greek than English. I cannot explain this. (SS159)

While working on the Sonnets, and with all 154 of them in his head, not surprisingly Butler found that he could write sonnets himself with some ease. In 1898, when he was deep in his past, writing about his father, about Pauli, beginning to transcribe his letters to Miss Savage, editing his correspondence with Jones, he wrote the following sonnet, 'An Academic Exercise'.

> We were two lovers standing sadly by
> While our two loves lay dead upon the ground;
> Each love had striven not to be first to die,
> But each was gashed with many a cruel wound.
> Said I: 'Your love was false while mine was true.'
> Aflood with tears, he cried: 'It was not so,
> 'Twas your false love my true love falsely slew –
> For 'twas your false love that was the first to go.'
> Thus did we stand and said no more for shame –

Till I, seeing his cheek so wan and wet,
Sobbed thus: 'So be it; my love shall bear the blame;
Let us inter them honourably'. And yet
　　I swear by all truth human and divine
　　'Twas his that in its death throes murdered mine.

This seems a more appropriate comment on his friendship with Pauli than on any other of his intimate relationships; he understood dead love and false love only too well.

Butler took some time to recover from the death of Pauli and its attendant revelations. The number of foreign excursions increased. A lengthy trip to Sicily in 1898 was followed by an outing to Flushing and a visit to Amsterdam to see the Rembrandt exhibition. The following spring brought another extensive tour of Italy. In the smelly smoking-room of a Venetian hotel, Charles Ricketts and Charles Shannon spoke to an 'old buggins who looked like a sea-captain': they found him delightfully arbitrary, deducing from his admiration for Gaudenzio Ferrari that he was Samuel Butler, 'a gouty angel in carpet slippers'.[7] Butler passed on one of his golden rules for appreciating a work of art: 'Ask yourself whether you would really like to see it a second time alone.' He also read them passages of his *Odyssey* alternated with Lang's, and outlined his views on the Sonnets.

Shakespeare's Sonnets Reconsidered did not appear until the end of 1899 when Longmans published it, once again at Butler's expense. In the intervening period, the *Iliad* came out, so there had been proofs to correct; and Butler's work rate was undoubtedly slowing down, or rather, he was taking more time to make decisions about business matters, and to deal with the numerous requests of friends and correspondents, many of them from Italy. There was little critical approval for the book or the theory, which was predictable. For the interpretation was yet another of Butler's demythologisings, and even in the restricted terms in which he expressed the 'catastrophe' and its sequel, he was suggesting that the great English poet, whose works were a Victorian source book of high thinking comparable with the Bible and Homer, wrote the Sonnets as a flesh and blood youth sowing his wild oats in sordid company and surroundings.

Although less subversive than Wilde's brilliant fiction 'Mr W.H.' (a text that Butler never alludes to, though he must surely have been aware of it), nevertheless his interpretation was an abrupt challenge both to politer biographical readings and to the 'literary exercise' school. Robert Bridges, who had been corresponding regularly with Butler since enjoying *The Authoress of the Odyssey*, wrote: 'I am very sorry indeed that you have been so clever as to make up so good (or bad) a story; but I willingly recognize that no one has brought the matter into so clear a light as you have done . . . It is not the logic that fails in this book.'[8] Butler was well disposed towards Bridges, for Rockstro had passed on the latter's opinion that Butler wrote better prose than any living author. They exchanged books, and Butler found himself having to comment on Bridges's verse dramas.

However, Bridges's was a rare approving voice. A meeting was arranged between Butler and the Shakespearean scholar, Dr Furnivall, 'a most amiable, kindly old gentleman, absolutely free from "side" or affectation, and very sensible (as I presently found) on some matters in respect of which most men are idiots'. It soon transpired that Furnivall had not properly read Butler's book at all but merely skimmed it, and had not understood his reading of Shakespeare's 'offence'. He then admitted he had never studied the Sonnets very closely. 'I liked the old gentleman well enough, but I parted with him in some depression – for I saw more plainly even than before that no one in my life-time is likely to read, mark, learn and inwardly digest either my book or the immortal poems of which it treats. The more universal writing becomes, the more do people seem to have utterly lost the art of reading. However, I shall go on writing just the same.' (M2.310–14)

Once again, Butler's theories have received more critical attention from later generations of readers, for instance from Robert Graves, who in his essay 'The Sources of *The Tempest* broadly accepted Butler's interpretation.[9] Once again, too, Butler deceived his audience, and possibly himself, by the form of the book, making it appear an orthodox volume of literary and textual criticism, rather than a fictional and imaginative act of re-creation. His fables of Nausicaa and Shakespeare, masquerading as criticism, were novels in disguise; and they brought him back to the fable of Erewhon still shaping itself in his mind, the world of his first imaginative creation.

CHAPTER 21

Erewhon Revisited

Butler was becoming conscious of the 'pretty roundness' of his literary career. *Erewhon Revisited* was his major occupation during 1900 and 1901, though the evidence suggests that he wrote it more fluently than any other of his books. According to Jones, the idea had been in his mind for many years; 'some of his notes for it are given in the Note-Books, but I cannot tell at what date he first contemplated it because he sometimes added the titles to his notes when copying them out at a date later than that of their composition. But he did not look through his Note-Books for materials; he wrote the book straight off.' (M2.353) Writing on August 8th, 1900 to the Dean of Bristol, who had referred to *Erewhon* in a paper, 'On the relation of Disease to Crime', Butler admitted: 'I am the more anxious to read your criticism, be it adverse or the contrary, because I am almost immediately about to make a second journey to Erewhon in the person of my supposed son and to report sundry developments.' (M2.330–1)

In February, 1901 he consulted Mrs Fuller-Maitland. He had shown her the manuscript and, because of her objections, he had altered some passages. The cause for offence was his treatment of the Sunchild, the Erewhonian name given to Higgs after his ascension in the balloon; the religion that had evolved around his life and sayings was known as Sunchildism.

> Pray believe me I never meant any allusion whatever to the Founder of Christianity. I fear you must have thought I meant to suggest likeness to him in the Sunchild. I meant to show how myth, attended both by zealous good faith on the part of some and chicane on the part of others, would be very naturally developed in consequence of a supposed miracle, such as the balloon ascent would be to a people who knew nothing about

such things; and I meant to suggest a parallelism not between the Sunchild and Christ (which never even entered my head) but between the circumstances that would almost inexorably follow such a supposed miracle as the escape of the Sunchild, and those which all who think as I do believe to have accreted round the supposed miracle, not of the Ascension, but the Resurrection. And I did not mean to poke fun at Christianity. Anything but. However, I must not do anything that can be mistaken for this. I do not and never did wish to do so. I have given the amended MS. to Streatfeild and have urged him to call my attention to anything that is even bordering on 'bad taste'. (M2.338)

This was familiar territory. Butler was ingenuous if he believed his book would not be interpreted as a satire on Christianity. While continuing his own search for God, he maintained a lifelong crusade against the wrongs done in the name of false myth. The distinction was not always so clear cut to others. Longman, who had published all three of the Homer books, was the obvious person to approach. He declined, according to Butler, 'for fear of giving offence to his connection among the High Anglican party'. (M2.339) On the suggestion of his friends Emery Walker and Sydney Cockerell, Butler sent the manuscript to Shaw for advice.

Butler was, unusually, in London during the spring of 1901, while Jones had already set off for Sicily. There had been a slight shift in their relationship, which is largely suppressed in Jones's *Memoir*. Jones's mother had died in January, 1900, and by her will had left him financially secure. Butler stopped the allowance he had been paying, and Jones offered to repay Butler everything he had received since Canon Butler's death thirteen years before, an offer that Butler initially refused. However, Jones later signed a covenant at Butler's insistence that the estate would be repaid. As Butler later confided to Gogin, he did not intend to have a second Pauli.[1]

The evidence of a cooling in the friendship is fragmentary, but unmistakable. Each travelled abroad separately in these last years, or spent less time in the other's company when they did go together. Jones would go round to Clifford's Inn on three, rather than five, nights a week, and dropped the regular Sunday walk because it tired him. Richard Streatfeild, whom Butler had met at the British

Museum, became more prominent as an adviser, and was eventually made literary executor, a rebuff for Jones, who for years had been so closely connected with Butler's writing. Butler believed that Jones's health was much more precarious than it proved to be: he noted later that his friend was 'obviously & rapidly failing. That there is serious brain mischief now I cannot doubt.' He wanted a healthy literary executor with a good life expectancy. Yet Butler, writing to Jones in September from Wassen, where he was editing Miss Savage's correspondence, confessed: 'I am shocked to see how badly I treated her, always thinking and writing about myself and never about her. If I have been as selfish and egoistic to you as I was to her, it will explain a good deal. I must endeavour, late as it is, to mend my ways.' (M2.349) That suggests there was something specific to explain. Jones loyally comments: 'To me he was the dearest, kindest, most considerate friend that any man ever had. He was never selfish or egoistic, nor was there anything that required explanation. If any one was selfish just at this time it was I for going off to Sicily to satisfy my curiosity about the procession on Mount Eryx', leaving Butler alone at Wassen 'to make stepping-stones of his dead selves'.

That exchange and confession came later in the year, during Jones's second solo visit to Sicily. Meanwhile, Butler wrote to Shaw about his book which he described as 'far more wicked than *Erewhon*'. (M2.339) Shaw responded enthusiastically and warmly: 'It is almost incredible that Longmans should be such a stupendous ass . . . My own publisher is a young villain named Grant Richards who has no scruples of any kind. You had better let me show you to him on approval. If you will come to lunch with us at 1.30 say, on Wednesday or Thursday, I will invite Grant Richards, too. If you can persuade Walker or Cockerell or both to come along with you, do. We shall then feel at home and independent, as Richards will be in a hopeless minority. My wife is a good Erewhonian, and likes Handel; you won't find her in any way disagreeable. And 10 Adelphi Terrace is within easy reach . . . I have started reading your MS. instead of doing my work. So far I am surprised to find that so confounded a rascal as your original hero did not become a pious millionaire; otherwise he is as interesting as ever. More of this when I finish him.' (M2.339–40) Shaw's approach was both generous and extremely tactful, designed to display Butler at his best, at ease and protected by friends. Richards, to whom Shaw described Butler as a 'polite and delicate old bird',[2] agreed to have it and, at the same time, to bring out a new edition of *Erewhon*, for which Butler would supply enough additional material to guarantee a fresh copyright. As Richards wanted to take the sheets with him to America in May, Butler immediately settled down to complete his tasks. Streatfeild and Alfred checked the proofs, Walker and Cockerell advised on the layout, and Butler was free to set off for the continent.

Butler's journeys were ritual retracings of his personal map of Europe. He stayed at Basel, to see the Faesches, and at Casale-Monferrato, where he called on his friends the Negri and Coppo families. Then he met Jones at Pisa, and they went south to Rome and Naples, and so to Sicily. Jones records the royal progress: 'Our friends Miss Bertha Thomas and Miss Helen Zimmern were in the hotel and Ingroja had come down from Calatafimi to meet us. We went to Trapani and up the mountain, saluting all our friends; then through Castelvetrano back to Palermo and on through Catania to Taormina where we found William Logsdail, the painter, with his family. We went to Aci Reale for a day and saw Mario Puglisi, then to Messina and returned by sea to Naples.' (M2.342–3)

The schedule was punishing, and Butler's health was now fragile. For some years Jones had accompanied him on his way back from his rooms to Clifford's Inn in the evenings, in case he felt dizzy. He did this, he hoped, unobtrusively, for Butler preferred to make light of his symptoms. In Naples, he admitted to feeling ill, but would not alter his plans. On they went north, until he was doing little more than be 'put into the train to travel by day and be put into the hotel to sleep by night'. At Bologna, he collapsed on a seat in the gallery while Jones, at his insistence, went to see the pictures. Back at Casale, he agreed to stay for several days, to consult a doctor, who diagnosed malaria. The higher altitude and fresher atmosphere revived him, and he was home, in better health, by the end of June.

There he took up the task of reconstructing his life, editing his notes and correspondence. He was also considering a new study of Tabachetti, or at least undertaking the translation of Avvocato Negri's monograph. In September he went to Wassen, while Jones returned to Sicily to see the procession of the Personnagi on Monte San Giuliano. Butler had seen this some years before, and in any event did not wish so long a journey. In Wassen, he sketched and worked on his correspondence with Miss Savage, writing the letter to Jones in which he expressed shock at treating her so badly, and at least one of the sonnets:

> And now, though twenty years are come and gone,
> That little lame lady's face is with me still;

In a Wassen sketchbook, another version begins:

> And now, though twenty years are come and gone
> Since I beheld her, I behold her still.

There was also the line:

> Death bound me to her when he set me free.

Back in London, he awaited the publication of *Erewhon Revisited*.[3] His health remained precarious, although he concealed the fact from his close friends as far as possible: 'My new book is to come out on Wednesday,' he informed Cesare Coppo, 'and I am very anxious to see how it is received. As regards my health, I am very fairly well, but I doubt whether I have ever quite shaken off the attack I got in the spring. When I was at Wassen I had a return of it, and at one time, was in half a mind to run over to Casale and show myself to Cavaliere Giorcelli, but I got better again – though I am still not quite as I should be.' (M2.352)

Erewhon Revisited was published on October 11th: it was more positively received than any of his works since *Erewhon*. In sending Mrs Fuller-Maitland a copy he referred to it again as 'my wicked book', but it did not cause much controversy. Quiller-Couch, reviewing it favourably in *The Daily News*, expressed one reservation:

> But when it comes to inventing for an Erewhonian woman named Yram (which is 'Mary' reversed) and her husband a situation which at once calls up, and scandalously, the nuptials of Christ's Mother with Joseph, then I must submit that he is either offensive by inadvertence almost incredible or . . .[4]

For once Butler was in a secure position. As he pointed out in a letter to the editor, the parallel could only come into the question if

Higgs, the Sunchild, was the son of Yram, not the father of her child. Quiller-Couch apologised in a private letter, offering to publish a retraction, but Butler was content to let the matter rest.

He provided *Erewhon Revisited* with the most complex narrative structure of all his books. The story is told by Higgs's son John from his father's diaries and notes dictated when he arrived back in England with fading memory and broken health. 'Remember,' he told John, 'that I thought I was quite well so long as I was in Erewhon . . .'

The first main theme is a return to Butler's early preoccupation with the Crucifixion and Resurrection of Christ. What might have happened in Erewhon after Higgs's apparently miraculous ascent into the heavens with his earthly bride Arowhena? Given a single great miracle, Butler argued, more would accrete around it, and, as with other religions, there would follow 'temples, priests, rites, sincere believers, and unscrupulous exploiters of public credulity'. Higgs discovers that he is worshipped as 'the Sunchild'; the Musical Banks have been swift to adopt the new movement; there is a flourishing Sunchild Evidence Society; and Professor Hanky is one of its chief exponents. The climax of Butler's treatment of this idea is Professor Hanky's sermon in the temple, during which Higgs proclaims that he is still alive, and has to be arrested and imprisoned to avoid being torn in pieces and burned.

The second theme is the story of a father trying to win the love of an unknown son. By declaring himself to be the Sunchild, Higgs faced possible death at the hands of the vested interests of Sunchildism. George is his child by Yram, daughter of his gaoler during his first months in prison, who had taught him the Erewhonian language. She had married Mr Strong, now the Mayor of Sunch'ston; and they had brought George up as their son. Much of the imaginative energy of the novel is directed towards the relationship between Higgs and George; and George is Butler's idealised portrait of the son he never had. Indeed, Yram and Strong represent a true marriage, in contrast to the false legitimacy of Theobald and Christina Pontifex; and Higgs's hard won, momentary love for George signifies the ultimate earthly happiness.

This second theme grows in importance as the book develops, so that, as Hugh Kingsmill suggests, Higgs, 'returning to Erewhon twenty years or so after his first visit, is no longer Higgs, but Butler in search of a son'.[5] George, the ideal man, owes something to the idea of the swell, to Towneley, and to Pauli as Butler first imagined him to be; in his simplicity, he reflects the qualities Butler saw in Hans Faesch; in his natural goodness – and he is, significantly, a 'natural child' – there is a touch of Alfred as well as of Hans. (Alfred makes an eponymous appearance in the book as the family solicitor.) Butler gave full rein to his sentiment in the description of Higgs's leave-taking. The prevailing form is that of melodrama, the kind of melodrama that left not a dry eye in the house:

> They then re-packed all that could be taken away; my father rolled his rug to his liking, slung it over his shoulder, gripped George's hand, and said, 'My dearest boy, when we have turned our backs upon one another, let us walk our several ways as fast as we can, and try not to look behind us.'
>
> So saying he loosed his grip of George's hand, bared his head, and turned away.
>
> George burst into tears, and followed him after he had gone two paces; he threw his arms around him, hugged him, kissed him on his lips, cheeks, and forehead, and then turning round, strode full speed towards Sunch'ston. My father never took his eyes off him till he was out of sight, but the boy did not look round. When he could see him no more, my father with faltering gait, and feeling as though a prop had suddenly been taken from under him, began to follow the stream down towards his old camp. (ER295–6)

The curtain might fall, and the strains of the orchestra die away; but Butler's withdrawal from Erewhon is never complete. First, he uses Higgs's farewell to his second, 'legitimate' son, John, to recall the fading vision, evoking with pathos the image of a poor, unhinged creature under the starlit calm of a great wilderness, conscious that on the other side of the great wall of mountain thousands of children were praying to him. He then moves surreptitiously into burlesque with Higgs's dying words: 'he seemed to see some horrible chasm in front of him which he had to cross, or which he feared that I must cross, for he gasped out words, which, as near as I could catch them, were, "Look out! John! Leap! Leap! Le . . ."'[6] When John is sleeping out on the mountainside, waiting to keep his father's promised appointment with George, he dreams he is by his father's bed-side, trying to catch his dying words: 'All of a sudden the bed seemed to be at my camping ground, and the largest of the statues appeared, quite small, high up the mountain side, but striding down like a giant in seven league boots till it stood over me and my father, and shouted out "Leap, John, leap." ' Sitting by the statues with George the following day, John asked him why he had not met him the day before, as was the arrangement: he learned that 1891 had been a leap year with the Erewhonians, and in the deliberately mundane explanation the aura of mystery is punctured.

Throughout the final section the sense of gain is finely balanced against the sense of loss. Butler offers images of unity only to under-line their fragility and impermanence; but he is reluctant to leave the idealised world of Erewhon, blessed now with the presence of George: the novel's final sentence introduces yet one more projected fictional journey, to the neighbouring country of Erewhemos. This vein of sentiment, never far below the surface, is more visible in this last book. But the comic ending is so idealised that it almost mocks itself, like those of Wilde's 'children's' stories. Butler's adroit wit never deserted him. He reminded the writer and journalist H.W. Nevinson, who visited him at Clifford's Inn in July, 1901, of a Greek comic mask: 'The mouth opened like a comic mask, and the humorous or ironic wrinkles in the reddish face were like a mask as well. There was something of Socrates about it, something, therefore, of the satyr. One expected to see pointed ears covered with fur. And I observed the satyr eyes – bluish or grey, but very bright, gleaming with a genial malice or a malicious cheerfulness, but revealing the sensitive shyness and melancholy common to humorists and monkeys and other wild animals. The appearance of attractive wild beast was increased by the short white beard and the thickets of black eyebrow . . .'[7] Towards younger writers, Butler showed a generosity and sweetness of nature that remained unsoured by personal disap-pointment; he asked Nevinson about the siege of Ladysmith, and called in Alfred to listen as he explained with a few heaps of books for hills and matches for guns. The talk soon drifted on to Homer, and Nevinson kept a discreet silence about his review in *The Daily Chronicle*, headed 'Miss Homer's Work'.

Nevinson commented that Butler's life was far from unhappy: 'He delighted in his own work, and was concentrated upon it.'[8] The comic mask, the gentle voice and old-fashioned courtesy, for the most part concealed the melancholy. In his last novel, a sense of failure, an evocation of the void, obtrudes. A more characteristic, but no less poignant, expression of the son he never had occurs in a note of October 13th, 1892:

> I knew we should never get on together; I should have had to cut him off with a shilling either for laughing at Homer or for refusing to laugh at him, or both, or neither, but still cut him off, so I settled the matter by turning a deaf ear to his importunities and sticking to it that I would not get him at all. Yet his thin ghost visits me at times, and though he knows it is no use pestering me further he looks at me so wistfully and reproachfully that I am half inclined to turn tail and ask him to let me get him after all. But I should show a clean pair of heels if he said this – besides he would probably be a girl.[9]

CHAPTER 22

Last Days

For the Christmas of 1901, Butler crossed the Channel with Jones to stay at Boulogne as so often in the past. On their return, Jones went to stay with his sister Lilian at Downshire Hill, Hampstead, and became seriously ill with pneumonia. Butler occasionally made the effort to visit him, bearing bottles of turtle soup, but he was far from well himself. Instead he wrote long letters, often to Lilian, sending whatever news and gossip would entertain the invalid. He described the Surrey Pantomime with the loving appreciation of a connoisseur. Even if the vulgarity was toned down, there were still the old familiar allusions to delirium tremens, and a baths and washhouse scene 'in which Victor Stevens in stays, bathing-drawers, and long dishevelled black hair, as also all the other protagonists in extreme dishabille, came almost up to the old Grecian level'. (M2.372–3)

He continued to delve into his own past; he was editing the 'very painful' years of his correspondence, 1883–86: 'I am at the point when I was sent for post-haste to Shrewsbury to a supposed perfectly hopeless illness of my father who recovered and lived three years longer. I see I wrote to Miss Savage that it was Orpheus and Eurydice only the other way about.' (M2.364) When he came to Jones's letters of 1883, he found they contained 'treasonable matter' about Butler's immediate family; he overscored them with lines from Milton, *Paradise Lost*, Book III, which he had learned by heart at Shrewsbury when copying them out over and over again as a punishment; of Jones's letters he said, 'Treated with a moderate application of "Hail, holy Light" they are quite safe; in all cases of doubt I apply the Milton.' Death filled his mind, though he had already clarified his philosophy in that respect. This sonnet appeared in *The Athenaeum* in January:

Μέλλοντα ταυτα

Not on sad Stygian shore, nor in clear sheen
Of far Elysian plain, shall we meet those
Among the dead whose pupils we have been,
Nor those great shades whom we have held as foes;
No meadow of asphodel our feet shall tread,
Nor shall we look each other in the face
To love or hate each other being dead,
Hoping some praise, or fearing some disgrace.
We shall not argue saying ''Twas thus' or 'Thus',
Our argument's whole drift we shall forget;
Who's right, who's wrong, 'twill be all one to us;
We shall not even know that we have met.
    Yet meet we shall, and part, and meet again
    Where dead men meet, on lips of living men.

He thought much about the past, and memories of New Zealand had been revived by the writing of *Erewhon Revisited*. A letter from the editor of the Christchurch Press, enclosing copies of the Jubilee *Weekly*, was particularly welcome:

> The *Weekly Press* is really an astonishing performance as well as a most interesting one – I need hardly say that I shall value it very highly. The illustration which affects me personally most is the one of Dr Sinclair's grave which is on my own run (that was). I was away down at Christchurch when poor Dr Sinclair, who was staying at my station, was drowned, and never heard of what had happened till I actually reached home and found that the body had been already buried – with a service, I blush to say, read from my bullock-driver's Mass-Book by Dr Haast, as he then was, no Church of England Prayer Book being found on the station. Possibly I had taken mine with me for use at Christchurch, but at this distance of time – nearly forty years – who can say? (M2.361–2)

In the Jubilee number, there were photographs of William Sefton Moorhouse, who dwelt in Butler's memory as one of the finest men whose path he ever crossed, 'but who also haunts me bitterly as one

of the very few men – at least I trust it may be so – who treated me
with far greater kindness than I did him . . . Not that I ever failed in
admiration and genuine affection but (it is true, under great stress)
I did not consider things which a larger knowledge of the world has
shown me I ought assuredly to have considered.' There was also a
flattering article about the announcement of *Erewhon Revisited*, and
Butler arranged for copies to be sent out. 'You will see reminiscences
of my own first crossing the hills above Lyttelton and riding across
the plains in chapter xxvii, but I have deliberately altered a good
deal, for I had to make the writer get up the Rakaia Gorge, whereas
I have really taken him to the Rangitata.' (M2.361–2)

In the intervals of editing his remains, and arranging alterations
and improvements to his house property, Butler was slightly more
sociable this winter. But he was also becoming more irritable, no
doubt a product of his deteriorating health. He quarrelled with Harry
Quilter, who had published some tactless remarks about his way of
life, and especially about his 'boy' Alfred, in *What's What*. He lunched
again with the Shaws, having agreed to eat vegetarian. He wanted
Shaw's advice about a new edition of *Ex Voto*, which he was trying
to persuade Grant Richards to undertake. Butler did not really like
Shaw, or the people he met there, but he was grateful for his interest
and energy on his behalf. 'Mr Shaw used to preach at the Governor,'
according to Alfred. 'There was none of your "What do you think
about this?" It was always, "I'm telling you about this." The Governor
used to say, "Alfred, I hate Irishmen." '[1] Shaw, in some respects,
was remarkably like Butler, not least in his dogmatism, and his
opinions clashed with Butler's; he would cry down Handel and cry
up Wagner, or attack Shakespeare in favour of Bunyan: 'If he means
it, there is no trusting his judgment. If he does not mean it I have
no time to waste on such trifling . . . there is something uncomfortable about the man which makes him uncongenial to me.'[2] In former
years, Butler might have avoided such a contact; now he was at least
tolerant enough to go to lunch, and repeat the encounter. Grant
Richards rejected the *Ex Voto* scheme, and Butler decided to pursue
the idea of a short book on Tabachetti to be called *Jean de Wespin*.

Since Jones was still not well enough to travel to Sicily that spring,
Butler decided to set out on his own on a final journey to Ithaca.
He planned to meet the Fuller-Maitlands in Rome, and show them
the Sicilian sites of the *Odyssey*, while Jones would join him later in

Varallo. At Casale-Monferrato, he felt sufficiently 'good for nothing' to send for Dr Giorcelli. The doctor gave him a prescription, which Butler never had made up, and advised him to take a couple of sulphur baths in Rome. His friends tried to persuade him to stay with them longer, to recuperate, but he insisted on continuing to Rome. He told them that his father, at the end of his life, had gone to his farm at Harnage against the advice of his family, where he had caught a cold from which he never recovered; he said that 'he was like his father and intended to go to Sicily if it cost him his life.' In Rome, he saw the Fuller-Maitlands and discussed plans. He also took a sulphur bath, which he claimed did him harm, and consulted a homoeopathic doctor, who prescribed quinine in heroic quantities. (M2.388–391)

There was an English doctor, Rowland Thurnam, in the Victoria Hotel, who fell into conversation over dinner with his neighbour on the subject of Sicily. Something was said about Trapani, and the *Odyssey*. Thurnam had read *The Authoress of the Odyssey*, and said:

'Oh! but in that case you ought to talk to old Butler.'

'I am old Butler,' replied his neighbour.

Butler was delighted to find an enthusiastic reader, and sat up talking with him till three in the morning. He also had a professional consultation as to whether he was strong enough to continue to Sicily. Another evening, recalled another guest at the hotel, 'my daughter called my attention to an old gentleman sitting near the head of the table who she said looked like a philosopher. I looked up and immediately knew that the old gentleman had been in my life sometime, but I could not quite place him. At the end of dinner someone sitting next to him left the table and taking my glass of wine with me I walked up to the vacant seat and began talking to my neighbour. I thought I knew his voice and asked him if he had ever been in New Zealand. "Oh yes," he said, "about forty years ago I was there." "Then perhaps," I said, "you are Sam Butler," and "by God," he returned, "you are John Baker." How we yarned the rest of the evening, and Butler, who had a wonderful memory, mentioned many incidents and conversations I had forgotten years before. We talked till long past midnight . . .'[3] It was with John Baker that Butler had discovered the pass through the Southern Alps, which became his entrance into Erewhon.

After a while, he felt sufficiently well to continue to Naples and

Palermo, arriving about the same time as the Fuller-Maitlands. He wrote to Jones asking for a supply of sixpenny novels – an alarming symptom – and even a volume of George Meredith: 'my blood be upon my own head'. Jones was by now in Nice, staying with his sister Cattie, and several times offered to join him. Butler would not hear of it: 'I miss you very much, but at the same time I am *most thankful* that you are not with me. It is a great relief to me and makes things much easier for me, for I can run myself quite well.'[4] He suffered a severe and prolonged attack of diarrhoea: he told May that his digestive organs were much insulted. Mrs Fuller-Maitland was also ill; Fuller-Maitland attended on both sick-beds, running backwards and forwards with prescriptions for the two invalids, who were suffering from diametrically opposite complaints, to the chemist's confusion. Butler's Sicilian friends were constant visitors, which was gratifying but tiring.

In his weak and depressed state, his suppressed resentment towards Jones welled up, and he wrote him a 'dreadful' letter.[5] He confided in Fuller-Maitland, who later noted tactfully that Jones 'had sprained an ankle in North Italy and could not come to succour his friend'. He also sent an account to Gogin, which he asked him to burn. Jones replied, saying that he had destroyed the letter. After a while, the doctor insisted that Butler had a nurse. On May 11th he was strong enough for the nurse to escort him over to Naples, and Alfred was sent for. A nephew by marriage of Harriet Bridges was cruising off Naples, on his yacht; Harriet would not even contact him, for fear the young man might be contaminated by her infidel brother.[6]

On May 14th Butler wrote to the Fuller-Maitlands from Bertolini's Palace Hotel, 'A perfect hotel':

I now write to say that there is no doubt that I am far more gravely ill than was suspected by any of us, and am only being hurried home as a prelude to consultations, operations, and artificial prolongations of what Christian charity should curtail.

So be it! Alfred starts from London today. He and the nurse are to accompany me both of them to Basle and Alfred to London. The doctor fully believes that I may reach London much as now, and there may be weeks or even months before the end comes, but I can see he has not the faintest doubt what the end is to be.

Therefore with infinite thanks for infinite kindness received from both of you and every cordial good wish for many years of happiness and health to you both, I bid you both heartily farewell. No answer, please. – Always very affectionately to both of you, S. Butler.

You will not forget the pretty roundness of my literary career! α *Erewhon*, ω *Erewhon Revisited*. (M2.393)

Alfred arrived in Naples on May 16th, and suggested sending for Jones, but Butler forbade him. They set off at once for London. The nurse went with them as far as Calais, and Butler was home in Clifford's Inn on May 19th. Although he had written to Fuller-Maitland from Naples, 'I doubt whether the doctor takes quite so gloomy a view of my ultimate chance as he did,' he responded to the editor of the Sicilian *Quo Vadis* on May 22nd with these words: 'Al medesimo tempo, saluto gli amici Trapanesi, li abraccio, alzo mio cappello, e li dico cordialmente addio.' (At the same time I salute my Trapanese friends, I embrace them, I raise my hat, and I bid them cordially farewell.) (M2.394)

As Butler clearly thought he was dying it is surprising that Jones did not insist on going to meet him: he was as near as Ancona by the time Butler had returned to Naples. His explanation in the *Memoir* is unconvincing: 'he started too suddenly and travelled too fast for me to join him on the Continent, but as soon as I knew he was in London I followed.' Butler had written to him from Naples: 'I don't see why you should come home sooner than you naturally would. Alfred and the nurse will get me home. I am feeling more hopeful today about getting home alive, about which yesterday I was almost despairing.'[7] On May 21st Butler wrote from London to Basel: 'I feel sure that I shall not ask you to do anything that does not commend itself to your sense of our ultimate happy relations. However, I shall be very glad to see you on your return...' He added, 'I am weaker than words can say.'[8] The strained phrasing points to Butler's decision to change his will. On May 24th Jones was still abroad, and Alfred wrote on Butler's behalf: 'Mr Butler will be very grateful if you could come home as soon as you can.' A telegram the next day urged Jones not to hurry; but, hearing that he was on his way, Butler wrote to his chambers suggesting he contacted Russell Cooke, Butler's solicitor, before coming to see him at the nursing home: 'I think it will be better all round.' He told Gogin that he had made Jones promise to refund all the money he had given him to his nephew.[9]

Butler made a new will on May 31st. Jones was not even appointed an executor: these were Reginald Worsley and Richard Streatfeild; Streatfeild was to be his literary executor, and was bequeathed 'all unpublished manuscripts notes etc and all his copyrights'. Alfred was left £2000, together with furniture, clothing and household effects, and his watch and chain and plate and photographic cameras. Charles Gogin and his wife Alma were left an annuity of £100 a year, and Mrs Cathie, his laundress, £1 a week. He gave his sister-in-law, Henrietta Butler, a life interest in his freehold estate in Northamptonshire; he had helped her considerably with financial advice in recent years. The bulk of the estate was left to his nephew Henry, who had been fruit farming in Florida. Each of his sisters received £200, the same sum as the executors. To Jones, he now left only '£500 and all interest in musical compositions upon which they had been jointly engaged and all copyrights etc in all works published in common by them'. (M2.402–3) When Jones arrived, they made their peace, and any residual hurt remained unspoken. On June 4th he told Harriet that he had 'made up all estrangement', and they were now as good friends as ever. Butler's estate was, by this time, substantial. In 1893 the capital had been calculated at over £50,000. Some of the house property was sold to pay for the annuities, but there were still thirty-eight freehold houses, and the residue, after all the bequests and annuities, came to over £33,000.

Dr Dudgeon had arranged to move his patient from Clifford's Inn to a nursing home in Henrietta Street, off Regent Street, close to where he had lodged as a young man just down from Cambridge. The night nurse made a fuss of him. According to Alfred, she went further than that, and persisted in getting on the bed on top of him – 'she was a gold-digger'. Butler demanded she should be replaced, but when nothing was done, Dudgeon found him a more peaceful alternative in St John's Wood. His windows looked on to Lord's cricket ground, and Alfred would sit and watch the cricket when he slept in the afternoons. 'I am much better today,' Jones reports him as saying. 'I don't feel at all as though I were going to die; of course, it will be all wrong if I do get well, for there is my literary position to be considered. First I write *Erewhon* – that is my opening subject; then, after modulating freely through all my other books and the music and so on, I return gracefully to my original key and publish *Erewhon Revisited*. Obviously now is the proper moment to come to a full close, make my bow and retire; but I believe I am getting well, after all. It's very inartistic, but I cannot help it. However, we shall see.' Jones tried to comfort him by telling him that his recovery would give him an opportunity for a coda of considerable length on a tonic pedal. 'You might make that very artistic indeed; you know you always liked a tonic pedal.' It was not of much use, Jones commented, 'for in himself he believed he was dying, but he was not going to say so'. (M2.397 *et seq*)

Dudgeon advised that, on his recovery, he must not go back to Clifford's Inn, but find a flat in a more airy locality. So it was arranged that both Butler and Jones would give notice, and search for neighbouring flats. Butler became worried that he would disturb his neighbours when he played the piano, so the flat was transformed into a house, first leasehold, and then freehold. Alfred and Jones found a suitable house in Hampstead, and Reginald Worsley was sent to prepare a report. 'I am not behaving like a man who is going to die,' commented Butler. 'I make my will, and tell my sisters all about it, and then here I am buying a freehold house at Hampstead!'

Doctor, patient and Jones discussed whether to seek a second opinion. Dr Dudgeon was eighty-two, and deaf. Butler said he was perfectly satisfied, but if Dudgeon wanted a second opinion, he had only to say so; Dudgeon was happy with the diagnosis and his patient's progress, but if Butler wanted to consult someone else, he would arrange it at once. On June 6th Dr Moir was called in, and diagnosed Butler's condition as pernicious anaemia. Alfred kept a careful note of all expenditure: grapes and flowers, 1s 9d; and each time a doctor called, the guinea fee was entered in the account book. On June 9th a third doctor was consulted. Alfred added after his name and fee, '(fraud)'.[10]

Butler had visits from his nieces, Tom's and Henrietta's daughters, Elsie and Maysie. Elsie Phillipson went with her soldier husband; she found Uncle Sam 'shockingly white and thin and weak': when Alfred arrived, he did not recognise him, and addressed him in Italian. She thought he would get better, 'but he was horribly pathetic

and was just going to cry, and we ran away'. Harriet and May sent
Maysie to find out whether they might be allowed to visit. Armed
with a bunch of red roses, Maysie arrived at the nursing home, to
find her uncle yellow and shrunken. When she removed his bedrest,
he was as light as a feather on her arm. He declined to see his
sisters. He was annoyed, she recalled, because May had written to
Alfred for news, instead of direct to him. 'I told him their anxiety
was not curiosity, but a real affection and anxiety to know what they
could do for him. This he derided; but knowing it to be true, I rather
pressed for a message to them, saying, "They want you to know that
they care for you." At this he smiled, and said, "I will take it at
that." '[11]

Butler grew slowly weaker. He complained that he did not want
to smoke, and that he was not allowed wine; but he had no real wish
to do either. He said he did not suppose he would ever drink another
glass of wine or smoke another cigarette. On June 18th, 1902 there
was a change for the worse. He had difficulty in breathing. Jones sat
with him in the late afternoon. When he got up to leave Butler
opened his eyes and said: 'I'm going away soon. I'm to be left alone.'
Jones fetched Worsley and Alfred, and told Butler:

'I've brought Reggie to tell you about your house. He has been to
Hampstead to see it.'

'Well, and what do you think of it, Reggie?'

'It's a very nice house, Sam; it will do very well for you.'

'Drains all right?'

'Yes, the drains are in very good order.'

'Very well; then you'll send your report to Russell Cooke.' The
next thing he said was that he knew he was dying.

Jones told him that he would come and see him in the morning.
Butler replied that he did not suppose he would be there in the
morning. Jones waited downstairs, and presently Alfred came to fetch
him.

'We went into the room. He knew us and said it was a dark
morning. It was really a very fine evening; I think he supposed it was
the next day. Then he said: "Have you brought the cheque-book,
Alfred?" '

There were really no last words, Alfred said in 1939. He sat in a
chair in front of the dressing-glass, and at about eight-forty, he
collapsed and his head fell backwards. Alfred noted in the account

book: 6d – Telegram to Mrs Bridges. The cause of death was entered as intestinal catarrh and pernicious anaemia. Dr Moir had diagnosed cancer.

The funeral was on June 21st. Four members of Butler's family attended; his cousins Reginald and Richard Worsley; Amy, Reginald's daughter, and Richard Phillipson. Present also were Jason Smith, William Beales, Alfred Marks, Gaetano Meo, Miss Patten and Nurse Cawley from the nursing home, Charles Gogin, Richard Streatfeild, Russell Cooke, Edward Tanner, who collected rents for Butler, Jones and Alfred.

At one time Butler had wished to be buried at Langar, with a musical quotation from a Handel fugue on his tombstone. Then he decided to be cremated, and for his ashes to be scattered over the grass court at Clifford's Inn. After the experience of his mother's cremation, Jones told Butler that there would be pieces of calcined bones, and that you could not scatter bones over the garden; besides, the laundresses used to 'lose their cats' there, which made it unsuitable. Alfred then said he would like to keep the ashes on his mantelpiece, but later had second thoughts.[12] Butler's last will stated firmly that he should be cremated and the ashes not preserved. So, the Saturday after the funeral, Alfred and Jones returned to the crematorium at Woking. They took the urn into the grounds. Alfred borrowed a spade, broke the seals, and looked at the ashes, which interested him. He sorted through them, and found what he thought was the knee-bone. Then, prompted by Jones, he dug a hole, dropped the ashes in, covered them over, and left nothing to mark the spot.

CHAPTER 23

Life After Death

Butler, the archetypal rebel, stood deliberately at an angle to his age, resisting its values and judgments. E.M. Forster described him as 'a master of the oblique',[1] but it is misleading to categorise him as simply eccentric, a quirky, prickly, unclubbable individual scratching away in the margins of intellectual and artistic life. Certainly the initial reception of his books, *Erewhon* excepted, indicates that early critics found a lack of centrality, a dogged insistence on moving against the flow. Butler nurtured a belief that the tide would one day turn in his favour, seizing on the most ephemeral incidents as evidence that he was gaining ground. His sonnet, 'Not on Sad Stygian Shore', expressed one approach to immortality:

> Yet meet we shall, and part, and meet again
> Where dead men meet, on lips of living men.

But even he underestimated his power in presuming that the drift of his arguments, 'who's right, who's wrong', would be ignored. In fact, his philosophical books are still referred to; *The Authoress of the Odyssey* is in print; volumes of letters, editions of the Notebooks, and his two major novels give him a readership beyond his wildest calculations.

His death did not make much stir beyond the boundaries of his private map. Significantly, of the ten obituaries that Streatfeild printed for private circulation, five came from Italy – Varallo, Trapani, Rome – one from New Zealand – the *Press* – and one from Cambridge – *The Eagle*. The first shift in Butler's reputation came with the publication of *The Way of All Flesh*[2] in 1903. Richard Streatfeild claimed in a prefatory note that Butler 'always intended to rewrite it or at any rate to revise it. His death in 1902 prevented him from doing this, and on his death-bed he gave me clearly to understand that he wished it to be published in its present form.' Whether he wished it published during the lifetime of his sisters is less clear. It caused them great hurt. Although they had studiously avoided reading any of their brother's books, and had been warned how painful this one would be to them, each privately bought a copy and surreptitiously read it.[3] The personal dimension was forcefully expressed by Robert Bridges in a letter to his sister, the Carrie with whom Butler had played Handel as a boy at Langar: 'It is very difficult to reconcile his wide charity of disposition with his bitter onesided almost venomous regard towards his own family, nor can I understand how he, who cannot possibly be suspected of anything like hypocrisy, can have, in his intercourse with them, maintained himself in their affection and good opinion (so far as family relations were concerned) till the last. I have not seen this last book, but I suppose from what you say that they have now got the riddle before them.'[4]

The riddle has continued to perplex. Mrs R.S. Garnett, the grand-daughter of Philip Worsley, Fanny Butler's brother, wrote *Samuel Butler and his Family Relations* partly as an act of reparation towards the well-meaning individuals he had handled so cruelly. But Butler was not only exacting revenge on his own family. His novel is an attack on the Victorian family as an institution, and a particular kind of family at that; middle class, complacent, propertied, and above all religious, with a peculiarly English and joyless form of religion, whose god is defined by negatives: sin; thou shalt not; deny yourself. May Butler wrote a hymn that characterises the spirit against which her brother fought:

> Not yet the struggle is ended,
>   Not yet the battle won,
> But well for thee if in earnest
>   Thou knowest it begun!
> Thro' many a year of sorrow
>   And yet unconquered sin,
> Thou must press to the gate of Heaven,
>   But thou shalt enter in![5]

Ernest Pontifex is the first-born child of parents, Theobald and Christina, whose names reflect the religion which binds them.

Enchained by experience, his self-will almost crushed, he makes his progress through the Victorian wilderness in search of his birthright. The characters are 'drawn from' their originals, rather than being true portraits; but the personal element is so raw and fierce that the feeling of shock persists.

Described by Shaw as 'one of the great books of the world'[6] and by Galsworthy as 'the best modern English novel', *The Way of All Flesh* is an uneven, extraordinary and unforgettable book, evoking strong emotions of recognition and horror, and shattering for ever the sacred English totem, the idea of the family. The novel seems to belong to the twentieth, rather than the nineteenth, century; sceptical and ironic, it is a product of the new, urban, godless world. Butler strips bare the old, out-worn structures, and is too honest to put much in their place.

Shaw, who had praised and encouraged Butler in his lifetime, remained his most influential champion: 'You will throw Shelley, Thompson, Meredith and all the rest out of the window and take Butler to your heart for ever,' he commented when *The Way of All Flesh* first appeared. His partisanship was echoed by Leonard Woolf, who wrote of his generation at Trinity College, Cambridge, that 'We read it when it came out and felt at once its significance for us,' and coupled Butler with Hardy as novelists 'whom we recognized with enthusiasm, not merely as writers and artists, but as our leaders'.[7] But the readership, if celebrated, was initially slight: there were only 1500 copies of the first edition. In 1905, however, Shaw gave Butler and his novel a generous puff in the preface to *Major Barbara*: 'Samuel Butler was, in his own department, the greatest English writer of the latter half of the nineteenth century. It drives one almost to despair of English literature when one sees so extraordinary a study of English life as *The Way of All Flesh* making so little stir that when, some years later, I produce plays in which Butler's extraordinarily free and future piercing suggestions have an obvious share, I am met with nothing but vague cackles about Ibsen and Nietzsche.'

Henry Festing Jones made important contributions to the long process of discovering Butler. His first efforts were modest, constrained by the precedence given to Streatfeild as literary executor. He went on a pilgrimage to Italy in the spring of 1903, distributing photographs and memorabilia to Butler's friends, and leaving the manuscripts of the Italian books in appropriate places: *Ex Voto* at

Varallo, *The Authoress of the Odyssey* at Trapani. In the next year, he published his diary of this journey, and in 1908 he arranged the first Erewhon dinner, a well-meaning if slightly cosy series of celebrations. But the real breakthrough came when A.C. Fifield agreed to publish four titles, including a new edition of *The Way of All Flesh*. This was another act of generosity on Shaw's part, because it was through him and his wife that Streatfeild was introduced to Fifield; Mrs Shaw lent Fifield the money to finance *The Way of All Flesh*, and Shaw, while refusing to write a new introduction, told Fifield 'what he had written, he had written'; Fifield lifted the *Major Barbara* preface, and 'plastered George Bernard Shaw all over the Butler leaflets and advertisements'.[8] Butler's sales and reputation began to mount. A.C. Fifield, whose office was in Clifford's Inn, gradually added the other works to his list. (Butler had more luck with his publishers after his death than during his life; Jonathan Cape bought up Fifield in 1921 to bring about the complete 'Shrewsbury' edition of 1923.) The Note-Books were the next revelation.[9] Jones arranged and edited the first selection in 1912 (a further volume followed in 1934). They were widely praised and read: 'perhaps,' wrote *The Times*, 'it will come to be the most read and valued of all his works'; 'He is excessively interesting to us . . .' (Edmund Gosse); 'They defy summary or analysis . . .' (Walter de la Mare). It made one more wry footnote to Butler's career, to be eulogised for a book he never prepared for publication, edited by the man he carefully excluded from the position of literary executor.

The Note-Books led to a major revaluation of Butler's stock, providing a third substantial and unignorable work to set beside his two satirical novels. They revealed him as a modern individual: frank, intimate, unconventional, provocative. They offered entry to the private workings of his unusual mind and, as with *The Way of All Flesh*, readers found an element of recognition in the apparently casual, unguarded thoughts and judgments, edited and revised but still giving the impression of a man talking personally. Butler's way of life, formed in New Zealand, gave him time to think: 'One's thoughts fly so fast that one must shoot them; it is no use trying to put salt on their tails' – so he captured them on paper. He functioned, too, like a camera, or recorder, noting the oddities of daily life and speech, and commenting upon them in his half-mocking, half-affectionate way, which sometimes moves from the trivial to the profound within the same sentence.

Of the triviality or untenableness of many of his notes, he was well aware – an author is the worst person to make selections from his own notes – 'or indeed even, in my case, to write them'; or, 'Our Ideas' – 'They are for the most part like bad sixpences and we spend our lives trying to pass them on one another.' Yet he also predicted their value: 'I think that, to some, such a record of passing moods and thoughts good, bad and indifferent will be more valuable as throwing light upon the period to which it relates than it would have been if it had been edited with greater judgment.' The attics and junk rooms of his mind are more interesting, perhaps, than the library; and Butler, of course, did without a library.

Before long, two members of the Bloomsbury set were planning to write on Butler. In 1913 Lytton Strachey, who had recently found *The Way of All Flesh* 'cheering', suggested an article on Butler to *The Edinburgh Review*; and the following year E.M. Forster made a proposal to his publisher, Edward Arnold, for a book, and was offered a £25 advance. Forster found himself in close sympathy with Butler. He corresponded with Jones and went to the last Erewhon dinner on July 3rd, 1914: there were 160 present, including, for the first time, ladies, and the speakers included the Hon. Mrs Richard Grosvenor (formerly Mrs Bovill, Butler's 'human Easter Monday'), Shaw, Gilbert Cannan and Desmond MacCarthy. The projected book made little progress, but Butler remained a potent influence for Forster. Years later he chose *Erewhon* as the subject for a radio talk, 'Books that have influenced me'. He named Butler with Jane Austen and Proust as the three authors who helped him most over his writing, 'and he did more than either of the other two to help me to look at life the way I do'.[10] P.N. Furbank comments that Forster's handling of the money theme in *Howards End*, 'the Schlegel frankness about money that so shocks the Wilcoxes, owed much to Butler';[11] and suggests that Mr Emerson in *A Room with a View* may be partly based on him. Other novelists whom Butler helped to form include H.G. Wells and Ivy Compton-Burnett. Ivy Compton-Burnett was so strongly affected by the Note-Books that 'she wrote in her copy, underneath Butler's description of people whose life is a partial death ("a long, living death-bed, so to speak, of stagnation and nonentity") her own terse confession: "I am a living witness of this crushing lifeless stagnation of the spirit." '[12] There are affinities between Ernest Pontifex and Felix Bacon in *More Women Than Men*.

Virginia Woolf, reviewing John Harris's study of Butler in 1916,[13] defined his distinctiveness: 'He is one of those rare spirits among the dead whom we like, or it may be dislike, as we do the living, so strong is their individuality . . .' She sensed that his success lay in 'being the master of his life', and by quite consciously treating life as an art. He achieved, in fact 'freedom of soul': 'To have by nature a point of view, to stick to it, to follow it where it leads, is the rarest of possessions.' She also praised 'the peculiar accent and power of his style', something she explored further in her review, 'The Modern Essay', taking as her example 'Ramblings in Cheapside', and Butler's starting-point of the turtles in Mr Sweeting's shop window. His method, the very opposite of Stevenson's imitation of the traditional eighteenth-century essay, is to think your own thoughts and speak them as plainly as you can; she adds, 'to write like oneself and call it not writing is a much harder exercise in style than to write like Addison and call it writing well'. W.B. Yeats made a similar point when he described Butler as 'the first Englishman to make the discovery that it is possible to write with great effect without music, without style, either good or bad, to eliminate from the mind emotional implication and to prefer plain water to every vintage . . .'[14]

After the Note-Books came Jones's monumental *Memoir*, completed by June, 1915 though not published until 1919, after the death of Butler's last surviving sister, Harriet Bridges. These two fat volumes, nearly a thousand pages, form an impressive memorial. They give the impression of being exhaustive, but there are, understandably, crucial omissions. Jones suppressed the breach of the final years, claiming to Gogin that 'he had been forbidden to say anything about it'.[15] Alfred's criticism – 'too much of Jones in his book and too little Butler' – is partly justified; but it is full of the insights born of twenty-five years' intimate friendship.

Throughout the twenties and thirties, there was a steady stream of books concerning Butler, including a significant number from abroad, notably Clara Stillman's 1932 study, *Samuel Butler: A Mid-Victorian Modern*. In Paris, Valéry Larbaud translated Butler's major works and organised a *conférence* at Mlle Monnier's bookshop, La Maison des Amis des Livres, which was another link with James Joyce and *Ulysses*. Several books greeted the centenary of Butler's birth, the most important being the edition of the correspondence with Miss Savage, edited by Geoffrey Keynes and Brian Hill. Jonathan Cape commissioned a new appraisal from Malcolm Muggeridge, but declined to publish the result, *The Earnest Atheist*, the first outright assault on Butler since Romanes. Muggeridge admitted that the more he explored Butler's life and outlook, the less he liked him. He wrote the book in his Calcutta office, where he was assistant editor of *The Statesman*, constantly interrupted, 'with the fan churning up the stagnant humid air', and his stagnant mind 'needing to be churned up likewise if it was to function at all'; in those circumstances, he saw Butler more luridly than he might otherwise have done, as symbolising everything he most abhorred. The research was done partly by his wife, who copied out 'what she thought would be of interest or significance', and sent it out to India.[16] Though full of isolated perceptions, the overall effect is a curiously personal act of demolition, in which Muggeridge labels Butler as a timid homosexual and a money-obsessed snob. Desmond MacCarthy was so incensed that he spread himself over two long reviews in *The Sunday Times*[17] to oppose these judgments. He chose to concentrate on the breach with Jones, which Muggeridge implied had hastened Butler's death. That was one area where Muggeridge had acquired new evidence, in the form of Alma Gogin's memories. Stung by MacCarthy's reference to her as an embittered old woman, she wrote to support that part of Muggeridge's book from her last address, 'Erewhon', Reigate.

The Earnest Atheist was answered critically by P.N. Furbank's incisive study of 1948, and in terms of his life by Philip Henderson's biography of 1953; while E.M. Forster crystallised Butler's significance for modern writers and writing: 'If Butler had not lived, many of us would now be a little deader than we are, a little less aware of the tricks and traps in life, and of our own obtuseness. His value, indeed, resides not in his rightness over this or that, not in his happy hits, not even in the frequent excellence of his prose and verse, but in the quality of his mind. He had an independent mind.'[18]

Since then, the pursuit of Butler's elusive and paradoxical figure has continued. His three great works, *Erewhon*, *The Way of All Flesh*, and the Note-Books, make a formidable and still valid attack on the hypocrisy of his age and society. His other, diverse interests and achievements survive in ways unpredicted even by himself. While he may, in spite of disclaimers, have predicted some kind of publication for his notes, he could never have envisaged *Erewhons of the Eye*, Elinor Shaffer's full-length study of him as painter, photographer and art critic, or the ensuing exhibition, 'The Way of All Flesh', at Bolton Museum, 1990. In the same year, a play based on his life was performed in Langar church, of all unlikely places, as the centre of a week-long Samuel Butler festival.

Yet Langar church is not an entirely inappropriate place to celebrate Butler. He set out repeatedly on his formative journeys, to New Zealand, Erewhon or Ithaca, and always returned. He liked to revisit places, in reality and in his mind, and while he rejected what his family stood for, he could never bring himself to break with them finally, acknowledging the continuity of his inheritance. His sexual and emotional life bore little resemblance to the Rectory traditions; he was more recognisably a true son in the way he could not stop thinking about God.

Butler's freedom and independence of spirit infuses his life and work. 'Work' seems a more appropriate word than art, for someone who compared Pater's style to the face of an enamelled old woman, and who never found the easy grace he admired in the swell and suspected in the artist. Yet the close relationship between his life and the full range of his art is oddly reminiscent of a man who was in many ways his opposite, Oscar Wilde, like Butler an exploiter of paradox, and creator of a comic Ernest, and like him an arch mocker of the deadlier conventions of his time. Each triumphantly overcame earnestness, which was for Butler 'the last enemy that shall be subdued'.

Butler was someone who did not, in the important things, compromise; who was almost crushed, but who remade himself, not as he would have liked to be remade – handsome, wealthy, lucky, healthy – but as best he could. In his own words, 'I had to steal my own birthright. I stole it, and was bitterly punished. But I saved my soul alive.'[19] The process of re-creation was a lonely one, dogged by suspicion and self-doubt, and his need to put everything to the test led to some bizarre exclusions and crabbed judgments. As Henry Nevinson wrote: 'Of him it may truly be said: "He touched nothing from which he did not strip the adornment"; and what higher praise could be given to any artist or any writer?'[20] Butler trained his mind and his eyes to look with a clear and penetrating gaze at the world around him; and it is this hard-won, free and personal vision that survives.

Notes

Chapter 1

1 *Samuel Butler's Note-Books: Selections*, ed. Geoffrey Keynes and Brian Hill, London, 1951, p.320.
2 *The Living Novel*, V.S. Pritchett, 1946, p.102.
3 *The Magic Lantern*, Ingmar Bergman, London, 1988, p.73.
4 *Fraser's Magazine*, August 1842.
5 The *Life and Letters of Dr Samuel Butler*, Samuel Butler, 2 vols, London, 1896, vol.1, p.9.
6 ibid., vol.1. p.355.
7 See D.S. Colman, '*Sabrinae Corolla: The Classics at Shrewsbury School under Dr Butler and Dr Kennedy.*' (A Paper Read to the Annual General Meeting of the Classical Association at Bristol on 14 April 1950). Shrewsbury, 1950, p.7.
8 ibid., pp.7–8.
9 *The Autobiography of Charles Darwin, 1809–1882*, ed. Nora Barlow, London, 1958, p.46.
10 *The Life and Letters of Dr Samuel Butler*, vol.1, p.46.
11 ibid., vol.1, p.125.
12 *Samuel Butler and his Family Relations*, Mrs R.S. Garnett, London, 1926, p.13.
13 *The Correspondence of Charles Darwin*, vol.1, 1821–1836, Cambridge, 1985, p.15.
14 *The Life and Letters of Dr Samuel Butler*, vol.1, p.298.
15 ibid., vol.1, p.302.
16 *The Autobiography of Charles Darwin*, p.58.
17 *The Correspondence of Charles Darwin*, op. cit., letter of 13 September 1828, p.65.
18 ibid., letter of 28 March 1834, p.376.

Chapter 2

1 *Nottinghamshire*, Nikolaus Pevsner, revised by Elizabeth Williamson, 2nd edn, London, 1979, pp.161–2. See also *Highways and Byways in Nottinghamshire*, J.B. Firth, London, 1916.

2 Letter to Charles Gogin, 7 December 1880 (Chapin Library).
3 *Life and Letters of Dr Samuel Butler*, vol.2, p.107. The letter is dated 7 May 1835; the subject is one on which Dr Butler remained sensitive throughout his career: 'Permit me, sir, to add that thirty-seven years' successful experience . . . is some guarantee to parents that their sons are not likely to be ill-taught or ill-treated under my care.'
4 *Samuel Butler and his Family Relations*, op. cit., p.45.
5 ibid., p.87.
6 *The Autobiography of Mark Rutherford* (William Hale White), 1881, ch. 1.
7 Note-Books, 28 November 1898.
8 *Under the Greenwood Tree*, 1872, ch. 4.
9 'The Sad Fortunes of the Rev. Amos Barton', *Scenes of Clerical Life*, ch. 1, first published in *Blackwood's Magazine*, 1857.

Chapter 3

1 Letter to W.E. Heitland, 20 June 1889 (*The Eagle*, XXXIV, pp.348–52). Kennedy, who reminded M.R. James of an apopleptic macaw, impressed himself on people's memories. When a Canon of Ely, he was in procession in the cathedral when his conversation with a neighbour became suddenly audible during a break in the organ music: 'Yes, I have found it a rather pleasant after-dinner wine.'
2 Shrewsbury School Prospectus, 1852.
3 ibid.
4 The Diaries of John Coker Egerton, quoted in *A Salopian Anthology*, ed. Philip Cowburn, London, 1964. See Chapter VI, 'A Good Specimen of a Shrewsbury Boy'.
5 *Samuel Butler and his Family Relations*, pp.53–4.
6 Note in Hound Book, quoted in *Shrewsbury School Register*.
7 There is one item which derives from this visit in the St John's Collection, a black and white outline sketch: Civita Vecchia, 1854.

Chapter 4

1 First published in *The Eagle*, vol.1 no.5, 1859. Reprinted in *A First Year in Canterbury Settlement, with other early essays*, ed. R.A.Streatfeild, 1914.
2 For a detailed description, see *Memories of a Long Life*, T.G. Bonney, Cambridge, 1921, pp.17–18.
3 *The Correspondence of Samuel Butler with His Sister May*, ed. Daniel F. Howard, Berkeley and Los Angeles, 1962, p.36.
4 See *The History of the Lady Margaret Boat Club, 1825–1890*, R.H. Forster and W. Harris, Cambridge, 1890.
5 'On English Composition and other Matters', *The Eagle*, vol.1, no.1, Lent Term 1858. See also *A First Year*, pp.205–10.
6 *The Eagle*, vol.1, no.5, Easter Term 1859. *A First Year*, pp.221–2.

7 *A First Year*, p.269. *The Cambridge Magazine*, 1 March 1913, A.T. Bartholomew.

Chapter 5

1 Autobiographical Notes, written c. 1883. Note-Books, vol.3.
2 There were opportunities at Shrewsbury for such experience. Even Dr Butler had conceded that 'immorality with women' 'existed and would exist' among a few older boys. (British Library, Add. Ms 34586.)
3 *Correspondence with May*, p.38.
4 *Samuel Butler and his Family Relations*, p.128.
5 *Correspondence with May*, pp.38–40.
6 'Our Emigrant', *The Eagle*, vol.2, 1861, pp.101–13. This was one of the sources which Canon Butler edited to form *A First Year in Canterbury Settlement*, where it appears in a somewhat condensed form.

Chapter 6

1 *A First Year in Canterbury Settlement*, London, 1863. References are to the 1914 edn. (A.C. Fifield, London). There is an annotated edition, edited by A.C. Brassington and P.B. Maling, published by Blackwood and Janet Paul (Auckland and Hamilton), 1964.
2 Letter of Mrs M.E. Orr, daughter of Professor Sale, quoted in *William Rolleston*, W.D. Stewart, Christchurch, 1940, p.10.
3 The definitive account is *Samuel Butler at Mesopotamia, together with Butler's 'Forest Creek' Manuscript and his letters to Tripp and Acland*, by Peter Bromley Maling, 1960, reprinted with corrections, Wellington, 1984. See also *Unclimbed New Zealand*, John Pascoe, London, 1939, and *Great Days in New Zealand Exploration*, John Pascoe, London, 1959; and *The Early Canterbury Runs*, L.G.D. Acland, rev. edn, 1975.
4 A newcomer to Canterbury would be attached to a station, working for nothing in return for his keep and the knowledge he gained.
5 The 'Forest Creek' manuscript, with two sketches by Butler, was found between the leaves of a book bought in the Caledonian Market in London in 1935. It was acquired by the Canterbury Museum in 1954. Butler sent the article to the editor of *The Eagle*, who published some of it after extensive editing. The remaining pages are in the Butler Collection at St John's.
6 Quoted in an article by W. Vance in the *Timaru Herald*, 9 February 1935.

Chapter 7

1 This copy is in the collection of the Canterbury Public Library, Christchurch, and contains manuscript notes by Wynn Williams.
2 *A Surveyor in New Zealand*, Noeline Baker, Auckland, 1932, p.31.
3 Letter from John H. Baker to J.J. Kinsey, 30 August 1896, Kinsey Papers, (MS Papers 22: Folder 53), Alexander Turnbull Library, Wellington.

4 ibid.

5 Letter of J.D. Enys, *Memoir*, vol.1, p.104. Like so many of Butler's New Zealand acquaintances, Enys kept in touch with him, calling on him at Clifford's Inn after his return to Cornwall, sending him pheasants, etc. He lent Butler a photograph of his cottage, taken soon after it was built in 1861.

6 *Five Years in New Zealand*, R.B. Booth, London, 1912. pp.73–4.

7 The two watercolours are in the Canterbury Museum, Christchurch. A letter of 1936 from the former manager of Mesopotamia, Mr F.S. Pawson, records: 'The pictures were hanging in the old cob hut. They were covered with dust and cobwebs and were quite smoke-dried (after more than 50 years). Being interested in Samuel Butler's works I investigated and found that they were painted by Butler while at Cambridge, and were framed there, and bear the framer's name on the back.' On the back of the seascape is written 'Budleigh Salterton'. Butler may have painted this on his traumatic visit to Torquay in 1859.

8 *The Life and Times of Sir Julius von Haast*, H.F. von Haast, Wellington, 1948, p.180.

9 *The Kettle on the Fuchsia*, Barbara Harper, Wellington, 1967, p.38.

10 Family tradition, communicated by Mrs Rosa Peacock (née Tripp).

11 *Diary of E.R. Chudleigh, 1862–1921*, edited by E.C. Richards, Christchurch, 1950, p.68.

12 ibid., p.125.

13 Letter to Sir Julius von Haast 24 February, 1865, (MS Papers 37: Folder 41), Alexander Turnbull Library.

14 Letters to J.B. Acland of 28 July 1862, and 4 October 1862, in Canterbury Museum. Published in *Samuel Butler at Mesopotamia*, op. cit., pp.58–9.

15 Comment of Mr Laurie Prouting, present owner of Mesopotamia, understandable from the point of view of a family who have worked to improve the property since 1945.

Chapter 8

1 The *Press*, 21 February 1863; *A First Year*, pp.167–78.

2 The *Press*, 13 June 1863; *A First Year*, pp.179–85.

3 Letters of Canon Butler in von Haast papers, Alexander Turnbull Library.

4 Haldon Station Diary, quoted in *High Endeavour, The Story of the Mackenzie Country*, William Vann, 1980, pp.106–8; see also *South Canterbury, A Record of Settlement*, O.A. Gillespie, Timaru, 1958, p.325.

5 See *Lyttelton Times*, 29 October 1863 and 12 December 1863.

6 The *Press*, 15 February 1864; *A First Year*, pp.199–202.

7 *A First Year*, pp.195–7.

8 See the Complaint Book of the Christchurch Club in Canterbury Museum. 'No sealing wax,' Butler complained at 4.25 on 31 January 1862 – 'I apologise – sealing wax found. 4.55.' 'The undersigned are wholly at a loss to conceive why colonial beer should be 6 a glass at the club and 3 a glass

every where else in the town.' Butler was the first of seven to sign this complaint of October 1863.

9 Note-Books, vol.3; reprinted with an introduction by A.T. Bartholomew in *Life and Letters*, vol. VII, no.41, October 1931, pp.259–99.
10 *Samuel Butler in Canterbury, The Predestined Choice*, A.C.Brassington, Christchurch, 1972, p.17.
11 *Diary of E.R. Chudleigh*, 19 March 1864, p.125.
12 Note-Books, vol.3.
13 *William and Mary Rolleston, An Informal Biography*, Rosemond Rolleston, Wellington, 1971, pp.35–6.
14 'A Peculiar Dream', *Crusts*, L.J. Kenneway, published in New Zealand in 1861 and London, 1874.
15 The copy is now in the Alexander Turnbull Library.

Chapter 9

1 *Correspondence with May*, pp.42–3.
2 Note-Books, vol.3.
3 *Samuel Butler (1835–1902)*, P.N. Furbank, Cambridge, 1948, pp.99–101.
4 Letter of 24 February 1865.
5 Letter of 20 April 1865 in Kinsey Papers, Alexander Turnbull Library.
6 Letter of 14 November 1865.
7 Letter of 28 February 1867.
8 *Oddities, Others, and I*, Henriette Corkran, London, 1904, p.208.
9 'Recollections of Samuel Butler', *Essays Irish and American*, J.B. Yeats, Dublin and London, 1918.
10 *A Player under Three Reigns*, Johnston Forbes-Robertson, London, 1925, pp.53–5.
11 *Painters of the Victorian Scene*, Graham Reynolds, London, 1953, p.21.
12 Memoranda from old account books, 2 December 1899 in Notebooks, vol.3. *Memoir*, vol.1, p.317. See also *My Life, A Record of Events and Opinions*, Alfred Russel Wallace, 2 vols., London, 1905.
13 *Essays Irish and American*, op. cit.
14 Memoranda, Notebooks, vol.3.
15 *Correspondence with May*, pp.43–5.
16 Letter of 16 May 1866.
17 Letter of 20 May 1866.
18 Letter of 27 December 1867.

Chapter 10

1 Autobiographical notes, written ca. 1883. Notebooks, vol.3.
2 *A Player Under Three Reigns*, op. cit., p.54.
3 *Diary of E.R. Chudleigh*, pp.125–6.

Chapter 11

1 *The Rock*, 25 April and 9 May 1873.
2 *Correspondence with May*, p.58.
3 ibid., pp.61–3.
4 *The Earnest Atheist: A Study of Samuel Butler*, Malcolm Muggeridge, London, 1936, p.168.
5 See *Erewhons of the Eye, Samuel Butler as painter, photographer and art critic*, Elinor Shaffer, London, 1988. Dr Shaffer makes a detailed study of the hitherto neglected area of Butler's art.

Chapter 12

1 *Correspondence with May*, p.66.
2 For Butler's Canadian dealings, see 'Samuel Butler in Canada,' Brian Hill, *Dalhousie Review*, April, 1936; and 'Samuel Butler's Canadian Investments,' A.W. Currie, *University of Toronto Quarterly*, 32 (Jan. 1963).
3 See 'Samuel Butler in Canada', Brian Hill; and volume of newspaper cuttings in British Library.
4 Note-Books, vol.3, reprinted in *Butleriana*, p.55.
5 ibid.
6 *Selections from Previous Works*, London, 1884. The poem was published in *The Spectator*, 18 May 1878. According to Edward Clodd, he first met Samuel Butler at the Century Club in March 1878, when Butler recited 'A Psalm of Montreal'. Clodd read it to the Rev. Charles Anderson, who read it to Matthew Arnold, then a school inspector, who in turn passed it to Hutton, the editor of *The Spectator*. *Memories*, Edward Clodd, London, 1916, pp.255–6.
7 *Life and Habit*, edition of 1910, pp.52–3.
8 'Recollections of Samuel Butler,' Desmond MacCarthy, *Life and Letters*, vol.VII, no.41, October 1931.
9 Note-Books, vol.6, 'Blackguardisms and Improprieties'.
10 Letter of 22 August 1903, in *The Selected Letters of Robert Bridges*, ed. Donald E. Stanford, 2 vols, Newark, 1983, vol.1, pp.437–8. Bridges, whose younger brother had been married briefly to Butler's sister Harriet before his sudden death, uses uncharacteristically strong language, in sharp contrast to his courteous, even expansive, letters to Butler. 'But Samuel Butler was both vain and ugly in mind. There was a meanness in his general mental attitude towards humanity, as in his actual social habits and personal appearance. – I do not care to speak more in detail about him, for he was familiarly unreserved towards me, and there is no use in dissecting out the badness of any one.'
11 *Henry Scott Tuke: A Memoir*, Maria Tuke Sainsbury, London, 1933, pp.39–41.
12 Note-Books, vol.3.
13 *Oddities, Others, and I*, op. cit., p.209.

14 Review of *The Earnest Atheist*, Malcolm Muggeridge, 1936, by Desmond MacCarthy in *The Sunday Times*, 6 and 13 September 1936.

Chapter 13

1 *Life and Habit*, London, 1878. New Edition, with Author's Addenda and Preface by R.A. Streatfeild, London (A.C. Fifield), 1910. Page references are to this edition, which was reprinted by Jonathan Cape in 1924 and 1935.
2 *Truth*, 31 January 1878.
3 *Unended Quest: An Intellectual Biography*, Karl Popper, London, 1976, pp.176–79.
4 Butler's account is in Chapter Four of *Unconscious Memory*.
5 Letter of 2 January 1880. See 'The Darwin–Butler Controversy', Appendix 2 in *The Autobiography of Charles Darwin*, op. cit., pp.167–219. This includes Festing Jones's pamphlet, '*Charles Darwin and Samuel Butler, A Step Towards Reconciliation*', published by A.C. Fifield in 1911. The expenses of publication were shared between Jones and Francis Darwin, at Darwin's request (*Memoir*, vol.1, p.322). Most of the letters are also printed in *Memoir*, vol.2, Appendix C, pp.446–67.
6 Darwin Correspondence, Cambridge University Library.
7 *Autobiography*, p.179.
8 Letter of 4 February 1880. *Autobiography*, op. cit., pp.187–8. Huxley's advice was to 'take no notice whatever of Mr Butler until the next edition of your book comes out – when the briefest possible note explanatory of the circumstances – will be all that is necessary . . . I am astounded at Butler – who I thought was a gentleman though his last book appeared to me to be supremely foolish. Has Mivart bitten him and given him Darwinophobia?' *Autobiography*, p.211.
9 *Autobiography*, p.176.
10 *Nature*, 27 January 1881, the same issue that contained Romanes's swingeing review of *Unconscious Memory*.
11 *Pall Mall Gazette*, 31 May 1887.
12 *Memories*, Edward Clodd, op. cit., p.256.
13 *My Life, A Record of Events and Opinions*, Alfred Russel Wallace, 2 vols, London, 1905. vol.2, pp.84–5.

Chapter 14

1 Note-Books, vol.3, 'Jones and Myself'.
2 ibid.
3 Note-Books, vol.6, 'Blackguardisms and Improprieties'.
4 ibid.
5 *Samuel Butler and his Family Relations*, op cit., p. 63.
6 Letter of Thomas Butler to How, the family solicitor, 10 November 1881.
7 The letter was sent to the George Inn, Shrewsbury.

Chapter 15

1 *Alps and Sanctuaries of Piedmont and the Canton Ticino*, London, 1882. A new edition was published by A.C. Fifield in 1913, incorporating Butler's revisions and index, with an introduction by Streatfeild, and an additional chapter 'Fusio Revisited' compiled by Jones from materials in Butler's papers. Butler had contemplated a third 'Italian' book. Page references are to the 1913 edition.

2 Letter to Jones, 6 August 1882.

3 Alluding to the song 'When the enterprising burglar isn't burgling – isn't burgling' in *The Pirates of Penzance*.

4 E.M. Forster, manuscript journal, Forster Collection, King's College, Cambridge.

5 Charles Gogin's frontispiece for *Alps and Sanctuaries* is also of Our Lady of the Snows, Santa Maria della Neva.

Chapter 16

1 *Correspondence with May*, p.98.

2 Letter of 28 January 1885.

3 Letter of 14 October 1883.

4 Letter of 19 October 1883.

5 Letter of 18 October 1883.

6 Letter of 8 September 1885.

7 Letter of 2 October 1885.

8 Letter of 8 October 1886.

9 Letter from Maysie Butler to her mother, 19 December 1886.

10 Letters of 26 and 28 December 1886.

11 Letter of 31 December 1886.

Chapter 17

1 Note-Books, vol.3, Memoranda from old account books.

2 Letter of 7 October 1891.

3 *Letters and Journals of Charles Ricketts*, ed. Cecil Lewis, London, 1939, pp.362–3.

4 As 'The Sanctuary of Montrigone'. This was the second of a series of articles which appeared between July 1888 and November 1890. They include 'Ramblings in Cheapside', 'The Aunt, the Nieces and the Dog' and 'A Medieval Girl School', and contain some of Butler's most enjoyable writing. Most of these articles were collected and published in *Essays on Life, Art and Science* (Grant Richards, 1904), and then, with additions and an introduction by Streatfeild, in *The Humour of Homer and other Essays* (A.C. Fifield, 1913). The editor of the *Universal Review* was Harry Quilter, like Butler an unsuccessful candidate for the Slade Professorship.

5 *Narcissus, A Dramatic Cantata in vocal score. With a separate accompaniment*

*for the pianoforte. The words written & the music composed by Samuel Butler &
Henry Festing Jones.* London: Weekes & Co., 1888.

6 In a letter to Charles Ricketts, 8 July 1907. Ricketts had written: 'I am glad
that you say charming exaggerated things about dear old Butler. I met him
in Venice, and we liked each other hugely though he loved Handel.' 'It is
true that Butler loved Handel,' replied Shaw, 'but don't forget that he hated
Raphael.' *Letters and Journals of Charles Ricketts*, op. cit., pp.142–4.

7 William Smith Rockstro (1823–95), was a highly regarded teacher, performer and composer. He was an authority on early music, and wrote a
biography of Handel. Butler took a striking portrait photograph of him,
which is reproduced in *A Door-Keeper of Music*, J.A. Fuller-Maitland,
London, 1929. Fuller-Maitland records that he tried to induce Butler to
give it to him 'by suggesting that it might be possible to arrange for a grand
performance' (of *Narcissus*) 'in the Albert Hall. He answered that "the Devil
had never before tempted him with so alluring an offer," and sent me the
gift,' p.85. Fuller-Maitland (1856–1936) was music critic successively for
the *Pall Mall Gazette, Guardian*, and (from 1889) *The Times*.

8 *Memoir*, vol.2, pp.117–120. These 'Reminiscences of my friend, Mr Samuel
Butler' were sent to Jones by the Hon. Mrs Richard Cecil Grosvenor,
formerly Mrs Bovill. Some unexplained breach occurred between Butler
and her. 'No more news of Mrs Bovill' wrote Butler to Hans Faesch (7
February 1896), 'things can never be patched up again between her & us
– and both Jones & I are very sorry about it but it is no way our fault.' All
was forgotten by the time she spoke at the seventh Erewhon dinner.

9 *Life and Letters*, October 1931.

10 See *Erewhons of the Eye*, Elinor Shaffer, Ch. 4.

11 *The Authoress of the Odyssey*, 2nd edn, 1922, p.6.

12 *Correspondence with May*, pp.207–8. *Memoir*, vol.2, p.106.

Chapter 18

1 'A lecture on The Humour of Homer', delivered at the Working Men's
College, Great Ormond Street, London, 30 January 1892. Reprinted, with
Preface and Additional Matter, from *The Eagle*. Cambridge, Metcalfe and
Co. Ltd, 1892; 'On the Trapanese Origin of the Odyssey', Cambridge,
Metcalfe and Co. Ltd, 1893; *The Authoress of the Odyssey, where and when
she wrote, who she was, the use she made of the Iliad, and how the poem grew
under her hands*, London, Longmans, Green, and Co., 1897; *The Iliad of
Homer rendered into English prose for the use of those who cannot read the original*,
London, Longmans, Green and Co., 1898; *The Odyssey rendered into English
prose for the use of those who cannot read the original*, London, Longmans,
Green, and Co., 1900.

2 *The Victorians and Ancient Greece*, Richard Jenkyns, Oxford, 1980, p.192.
See also *The Greek Heritage in Victorian Britain*, Frank M. Turner, New
Haven and London, 1981.

3 See *Olympian Dreamers: Victorian Classical Painters 1860–1940*, Christopher Wood, London, 1983.

4 *The Humour of Homer and Other Essays*, ed. R.A. Streatfeild, 1913, p.96.

5 Letter to Mrs Bovill, 17 June 1892.

6 Jane Ellen Harrison (1850–1928), classical, linguistic and archaeological scholar, had published *Myths of the Odyssey in Art and Literature* in 1882.

7 *Correspondence with May*, 26 April 1892, pp.215–16.

8 *Spectator*, 23 April 1892, no.3330.

9 *The Complete Poems of C.P. Cavafy*, translated by Rae Dalven, London, 1961, pp.36–7.

10 *Homer's Daughter*, Robert Graves, 1955. The dust-jacket says: 'Apollodorus, the leading Classical authority on Greek myths, records a tradition that the real scene of the poem was the Sicilian seaboard, and in 1896 Samuel Butler, the author of *Erewhon*, came independently to the same conclusion. He further suggested that the poem, as we now have it, was composed at Drepanum, the modern Trapani, in Western Sicily, and that the authoress was the girl self-portrayed as Nausicaä ... Robert Graves, while working on his *Penguin* dictionary of Greek Myths, found Butler's argument for a Western Sicilian setting and for a female authorship irrefutable.'

Chapter 19

1 The letter was written to Rémi Faesch, younger brother of Hans Faesch, 15 November, *Memoir*, vol.2, pp.256–7. See also Jones's account of Butler's daily routine in the sketch prefaced to *The Humour of Homer*, pp.41–3.

2 Memoranda from old account books, 2 December 1899, in Notebooks, vol.3. Butler comments, 'I had been intimate with her for near 20 years.'

3 Interview with Alfred Cathie by A.G. Macdonell in *John O'London's Weekly*, vol. XXXIV, no.867, 23 November 1935 (Samuel Butler: Centenary Number).

4 Letter of 13 October 1888.

5 Interview with A.G. Macdonell, see above.

6 *Things are Waking Up at Mudham*, Charles Gogin, London, 1929, p.171. Among the illustrations is a photograph by Butler.

7 Letters of August, and 7 September 1886, to Jones.

8 Letter from Hans, 7 March 1895.

9 Letter to Hans, 8 March 1895, partly reproduced in *Memoir*, vol. 2, pp.204–5.

10 Letter to Jones, 5 April 1895.

11 *Reminiscences of a Student's Life*, Jane Ellen Harrison, 1920, p.70.

12 Letter from Jones, 4 April 1895.

13 Letter to Jones, 17 April 1895.

14 Letter to Watt, 17 April 1895.

15 Letter to Jones, 20 April 1895.

16 Letter to Hans, 6 June 1895.

17 Letter to Hans, 10 July 1895.

18 Letter from Mayor, 10 October 1896.
19 Letter to Hans, 17 December 1896.
20 Letter of 26 April 1897.
21 *The Pound Era*, Hugh Kenner, 2nd edn, London, 1975, pp.46–50.

Chapter 20

1 Letter to Jones, 10 June 1898.
2 See Note-Books, vol. 3; *Life and Letters*, op. cit.; and *Memoir*, vol. 2, pp.283–7.
3 Letter to Jones, 30 December 1897.
4 Letter to Gogin. 7 January 1898.
5 *Times Literary Supplement*, 30 October 1919.
6 *Shakespeare's Sonnets Reconsidered*, new edition of 1927, Preface.
7 *Letters and Journals of Charles Ricketts*, op. cit., pp.26–7. In 1926, recalling the meeting in a letter to Cecil Lewis, Ricketts commented: 'He was insulted there by a bellied commercial-looking Briton to whom he had spoken, and, being nice, well-bred young men, we instantly handed him matches, a recent English newspaper, and in addressing him used the conventional "Sir".' (p.363)
8 *Selected Letters of Robert Bridges*, vol. 1, p.359.
9 'The Sources of *The Tempest*' (1925), in *The Common Asphodel*, Robert Graves, London, 1949.

Chapter 21

1 Typescript/manuscript by Mrs Charles Gogin and Alfred Cathie, Chapin Library, Williams College, Williamstown, Massachusetts. 'He said to my husband, when the latter saw him at the Nursing Home: "Gogin, I have made Jones promise that the money I have given him should all be refunded to my nephew. *I do not intend to have a second Pauli.*" Imagine the bitterness Butler must have felt in saying that!'
2 Letter of Shaw to Grant Richards, 28 March 1901. *George Bernard Shaw, Collected Letters*, 1898–1910, vol. 2, ed. Dan H. Laurence, London, 1973, p.225.
3 *Erewhon Revisited Twenty Years Later Both by the Original Discoverer of the Country and by his Son*, London, Grant Richards, 1901. References are to the Third impression, published by A.C. Fifield in 1908.
4 *The Daily News*, 30 October 1901.
5 *After Puritanism*, Hugh Kingsmill, London, 1929, p.107.
6 *Erewhon Revisited*, chs. XXVI and XXVII, which have, as throughout the book, expansive and parodic headings: MY FATHER REACHES HOME, AND DIES NOT LONG AFTERWARDS; and I MEET MY BROTHER GEORGE AT THE STATUES, ON THE TOP OF THE PASS INTO EREWHON.
7 *Changes and Chances*, H.W. Nevinson, London, 1923, p.305. Nevinson was

at school at Shrewsbury, and Butler had followed his literary career with interest.

8 Review of Jones's *Memoir*, *The Nation*, 25 October 1919, pp.123–4.

9 *The Note-Books of Samuel Butler*, p.366.

Chapter 22

1 Alfred Cathie in the interview with A.G. Macdonell.

2 *Note-Books*, selections edited by Geoffrey Keynes and Brian Hill, p.45.

3 *A Surveyor in New Zealand*, op. cit., pp.39–40.

4 Letters to Jones, such as that of 22 April 1902.

5 Letter of Jones to Charles Gogin, 14 October 1921, Chapin Library, Williams College. 'He wrote me a dreadful letter about it from Palermo in April or May 1902, and I replied from Ancona where I then was. In my reply I told him that I had destroyed his letter. He did not reply to my letter, but when I saw him in May in London, in that Nursing Home in New Cavendish Street, one of the first things he told me was that he had destroyed my letter, and also all other letters referring to that particular subject, and that he wished the matter never to be mentioned. It would have been a difficult thing to speak of in the *Memoir* and I was glad to feel that I had been forbidden to say anything about it.'

6 *Samuel Butler and his Family Relations*, op. cit., p.140.

7 Letter of 11 May 1902.

8 Letter of 21 May 1902.

9 As reported by Mrs Charles Gogin.

10 Butler's account books, Butler collection, St John's College, Cambridge.

11 *Samuel Butler and his Family Relations*, p.141. She added, 'think of the horror of being told such a thing as that one had a cancer.'

12 See Betty Miller's sympathetic article on Alfred Cathie in *Horizon*, vol. XVIII, no. 107, November 1948. When Alfred died on 30 March 1947, at Manor Park, Ilford, there were, at his request, no pall, no flowers, no service. His ashes were scattered in the grounds of the crematorium, and nothing remains to mark the spot.

Chapter 23

1 'Books That Have Influenced Me,' radio talk by E.M. Forster, 17 April 1944. Forster Collection, King's College, Cambridge.

2 *The Way of All Flesh* was first published in 1903 by Grant Richards, with an introductory note by R.A. Streatfeild. The full title on Butler's manuscript is 'Ernest Pontifex/ or/ The Way of all flesh/ a story of English Domestic life.'

3 *Samuel Butler and his Family Relations*, op. cit., p.138.

4 Letter of Robert Bridges of 22 August 1903, to his sister Mrs Glover – the 'Carrie' with whom Butler had played Handel as a boy at Langar. *Selected Letters of Robert Bridges*, op. cit., vol.1, p.438.

5 *Samuel Butler and his Family Relations*, p.84.
6 Letter to Henry Salt, *George Bernard Shaw, Collected Letters*, op. cit., vol.2, p.341.
7 *Sowing*, Leonard Woolf, 1960, p.166.
8 'Butler and his Publishers', A.C. Fifield, in *Now & Then*, October 1923, no.9.
9 *The Note-Books of Samuel Butler/ Author of 'Erewhon'/ Selections arranged and edited by Henry Festing Jones*. A.C. Fifield. London, 1912.
10 *The Listener*, 12 June 1952. 'The Legacy of Samuel Butler', E.M. Forster. pp.955–6.
11 *E.M. Forster, A Life*, P.N. Furbank, 2 vols, London, 1977–8. vol.2, pp.3–4.
12 *Secrets of a Woman's Heart*, Hilary Spurling, London, 1984, pp.119–21.
13 'A Man with a View', *Times Literary Supplement*, 20 July 1916.
14 'More Memories', W.B. Yeats, *The London Mercury*, vol.VI, no.33, July 1922.
15 Letter of Jones to Charles Gogin, 14 October 1921, Butler Collection, Chapin Library, Williams College, Williamstown.
16 *The Infernal Grove, Chronicles of Wasted Time: Number 2*, Malcolm Muggeridge, London, 1973. See pp.32–5.
17 *The Sunday Times*, 6 and 13 September 1936. The correspondence rumbled on until 4 October.
18 *The Listener*, 12 June 1952.
19 *The Note-Books of Samuel Butler*, p.182.
20 *The Nation*, 25 October 1919, p.123.

Sources

The materials for a life of Butler are extensive. Many of his letters are preserved in bound volumes in the British Library. Some of these have been published: the correspondence with Miss Savage (*Letters Between Samuel Butler and Miss E.M.A. Savage, 1871–1885*, ed. Geoffrey Keynes and Brian Hill, 1935); a selection of family letters (*The Family Letters of Samuel Butler, 1841–1886*, ed. Arnold Silver, 1962); and *The Correspondence of Samuel Butler with His Sister May*, ed. Daniel F. Howard. In addition, many letters were included in the two volume *Memoir* by Henry Festing Jones. I have referred to printed sources where possible; for unpublished letters, I have given the date of the letter, and it may be found in the British Library except where otherwise indicated.

The six volumes of Note-Books, which contain many autobiographical incidents and portraits, are in the Butler Collection of the Chapin Library, Williams College, Williamstown, Mass. There are copies in the British Library, and in the library of St John's College, Cambridge. Selections of the Note-Books have been published, and many notes are also included in the *Memoir*, though sometimes in a slightly altered form. There is also one complete volume published to date, Vol. 1, 1874–1883, ed. Hans-Peter Breuer. Again, I have referred to printed sources wherever possible, since so many quotations must of necessity be short excerpts.

I have also been given generous access to the Butler Collection at St John's, and have used information from, for example, Butler's Account Books.

Jones's *Memoir* remains an indispensable source. I am also in debt to my many predecessors in the field of Butler studies. For quotations from Butler's own works, I have used what I hope are the most widely available popular editions, rather than the Shrewsbury Edition. *The Way of All Flesh*, ed. by James Cochrane, and *Erewhon*, ed. by Peter Mumford, are in Penguin Classics. For the rest, I have used the Fifield/Jonathan Cape editions.

Select Bibliography

Collected Edition

The Shrewsbury Edition of the Works of Samuel Butler. Edited by H. Festing Jones and A.T. Bartholomew. 20 vols. Jonathan Cape and E.P. Dutton, London and New York, 1923–6.

Separate Works

A First Year in Canterbury Settlement. Longman, Green, Longman, Roberts, and Green. London, 1863. New edition, with other early essays, and an introduction by R.A. Streatfeild, A.C. Fifield, London, 1914. Ed. A. Brassington and P.B. Maing, Blackwood and Janet Paul, Auckland and Hamilton, 1964.

Erewhon, or Over the Range. Trübner and Co., London, 1872. New and revised edition, Grant Richards, London, 1901. Ed. Peter Mumford, Penguin, Harmondsworth, 1970. Ed. Hans-Peter Breuer and Daniel F. Howard, University of Delaware Press, Newark, 1981.

The Fair Haven: A Work in Defence of the Miraculous Element in our Lord's Ministry upon Earth, both as against Rationalistic Impugners and certain Orthodox Defenders, by the late John Pickard Owen. Edited by W.B. Owen, with a Memoir of the Author. Trübner and Co., London, 1873. New edition, with an introduction by R.A. Streatfeild, A.C. Fifield, London, 1913.

Life and Habit. Trübner and Co., London, 1878. New edition, with author's addenda and a preface by R.A. Streatfeild, A.C. Fifield, London, 1910.

Evolution, Old and New; or, the theories of Buffon, Dr Erasmus Darwin, and Lamarck, as compared with that of Mr Charles Darwin. Hardwicke and Bogue, London, 1879. Second edition, with a new preface, David Bogue, London, 1882. New edition, with author's revisions and an introduction by R.A. Streatfeild, A.C. Fifield, London, 1911.

Unconscious Memory: A Comparison between the Theory of Dr Ewald Hering, Professor of Physiology at the University of Prague, and the 'Philosophy of the Unconscious' of Dr Edward von Hartmann, with Translations from these Authors and Preliminary Chapters bearing on 'Life and Habit', 'Evolution Old and New', and Mr Charles

Darwin's edition of Dr Krause's 'Erasmus Darwin'. David Bogue, London, 1880. New edition with a Note by R.A. Streatfeild, and an Introduction by Professor M. Hartog, A.C. Fifield, London, 1910.

Alps and Sanctuaries of Piedmont and the Canton Ticino. David Bogue, London, 1882. New edition, with author's revisions and index, an Introduction by R.A. Streatfeild, and an additional chapter 'Fusio Revisited' compiled by H. Festing Jones, A.C. Fifield, London, 1913.

Selections from the previous works with remarks on Mr G.J. Romanes's 'Mental Evolution in Animals' and a Psalm of Montreal. Trübner and Co., London, 1884.

Luck or Cunning, as the main means of Organic Modification?: An Attempt to throw Additional Light upon the late Mr Charles Darwin's Theory of Natural Selection. Trübner and Co., London, 1887. Second edition, re-set and corrected, A.C. Fifield, London, 1920.

Ex Voto: An Account of the the Sacro Monte or New Jerusalem at Varallo-Sesia. With Some Notice of Tabachetti's Remaining Work at the Sanctuary of Crea. Trübner and Co., London, 1888. Re-issue, with 'Additions and Corrections', Longmans, Green, and Co., London, 1890.

The Life and Letters of Dr Samuel Butler, Headmaster of Shrewsbury School 1798–1836, and afterwards Bishop of Lichfield, in so far as they illustrate the Scholastic, Religious and Social Life of England, 1790–1840. 2 volumes. John Murray, London, 1896.

The Authoress of the Odyssey, where and when she wrote, who she was, the use she made of the 'Iliad', and how the poem grew under her hands. Longmans, Green, and Co., London. 1897. Second edition, corrected and with a Preface by H. Festing Jones, Jonathan Cape, London, 1922.

The Iliad of Homer rendered into English prose for the use of those who cannot read the original. Longmans, Green, and Co., London, 1898.

Shakespeare's Sonnets reconsidered, and in part rearranged; with introductory chapters, notes, and a reprint of the original 1609 edition. Longmans, Green, and Co., London, 1899. New edition, with a note by H. Festing Jones and A.T. Bartholomew, Jonathan Cape, London, 1927.

The Odyssey rendered into English prose for the use of those who cannot read the original. Longmans, Green, and Co., London, 1900.

Erewhon Revisited Twenty Years Later, Both by the Original Discoverer of the Country, and by his Son. Grant Richards, London, 1901.

The Way of All Flesh. Grant Richards, London, 1903. New edition, edited by Daniel F. Howard. New edition, edited by James Cochrane with an introduction by Richard Hoggart, Penguin, London, 1966.

Essays on Life, Art and Science. Edited by R.A. Streatfeild. Grant Richards, London, 1904.

God the Known and God the Unknown. With a prefatory note by R.A. Streatfeild. (This work first appeared as a series of articles in *The Examiner*, May to July, 1879.) A.C. Fifield, London, 1909.

The Humour of Homer and Other Essays. Edited by R.A. Streatfeild, with a biographical sketch of the author by Henry Festing Jones, A.C. Fifield, London, 1913.

The Note-Books of Samuel Butler, Author of 'Erewhon'; Selections arranged and edited by Henry Festing Jones. A.C. Fifield, London, 1912. Republished with an introduction by P.N. Furbank, The Hogarth Press, London, 1985.

Butleriana, edited by A.T. Bartholomew, Nonesuch Press, London, 1932.

Further Extracts from the Note-Books, chosen and edited by A.T. Bartholomew, Jonathan Cape, London, 1934.

Note-Books. Selections edited by Geoffrey Keynes and Brian Hill, Jonathan Cape, London, 1951.

The Note-Books of Samuel Butler, volume I (1874–1883), edited by Hans-Peter Breuer, University Press of America, Lanham, New York and London, 1984.

Letters

Letters Between Samuel Butler and Miss E.M.A. Savage, 1871–1885, edited by Geoffrey Keynes and Brian Hill, Jonathan Cape, London, 1935.

Samuele Butler e la Valle Sesia, de sue lettere inedite a Giulio Arienta, Federico Tonetti ed a Pietro Calderini, Alberto Durio, Varallo Sesia, 1940.

The Correspondence of Samuel Butler with his sister May, edited with an introduction by D.F. Howard, University of California Press, Berkeley and Los Angeles, 1962.

The Family Letters of Samuel Butler, 1841–1886, selected and edited with an introduction by Arnold Silver, Jonathan Cape, London, 1962.

Musical Works

Gavottes, Minuets, Fugues, and other short pieces for Piano (with Henry Festing Jones). Novello, Ewer and Co., London and New York, 1885.

Narcissus: A Dramatic Cantata in Vocal Score with a separate accompaniment for the pianoforte (with Henry Festing Jones). Weekes and Co., London, 1888.

Ulysses: A Dramatic Oratorio in Vocal Score with Accompaniment for the Pianoforte (with Henry Festing Jones). Weekes and Co., London, 1904.

Selected Shorter Works

The Evidence for the Resurrection of Jesus Christ, as given by the Four Evangelists, Critically Examined. Privately printed, London, 1865.

Holbein's Dance. London, 1886.

The Humour of Homer. A Lecture delivered at the Working Men's College, Great Ormond Street, London: January 30th, 1892. Metcalfe and Co. Ltd., Cambridge, 1892.

On the Trapanese origin of the Odyssey. Metcalfe and Co. Ltd., Cambridge, 1893.

Bibliography and Catalogues

The Samuel Butler Collection at St John's College, Cambridge, a Catalogue and a Commentary by H.F. Jones and A.T. Bartholomew, W. Heffer and Sons Ltd, Cambridge, 1921.

A Bibliography of Samuel Butler, A.J. Hoppé, The Bookman's Journal, London, 1925.

Samuel Butler, Catalogue of the Collection in the Chapin Library, Williams College, Williamstown, Massachusetts. The Southworth-Anthoensen Press, Portland, Maine, 1945.

The Career of Samuel Butler: A Bibliography, Stanley B. Harkness, The Bodley Head, London, 1955.

Samuel Butler: An Annotated Bibliography of Writings About Him. Compiled and edited by Hans-Peter Breuer and Roger Parsell. Garland Publishing, Inc., New York and London, 1990.

Biographical and Critical Works

Bekker, W.G. *An Historical and Critical Review of Samuel Butler's Literary Works,* Rotterdam, 1925.

Blum, J. *Samuel Butler,* Paris, 1910.

Brassington, A.C. *Samuel Butler in Canterbury: The Predestined Choice,* Christchurch, 1972.

Breuer, Hans-Peter. 'A Reconsideration of Samuel Butler's *Shakespeare's Sonnets Reconsidered', Dalhousie Review,* LVII (1977) 507–24.
——'Samuel Butler's "The Book of the Machines" and the Argument from Design', *Modern Philology,* LXXII iv (May 1975) 365–83.
——'The Source of Morality in Butler's *Erewhon', Victorian Studies,* XVI iii (March 1973) 317–28.

Cannan, Gilbert. *Samuel Butler: A Critical Study*, London, 1915.

Cole, G.D.H. *Samuel Butler and 'The Way of All Flesh'*, London, 1947.
———*Samuel Butler*, London, 1952 (revised, 1961 and 1971).

Currie, A.W. 'Samuel Butler's Canadian Investments', *University of Toronto Quarterly*, 32, January 1963.

De Lange, P.J. *Samuel Butler et le Bergsonisme, avec Deux Lettres inédites d'Henri Bergsoné*, Paris, 1936.

Farrington, B. *Samuel Butler and the Odyssey*, London, 1929.

Fort, J.B. *Samuel Butler, L'Ecrivain: Etude d'un Style*, Bordeaux, 1935.
———*Samuel Butler, 1835–1902. Etude d'un Caractère et d'une Intelligence*, Bordeaux, 1935.

Furbank, P.N. *Samuel Butler, 1835–1902*, Cambridge, 1948.

Garnett, Mrs R.S. *Samuel Butler and his Family Relations*, London and Toronto, 1926.

Giovanni, Angelo. 'Samuel Butler in Sicily', *A Review of English Literature*, vol. 3, no. 1, January 1962, 47–52.

Gosse, Edmund. 'Samuel Butler', *Aspects and Impressions*, London, 1922.

Harris, John F. *Samuel Butler, Author of 'Erewhon': The Man and His Work*, London, 1916.

Henderson, Philip. *Samuel Butler: The Incarnate Bachelor*, London, 1953.

Hill, Brian. 'Samuel Butler in Canada', *Dalhousie Review*, April 1936, 54–7.

Holt, Lee E. *Samuel Butler*, New York, 1964.

Jeffers, Thomas L. *Samuel Butler Revalued*, Pennsylvania, 1981.

Joad, C.E.M. *Samuel Butler (1835–1902)*, London and Boston, 1924.

John O' London's Weekly, (Samuel Butler Centenary Number), vol. XXXIV, no. 867, 23 November 1935.

Jones, Henry Festing. *Diary of a Journey through North Italy to Sicily in the Spring of 1903, undertaken for the purpose of leaving the MSS of three books by Samuel Butler at Varallo-Sesia, Aci-Reale and Trapani*, privately printed, Cambridge, 1904.
———*Charles Darwin and Samuel Butler: A Step towards Reconciliation*, London, 1911.
———*Samuel Butler: Author of 'Erewhon' (1835–1902). A Memoir*, 2 vols, London, 1919.

Jones, Joseph. *The Cradle of 'Erewhon': Samuel Butler in New Zealand*, Austin, 1959.

Kingsmill, Hugh. *After Puritanism, 1850–1900*, London, 1929.

Knoepflmacher, U.C. *Religious Humanism and the Victorian Novel: George Eliot, Walter Pater, and Samuel Butler*, Princeton, 1965.

Larbaud, Valéry. *Samuel Butler, Conférence faite le 3 novembre 1920*, Paris, 1920.

Life and Letters (Samuel Butler Number), vol. VII, no. 41, October 1931.

MacCarthy, Desmond. 'Samuel Butler: An impression', *Remnants*, London, 1918.

Maling, Peter Bromley. *Samuel Butler at Mesopotamia* together with Butler's 'Forest Creek' Manuscript and His Letters To Tripp And Acland, Wellington, 1984 second edition.

Meissner, K.W.P. *Eine Studie zur Kultur des angehenden Viktorianismus*, Leipzig, 1931.

Muggeridge, Malcolm, *The Earnest Atheist: A Study of Samuel Butler*, London, 1936.

Norrman, Ralf. *Samuel Butler and the Meaning of Chiasmus*, London, 1986.

Pestalozzi, Gerold. *Samuel Butler, der Jungere, 1835–1902: Versuch einer Darstellung seiner Gedankenwelt*, Zurich, 1914.

Pritchett, V.S. 'A Victorian Son', *The Living Novel*, London, 1946.

Rattray, R.F. *Samuel Butler: A Chronicle and an Introduction*, London, 1935.

Salter, W.S. *Essays on Two Moderns: Euripides, Samuel Butler*, London, 1911.

Shaffer, E.S. *Erewhons of the Eye: Samuel Butler as painter, photographer and art critic*, London, 1988.
———'Samuel Butler's Fantastic Maps: Erewhon, the "New Jerusalem", and the Periplus of Odysseus', *Word and Image*, IV/2, 1988.

Stanford, Donald E. 'Robert Bridges on His Poems and Plays: Unpublished Letters by Robert Bridges to Samuel Butler', *Philological Quarterly*, L (April 1971) 281–91.

Stillman, Clara G. *Samuel Butler: A Mid-Victorian Modern*, New York, 1932.

Stoff, R. *Die Philosophie des Organischen bei Samuel Butler, mit einer Biographischen Übersicht Zusammengestellt*, Vienna, 1929.

Streatfeild, R.A. (ed.) *Samuel Butler: Records and Memorials*, privately printed, Cambridge, 1903.

Vita-Finzi, Claudio. 'Samuel Butler in Italy', *Italian Studies*, XVIII, 1963.

Willey, Basil. *Darwin and Butler: Two Versions of Evolution*, London, 1960.

Wilson, Edmund. 'The Satire of Samuel Butler', *The Triple Thinkers: Ten Essays on Literature*, London, 1938.

Woolf, Leonard. 'Samuel Butler', *Essays in Literature, History, Politics*, London, 1927.

Yeats, John Butler. 'Recollections of Samuel Butler', *Essays Irish and American*, Dublin and London, 1918.

General

Acland, L.G.D. *The Early Canterbury Runs*, Christchurch, 1951.

Allen, D.E. 'The botanical family of Samuel Butler', *Journal of the Society for the Bibliography of Natural History*, vol. 9, pt 2, April 1979, pp. 133–6.

Baker, Noeline. *A Surveyor in New Zealand*, Auckland, 1932.

Barlow, Nora (ed.) *The Autobiography of Charles Darwin, 1809–1882*, London, 1958.

Bonney, T.G. *Memories of a Long Life*, Cambridge, 1921.

Booth, R.B. *Five Years in New Zealand*, London, 1912.

Clodd, Edward. *Memories*, London, 1916.

Colman, D.S. *Sabrinae Corolla: The Classics at Shrewsbury School Under Dr Butler and Dr Kennedy*, Shrewsbury, 1950.

Corkran, Henriette. *Oddities, Others, And I*, London, 1904.

Cowburn, Philip (ed.) *A Salopian Anthology*, London, 1964.

Forbes-Robertson, Johnston. *A Player under Three Reigns*, London, 1925.

Fuller-Maitland, J.A. *A Door-Keeper to Music*, London, 1929.

Graves, Robert. 'The Sources of *The Tempest*', *The Common Asphodel*, London, 1949.
————*Homer's Daughter*, London, 1955.

Haast, H.F. von, *The Life and Times of Sir Julius von Haast*, London 1948.

Jenkyns, Richard. *The Victorians and Ancient Greece*, Oxford, 1980.

Lewis, Cecil (ed.) *Letters and Journals of Charles Ricketts*, London, 1939.

Miller, Betty. 'Alfred', *Horizon*, vol. XVIII, no. 107, November 1948.

Nevinson, H.W. *Changes and Chances*, London, 1923.

Newton, Peter. *Mesopotamia Station*, Timaru, 1960.

Pascoe, John. *Great Days in New Zealand Exploration*, London, 1959.
——*Unclimbed New Zealand*, London, 1939.

Pocock, L.G. *The Landfalls of Odysseus – Clue and Detection in the Odyssey*, Christchurch, 1955.

Popper, Karl. *Unended Quest: An Intellectual Autobiography*, rev. edn, London, 1978.

Quilter, Harry. (ed.) *What's What*, London, 1902.

Reynolds, Graham. *Painters of the Victorian Scene*, London, 1953.

Richards, E.C. (ed.) *Diary of E.R. Chudleigh, 1862–1921*, Christchurch, 1950.

Sainsbury, Maria Tuke. *Henry Scott Tuke, A Memoir*, London, 1933.

Stanford, W. *The Ulysses Theme: A Study in the Adaptability of the Traditional Hero*, 2nd rev. edn, Oxford, 1963.

Turner, Frank M. *The Greek Heritage in Victorian Britain*, New Haven and London, 1981.

Wallace, Alfred Russel. *My Life*, 2 vols, London, 1905.

Wood, Christopher. *Olympian Dreamers: Victorian Classical Painters 1860–1940*, London, 1983.

Index